Saudi Arabia's Development Potential

Saudi Arabia's Development Potential

Application of an Islamic Growth Model

Robert E. Looney
Naval Postgraduate School

LexingtonBooks
D.C. Heath and Company
Lexington, Massachusetts
Toronto

Library of Congress Cataloging in Publication Data

Looney, Robert E.
  Saudi Arabia's development potential.

  Includes bibliographical references.
  1. Saudi Arabia—Economic policy. 2. Islam and economics. I. Title.
HC415.33.L66   338.953'8   79-2274
ISBN 0-669-03083-x   AACR2

Published simultaneously in Canada

Printed in the United States of America

International Standard Book Number: 0-669-03083-x

Library of Congress Catalog Card Number: 79-2274

For Anne

Contents

List of Figure
and Tables

Preface

The increase in the export earnings of Saudi Arabia, from about $8 billion in 1973 to about $32 billion in 1974 and thereafter, is one of these extremely rare historical events that fundamentally alters economic and political relationships both within and outside of a country.[1] One result is that Saudi Arabia has regained an influence on the world similar in many ways to that possessed in historic times following the spread of Islam westward across North Africa and eastward beyond Persia. Saudi Arabia's very recent rise to preeminence and influence has been more dramatic and certainly swifter than the early Islamic conquests.

The country's new status, however, is proving to be a mixed blessing. Given its economic, political, social, and bureaucratic makeup, Saudi Arabia has been—and still is—singularly ill-equipped to cope with the importance thrust on it. While the nation possesses one-quarter of the world's proven oil reserves, its large geographic size and comparatively small population pose a number of unique and difficult problems for its leaders.

Oil-exporting countries, such as Saudi Arabia, are often discussed as if they are purely bonanza countries, having received a gift from the gods that permits them to live a never-ending life of ease, leisure, and luxury. A widely held belief is that Saudi Arabia has obtained its position as one of the richest countries of the world without having undergone all the pains of an industrial revolution. This image is so well popularized in the United States that it not only creates a certain degree of hostility toward the kingdom, which along with the other OPEC countries has become an easy scapegoat for all the failures of the industrialized world to manage production and distribution of energy, but it has also largely prevented any Western analysis of the various social and economic constraints that the kingdom has faced.

With the phenomenal development of Saudi Arabia during the last decade, there has been an accompanying proliferation of literature on the country. It was with some trepidation, therefore, that I embarked on a study to add to this literature. Apart from a few general works of reference, however, most of the studies have been concerned with particular sectors of the economy or aspects of its development rather than the economy as a whole. Thus there seemed to be need for an in-depth analysis of the overall economy that was broader in its scope than the earlier studies. Also, much of the existing literature was descriptive rather than analytical, and often not written by economists. When economic theory was applied in the Saudi Arabian context, it was usually a particular model rather than economic principles in their more general sense.

For over a decade I have studied the economies of the Middle East and their development.[2] The absence of an in-depth examination of the Saudi

Arabian economy led me to prepare this volume, the goal of which is to present the economic underpinnings of that country's present growth and future development.[3]

The book seeks to survey the basis and extent of economic development in Saudi Arabia, the need to translate the petroleum-generated rapid growth into viable development, and the prospects that growth will in fact be self-sustaining. The country's planners face a delicate balancing of considerations stemming from the nonrenewable nature of oil and natural gas and the necessity of meeting current requirements while planning for future generations. The chapters offer an introductory overview, trace the development of the Islamic economic system, outline public financing and economic policy, sketch issues involved in industrialization, agricultural development, regional growth, and finally, attempt to forecast the likely growth path of the economy to the end of the century.

In this book I have concentrated on those aspects of the kingdom's development that I feel will be crucial in determining the future shape of the economy. My aim has been to enable the educated but not technical reader to distinguish what is significant in the material and data that is becoming available on Saudi Arabia. Hopefully, the end result will provide the reader with a clear insight as to how the economy actually functions and differs from that of most developing countries.

The kingdom is a vital and tremendously dynamic country. Data on the country is still relatively scarce; this volume is also meant to bridge at least in part that knowledge gap.

Notes

1. Donald Wells, *Saudi Arabian Development Strategy* (Washington: American Enterprise, 1976), p. 1.

2. See for example, Robert Looney, *The Economic Development of Iran* (New York; Praeger Publishers, 1973); *Income Distribution Policies and Economic Growth in Semiindustrialized Countries: A Comparative Study of Iran, Mexico, Brazil, and South Korea* (New York: Praeger Publishers, 1975); *Iran at the End of the Century: A Hegelian Forecast* (Lexington, Mass.: Lexington Books, D.C. Heath and Company, 1977); and *A Development Strategy for Iran Through the 1980s* (New York: Praeger Publishers, 1977).

3. The notable exception is Faisal S. Al-Bashir, *A Structural Econometric Model of the Saudi Arabian Economy: 1960/1970* (New York: John Wiley, 1977).

Acknowledgments

My appreciation is due to many individuals who have assisted in the collecting of materials and information. In Saudi Arabia, Ray Kelly of Stanford Research Institute and the Ministry of Planning was especially helpful in providing background information on the economy. At the Ministry of Planning, Faisal Al-Bashir, deputy minister, and Michael Gillibrand also provided invaluable assistance. Much of the original data on the economy is from the Central Department of Statistics (CDS). Ali Rashid was extremely helpful and cooperative in supplying me with some of the more-difficult-to-obtain sources. Also at CDS, Dunstan Perera furnished detailed information on the national income accounts and their method of compilation. Talks with William Hosteller at Aramco were particularly helpful in initially orienting me to the workings of the economy.

Dr. Jameel Al-Jishi, director of the Royal Commission for Jubail, assisted me in obtaining much of the basic information on that project. His evaluation of the project was extremely helpful in putting it into perspective. Paul Eckbox and Martin Yates of the Norwegian Petroplan provided useful critiques of the forecasting model.

At the Naval Postgraduate School (NPS), talks with Ralph Magnus aided my understanding of the many political dimensions in Saudi decision making. Also at the NPS Peter Frederiksen helped with much of the initial computer work.

Finally, special gratitude goes to my wife, Anne, who processed the many versions of the manuscript with patience, efficiency, and good cheer. Her help and encouragement made the book possible.

The author wishes to especially thank the Research Foundation at the NPS for its financial assistance during the summer of 1980, enabling me to complete the empirical sections of the study.

The responsibility for any errors, shortcomings, or discrepancies are solely mine. Also, it should be added that this study does not necessarily in any way reflect the views of the Research Foundation of the NPS, or those persons mentioned here.

Saudi Arabia's Development Potential

1 Introduction

This study will be concerned with economic development in an oil-based economy; that is, an economy for which petroleum acts as the principal source of revenue. Any economy that depends almost exclusively on one source of income, even oil, invites a long-term risk. Such a risk is seldom encountered in other less-developed countries that are not so fortunate as to have Saudi Arabia's natural bounty, and therefore have to resort to the more traditional means of growth. The obvious danger in the kingdom's dependence on oil revenues is the incongruity that may emerge in the long run between the mounting requirements for development and the risk that if anything should reduce oil revenues, the country's inability to generate sufficient alternative sources of income. Therefore, whether oil will act as a stimulant or a possible barrier to the economy's development is a question that in the long run will depend entirely on its expenditure policies. In this study we examine the government's past expenditure policy and also assess the possible investment strategies open to the authorities, assuming that they wish the country to become somewhat independent of oil revenues in the foreseeable future.

Most Saudis would admit that their important position in the world is not immediately and directly the result of their own efforts, but more the effect of their vast oil wealth. The country's real achievement—and this is a prolonged and unfinishing process—will be to come to terms with the effects of this wealth. This involves economic development inside the country, investment in the West, and the resulting exposure to alien social and political systems without damaging the fabric of Saudi society, which is based on the tight rules and regulations of a fundamentalist interpretation of Islam.

It is inevitable and desirable that these developments be followed by evaluations of their consequences. Thus a major aim of this book is to provide an analysis and description of the economic consequences of the oil boom on the Saudi Arabian economy, with implications for the United States and the Western world.

Relevance of Saudi Arabia

The emerging economic power of the Arab states has been recognized and demonstrated by many able Middle East analysts. Among the Arab oil nations, Saudi Arabia stands as the key state. Its role in the world economy

1

at present and in the future cannot be overemphasized. It is the world's leading exporter of oil. Because it produces one-quarter of the world-proven reserves, it has the capacity to expand oil production long after most of the Organization of Petroleum Exporting Countries' (OPEC) production peaks in the 1980s.

There are a number of additional reasons why an examination of the Saudi Arabian economy at this time should be of particular interest. No country in the world has seen as much development activity in the last 10 years as has Saudi Arabia. Needless to say, the rapid structural changes which have taken place and will continue to occur in the near future are the result of the post-1973 oil boom. A more important aspect has been the greater degree of attention government has devoted to the economy.

In addition there are at least six conditions.[1] In the study of its economy it will be of interest to see the general applicability of many of the standard principles of development economics. The kingdom's special characteristics are as follows:

1. Its cultural, religious, linguistic, and ethnic cohesion is unparalleled, though it is now confronted by the utilization of resident foreign manpower, the magnitude of which adds to its uniqueness and may alter the nation's relatively homogeneous cultural mix.

2. It is the only major nation whose constitution is sacred scripture (the *Holy Qu'ran*) and whose political system does not embrace such institutions as political parties or legislatures (functional equivalents, however, do exist).

3. The government has attempted and thus far been successful in controlling the flow of foreign values into the country. Few other nations have successfully based their development on varying degrees of independence of foreign powers.

4. Development is taking place in the context of enormous wealth rather than abject poverty, thus creating a totally different environment than encountered elsewhere. The dilemmas and strains of wealth handled by an administrative-economic infrastructure still emerging from a feudal-type society, have captured attention in the popular press but have not been dealt with in scholarly literature.

5. The sequence of emphasis in the developmental process has been different from most systems. An institutional infrastructure is being built before the expansion of mass participation produces an escalation of demands incapable of being met.

6. The country has evolved in less than fifty years unimpeded by either a single or mixed colonial tradition. Thus the economy starts with almost a clean slate on which are inscribed only the allegiance to Wahhabi Islam and a markedly favorable attitude toward American values and technology—the latter partly in consequence of amicable and constructive relations with the Arabian American Oil Company.

Scope of the Study

This study is largely an attempt to assess the country's growth prospects. Throughout the study there are seven basic tasks involved in this attempt. First, the Islamic economic doctrines which underlie the government policy are outlined to see if they pose any particular constraints on future economic development. Second, the role of the government in the development of the major sectors is analyzed and its economic philosophy evaluated for its relevance in dealing with the problems likely to confront these sectors. Third, the progress made toward economic planning together with an analysis of the objectives, policies, and investment criteria associated with planning is undertaken. Fourth, the major instruments of the nation's development policy are identified. Fifth, an assessment of the performance record of development planning is presented. Sixth, an identification of the current constraints facing the authorities is performed. Finally, a series of forecasts of the country's likely growth paths over the period to the year 2000 are presented.

Among the specific results of the forecasts are that:

1. Crude oil and refining will constitute a decreasing share of GDP.
2. Government revenues will continue to exceed greatly the government's spending capacity for internal development over most of the forecast period.
3. Personal consumption will rise, but private investment will decline as a percentage of national income, whereas nonoil income will constitute a larger share of GDP.
4. While private consumption and investment will decline as a percentage of nonoil GDP, the share contributed by the government will increase.
5. Imports will probably grow at a faster rate than exports during this period.
6. The domestic gap between savings and investment will continue to be larger than the external gap between exports and imports.
7. Most importantly, the economy should be nearing self-sustained nonoil based growth by the end of the century.

The major focus of the study is on the likely character of Saudi Arabia's economy in the 1980s and 1990s. This is done by:

1. Examining the long-term problems which help to define, along with certain social, philosophical and institutional knowns, the necessary development strategy for Saudi Arabia as seen in 1981 is developed.
2. Analyzing and appraising the Second Plan (1975–1980) goals so as to specify more correctly the most probable Third Plan (1980–1985) scenario and its concomitant policy requirements.

3. Projecting on a preliminary basis the major macroeconomic variables of the Third Development Plan with an eye to extending these into the Fourth, Fifth, and Sixth Development Plans.
4. Reemphasizing in the light of present developments, the key problems in the macroeconomic area that are most likely to be a cause of concern.

Because the foreign-exchange surpluses made possible by the oil revenues are essentially a transfer of income to the future, the three main policy issues examined at length are

1. How rapidly should oil production be increased;
2. How much of the oil revenues should the government allocate to domestic spending to increase current benefits, and how can this best be done;
3. How should the government encourage the private sector's participation in the economy after policy issues 1 and 2 have been resolved?

In examining these issues it was necessary to take into account the limitations to growth imposed by natural bottlenecks such as the transport system, the scarcity of physical resources (other than hydrocarbon), and of trained people—administrators, managers, technicians, and skilled workers. These are discussed at length with the concluding chapters devoted to identifying:

1. Sectors in which massive spending would be most economically rational and could be successfully implemented.
2. The impact of this expenditure on living standards and personal disposable income.
3. The spatial pattern of growth best suited for the country.
4. The best means available to the country to improve its absorptive capacity.
5. The role of external resources—in particular foreign expertise, skills, and technology—in building a more self-sustaining economy.

It is concluded that Saudi Arabia's major economic problem is not capital, but rather its optimal allocation. Therefore a major task in the chapters that follow is to analyze the Saudi Arabian situation within the concept of a capital-surplus-developing economy and to suggest the necessary considerations—from a Saudi Arabian viewpoint—which must be taken into account to manage the oil-based financial surplus. This task is to be accomplished by:

1. Describing the relationship between growth, inflation, and oil revenues in the Saudi Arabian economy.

2. Discussing some of the international political and economic considerations which are likely to determine the size of future oil revenues.
3. Presenting some elementary theoretical considerations in the determination of absorptive capacity.
4. Attempting to empirically determine the approximate size of the financial surplus according to different sets of assumptions.
5. Suggesting an approach for surplus management.
6. Indicating broadly the type of approach to be taken by the government toward the private sector to assure that sector's full participation in the country's development.

It might be argued that this approach totally ignores the political ramifications of the development process, and that an Iran-like revolution is likely to occur, thus undermining the government's whole development effort and invalidating the economic forecasts made throughout the study.

At this point it should suffice that the differences between the political dynamics of Iran and Saudi Arabia are too pronounced for anything like the set of forces undermining the Shah to befall the Saudi monarchy. In addition:[2]

1. Iran has over ten times the population of Saudi Arabia (over 40 million compared to approximately 4 million, respectively). (See table 1-1.) Thus Saudi Arabia's greater oil revenues are spread over far fewer people, vastly reducing the chances of the serious economic recession which helped to undermine the Shah's regime. Moreover, with a smaller population, Saudi Arabia depends to a greater degree on foreign laborers who can be sent home if economic activity declines.

2. Islam provides a major element of legitimacy for the Saudi monarchy, whereas in Iran the regime attempted to exclude the Islamic leadership from the political process.

3. The pace of economic development has been more measured in Saudi Arabia, thus avoiding the extreme dislocations in its economy that Iran experienced (such as massive inflation, the creation of an industrial labor force with high wages and low productivity, and mass migration to the cities). While these developments are occurring in Saudi Arabia, they are not doing so at nearly as rapid a pace as occurred in Iran.

4. Saudi Arabia, despite some regional differences, is a far more homogeneous society than multiethnic Iran.

While it is not probable that the Saudi monarchy will be faced with the same sort of situation that toppled the Shah, this is not to say that Saudi Arabia is experiencing no social change. All developing countries that are rapidly introducing modern technology and education to traditional and largely illiterate societies face the problems of change. In this process,

Table 1-1
Comparative Economic Positions of the Arab Countries, 1975 and 1985
(Constant 1975 dollars)

Country	Gross Domestic Product (billions)		Nonoil GDP (billions)		GDP Per Capita (thousands)		Nonoil GDP Per Capita (thousands)		Accumulation (billions)		Population (millions)	
	1975	1985	1975	1985	1975	1985	1975	1985	1975	1985	1975	1985
Saudi Arabia	38.0	61.1	5.6	15.2	6.1	7.3	0.9	1.8	56	79–121	6.2	8.4
Kuwait	10.9	15.6	2.3	3.4	10.9	12.0	2.3	2.6	27	63–115	1.0	1.3
Iraq	13.6	22.5	5.3	10.8	1.2	1.5	0.5	0.7	4	26–42	11.1	14.9
Libya	14.7	23.6	7.0	15.6	6.1	7.3	2.9	4.9	Small		2.1	3.2
Egypt	12.4	21.4			0.3	0.4					37.1	47.6
Syria	4.7	9.0			0.6	0.9					7.4	9.9
Jordan	0.9	1.7			0.5	0.6					2.0	2.7

Source: Arthur Smithies, *The Economic Potential of the Arab Countries*, The Rand Corporation, R-2250-NA, November 1978.

Notes: The 1985 GDP figures for the oil rich assume export income increasing at 3.5 percent annually. Population figures assume 1975 population increase at 3.0 percent annually, with the exception of Egypt, which is assumed to increase at 2.5 percent.

expectations typically rise and frustrations increase in proportion to the degree that they are not met. The central question underlying the analysis in the following chapters, therefore, is to what degree can the kingdom's social, political, and economic institutions collectively meet rising and changing expectations?

Notes

1. Ralph Braibanti and Fouad Abdul-salam Al-Farsy, "Saudi Arabia: A Development Perspective," *Journal of South Asian and Middle Eastern Studies* (September 1977): 7–8.

2. David E. Long, "Saudi Arabia," in Joint Economic Committee, Congress of the United States, *The Political Economy of the Middle East: 1973–1978* (Washington: U.S. Government Printing Office, 1980), p. 181.

2
Natural Resources—
Physical Environment

The size and structure of available resources and their utilization are fundamental to every analytical and growth model of the economy. No economy can spend more than it produces and imports; neither can it in the short run radically change the spending proportions among private consumption, public consumption, and savings. If sudden security decisions put heavy demands on public expenditure or if accelerated planned development is undertaken, these usually end up—at least in the short run—in inflation.

The economic progress of any society, therefore, depends in large measure on its ability to adapt its productive structure to its wants and to its available natural resources. The natural endowment is usually less important to this progress than the human contribution, but the quality and character of natural resources have an important effect on the pattern and production and often on the level of incomes achieved.[1] The effect of resources on the level and pattern of growth has probably been more significant in Saudi Arabia's case than nearly any other country.

Saudi Arabia's development pattern has been formed by two broad factors: those that can be classified as internal and those that might be traced to the external environment. Poverty of nonoil natural resources such as the limited availability of land for agriculture and lack of many of the essential materials for industrial output have historically characterized Saudi Arabia and been major impediments on the kingdom's growth. Only very recently has the severe paucity of the country's nonoil resources begun to be successfully overcome. This development is partially the result of institutional adaptation or innovation within, and partly by resorting to solutions which have depended on the external environment; that is, the importation of technology and manpower made possible by developments in the oil sector. The interaction between the internal and external has had a profound effect on the country's process of development as well as its course over the last several decades. It is, therefore, with reference to this interaction that we first consider the internal barriers to development.

Topography

The whole of Arabia is tilted—a great slab of ancient rock pushed up into high mountains in the west, down almost to sea level in the east. Inland, a sandy plateau slopes downward to the Gulf, broken up by wadis, broad valleys carved out by the rainfall of a time (perhaps only 15,000 years ago) when the area was much wetter than at present. The extreme is reached in the *Rub al Khali*, the Empty Quarter, where often rain does not fall for several consecutive years. This area is literally a sea of sand, with sand mountains up to 1,000 feet high. Although there is some interest in the area because of the likely presence of oil, its harsh conditions have resulted in it being still largely unexplored. There are a few mountains on the east coast. Those that do exist are geologic extensions of their Iranian counterparts on the opposite side of the Gulf.[2]

Along the Red Sea and extending inland 15 to 75 miles is a hot, dry, desolate coastal plain known as Tihama. It is occasionally traversed by dry river valleys (or wadis) which provide sufficient underground water (and occasional runoff water from occasional rains) to support limited agriculture.

The largest city in the region is Jeddah (1974 population, 561,104),[3] a commercial center for the entire kingdom and the port for Mecca (366,800), the holiest city in Islam. Mecca is about 50 miles east of Jeddah and is surrounded by barren rocky hills. Slightly to the east of Mecca and rising abruptly from the plain is a relatively narrow escarpment running the entire length of Saudi Arabia. Altitudes vary from 3,000 to 4,000 feet in the north and reach 10,000 feet in the south. In neighboring Yemen, further to the south, the mountains exceed heights of 12,000 feet.

The region south of al-Taif (204,857) is called Asir. Its regional capital is Abba (50,150), 8,000 feet up in the mountains. Nearby on the coast is the seaport town of Jizn (32,812) which has recently been connected to Abba by a modern road. Southeast of Abba is the Wadi Najran, a fertile dry-river valley extending toward Yemen.

Writing of southern Arabia, Wilfred Thesiger referred to it "as a bitter desiccated lad which knows nothing of gentleness or ease."[4] Lawrence described the life of the Saudi Arabian bedouin as a "death in life."[5] And in a way the early explorers and travellers in Arabia saw the problems of the area, which have by no means essentially changed, with greater clarity than many modern analysts. Thesiger puts the situation most aptly: "Men live there because it is the world into which they were born; the life they lead is the life their forefathers led before them; they accept hardships and privations; they know no other way."[6]

The Asir is the only part of Saudi Arabia to receive regular rainfall, most of which comes from the Indian Ocean monsoons. Its terrain, terraced fields, and stone-built villages resemble sectors of Yeman and Lebanon rather than the rest of Saudi Arabia. Rainfall is undependable, however, and it is not uncommon for the region to experience droughts of several years' duration.

As noted, east of the mountains the terrain slopes away gradually until it reaches sea level along the shores of the Persian Gulf. Central Arabia is called Najd. Its most prominent land feature is Jubal Tuwaiq, a westward facing escarpment which extends 600 miles in a shallow arc from north to south. The major population center of the Najd is Riyadh, the capital. In the last 10 years, Riyadh has grown from an isolated mud-brick oasis town to a modern sophisticated city of 666,840 (1974).

Northeast of Riyadh in the Qasim district are the rival major towns of Anayzah and Buraydah (169,940). Beyond them in the Jabal Shammar district is al-Hayil (40,502), seat of the Al Rashids, historic rivals of the House of Saud. Southwest of Riyadh is the oasis of al-Kharj, a major military center.

Along the Arabian Gulf coast lies the Eastern Province. A low barren plain dotted with rocky outcrops, its chief population centers are the vast Hasa (*al-Ahsa*) Oasis with its principal town Hufuf (101,271), and the smaller Qatif Oasis. Hasa once give its name to the entire area, but with the development of Dhahran, it has fallen from prominence. Dhahran is not really a traditional Saudi town but instead comprises the spiraling Arabian American Oil Company (ARAMCO) headquarters and residential area, the Petroleum and Minerals University campus, the American consulate general compound, and the Dhahran airport complex.

The two population centers in the vicinity are Dammam (127,844), the capital of the Eastern Province, and al-Khobar (48,817), south Dammam and east of Dhahran, and the Qatif Oasis is Ras Tanura, the site of Saudi Arabia's major oil refinery and oil-loading terminal.

Weather

Of all the sizable countries on earth, Saudi Arabia is probably the driest. Its weather is climatically linked to the eastern Mediterranean and adjacent lands, in that it has a long, hot, and almost totally dry summer, with a short, cool winter season during which little rain occurs because the air masses reaching Arabia have been largely exhausted of their moisture. Although Arabia is surrounded on three sides by the sea, aridity remains the dominant feature.

Although nearly all Saudi Arabia is hot and dry, there are great variations in climate. Winters are generally balmy, but nights can be quite cold in the mountains and interior. Subfreezing temperatures often occur at night during the winter. Summers are very hot, and often reach 140°F in the desert. Temperatures do, however, drop rapidly at sunset in the desert interiors. Along the coasts, the high humidity militates against such extremes, but summers are quite oppressive with temperatures ranging from 100°F to 115°F, while the humidity is usually in the high 90s.

Water

Until recently, the difficulty of the terrain, its aridity, and the consequent scarcity of good soil sharply controlled the ways of life within the kingdom. Apart from a few fishermen and traders, Saudi Arabia was able to support only a small population, estimated at 1.5 to 2 million in the 1930s. Possibly half of this could be regarded as rural cultivators, village craftsmen, and sheperds moving locally over short distances with their animals. At least one-quarter of the population was entirely nomadic, following a regular pattern of rough grazing of sheep, goats, and camels, involving considerable annual movement.[7] Both ways of life depended on the use of wells which tapped water tables at moderate or shallow depth, for there is no permanent river. Today, with the advent of planned irrigation and the exploitation of underground water resources, four or five times the former population is supported and the major cities previously noted have evolved.

Most of Saudi Arabia's problems, therefore, stem from internal resource deficiencies. From a surface area of some 2.3 million kilometers, only 0.2 percent of the total is cultivated, and of this less than 20 percent can be worked under rain-fed agriculture. Outside of the Asir all agriculture takes place in irrigated areas of the wadi basins and coastal plains, and in scattered oases where subsurface water supplies can be economically raised for use in cultivation. All other water sources, including deep-lying aquifers and desalination plants, tend to produce water too expensive for use in all but high-technology irrigation units. The same arguments apply equally to the supply of industrial water. It is possible and there are several examples in operation to subsidize water for agriculture and industry, though such activities clearly increase rather than diminish the kingdom's dependence on oil income.

Geology

Because of its importance as a major oil producer, the geology of Saudi Arabia has been thoroughly studied. Our knowledge of it has vastly improved in the last 20 years. Most of Saudi Arabia is situated in a huge sedimentary basin extending from the Anatolian Highlands of Turkey to the Hajar Mountains of Oman, and from the Hijaz Mountains in the west to the Zagros Mountains of Iran in the east.

The Hijaz Mountains are volcanic and geologically a part of the pre-Cambrian shield, one of the oldest formations known. To the east, the geology, though ancient, is of more recent origin than the Hijaz. The Arabian Gulf covered this area at one time, and sedimentary marine deposits accumulated on top of the shield. Over time, this great sedimentary basin began to sink gently toward the east, and the fossilized remains of marine life were gradually transformed into oil deposits caught in pockets in the limestone and sandstone rock strata. These pockets (known as domes or anticlines) are the present-day oil fields.

Raw-Material Base

Fortunately for Saudi Arabia, economic development of the country is influenced not only by its geography, but also by the availability, richness, and variety of its raw-material endowments.

Saudi Arabia is the richest, yet possibly the most engimatic country in the Middle East because although its crucial role in the world petroleum industry is much publicized, far less is known about its other economic resources. In fact it has only been fairly recently that nonoil minerals have attracted much attention.

The 1972 mining law (revised in 1973) offers important incentives to overseas mining companies, and French, British, Canadian, and Swedish companies are surveying the prospects for various minerals.

So far relatively few nonoil minerals have been discovered. Deposits of gold, silver, iron, sulfur, phosphates, and rare metals have been found. Low-grade iron-ore deposits at Wadi Fatimah, near Jeddah, are estimated to contain about 1 to 2 billion tons. Large quantities are also believed to exist in the Wadi Sawanin and Jebel Idsa areas. Other known mineral reserves include deposits of phosphates along the Jordanian border, concentrations of heavy metal on the Red Sea floor, and deposits of copper in the Jabal Sayid area.

As things stand in 1981, however, gold is the only nonpetroleum mineral commercially mined in Saudi Arabia. Although the new mining law provides substantial incentives for investment, the lack of infrastructure and shortages of labor make it unlikely that the private sector will undertake significant investment in this field. The government intends to exploit some of the iron deposits. A steel mill with an annual capacity of 3 million tons of pellets and 1 million tons of steel products is planned for Jubail. On the whole, however, minerals other than oil and gas are not expected to play an important role in the Saudi economy until the mid-1980s. They should begin to provide a practical-investment outlet for a significant portion of Saudi oil revenues at that time. On the other hand, the importance of natural gas is destined to increase more rapidly as plans for the Jubail and Yenbo industrial centers are implemented during the 1980s. Over the long run exploitation of nonoil minerals may become a significant foreign-exchange earner.[8]

Oil and Gas

Ultimately the special Saudi role in the world economy is founded upon its ownership of nearly 25 percent of total known reserves of crude. At the end of 1977 its proven reserves were estimated at 153 billion barrels out of 646 billion for the world as a whole, and 548 billion for the noncommunist countries. Historically, there have been differences in the official Saudi estimates and those of Aramco so that the precise figure is not clear.

Exploration is still continuing and the government's own geologists are compiling as much seismic data as possible—especially about the *Rub al Khali*, the Empty Quarter, where many experts predict substantial oil deposits. Many Saudi officials feel that oil not yet discovered will be equal to the 110 billion barrels of existing reserves.

Oil was first discovered in 1938, but large-scale development did not take place until after World War II. Since that time production has grown rapidly, with output in 1971 averaging 4.77 million barrels per day, rising to over 6 million barrels per day in 1972. By September 1973 output had reached 8.3 million barrels per day and was expected to reach 10 million barrels per day by the end of the year. Production, however, was interrupted by the Arab oil restrictions, introduced after the October 1973 Middle East war. As a result, production averaged 7.6 million barrels per day for the whole of 1973. The restrictions were progressively relaxed during the first half of 1974, and output was back at September 1973 levels by the middle of the year.[9]

Output fell steadily from the end of 1974 onward and averaged only 6.97 million barrels per day in 1975. Recovery set in, however, in 1976 when output was 8.6 million barrels per day. The following year saw a substantial recovery to 9.2 million barrels per day, but a slack world economy caused a sharp reversal in the first half of 1978 to 7.7 million barrels per day. Increases following the Iran shortfall brought production to nearly 11 million barrels per day by the end of 1980.

The kingdom is clearly the largest producer of oil in the Middle East and the largest exporter in the world. The main purchasers of Saudi crude are Japan, the Netherlands, Italy, France, the United Kingdom, and to a growing extent the United States.[10]

The government is anxious to establish in broad outline the extent of its oil wealth to plan systematically its depletion policy. This policy will ultimately be dependent in large part on technical factors. There is a certain maximum rate of depletion that corresponds to good oil-field practice, which on 1981 reserves is probably around 20 million barrels per day. But, as noted, 1981 production is considerably below this.[11]

One consideration that determines the level of production is the technical capacity of the oil-field equipment. In 1981 the Saudis are capable, if they want to, of producing over 12 million barrels per day. By the mid-1980s the technical capacity of their equipment will rise to 14 million barrels per day. There are no plans at the moment to raise capacity further, once this point is reached. Much depends on the level of production the Saudis actually attain in the early 1980s when the demand for Middle East oil is expected to increase sharply again after the pause caused by the increased supplies from the Alaskan and North Sea fields. If political considerations in the Middle East or concern for the American economy lead the government to allow production to rise to the 14 million-barrels-per-day target, then the Saudis might have to increase capacity even further to retain some of their control over the OPEC pricing process.[12]

One factor which will influence the levels of output is the kingdom's determination to alter the production balance between the light and heavy crudes. Per refined barrel, light, low-sulphur crude produces more high-value products (such as gasoline) and less, low-sulphur residual-fuel oil. Also the cost of removing sulphur from light crude is much less expensive. Heavy, high-sulphur crude is thus considerably less attractive, especially to refiners—such as most of those in the United States—that in any case are not technically equipped to process it. Since much of the incremental demand for OPEC oil is likely to come in the future from America (rather than from the more traditional customers such as Europe or Japan), demand for light oil is likely to be rising just at the time when the OPEC members are trying to sell more heavy oil. From the Saudi point of view, the priorities are clear: the ratio of production to reserves is very small for heavy crudes and quite large for light crudes. To try to shift the balance, Saudi policy should permit almost no increase in production of light crude. In the immediate future, any extra production should be that of heavy crude.

The present balance is still tilted firmly toward light crude. Production in September 1977, for example, ran at 6,486,000 barrels per day for Arab light, 553,000 barrels per day for the exceptionally light Berri crude, and 1,460,000 barrels per day for the heavier crudes. This is a ratio of nearly 5:1 light to heavy.

The capital cost of converting refineries to handle heavy, high-sulphur crude is considerable, and it looks as though the present price differential between light and heavy crudes is not sufficient to encourage refiners to convert. Heavy crudes have been rising in price much less rapidly than light crudes, and this trend is likely to continue in the 1980s. It is a development that will help to even out the depletion of Saudi Arabia's resources—but it will mean increased competition at the heavy end of the market. This is especially troublesome for one of Saudi Arabia's major rivals, Kuwait—the only producer in the world 100 percent dependent on heavy crude.

Of particular interest to the government is the development of improved methods of obtaining maximum recovery from its existing fields. Traditionally expensive methods of boosting recovery by injecting gas or water to push the oil to the surface have tended to be introduced toward the end of a field's life. When ARAMCO was American-owned, these techniques were usually only used as a last resort to prevent a decline in production. But now that control of the oil lies in most cases with the government, these techniques are being used even at the initial stages of exploration. The country is tending to use its gas for industrial fuel or petrochemical feedstock, and thus is relying mainly on water to push the oil out of its producing-formations.

Because water itself is scarce, this method has obvious limitations. The traditional technique—known as "dump flooding"—usually has entailed finding natural stores of water several thousand feet above the oil-producing formations. This is done by drilling a hole to link the two strata, then allowing the water to flow down into the oil-bearing levels from above. This technique has been mainly useful at the early stages of a field's life when the water pressures need to be low. Other means of getting a higher pressure into the fields are needed as many fields reach a mature stage of production.

At the end of 1976, ARAMCO was injecting over 12 million barrels per day of water into eleven fields—handling much more water, therefore, than oil. A huge desalination plant is being constructed to replace the dwindling supplies of underground water. A 60 mile-long pipeline from the coast will carry the treated water to the field. The first stage of the project began operation in 1978, and underground water sources then started to be replaced with treated seawater. A treatment plant that can handle 5.5 million barrels per day of seawater is now being built but the facilities can be expanded to cope with 15 million barrels per day if necessary.

The huge scale of such undertakings—designed in this instance to provide water for just one area of one field—underlies the care that is being taken by the Saudis to get the most oil possible out of the ground. These methods will obviously raise the average cost of producing crude oil, which in 1981 is approximately 30 cents a barrel. Still, the incremental barrels will cost far less than they do in Alaska or the North Sea.

Saudi Arabia's oil reserves are adequate to finance the economic objectives of the government. The huge and prolific oil fields have so far sustained the country's rapid economic development, largely through the provision of foreign exchange. But as the country's industrialization advances at a rapid pace, oil and gas reserves will increasingly be called on to take on the added function of supplying part of the raw material and energy requirements of the domestic economy. In the same vein, nonoil minerals will be increasingly tapped to provide raw materials needed by domestic industries. To be sure, however, Saudi Arabia will by no means be self-sufficient in many of its nonoil needs; foodstuffs in particular, in the near future. But the country's capacity to use its oil and gas revenues in the the service of diversification and industrialization is vastly superior to most of its oil-producing neighbors in the Persian Gulf.

The Saudi reserves-to-capacity ratio in January of 1981 is about 45:1. The government has never given any official indication of the ratio that it would consider desirable. At times however, prominent officials have indicated that a 2 to 3 percent annual depletion is desirable. This rate would mean reserves to production ratios of approximately 33 to 50 years.[13] There is every reason to believe, however, that reserves in the kingdom will increase with exploration and that new discoveries and revisions will exceed annual production for many years in the future. Thus reserves should continue to rise during the foreseeable future.

Debate about this issue within the Saudi hierarchy has often been reported, though focusing on a different aspect—namely, the rate at which it is wise to turn oil in the ground into another kind of Saudi wealth, the nation's holdings of foreign exchange. For some years at least, the kingdom will continue to have more current income that it can practically spend at home on welfare and development (see forecasts in chapter 16) or dispense in aid to Arab and Muslin developing countries abroad. Hence, much of each year's income ends up as petrodollar surpluses, holdings of foreign exchange, bonds, and securities.

What the Saudis do with their oil is of such importance to the rest of the world that their policies are often discussed as if these external consequences and implications ought to be their ruling considerations in policymaking. That is, of course, preposterous. Saudi policy regarding oil or anything else is and must continue to be directed primarily toward furthering the kingdom's own national objectives.

Conclusions

Saudi Arabia's natural resource endowment is probably too narrow to support a high degree of diversification. The huge and prolific oil fields have so far sustained the country's rapid economic development largely through the provision of foreign exchange. But as the kingdom's industrialization advances at a rapid pace, oil and gas reserves will increasingly take on the added function of supplying part of the raw material and energy requirements of the domestic economy. In the same vein, certain nonoil materials will be tapped to provide raw materials needed by domestic industries. Certainly Saudi Arabia will by no means be self-sufficient in many of its nonoil needs in the near future. But the country's capacity to use its oil and gas revenues in the service of diversification and industrialization is, with the exception of Iran and Iraq, vastly superior to that of its oil-producing neighbors on the Gulf.

Notes

1. Hollis Chenery, "Land: The Effects of Resources on Economic Growth," in Kenneth Berrill, ed., *Economic Development with Special Reference to East Asia* (London: Macmillan, 1965), p. 19.

2. Peter Mansfield, *The Middle East*, 5th ed. (New York: Oxford University Press, 1980), pp. 105–106.

3. Unless otherwise specified, all population figures are from the 1974 census. See Saudi Arabia: Ministry of Finance and National Economy, Central Department of Statistics Census of Population in the Kingdom of Saudi Arabia, 1974 (Dammam: 1978).

4. Wilfred Thesiger, *Arabian Sands* (New York: Dutton, 1959), p. 7.

5. Cited in Thesiger, *Arabian Sands*, p. 18.

6. Ibid., p. 19.

7. Sir Norman Anderson et al., *The Kingdom of Saudi Arabia* (London: Stacey International, 1977), p. 18.

8. F. Abolfathi et al., *The OPEC Market to 1985* (Lexington, Mass.: Lexington Books, D.C. Heath and Company, 1977), pp. 248–249.

9. An excellent account of this progress is given in J.E. Hartshorn, *Objectives of the Petroleum Exporting Countries* (Nicosia: Middle East Petroleum and Economic Publications, 1978), pp. 75–101.

10. The Economist Intelligence, Unit, *A Study of the Middle East Economies: Their Structure and Outlook into the 1980s* (London: The Economist Intelligence Unit, 1978). p. 202.

11. Hartshorn, *Objectives*, p. 89.

12. Saudi Arabia's role in and relationship to OPEC are discussed at length in chapter 6.

13. Hartshorn, *Objectives*, p. 91.

3

An Islamic Growth Model—Theoretical Considerations

National economic performance is influenced not only by natural and raw material resources, but also by its religious and other social institutions, and the overall philosophy supporting the sociopolitical superstructure. Even a resource-rich country such as Saudi Arabia may be hampered in its development efforts by its own religion-derived institutional-philosophical underpinnings. A rigid, doctrinaire philosophy may not only make it difficult to attain development objectives; it may also perpetuate suboptimal allocation of resources. On the other hand, a flexible, pragmatic, and generally utilitarian economic order can greatly facilitate economic performance and help optimize the utilization of scarce resources.

The kingdom of Saudi Arabia was, until the Iranian Revolution, perhaps the nearest equivalent in the world today of the old Islamic ideal of theocracy: a community of believers who have benefited from divine revelation to the Prophet Mohammed and who seek to implement God's will through the application of the Holy Law, or the *Shari'a*.

Islamic principles permeate all aspects of Saudi Arabia—its political institutions, social philosophy, and its economic organizations. Together these combine to yield the country's Islamic economic system, a unique and often misinterpreted method of organizing economic activity. Identifying the fundamental nature of the Islamic economic system entails addressing several basic issues. First, what essential characteristics of the economic framework are and must be consistent with the Islamic philosophy of life and in what manner? Presumably the economic system is designed to reflect the Islamic point of view about the basic economic processes. Second, what policy objectives appropriate to an Islamic society are advocated by the authorities? Third, what policy instruments have been chosen by the kingdom, presumably with a view toward achieving these specified policy goals, while at the same time satisfying the ethical constraints Islam prescribes? Without pretending to be authoritative, the objective of what follows is to examine each of these fundamental issues in a general abstract way. This involves the identification of what might be referred to as the ethical foundations of Islamic economies and will comprise the remainder of this chapter.[1] This chapter attempts to determine how Islamic principles arise in the Saudi Arabian context.

Political Institutions

Saudi Arabia as a political entity dates from 1924–1925 when Abdul-Aziz ibn Saud completed his conquest of the country. He first took the title of King of Hegaj, then of Jejd, and finally in 1932 of Saudi Arabia. When he died in 1953, he was succeeded by his son King Saud, who was deposed in November 1964 by his brother, King Faisal ibn Abdul-Aziz. In March 1975, King Faisal was assassinated and was succeeded by his brother, Crown Prince Khaled.[2]

Saudi Arabia is an absolute monarchy. King Khaled heads the government as prime minister and minister of foreign affairs in the Council of Ministers. Many of the other ministers are members of the king's family. Ministers are responsible to the king, and the apparatus of modern government—ministries, civil service, budgeting, and so on—has been built up in less than a decade.

Saudi political institutions consist of three distinct though closely related areas: royal family politics, national politics, and Saudi bureaucratic politics. In all three, two traditional practices form the core of the decision-making process: consultation or *shura* and consensus or *ijma*.

The royal family serves as the constituency of the kingdom. The king is far from being an absolute monarch in that he must secure a consensus of support from the family. No one is quite sure how the family operates to create such a consensus or even how large it is (probably several thousand).

Islam has always provided the ideological base of the regime and hence a good measure of its legitimacy. *Shari'a* or Islamic law serves as the law of the land, and the religious leadership under the aegis of the Al al-Shaykh family (descendants of Muhammed ibm Abd al-Whhab) has always controlled the judicial system. One of the constraints on establishing a Western-type legislature is that Islamic law is holy and only God can legislate. Regulatory or administrative law outside the purview of Islamic law is presently promulgated in the form of royal decrees. There is talk, however, of creating a consulative assembly of *Majlis al-Shura*.[3]

The national political system in Saudi Arabia revolves around the king. In classical Islamic political theory, he is the *Imam* or leader of the faithful, the *ummah*. Besides maintaining the support of the royal family, the only other constraint on the king is Islamic law. Theoretically, he can be sued in his own courts.

There are no political parties or franchises. There is a constitution, an independent judiciary, and a modern judicial system—the result of an important reform program begun in 1962. King Khaled has promised a consulative council to "lay the foundations of justice." Oil revenues have changed the face of Saudi Arabia but not its social structure. While the government is committed to a policy of developing the economy as rapidly as possible, it is trying to do so without straining the existing political and social fabric.

Social Philosophy

One of the most impressive features of Saudi Arabia is the way in which, generally speaking, the Saudis enforce their Islamic form of rule. By any rule Saudis are a very conservative and conformist people, not because they are easily led or unduly passive, but because most of them believe in a real and positive sense in the type of society which Saudi Arabia is trying to become. This is as true of young people who have been educated abroad as it is of their elders—and it is striking how many young people return to the kingdom as soon as they have finished their education and fit back into Saudi society without any difficulty at all.[4]

Development economists may be somewhat surprised by the ordering of priorities in the country's official five-year plans, for the first of their guiding principles is to maintain the values of Islam, and the second is to ensure the defense and internal security of the kingdom.[5] Islamic political theorists, however, would find this ranking of goals quite natural. For if the Islamic community is to prosper, there must be constant interaction between religious authority and political power. The religious authority gives legitimacy to the political power, and the political power is in itself a form of religious prestige, for it is through this power that the ruler maintains the conditions in which the *Shari'a* may flourish. This explains the interdependence of state and religion in the traditional Islamic community. This is the situation which the modern kingdom of Saudi Arabia seeks to preserve.

Economic System

It is possible to develop arguments that might categorize the country as either socialist or capitalist. Those who cite the socialist aspects of the economic system usually point to the large share of the public sector in gross national product and to state ownership of a large proportion (in terms of value) of industrial production.

In fact the Saudi public sector totally dominates the economy by virtue of oil receipts. Not only does the government initiate nearly all domestic development projects but it is the fountainhead of nearly all funds entering the private sector as well. The mechanism in the system of public tenders through which all services are performed for the government by private contractors must be channeled. To obtain contracts may bidders retain middlemen to use their good offices with those who will price the contractor.

Although the system of agents has been officially curtained by the Saudi government, it is still highly prevalent.[6]

Also, the government is involved in extensive direct subsidization of consumption. Beginning with the Second Development Plan (1975–1980), the government assumed the responsibility for improving the economic and social well-being of Saudi citizens. This was not a sharp break with past policy made possible by the increase in oil revenues. Instead the major expansion of such programs as education and the provision of health care for all citizens (without direct cost) was in large part an extension of past policies. With the addition of many new programs and the extension of old ones, the government was able to develop a social security program capable of eventually meeting the basic requirements of all Saudis. Many foods are now subsidized, housing is provided at subsidized rates, and utilities have been extended and are provided by the government at low rates. In addition a wide range of recreational and social programs are offered at no cost by the government. In short the government now has the means to accept major responsibilities it was incapable of previously undertaking. These new responsibilities and program increases represent a potential commitment of resources of great proportions given the lack of marketable skills and the low standard of living of many Saudis.[7]

On the other hand, the Saudis have usually maintained that they prefer not to duplicate the Kuwaiti experience with its aspects of the welfare state. They assert that with the increased oil revenues, only minimum standards will be guaranteed by government actions and programs.[8]

Clearly, with its large revenues accruing directly to the state, the government has little reason to avoid such responsibilities. Saudi Arabia with its larger population and more varied resources has more scope for providing productive employment for its citizens than does Kuwait. But with economic welfare in the foreseeable future of the kingdom dependent upon the revenues from petroleum it seems natural for the government to share this wealth through welfare programs. To call the system socialistic misses the point.

In fact Saudi Arabia has one of the most laissez-faire economies in the world. The same Hanibali school of Islamic law which is so strict on social behavior is ironically the most liberal of all schools on business and economic matters. Similarly, there are few political restrictions on commerce.

Certainly "people's capitalism" is a better description of the situation than "state socialism." With the notable exception of petroleum, a few oil-related industries and certain manufacturing activities planned by the government and financed by state oil revenues, all traditional economic activities are privately owned and operated. The theocratic nature of the Saudi government based on Quranic scriptures and the devoutly religious makeup of its Islamic monarchy also place the Saudi kingdom in the nonsocialist group.[9]

Religion and Development

An identification of the linkages between religion and the kingdom's development has more importance than simply contributing to our theoretical understanding of the country's development process, however, for there can be little doubt that the objective conditions which relate development processes with religious impulses have changed dramatically in recent years.[10] In fact the best example of this is found right in the Islamic world and next to Saudi Arabia with the events in Iran providing the most tangible impact of religion on development. The importance played by religious forces not only in the overthrow of the Shah but more importantly in apparently mobilizing public frustrations with the country's Western-oriented, high-growth development strategy have obvious implications for the success of Saudi Arabia's current development strategy.

In fact, drastic revaluation of values is in process in the study of economic and political development. It has been forced upon economists by a series of disasters that have occurred in countries in which development seemed to be vigorously under way. The Iranian Revolution, the civil war in Nigeria, and the bloody falling apart of Pakistan are only the most spectacular instances of such development disasters.

As a result one reads with increasing frequency, pronouncements about the bankruptcy of the old development economics with its accent on growth rates, industrialization, and integration into the world market, and about the need for a wholly new doctrine that would emphasize the total, not just material, improvement of the individual.

On the surface it appears that many aspects of the Saudi development strategy resemble those of the countries noted previously.

There is some evidence of a fundamentalist Islamic revival in the kingdom, although not nearly on the level experienced by Iran or even that of some of the other Middle Eastern countries such as Egypt and Syria. Undoubtedly, these movements are a consequence of accumulated frustrations that are not rooted in, but are often inimical to social and religious values that command their allegiance. Revelations about the limitations of the overwhelmingly Western-oriented materialistic modern models of development have served to reinforce and support their quest for genuineness rather than transplantation. Moughrabi among others has contended that:

> The old model of development seems to be collapsing under the weight of contradictions and of scarcity. . . . [No longer is it] desirable or feasible to

sustain the social costs imposed by this model namely the social and economic inequalities, the imbalance in the human and ecological environment, the existence of industrial ghettos and of massive urban problems.[11]

The Iranian experience demonstrates, however, that an understanding of the likely success or failure of the kingdom's development strategy can only be obtained within the context that takes into account the linkages between religion and development. An approach which makes religion instrumental in development can still be congenial to the economist, for it suggests that religion may be constructive in the sense of playing a role in defining development and putting limits on the growth of various macroeconomic variables. If one accepts the idea that the kingdom's religious values are the source of the moral base of Saudi society, then it is an easy extension to view patterns of development as acceptable to religious and political authorities when those patterns reinforce that moral base.

This line of argument can be used to show that there are social limits to development. Again using Iran as an example, it is clear that certain development strategies, while seemingly successful from a superficial point of view, were generating the seeds of their own failure. For example, the social limits in Iran's case were apparently generated by the incompatibility between the inherited moral base of society and the type of growth characteristic adopted by the Shah. Thus one might argue that the kingdom's Islamic strategy of development will be more successful. This is at least partially and implicitly a hypothesis often advanced by Saudi planners to the effect that the methods used to implement growth in the country will provide or reinforce the moral base which is essential to Saudi society's functioning. The implication is that while growth is important to the country's leaders, it must still be limited or modified by such considerations for a valid development to occur. Otherwise growth will cause instability or at best a type of development that is transitory in nature and not capable of enabling the kingdom to achieve self-sustained material progress.

Whether these relationships themselves result in any positive correlation or possible link with economic development must in the last analysis be based on the ability of such a system to: (1) reinforce the factors conducive to growth; (2) serve as a deterrent to factors that are growth inhibiting; or (3) accomplish both.[12]

While economists do not always agree on the reasons for differences in national growth rates, there is sufficient agreement among them on the factors that are more or less relevant to growth or stagnation. In broad qualitative terms, five factors may be considered conducive to economic development:

1. Ample supply of natural and human resources.
2. Advanced technical know-how or willingness to adopt new technology.
3. Wise use of resources (that is, full employment and efficiency).

4. A favorable sociocultural value system (for example, dignity of labor, work ethics, and a sense of national purpose and will to progress).
5. Sociopolitical stability (that is, absence of internal strife or external conflicts).

By contrast, five factors may be regarded as growth impediments:

1. Paucity and low quality of natural resources or their inefficient use.
2. Wide gaps between educational programs and national economic needs.
3. Inordinately high propensity for conspicuous consumption or for leisure.
4. Market imperfections and the existence of supply bottlenecks.
5. Uncertainties about the political future of the economy and/or inadequate incentives for investment.

Perhaps none of these factors is totally immune from the long-term effects of a religious value system and short-term influences on the system are rather limited. It is difficult to see how, for example, a religious system can alter such factors as the resource base, the state of technology, business traditions and cultural values in the short span of a few years. In the short run a given religious-political-economic ideology can possibly: (1) help (hinder) efficient use of natural resources, (2) promote (or upset) political stability, and (3) increase (or decrease) the net accumulation of real productive resources.

Several basic issues arise before it is possible to even begin assessing the impact of the kingdom's economic system on the country's overall economic performance.

Framework for Analyzing the Islamic System

Before defining the Islamic economic growth model and its salient characteristics, it is necessary to define precisely the terms: (1) economic policies, (2) objectives, (3) means, and (4) targets.[13]

Economic policy can be viewed as a process by which the government in the light of its general policy aims decides on the relative importance of certain objectives, and if necessary uses instruments or institutional changes in the attempt to obtain those objectives. By government we mean the entity which has the right of coercion whose duties is to provide for collective needs, and which is held responsible for measures of economic policy; it comprises the central government (including the central bank), the local authorities, and state agencies.

Policies and policy instruments are magnitudes fulfilling three conditions. First, policymakers can use them. Second, they are not normally considered as desirable ends in themselves—that is, they are not objectives, although this has not always been the case in Saudi Arabia. Third, their function is to bring about the targets set for the objectives.

General policy objectives include economic welfare, equality, law and order, external security, and similar goals. Usually these aims are not precise enough to be quantified, but must be translated into objectives before this can be attempted. Economic objectives, on the other hand, refer to the desired rate of economic growth, a certain maximum rate of unemployment of price stability, and so on.

For a variety of reasons—such as the scarcity of resources, the nature of the economic system, or the conflicting views of various policymakers—it is usually impossible to reach all targets simultaneously. Some will be sacrificed entirely, or as is more often the case, partially, for the sake of others. The relative importance of objectives and the trade-offs between them are therefore an important element that helps to distinguish an Islamic economic system such as Saudi Arabia's from either capitalism or socialism.

Instruments are not in themselves objectives, but instead usually include such measures as tax rates, interest rates, and the exchange rate which the government can manipulate within a certain range to attain the objectives. Institutional changes, on the other hand, involve qualitative changes in the operation of the economy. Nationalization of industry and land reforms are measures commonly found in the Middle East. These changes are usually employed when the government decides that normal policy instruments would not be capable of reaching the country's main policy targets.

This discussion of policies, objectives, means, and targets is by no means complete but should provide a sufficient framework for discussing and elaborating the Islamic economic system, and highlighting those critical aspects associated with the Islamic system that distinguish it from other systems.

As a starting point, several basic axioms underlying Islam set a number of constraints and limitations on the possible nature of the economic system. These axioms are (1) Islam assigns central place to the individual in the universe, and (2) this freedom entails a responsibility which in turn implies ethical and social constraints on the individual's natural freedom.

Having accepted these axioms, it is possible to begin to understand the manner in which an Islamic economic system tends to differ from other economic organizations.

Characteristics of an Islamic Economic System

The basic philosophy underlying an Islamic economic system is that action in every field of human activity, including the economic, is spiritual as long as it is in harmony with the goals and values of Islam.[14] It is really these goals and values that determine the nature of the economic system of Islam. The major goals and values of Islam include:

1. economic well-being within the framework of the major norms of Islam;
2. universal brotherhood and justice;
3. equitable distribution of income;
4. freedom of the individual within the context of social welfare.

Islam is concerned with the establishment of an economic system which is viable enough to ensure, under all the progressive stages of economic development, two broad objectives: (1) the satisfaction of basic needs of life for all the members of society including those who may be incapacitated or handicapped in one way or another, and (2) a reward in the form of extra comfort or elegance to the talented members of society for their superior skill and enterprise.

The fundamental assumption of the Islamic economic system is that if a man is given the opportunity of applying his intelligence and physical abilities to economic activity, he will always be able to produce, at the minimum, enough to satisfy his basic needs of life. One of the tenets of Islam, however, is that if a man is capable of work, possessing a sound mind in a sound body, but would not engage himself in productive activity, the society and the state shall refuse to support him until he is compelled to work for himself. If a man is incapable of work, the society and state shall help and support him.

The major objectives of economic policy—(1) special justice, (2) economic growth, (3) employment and education, (4) positive public participation—are much more difficult to separate in the Islamic economic system than in the pure versions of socialism or capitalism.

Social Justice

The basic guiding principle regarding economic social justice in Islamic thought in general and in Saudi Arabia in particular is ultimately based on the two basic rules of welfare economics:[15] (1) production should be extended in various branches of production in such a way as to equalize marginal social productiveness among them; (2) the distribtution of income for all consumers must be such as to equalize the marginal utilities of consumption among all consumers. While never stated in these terms, Saudi policy of free trade seems to conform to these principles which if achieved will maximize social welfare—the principal aim of any Islamic society.

Note that the system of laissez-faire capitalism fails to meet these conditions because the market mechanism makes no provision for institutions that can satisfy the second rule. To correct this failing a redistribution of income in favor of those harmed must be effected as a matter of deliberate policy by the government.

The system of free markets also fails to satisfy the first rule of welfare economics, noted earlier, because external economies drive a wedge between the social and private profitabilities of investment in certain types of production. Standard economic theory tells us that in such a circumstance, the state must intervene to maximize social welfare by subsidizing those industries for which the gain to society from additional investment exceeds the gain to private investor.

A number of principles from the *Qu'ran* explicitly form the basis of the free enterprise system in Saudi Arabia. The first of these principles pertains to the right to private ownership of the means of production and the right to inheritance.[16] Second, the *Qu'ran* explicitly states that inequalities of property distribution and hierarchic social stratification are permissible. Third, engagement in gainful employment or labor-wage relations are encouraged. Fourth, commercial activity is singled out as commendable endeavor if it is conducted fairly. Fifth, profit or fair gain is an acceptable source of income.

Employment and Education

It follows that the Islamic economic system requires: (1) that an absolute minimum needed for the barest existence be ensured to every individual; (2) once this minimum is provided for, work must be the precondition of a more comfortable living; (3) the opportunity for work must be provided to all on an equal basis. Islamic economic policy, therefore, aims at the maximum generation of employment opportunities subject to the constraints of economic efficiency.

The published objectives of the education programs in Saudi Arabia are to preserve and transmit the religious heritage of Islam and the cultural traditions of the kingdom based on Islamic principles, while at the same time equipping its citizens for life in a modern and rapidly changing world of materialism and technology.

All education is free and all school materials are mainly provided by the Ministry of Education. Poor students may obtain financial assistance to stay at school and grants are given to all those at vocational or teacher training institutes and other higher education centers. Even private schools taking fee-paying students receive generous subsidies from government funds.

A possible contradiction has begun to develop, however, between the kingdom's education and growth goals. Of the possible one million Saudi women of working age, the Second Plan estimates 27,000 were working in 1975 and that only 48,000 of them would be working in 1980. Women may not work in public places and are not eligible for government scholarships outside the kingdom. Schools for girls did not open until the early 1960s. While these schools are increasing, they remain under the control of the *Ulema* (Muslim religious scholars), rather than the Ministry of Education. Curricula tends to emphasize religious values and the proper role of women. Ironies abound. Women are now permitted to study medicine at the University of Riyadh but are not permitted in the same room with a male professor; all classes are via closed circuit television. Teacher training classes are operated in a similar manner.

Economic Growth

A policy that aims solely or even primarily at securing social justice but does not contain any practical prescription for economic growth dooms the society to stereotyped traditionalism. For the essence of all life, including economic life, is the vitality that social change promotes through a combination of desire, activity, and conscious purpose. Therefore the reactivation of the vital impulses of growth should be the primary concern of an Islamic economic system. How can this be done? According to the basic philosophy of Islam the individual is the primary economic unit. Hence anything that deprives him of the zest for life that all creativeness stipulates and that dulls the spirit of adventure ultimately constitutes the negation of economic growth.

Positive Public Participation

Inasmuch as it destroys the individualistic character of social organisms, a complete socialization of the means of production can find no place in an Islamic society. By the same token a sizable role of private initiative is an essential part of such a society (for the primary growth impulses must emanate from the micro-units of the economic universe—that is, the individuals).

As pointed out, this is not the same as maintaining that laissez-faire characterizes the Islamic economic system. In fact the government will have to assume a bigger role, but only in areas such as education, health, and heavy industries. According to the principles of welfare economics, this applies to all those industries that create sizable external economies—that is, that accrue free of cost to society. However, the government control of business must be sharply distinguished from the government undertaking of the business itself.

The Saudi Arabian government uses public enterprises as an institution of last resort to cover areas where private entrepreneurs are not able or willing to penetrate:

1. To establish the petrochemical industry which is characterized by huge requirements of capital and expertise. PETROMIN offers an example of this type.
2. To stabilize prices and maintain adequate commodity reserves, a task that requires more capital than the private sector can afford. Grain Silos and Flour Mills Organization and the National Supply Corporation are examples of this type of public enterprise.
3. To provide basic transportation and communications services, particularly to those that have strong relation to national security. Saudi airlines and Saudi railroads are examples.

Principles of Islamic Economics

More specifically and apart from the set of values previously discussed which demarcate a large area of freedom for economic action, Islam furnishes a specific set of rules, some positive and other prohibitive, meant to guide action. These include:[17]

1. The payment of the *zakat* is an alms-giving duty amounting to 2.5 percent annually on income and savings. Ten percent is due on an agricultural harvest if irrigation was at no cost and no effort to the farmer; otherwise, only 5 percent is due. Unlike modern taxation *zakat* is a flat rate and does not increase at a progressive scale. Equity is achieved by encouraging voluntary charities. Moreover, in case of need, the state may levy more taxes on the richer.
2. The maintenance costs for certain categories of relatives must be paid— particularly for one's wife, needy parent, and female children until they marry.
3. One has an obligation to provide charitable assistance to one's kin, to one's neighbors, to orphans, and to the needy.
4. Working hard to earn one's own living and the living of dependents is highly praised.
5. Workers, manufacturers, and administrators should exert the utmost effort to make their product as perfect as possible.
6. The conditions laid down in the *Shari'a* law for the validity of business and financial transactions must be fulfilled. These laws make the transfers of goods safe and easy, and facilitate the conclusion of economic transactions between the contracting parties.
7. Pledges, trusts, and terms concluded with other parties must be kept.
8. Estates of deceased persons must be distributed among their heirs and must be respected as laid down in the *Qu'ran*. A person may not make a

will which deprives one of his heirs or which favors one heir over another, nor may he make a will involving more than one-third of his estate.

9. Usury is among the serious sins and all usurous practices should be avoided.

10. There must be respect for other people's property and abstention from unproductive malpractices, profiteering activities, deceiving, gambling, hoarding, monopoly, and the like. Earning through expediency and manipulation of the law is not legitimate.

These ten fundamental and distinct rules give the Islamic system of economics its unique character. The underlying concept is that the economic community is like an organic body in which each cell grows and contributes to the well-being of the other cells.

Differences from Capitalism and Socialism

Both socialism and capitalism have been held to reflect the Islamic ideal of an appropriate economic order. Socialism is often regarded as closer to Islamic tenets than capitalism and presumably would offer Saudi Arabia the possibility of achieving in a relatively short period of time, high rates of real economic growth. Chronic problems such as open inflation, that plague capitalistic society and are held in low regard by the Saudis, are effectively bypassed in socialistic economies by combining productive processes with overall monetary creation.

Furthermore, by directly controlling both the savings and the investment decisions, the need for interest payments becomes redundant in a socialistic economy. Unemployment is also attacked efficiently by socialism through the large-scale mobilization of the labor force for community development projects. A fairer distribution of both income and opportunities is said to have been created in socialism through abolishing private property, and providing free universal education and medical services. Furthermore, there is an air of simplicity about the ruling classes that has appealed to men of austere morals.[18] It is for these reasons that some have said that socialism is nearer than capitalism to the Saudi brand of Islam.

The fact is that Saudi Arabia has been one of the strongest bulwarks against socialism. The reasons for this go to the very heart of the Islamic vision of a social order. It is not only the atheistic tendencies of socialism that are an anathema to Islam and the Saudis. At a deeper level, it is the rejection by Islam of turning man into a cog in a gigantic social machine, even though this may work for the good of society. The creative impulse according to Islam must emanate from the individual, while organization directs it into socially desirable channels. It seeks in addition a judicious distribution among individuals of both the economic and political power that socialism would counter.

Fundamentally, it is the oppressively heavy human cost of economic development socialism imposes on society that is not acceptable to Islam or the Saudis. While Islam professes more work but allows enough leisure to maximize human happiness and help intellectual creativity, in an Islamic economy voluntary work rather than forced mobilization is seen as the best means of mobilizing work for the reconstruction of society. However, Islam does not accept unlimited unconstrained individualism; nor does it tolerate wasteful leisure. The essential waywardness of individual initiative is subjected to a dominant moral purpose so that respect for human dignity is compatible with the overall good of the society.[19]

Conclusions

A definitive treatment of all aspects of an Islamic growth model is beyond the scope of this book and the competence of the author.[20] An examination of its application in Saudi Arabia is at any rate feasible given the current state of knowledge about the basic characteristics of the country's economy. It should offer a convenient framework for examining the country's long-run growth prospects.

Issues of importance for the chapters that follow are:

1. More precisely what is the specific content of the Islamic economic system as adopted by Saudi Arabia?
2. How has this system effectively adjusted over time to new situations?
3. Is there any evidence that the Saudi Arabian brand of Islamic economic system will be any more efficient or inefficient than other systems in meeting the kingdom's major objectives?

Notes

1. Syed Nawab Haider Naqui, "Ethical Foundations of Islamic Economic Study," *Islamic Studies* 27 (1978): 106.

2. An excellent description of these developments is given in Peter Hubday, *Saudi Arabia Today* (New York: St. Martin's Press, 1978), pp. 11–36.

3. David Long, "Saudi Arabia," in Joint Economic Committee, Congress of the United States, *The Political Economy of the Middle East: 1973–78* (Washington: U.S. Government Printing Office, 1980), pp. 181–183.

4. Ralph Braibanti and Fouad Abdul-salam Al-Farsy, "Saudi Arabia: Development Perspective," *Journal of South Asian and Middle Eastern Studies* (September 1977): 21.

5. A detailed description of these priorities and their implications is given in Robert Cranes, *Planning the Future of Saudi Arabia: A Model for Achieving National Priorities* (New York: Praeger Publishers, 1978).

6. Long, "Saudi Arabia," p. 185.

7. Donald Wells, *Saudi Arabian Development Strategy* (Washington: American Enterprise Institute, 1976), p. 55.

8. Ibid. p. 63.

9. Jahangir Amuzegar, "Ideology and Economic Growth in the Middle East," *The Middle East Journal* (Winter 1974): 3.

10. An excellent survey is given in Ibrahim Ragab, "Islam and Development," *World Development* (July/August 1980): 513–521.

11. F.M. Moughrabi, "The Arab Basic Personality: A Critical Survey of the Literature," *Journal of Middle East Studies* (1978): 103.

12. This analysis is based on Amuzegar, "Ideology and Economic Growth," pp. 6–7.

13. These definitions are based on the approach taken in E.S. Kirschen, ed., *Economic Policies Commpared: East and West* vol. I, *General Theory* (New York: American Elsevier Publishing Company, 1974), pp. 8–44.

14. See M.N. Siddiqui, *Some Aspects of the Islamic Economy* (Lahore: Islamic Publications, 1978), pp. 11–26.

15. A good elaboration of these points is given in S. Abul A'La Mavdavdi, *The Economic Problem of Man and Its Islamic Solution* (Lahore: Islamic Publications, 1978).

16. See Muhammad Muslehuddin, *Economics and Islam* (Lahore: Islamic Publications, 1974), ch. II.

17. Muhammad Abdul-Rauf, *The Islamic Doctrine of Economics and Contemporary Economic Thought: Highlight of a Conference on a Theological Inquiry into Capitalism and Socialism* (Washington: American Enterprise Institute, 1978), pp. 9–10.

18. For an elaboration of these parts, see Solayman S. Nyana, "The Islamic State and Economic Development: A Theoretical Analysis," *Islamic Culture* (January 1976): 1–23.

19. See Syed Nauab Haider Nazui, "Islamic Economic System: Fundamental Issues," *Islamic Studies* (Winter 1977): 332–334.

20. An excellent treatment is given in Afzul-ur-Rahman, *Economic Doctrines of Islam*, 3 vols. (Lahore: Islamic Publications, 1974). For an introduction to the issues, see Agdul Zuades Shaikh et al., *Outlines of Islamic Economics* (Indianapolis: Association of Muslim Social Scientists, 1977).

4

An Islamic Growth Model—Industrial and Tax Policies

The Saudis want to create a new and unique type of nation—the first genuinely Muslim industrial power, a country which retains its old values at the same time that it develops economically. The Saudis do not want simply to modernize without regard to cultural developments as so many other countries have done. This view is given formal expression in their development plans, which have as their first objective the maintenance of the moral and religious values of Islam. This objective seems to be shared by all of the leading Saudi officials.[1] In addition to holding this common goal, Saudis in both the private sector and government are in many respects remarkably similar to each other in manner and style.

Apart from devotion to Islam, there is a fervent belief in free enterprise running throughout the Saudi ideal of the new society. Self-discipline in social matters is to be matched by economic self-reliance. The rulers of Saudi Arabia feel that their citizens should stand on their own two feet, and they have no intention of adopting the policy, seen most strikingly in Kuwait, of distributing revenues among the people as an end in itself. The development plan states that its principal social objective is to assure all Saudis "an adequate dignified minimum standard of living. Levels about this minimum will continue to be the reward of individual effort and achievement."

Many of the details concerning the working of the economic system of Saudi Arabia, and the corresponding Islamic growth model that they form are dealt with precisely in the chapters that follow. It suffices here to say that the basic foundations of the country's economic system include:

1. The Islamic economic order which is based on private ownership and free enterprise.
2. The pattern of resource ownership which put oil resources under public ownership.
3. The tremendous economic power that the government derives from oil revenues and their use.

Note: Throughout the text "riyal" and "Saudi riyal" (or SR) are used interchangeably. The history of the riyal for conversion purposes is: from 1954 to January 1960, SR3.75 per US$1; January 1960 to December 1971, SR4.50 per US$1; December 1971 to February 1973, SR4.14 per US$1; February 1973 to March 1973, SR3.73 per US$1; March 1973 to early 1976, SR3.55 per US$1. Since 1976 the riyal has fluctuated with a market rate of 3.53 in 1977, 3.40 in 1978, 3.36 in 1979, and 3.33 in 1980. International Monetary Fund, *International Financial Statistics* (June 1981), pp. 334–335.

4. The use of economic planning for the development of both the public and private sectors.
5. The decrees, regulations, and incentives which the government uses to solicit the participation of the Saudi and foreign private entrepreneur and to fight inflation, improve income distribution, and raise the standard of living.[2]

The application of Islamic principles to the organization of the Saudi Arabian economy is most apparent in three general areas of policy: (1) state expenditures and subsidies; (2) tax policy, and (3) banking policy. These subjects are examined below (with banking policy in chapter 5) to provide a general introduction to the kingdom's economic framework.

The Economic System—Roles of the Private and Government Sectors

The Saudi Arabian economic system is a mixture of public planning and private enterprise. It recognizes the value of private initiative and efforts within the framework of state guidance and direction. The government's economic philosophy, based on these principles, is oriented toward economic development within the framework of free enterprise and the individual's right to pursue his own financial destiny.

Saudi Arabia's private sector embraces a wide spectrum of activities including traditional agriculture, modern farming, medium and small manufacturing, cottage industries and handicrafts, mining and quarrying, residential and commercial construction, motor transportation, banking and insurance, wholesale and retail trade, importing and exporting, and shipping. In some of these activities the private sector shares the market with the government. The exclusively private domain consists mainly of household services, small retail outlets, and speciality shops, brokerage and middlemen agencies, and the professions.

The attitude of Saudi businessmen is one of cooperation based on self-interest. This attitude is consistent with the strong profit motivation of risk-averting Saudi entrepreneurs. Most government measures vis à vis the economy are intended to lessen risk and to reduce private cost by subsidizing a great part of it.

The industrial philosophy of the government is that once an industry backed by the state (except, of course, the oil industry) becomes profitable, then shares in it should be sold to Saudi citizens.[3]

In a state where the absolute monarchy dominates the system and where political and social powers are mobilized by the royal family, economic power is sought by the Saudi businessmen as a matter of fair play.

Many merchants are in fact richer than some of the most influential members of the royal family; most are richer than the king. To them, free enterprise sets no limit on monopoly power in a few influential private hands.

For the majority of business establishments, their role is equivalent to their size; that is, very small. The government does not expect much from them in terms of plan fulfillment, and they are mostly affected by government regulation in their capacity as consumers rather than businessmen.

On the other hand, the government has set a number of goals for the larger, more modern businessmen with the general objective of utilizing their efforts to enable the kingdom to obtain a degree of economic self-sufficiency never before realized. These objectives include:[4]

1. To increase the economy's capacity to produce at competitive costs a wide range of products for domestic use as well as for export markets.
2. To exploit industrially the substantial comparative advantages arising from low cost energy, raw materials from hydrocarbon-related industry, minerals, agriculture, and fishing resources.
3. To widen and deepen the kingdom's access to modern technology.
4. To encourage fuller utilization of capacity in the private manufacturing sector.
5. To increase productivity through closer approaches to optimal size plants.
6. To secure regionally balanced development of industry.
7. To promote interlinkage among industries.
8. To reduce dependency on expatriate workers by national skill-creation through the development of general and technical education and on-the-job training of national workers.

The general government orientation is to:[5]

1. Encourage the expansion of manufacturing industries, including agricultural industries, that can effectively contribute to increased national income and raise the standard of living by increased employment and diversification of the economy of the kingdom.

2. Rely on the private sector for implementation; that is, the authorities feel that goals of industrial development can be realized most effectively if private enterprise bears the primary responsibility for industrial projects.

3. View competition as serving the interests of the local consumers and being the best means of influencing the business community in the industrial field toward beneficial manufacturing and market-oriented projects. The government also considers that competition is the most effective means for selecting the investment schemes which suit the market requirements for encouraging low-cost production and for fixing fair prices for both consumer and producer.

4. Welcome foreign capital and skills and invite them to contribute to industrial development in collaboration with Saudi investors.

A number of specific incentives have been devised by the government to stimulate private industrial activity including:[6]

1. *Land sites:* Industrial estates are available at an annual rental of Rls 0.08 per square meter. There are a number of estates which are currently being developed by the government.
2. *Utilities:* Electric power is supplied at a subsidized cost of Rls 0.05 per kwh. Water rate is also subsidized, presently costing Rls 0.25 per cubic meter. Gas and fuel are very cheap in the kingdom.
3. *Duty Exemption:* There is custom-duty exemption for virtually all imported goods used by industry.
4. *Company Tax:* Pure Saudi companies, whether in industry or trade, are fully exempted from company taxes. However, they pay a small rate for *Zakat* (a religious levy amounting to 2.5 percent on liquid assets). Foreign companies are taxed at the rate of 25 to 45 percent on their profit.
5. *Industrial Loans:* The Saudi Industrial Development Fund makes loans of up to 50 percent of the total project cost for a term of 5 to 10 years, with a grace period of about one to 1.5 years and at an administrative fee of 2 percent.
6. *Government Preference for Domestic Products:* Domestic firms receive a preference of 10 percent over others on government contracts.

The significance of these investment incentives can be seen in the following example:[7]

Product to be made:
   Small-diameter steel pipe, annual capacity 40,000 tons.

Capital investment:
   Foreign partner—40 percent; Saudi partner—60 percent.

Annual return on equity at full capacity:
   With full incentives—46.4 percent.
   If 50 percent SIDF funding at 2 percent—34.2 percent.
   If land had to be bought at SR 50 a square meter—39.8 percent.
   If duties had to be paid on equipment and raw materials—37.6 percent.
   If taxes had to be paid on foreign partner's income, foreign partner—25.5 percent; Saudi partner—37.6 percent.

Though it is clear that one significant emphasis of the Third Five-Year Plan will be the further development of the private sector of the Saudi economy, severe doubts persist whether even these incentives will be sufficient to elicit adequate response from the sector. According to a 1979 survey of Saudi businessmen prepared for the government, the private sector prospers not because of any particular excelling features, but in spite of itself.[8]

The same survey finds that no major area of private business activity has been able to avoid manpower shortages, inadequate financing, confusing and contradictory government regulation, poor management and marketing skills, and lack of information concerning government policy.

In addition, business has traditionally been conducted in a highly centralized fashion. While not a particular hindrance in a simple trading economy, this practice now appears to be a major constraint to better management in a more sophisticated economy. Although foreign employees are handling much of the management tasks in some Saudi companies, the norm is for all paperwork and all decisions to lead to one man's desk.

As far as vitality goes, one of the most common criticisms of the private sector is that managers have little imagination. This is evidenced by the rapid duplication of hotels, supermarkets, and dairy recombination plants. In industry, a quick return for plants manufacturing construction materials seems to have brought about a concentration in that area.[9] The conclusion many draw is that it will be a long time before the basic inclination of the Saudi businessman for a quick return on a low volume of sales will be replaced by a longer-run view of investment in productive plant and equipment.

As noted, the basic foundations of the present economic system of Saudi Arabia are:

1. Islamic scriptures stressing the benefits of ownership and free enterprise.
2. The exclusive control of petroleum resources by the state.
3. The obligation to the economy that the government assumes as the sole recipient of the oil revenues.

Operationally, the government's socioeconomic objectives are incorporated in the country's five-year plans. In these plans the ultimate objectives of development are stated as: (1) preservation of religious values and traditions; (2) improving welfare and standards of living of the Saudi people; (3) preservation of national security; and (4) attainment of social and economic stability. These objectives are pursued by a strategy which calls for Accelerating the growth rate of GDP, manpower development, Diversification of sources of income for the purpose of reducing the economy's dependency on oil by increasing the contribution of the nonoil domestic production.[10]

The development policy is based on free enterprise and free trade, a balanced budget, and building an emergency reserve of foreign exchange sufficient for maintaining the country's imports for 1.5 years. Development programs and projects correspond to these basic objectives. Accordingly, government expenditures flow in three directions:

1. To finance physical and social infrastructure.
2. To extend financial assistance to private enterprises and private consumers.
3. To build the government's holding of foreign exchange and foreign assets.

In a broad sense these objectives and goals are reflected in several fiscal trends.

1. The growth of government expenditure in both absolute and percentage terms in Saudi Arabia over the period 1974–1978 has, by any standard, been spectacular with the ratio of government expenditure to gross domestic product (GDP) increasing from 19 percent in 1974 to 63 percent in 1978. Government expenditures in both consumption and investment have increased more rapidly than GDP.

2. The ratio of government revenue to GDP, however, has been on a declining trend since 1976, reflecting the changing composition of GDP with an increase in the share of the comparatively lightly taxed nonoil sector in total GDP. As a result the overall budget surplus was reduced to less than 4 percent of GDP in 1977, and a budget deficit was projected for 1978.

3. During the period since 1972, there has been a close relationship between the overall budget surplus/deficit and the balance of payments surplus/deficit.

4. In addition there appears to be a close relationship between domestic budget deficits, domestic liquidity-expansion, and inflation. As is shown in chapter 11, fiscal policy is the primary determinant of domestic liquidity and aggregate demand.

5. The composition of expenditure has undergone several significant changes:

a. Capital expenditures as a proportion of total stage outlays have been rising for more than a decade.
b. Expenditures on economic affairs (particularly for industry, transport, and communications) have had a marked increase over the years and in 1981 account for the largest share of the general budget.
c. Defense and security expenditures have claimed an increasing share of the budget in recent years owing to Saudi Arabia's increasing involve-

ment in the security of the Arabian Gulf and political instability in the Middle East.

d. In social affairs, large increases have been budgeted especially for housing, education, and health care.

e. In 1974 a new item, foreign grants, investments, and loans was added to the annual budget expenditure.

The Tax System

Oil dominates the sources of government income in Saudi Arabia to such an extent that one may be tempted to ignore the analysis of the revenue structure; nonetheless, the Islamic tax codes do have an impact on the tax structure, providing another unique aspect to the kingdom's economic system.

Saudi Arabia's tax system is quite simple.[11] There is no tax on wages or salaries (whether the employee is a Saudi national or a foreigner). Only commercial and industrial gains are taxed. The nature, base, and nomenclature of the various Saudi taxes differ according to the nationality of the taxpayer and whether he is an individual or a legal entity. If he is a Saudi, his gains are subject to *Zakat* (the Islamic tax which is levied on gains and invested capital) whereas foreigners pay an income tax only on realized profits.

Three kinds of income taxes are levied in Saudi Arabia:

1. *Zakat:* Only Saudi nationals and Saudi firms are subject to this type of income tax. Non-Saudis have no right to require substitution of this tax for other types of taxes, and Saudis are not entitled to request application of other types of taxation in lieu of this one. The *zakat* is due on the total income and capital that has been retained for one year or more and is charged at the rate of 2.5 percent of this total income. The details of this type of tax and its application are determined by the *Shari'a* law.
2. Additional income tax: This tax is levied on petroleum and hydrocarbon-producing companies. Additional income tax has its special regulation and as such requires a special treatment.
3. Income tax: This tax is levied on the incomes of foreign firms and individuals.

The distribution of *zakat* gives a view of the role of the government in correcting for the first welfare inequality outlined above. The distribution includes mainly: (1) the poor or those who cannot earn income to pay for their needs, and (2) the needy or those who are unable to support themselves fully.

Because of its oil revenues, Saudi Arabia is one of the few less-developed countries which does not need foreign capital to finance its development program. As a result, the government has reserved many business activities for Saudis, particularly those types of business of a purely commercial nature. Non-Saudis, however, may invest in the fields of industry or agriculture. This policy was adopted to obtain foreign skill, experience, and technology.

To encourage foreign investment (for the purpose of technology transfer) while at the same time implementing the tax codes of the Islamic *Shari'a*, the government has incorporated a number of subsidies and benefits into its fiscal policy:

1. Agricultural investment is totally and permanently exempted from both direct and indirect taxes.
2. The exemption of income tax due on industrial products realized during the first five years, if at least 25 percent of the total amount of industrial investment is contributed by a Saudi, is granted to foreign investors.
3. The government provides sufficient areas of land required for industrial projects in return for payment of a nominal rent.
4. There is a permanent exemption of individual income from tax on salaries and wages.

The actual Saudi system does not allow any foreigner, whether an individual person or a legal entity, to operate a business in Saudi Arabia. There are, however, two notable exceptions to this rule: (1) when a foreign investor wins a tender and enters into a contract with a Saudi Ministry or a public sector body, and (2) when a foreign investor is granted a license from a ministry to do business under the provisions of forming investment and regulation to establish any project that the country needs for its progress.

The profits derived by a foreign investor from industrial activities or from contracts signed with the Saudi government are subject to income taxes at the following rates:

1. 25 percent of profits not exceeding SR 100,000 (3.5 SR = 1.00).
2. 35 percent on profits between SR 100,000 and SR 500,000 per annum.
3. 40 percent on profits between SR 500,000 and 1,000,000 per annum.
4. 45 percent on profits exceeding SR 1,000,000 per annum.

The country's tax policy has undoubtedly been successful in its allocative objectives, but has left the tax base rather narrow, and the tax burden still somewhat tilted against the salaried middle classes in the private sector and consumers as a whole. The heavy and continued reliance by the government on the easy and abundant income from oil and gas has thus been a mixed blessing. On the one hand, a relatively low level of direct taxation enables the government when encountering a potential budget deficit to increase direct taxes without an unduly burdensome effect on the economy. On the other hand, the propagation of the easy life for most Saudis may make a smooth and effective enlargement of the tax base and tax rates politically painful and unpopular. For this reason efforts should be made to gradually widen the tax base and increase tax collection.

Conclusions

It is apparent from this account of principles and constraints that a case could be made that Islam's economic foundations are compatible with free enterprise and fair gain as a basic means of resource allocation. The particular Saudi model of resource allocation was developed in response to its own set of particular circumstances:

1. The relatively recent emergence of the country within its present boundaries as a sovereign state (1932) and the mass resources which the state cntrols.
2. The dominance of the Wahabi School of Islamic Thought—an extremely individualistic conservative school.
3. The desert environment places the family as the central institution around which political, social, and economic relations are built.
4. The role which the Saudi government assumes vis à vis the rest of the Islamic world makes it committed to developing the country as a model Islamic showcase.

As noted in the first five-year plan:

> The Kingdom's commitment to the free enterprise economy is founded basically in Islamic guidelines and tradition. The kingdom has concluded that the economy could not exploit fully the opportunities open to it except through the full utilization of private initiative, and by including private enterprises of all sizes and forms to perform the activities which it could perform more eficiently than the government.[12]

Tentatively and as a working hypothesis for much that follows we conclude that Saudi Arabia's high growth rate in turn is easily traceable to its net favorable assets. Sizable incomes from oil, a resilient and eager-to-learn people, unused natural resources, and a confident private sector have sufficiently overshadowed such growth-inhibiting elements as a small industrial base, shortages of skills, newness of advanced technology, shortages of water, bad weather, and so on.

The country's development, however, seems to be related in particular to two specific factors: (1) sustained political stability and (2) pragmatism with the possible exception of female labor in internal socioeconomic policies. The kingdom has largely been characterized by a situation where internal social frictions and external political conflicts have been minimal, and domestic socioeconomic policies have been tailored to fit national requirements relatively free from ideological constraints.

The kingdom has also been able to maintain a high degree of political stability and domestic social accord within its borders, thus ensuring its sustained economic growth. The wide latitude given to the private sector, a pragmatic course followed between laissez-faire and top-heavy bureaucracy, and the wise use of foreign-exchange earnings have all been important elements in the country's successful progress to development.

In sum, Saudi Arabia's oil wealth, institutional framework, and philosophical ideals are compatible to sustained economic growth and development. The socioeconomic superstructure is flexible, pragmatic, and tailor-made for indigenous Saudi Arabian conditions. The prevailing economic system is relatively nondoctrinaire in nature and capable of responding and adapting to changes in the underlying circumstances.

Notes

1. Ralph Braibanti, "Saudi Arabia in the Context of Political Development Theory," in Willard Beling, ed., *King Fisal and the Modernization of Saudi Arabia* (Boulder: Westview Press, 1980), pp. 36–37.

2. For a similar approach see A.M. Shashar, "Oil, Religion, and Mercantilism: A Study of Saudi Arabia's Economic System," *Studies in Comparative International Development* (Fall 1977): 46–64.

3. David Shirreff, "Manufacturing: Rich Incentives Ensure Quick Returns," *Middle East Economic Digest* (July 1980—Special Report): 39.

4. As listed in *The Second Development Plan 1395–1400 A.H.* (Riyadh: Ministry of Planning, 1975), ch. 1.

5. *A Guide to Industrial Investment in Saudi Arabia* (Riyadh: The Industrial Studies and Development Center, 1977), pp. 35–39.

6. Shirreff, "Manufacturing," p. 39.

7. Ibid.

8. Cited in "The Barriers Faced in Private Sector Economic Development," *Saudi Business and Arab Economic Report* (November 30, 1979): 11.

9. Timothy Sisley, "The Evolution of the Private Sector," *Saudi Business and Arab Economic Report* (February 15, 1980): 22–24.

10. As discussed in *The Second Development Plan*, ch. 1.

11. The following information on taxes is taken from *Regulations for Income Tax, Road Tax and Zakat* (Riyadh: Ministry of Finance and National Economy, Zakat and Income Tax Department, 1978).

12. *Development Plan 1390 A.H.* (Riyadh: Central Planning Organization, 1970), p. 21.

5

An Islamic Growth Model—Applications to Monetary and Banking Policy

Perhaps no other area of Islamic economic thought has been more misunderstood than that concerning the role of the rate of interest. Any economic system concerned primarily with the welfare of the individual must not only encourage allocative efficiency but also promote economic growth if it is to avoid social injustice, economic stagnation, and widespread unemployment.[1] The method of state allocation utilized in the Eastern-block countries is one possible way of avoiding the widespread use of interest rates. Given that complete or near-complete socialization of the means of production that this system requires is contrary to the individualistic moralistic philosophy of Islam, the Saudi government (given its concern for the welfare of the economy) is left with little choice but to somehow direct savings through the organized capital markets to the private sector. The difficult problem from an Islamic point of view arises because the only known method of encouraging the productive use of savings is to raise the interest rate to the point where the discounted marginal social cost of investment is equal to the discounted marginal social benefit of investment.

If the interest rate is not permitted to rise to some positive value to discourage marginal and inefficient projects, it is likely that the kingdom's objectives of social justice with material betterment for its citizens will not be met.

The simple fact is that the interpretation of Islamic doctrine to abolish the interest rate is not only not as straightforward as it is supposed to be, but quite naive given the fact that alternative policies may generate greater social inequalities than the existence of interest is alleged to promote—the inequality of income between labor and capital. While accepting that positive interest rates help in achieving economic efficiency and economic growth, Islamic scholars often contend that its use can still not be justified on moral grounds.[2] If we accept the fact that given our present state of knowledge, other policy alternatives create economic inefficiency and inhibit economic growth, then it is incumbent that Islamic countries create some sort of institutional arrangement whereby the positive aspects of the interest rate are allowed to function while simultaneously its negative or morally objectionable features are suppressed. Attempts at creating this type of institutional system largely describe Saudi monetary and banking policy over the years.

The Saudi Arabian financial system comprises five major institutions:

1. The Saudi Arabian Monetary Agency.
2. The money changers.
3. The commercial banks.
4. Public specialist institutions.
5. The Islamic banks.

The development of a modern monetary system in Saudi Arabia is a relatively recent phenomenon. A short review of the evolution of the present institutions is necessary for a better understanding of the workings of the kingdom's financial system; especially those factors that impinge on the government's ability to stabilize the economy while meeting the major objectives of the development plans.

Early Monetary Development

The early development of banking and financial institutions in Saudi Arabia took place within the country's regional context; that is, within the framework of currency developments in the Arabian peninsula.[3] The history of money in the Arabian peninsula followed the pattern found in other parts of the world. After experimenting with several objects as means of exchange, metallic coins came into use as money. The most widely circulated of these coins were the Maria Theresa thaler and the Indian rupee; the former was first minted in Austria in 1790.

In 1927 the Saudi Arabian government introduced a Saudi Arabian silver riyal to replace various silver coins that had previously circulated in the country. At that time the British gold sovereign was established as the standard base, and the riyal/sovereign ratio was fixed at 10:1. However, as changing international prices for gold and silver resulted in the smuggling out of silver in 1931 and in speculation by money changers, the government withdrew the silver riyal and minted another silver coin of smaller weight and size. This new riyal was minted in 1935 and went into circulation in 1936.

These early coins, particularly the riyal, suffered from several disadvantages. First, they were heavy in relation to value, thus making large transactions inconvenient due to the weight of the metal. Second, because of their inelastic supply, the value of the coins was not stable but varied seasonally with demand (particularly during the Haj) for the currency. Finally, the coins were melted down whenever metal prices were sufficiently high. Despite these limitations, Saudi Arabia continued to use metal coins long after the other Arabian peninsula countries had abandoned their widespread use.[4]

Until the early 1950s the entire banking system in Saudi Arabia consisted of a few money changers and a branch office of the Netherlands Trading Society. An organization of private bankers did exist, but its scope was extremely limited. There was no central bank, nor any supervision of the private banks.

While the Ministry of Finance exercised some central banking and public finance functions such as the issuing of coins, the collection and disbursement of public revenue, and the management of the public debt, it was not properly organized to handle the rapid increases in transactions. These problems made it incumbent that the government move in the direction of formalizing the country's monetary and financial relationships.[5]

Saudi Arabia's period of early financial development thus ended in 1952 with the creation of the Saudi Arabian Monetary Agency (SAMA).

The Current Institutional Framework

The legal framework of the present monetary system of Saudi Arabia consists of: (1) the 1952 charter of SAMA; (2) the currency reform statutes of 1960; and (3) the Banking Control Law of 1966.

The royal decrees of April 20 and August 5, 1952, established SAMA, which was conceived as a modified central bank. According to its charter SAMA was to:[6] (1) strengthen the currency of Saudi Arabia and stabilize it in relation to foreign currencies, and avoid the losses from fluctuations in the exchange value of Saudi Arabian coins; and (2) aid the Ministry of Finance in centralizing the receipts and expenditures of the government in accordance with the items of the authorized budget, and help it to control payments so that all branches of the government would abide by the budget.

This early legislation stipulated that SAMA would conform in all of its actions with the teachings of Islamic law. SAMA was not to be a profit-making institution, and it was not permitted to pay or receive interest, make advances to government or to private entities, engage in trade, or have any interest in any commercial, industrial, or agricultural enterprise. It could not buy or hold fixed property (except for its own uses), and it was not permitted to issue currency notes.

In carrying out its function of stabilizing and maintaining the external and internal value of the riyal, SAMA has relied on three major policy initiatives:

1. The management of monetary reserve funds as separate funds earmarked for monetary purposes only.
2. The buying and selling of gold, silver coins, and bullion for the government account.
3. Regulation of commercial banks, exchange dealers, and money changers.

SAMA's fiscal responsibilities consist largely of assisting the Ministry of Finance, and include: (1) acting as a depository for all government funds; (2) maintaining deposit accounts under such heads as the Minister of Finance might direct, and (3) acting as agent for the government in paying out funds for purposes duly approved by the government through the Minister of Finance.[7]

One of the first crises faced by SAMA was the increasingly good counterfeits of the gold sovereign that began to appear. SAMA was forced to remove it from circulation in 1953. In 1955 a substantial rise in the price of silver in New York began to drive silver coins out of circulation. The riyal was withdrawn in October 1955 by SAMA and replaced by the one riyal "pilgrims receipt." Because SAMA was not empowered at this time to issue a currency, these one-riyal notes were, strictly speaking, warehouse receipts rather than currency. Finally in 1960 SAMA was permitted to issue paper currency. At the same time gold and silver coins were officially demonetized.

In addition to the problems surrounding the use of metal coins, several other events lead up to the currency reform of 1960. Starting in the mid-1950s the Saudi Arabian government budget and balance of payments began to run large deficits. As a result SAMA's charter was amended enabling the agency to lend to the government. The agency's holdings of government paper soon rose to 86 percent of the currency issued.[8] The pilgrim's receipts were no longer fully backed by metallic coinage, and the free-market rate of the riyal depreciated considerably. A stabilization program initiated in May 1958 imposed stringent controls on government spending. A dual exchange market was set up, with imports of foodstuffs and other essential commodities permitted at the official rate, while other transactions were included in the free market to which SAMA channeled part of its foreign-exchange reserves. These measures succeeded in liquidating the government's indebtedness, and in January 1960 the riyal was made convertible at the unified official rate of SR 4.50 to US $1 (which had prevailed on the free market for some time).

It was against this background that SAMA's charter was amended in January 1960. Royal Decree No. 6, known as the Currency Statute, (1) authorized SAMA to issue a paper currency in place of the pilgrim's receipts in circulation (subject to regulations and decisions of the council of ministers), (2) required that the currency be backed 100 percent by gold or by currencies convertible into gold, and (3) authorized SAMA to invest foreign-exchange reserves in foreign securities in accordance with the usual practice of central banks (a provision that could be interpreted to mean that SAMA would not forego interest on its foreign investments).

Under this decree, the paper riyal was issued for the first time in June 1961, following Saudi Arabia's acceptance in March of the obligations of Article VIII of the International Monetary Fund's articles of Agreement. The second important amendment to the SAMA Charter was Royal Decree

No. 10, which empowered SAMA to buy and sell gold and foreign exchange for the purpose of maintaining the stability of the currency.

In addition to designating a gold content for the currency, SAMA's charter specified the method by which its parity may be changed. The charter also defined the assets that qualify as external reserves, what minimum proportion of the currency in circulation (or of total demand liabilities) is to be backed by external assets, and the method by which this proportion may be altered.

The Banking Control Law of 1966 further empowered SAMA with a number of powers giving it authority to regulate financial institutions in the kingdom. Thus SAMA in 1981 determines the structure and capital requirements of the commercial-banking system and supervises many of its operations.

SAMA is also empowered to maintain monetary stability. For this purpose the agency can establish statutory reserve requirements and domestic asset ratios. In addition, SAMA can regulate the discount and interest rates.

While religious restrictions concerning usury permeate the whole banking sector of the kingdom, commercial banks often bend the law and charge a "commission" rather than interest, and pay approximately 2 percent per annum to depositors holding not more than approximately $25,000. The Saudi Arabian Monetary Agency or other government bodies, however, cannot legally accept interest on money they lend.

In addtion to extending SAMA's regulatory powers over commercial banks, the Banking Control Law stipulates that deposit liabilities of a bank cannot exceed fifteen times its reserves and paid-in capital. When deposits exceed this ratio the bank must, within one month, deposit 50 percent of the excess with SAMA. The banks are required to maintain with SAMA deposits equivalent to 15 percent of their total-deposit liabilities; this action can be varied within the range of 10 to 17.5 percent, or by more than these limits with the approval of the Minister of Finance.

In addition to the statutory deposit, banks are required to maintain liquid assets equivalent to not less than 15 percent of their total deposit liabilities; SAMA can increase this ratio up to 20 percent. Most important, SAMA has the power to place restrictions on the volume and uses of credit and to specify its conditions and terms of credit.

There is no specific regulation of the interest rate charged by commercial banks. Social and religious pressures, however, have resulted (as of early 1980) in a three-tier prime rate:

1. For the best customers, rates vary from 7.5 percent or less to about 9.0 percent on long-standing facilities.
2. For additional loans, rates are 12 to 14 percent.

3. For new Saudi customers and for non-Saudis, loan rates reflect the 17 to 18 percent which prevail (early 1980) in the interbank market.[10]

To summarize, SAMA has evolved to the point where it has assumed responsibility in nine major areas:

1. The issue and regulation of bank notes and coins in the kingdom.
2. The management and consolidation of all government accounts.
3. The maintenance and management of the government's foreign-exchange reserves and the overseer of investments on behalf of the Ministry of Finance.
4. Advice to the government on implementation of financial and monetary policy.
5. Maintenance and regulation of commercial-banking system and credit policy.
6. Acting (in a very restricted sense) as lender of last resort to the commercial banks, although not through rediscounting or swap facilities.
7. Banker to the commercial banks for interbank settlements.
8. Publication of the consolidated financial position of the members of the banking system.
9. Granting permits to establish local banks, investment and financial institutions, and branches of foreign banks.

In general the agency has traditionally been very conservative in all areas of policy, particularly with regard to its role of supervising the kingdom's thirteen domestic banks.

Money Changers

Historically, money changers' main business in the kingdom was the pilgrim traffic. Over the years, however, they have gradually diversified into many of the activities normally carried out by commercial banks; that is, exchanging foreign currency notes, cashing travelers checks, maintaining interest-free accounts for devout Moslems, and providing short-term financing. As of 1981, their main source of funds is the commercial banks (they are precluded by the banking laws from buying foreign exchange from that agency). While not legally subject to regulation, moneychangers operate under the constant threat of SAMA extending its regulatory authority to include them if their actions cause any instability in the financial system.[11]

While no official statistics exist, there is little doubt that moneychangers, unlike their counterparts in most other developing countries, have increased their scope and size of operations. In fact they play a major role in financing much of the kingdom's domestic and foreign trade. Recently their operations have expanded to the financing of industry. It is possible that due to lack of government regulation, they have even grown relative to the commercial banks. While not significant holders of deposits, they are now major sources of credit and, in addition to industry and trade, currently provide advances for agriculture and commercial building materials. They are especially active in assisting traders in the *souks*.

Money changers are currently thriving in the kingdom for the simple reason that they are extremely profitable. Because they do not come under SAMA, they do not have a large proportion of their funds tied up as nonincome-yielding reserve requirements. In addition, their operating expenses are generally lower than those of the banks because they pay their employees below-bank rates and usually maintain less-prestigious establishments.[12]

The larger moneychangers are usually very competitive with the commercial banks, particularly in foreign-exchange dealings. They offer more competitive rates than the commercial banks and often provide speedier services. The larger dealers also offer a similar set of corresponding services abroad to those offered by the commercial banks.

A major problem in identifying the precise nature of the moneychanger's role in the financial system is that of distinguishing their banking roles from their other activities. Even where moneychanging establishments have not diversified into other activities, tied loans are common; that is, borrowers are often expected to purchase supplies from other clients of the moneychangers.

Because they usually do not take deposits, much of the moneychanger funding, however, is financed by their own reserves, or by funds generated within the family businesses. In contrast to the commercial banks, therefore, moneychangers have somewhat limited ability to expand credit in the short run. As a result, they do not appear to pose much of a threat to the kingdom's financial stability, and there is little likelihood that SAMA will find it necessary to control their operations.

Commercial Banks

As noted earlier (and as is well-known), Saudi-banking practices, particularly those involving interest on loans, are greatly modified by social and religious forces. The basis for Islamic banking and the prohibition of interest is the belief of the Moslem that capital itself should not generate a profit without any human effort being exerted. Financial gains, either through interest-bearing deposit accounts or interest-changing commercial loans, are referred to as *Riba* by Islamic banks and are strictly forbidden by the *Qu'ran*. Islamic law, however, does not imply that banks must receive negative or extremely low rates of return on equity. Under the *Mudaraba* system (otherwise known as profit-sharing), it is possible for banks to do extremely well financially.[13]

Under Islamic codes, banks can lend capital to entrepreneurs with the understanding that the bank will receive a certain fixed percentage of the profits generated by the loan. Banks stand to make a large profit through this practice, or conversely to share the losses if the new venture proves a financial failure. The *Mudaraba* system, therefore, assumes that a social balance is struck between the value of capital and the value of human endeavor, a balance that in no way reduces the overall level of investment that would likely take place under alternative Western-type banking practices. Many of the *Riba*-free banks (RFBs) operating in Saudi Arabia provide a full range of normal commercial-banking services. Credit provision and trade financing are undertaken on a profit-sharing basis, while transfers, foreign exchange, checking accounts, and other noncredit services are provided on a commission or fee basis. Fees for services are permitted by Islamic codes if they are payment for services that involve a real exertion of effort on the part of the bank.[14] In short, there is no inherent reason why Islamic restrictions should limit bank activity or profitability.

Pattern of Growth

Commercial banking in Saudi Arabia grew up largely through the provision of import finance. This type of activity still predominates, although there is a trend toward diversification of bank assets. Deposits are still largely short term, however, and as a result many banks are still reluctant to undertake a very large number of long-term commitments. Bid bonds and contract guarantees have become another lucrative area, although bonds for the big contracts must be syndicated abroad (since the Saudi banks do not have a large enough capital base to undertake them). Despite these changes commercial banking has not expanded as dramatically as the rest of the economy. Several reasons are responsible:

1. Because of restrictions on interest rates, banks have not been able to attract as many funds as would normally be the case.
2. The banking system itself is largely oligopolistic (only two Saudi banks) with little competition to force expanded service and coverage.
3. SAMA has been extremely conservative in issuing new licenses (only one was issued during the last decade).
4. Stiff competition still exists from the moneychangers who perform many of the services provided for by the banks.

5. Foreign or suitcase banking has become an important element in the system.
6. State-owned credit banks are major lenders in certain areas.
7. SAMA has not allowed offshore banks to open, but instead has preferred to see offshore Saudi riyal-financing develop in Bahrain with Saudi bank's opening subsidiaries there.
8. Qualified labor is quite scarce with many Saudi families discouraging a career in banking for religious reasons.

Several characteristics set the Saudi Arabian banking system apart from its counterpart in Kuwait, Bahrain and the UAE. These include:

1. The absence of interest rate regulations.
2. The lack of domestic capital market.
3. The slow progress toward any investment banking activity—relying, that is, on management skills rather than balance sheet optimization.

Lending Activities

While perhaps not expanding as fast as one might have anticipated because of the overall rate of growth of the economy, the sheer size of the expansion of assets in recent years clearly indicates the dynamic conditions prevailing in the country's financial markets. Private-sector loans and investments have increased by almost twenty times during the 1965–1979 period.[15]

Domestic loans and investments comprised over 40 percent of the banks' assets in 1979. This figure has been relatively constant with fluctuations approximately five percent of this figure through the 1970s. Bank assets are, despite the Islamic preference for direct equity investment, mainly comprised of loans. In fact Saudi commercial banks, as have their Western counterparts, have a strong preference for revolving credit loans rather than longer-term commitments.

A breakdown of the lending by the commercial banks shows that, as in most developing countries, trade credit is of greatest importance. This activity accounted for one-third of total bank loans in 1978. In large part these loans are used to finance local merchants' stocks of imported goods (as they often have to meet the payment to the foreign supplier before the goods are actually sold). Banks can, of course, provide letters of credit and guarantees for imports, but these are usually for only short periods. Saudi imports often require longer periods to turn their stock over. While importers have a number of financial options, it is apparent that the commercial banks are now playing a growth role in this area. Between 1977 and 1978, for example, the value of trade credit increased by over one-third.

The second most important area of bank credit is construction finance, comprising over one-fifth of the bank's total loans in 1978. Commercial-bank lending for construction takes place in spite of the activity of the state-run Real Estate Development Fund, which provides interest-free loans to private home buyers. In addition, another agency, the Credit Fund for Contractors, gives highly subsidized short- and medium-term loans to Saudi-building firms. There are a number of areas not covered by the public agencies, however, thus providing banks with a number of profitable lending areas. Housing and other facilities for immigrant workers, for example, are not covered by these funds, and in recent years there has been a boom in apartment building for these workers. In addition, bank lending for the construction of commercial buildings and other urban nonresidential development has filled an area also not covered with public lending.

Finally, in spite of the very generous financial provisions made for manufacturing ventures available by the Saudi Industrial Development Fund, commercial-bank lending to industry has been expanding rapidly in both absolute and relative terms. In large part this expansion is a response to several gaps in the government's industrial-financing program. The State Industrial Development Fund, for example, provides up to 50 percent of the financing available for the ventures it selects for credit. In addition, these loans are usually only for medium- and longer-term fiscal-capital formation. As a result borrowers have to turn to commercial banks for working capital.

Total foreign assets of the Saudi commercial banks amounted to almost 13 million riyals in 1979. Most of these are in the form of deposits with other banks in the principal world financial centers, particularly London. Saudi Arabia's two indigenous banks have only recently extended their operations outside the country. Their operations are largely confined to the wholesale interbank market rather than retail banking. The foreign assets are largely in the form of liquid placements. Most of these deposits are withdrawable on demand and involve only a few major Western-owned banks.

Foreign assets of this type do not qualify as reserves with SAMA. Yet, there is no evidence that banks have had much trouble in complying with SAMA's required reserve ratio. These domestic liquid assets were almost as great as loans outstanding in 1975 and 1979. This pattern reflects the commercial bank's tendency to maintain large cash holdings and deposits with SAMA in excess of their reserve requirements. The major component of bank liabilities is current account deposits (on which no interest is paid). The sheer magnitude of these deposits and their growth over the last decade indicate that they are well in excess of what depositors require for transactions or even precautionary purposes. Clearly, many customers are using current accounts for their savings. In doing so they are apparently willing to accept the opportunity costs involved (due to high interest rates abroad and domestic inflation domestically).

Saudization

In addition to the reasons given previously for the slow expansion of banking in the kingdom, foreign banks were somewhat reluctant to expand until quite recently because of the government's Saudization policy.[16]

Under this plan, majority ownership has been transferred to Saudi nationals with the usual equity pattern being 40 percent to the foreign bank, 15 to 20 percent to the Saudi sponsors, and 35 to 40 percent to the Saudi public.

For several years foreign banks were prohibited from either opening new branches or increasing their capital. Branching restrictions are not in effect for Saudiized banks. Through enabling foreign banks to increase their capital and branches, Saudization has enabled the foreign banks to begin competing with the two original Saudi banks, National Commercial Bank (NCB) and the Riyadh Bank.[17]

In 1980 the two Saudi banks still dominated the financial system. Combined they accounted for approximately 70 percent of the country's commercial bank assets, 80 percent of its deposits, and approximately 90 percent of all commercial demand accounts.[18]

The dominant position of the two Saudi banks may diminish as the Saudiized banks pursue an aggressive policy of opening new branches and generating loans. Because of the relatively long time needed to build branch offices and train new staffs, it may be 5 to 10 years before competition in banking increases by a substantial amount.

Bank Profitability

As noted earlier, although there is no official data, most experts on the kingdom's financial structure consider money-lending activities to be quite profitable. Official data collected by SAMA indicates that commercial banks are also quite lucrative as evidenced by three key ratios: (1) return on assets (ROA); (2) return on equity (ROE), and (3) leverage—the ratio of total assets to the equity of the bank's shareholders or partners. The most important indicator of bank profitability is ROA.

According to the most recent financial statements of the banks, the ROA of the two Saudi banks averages 2.6 percent. This is approximately 70 percent higher than the average 1.5 percent generated by the Saudiized banks. When the leverage factors of the banks are incorporated and the ROA is calculated, the difference between the two classes of banks is even more dramatic. NCB has the highest ROA at 47 percent. Three of the four Saudiized banks, on the other hand, average about 20 percent.[19]

Clearly, the Saudi banks operating with their massive deposit bases and low costs of funds are able to produce profitability ratios far in excess of the Saudiized banks. Although the relative size of the Saudi banks alone accounts for some of the difference in figures, that they are sole bankers in many locations in the kingdom (the Saudi banks have approximately 70 percent of all branches in the kingdom) must also contribute to their relative success.

Finally and probably most important, the Saudi banks seem to have an advantage in obtaining funds. While the Saudi banks do not specify the cost of funds (COF), (the amount banks must spend to maintain their deposits), a reasonable proxy for the COF for comparative purposes can be derived by dividing total service charges including interest paid on savings accounts by total funds. The calculation of COF indicates that the funds of the Saudi banks cost approximately one-half of what funds cost the Saudiized banks. Individual comparisons are even more dramatic. While Riyadh Bank's funds cost approximately 0.7 percent, those of Bank al Saudi al Hollandi cost 2.2 percent.[20] This is a difference of over 200 percent. By comparison the COF for most U.S. banks during 1979 was in the neighborhood of 10 percent.

The relatively low COF must in part account, therefore, for the high profitability of Saudi banks. In spite of their low COF, the Saudi banks are not very aggressive in making loans. Loans and advances as a percentage of total deposits is much lower than for Saudiized banks. NCB, for example, loans only 36 percent of its deposits, while the Saudi French Bank and the Saudi British Bank advance 83 to 84 percent of their deposits, respectively.[21]

Apparently, these ratios reflect a major difference in philosophy between the Saudi and Saudiized banks. While the Saudi banks are content to loan a relatively small percentage of their deposits, the Saudiized banks are aggressively granting loans to gain an increased market share. The disparity between loan-deposit ratios may narrow as the Saudiized banks increase their deposit base through their planned branch expansion.

Clearly, this deposit pattern benefits the banks and is a major reason for their high profitability. The value of time and savings deposits in which a fixed commission is paid in lieu of interest to the depositor (in accordance with Saudi law) remains relatively modest. There seems little desire on the part of customers to switch from demand to time deposits. The banks for their part seem reluctant to promote alternative methods of saving.

Reluctance of the banks in promoting savings makes a certain amount of sense given the greater profitability on current account deposits. However, expansion in savings deposits might not necessarily be at the expense of their current accounts. Large volumes of Saudi funds are held overseas. Some of these would likely flow into savings if the terms were improved. Clearly, the banks are aware of this. A major explanation of their lack of enthusiasm for savings promotion must be concern over antagonizing the more conservative sections of the community. Vigorous promotion by offering high premiums for savings may be viewed as an indirect form of interest. Sanctions might follow even though religious principle would not be undermined (as long as the higher charges are not passed on to borrowers). The banks' long-run strategy should be one of education; that is, since Muslim concern is with any hardships that might be inflicted on the latter, the banks should stress that potential gains might be made by depositors as long as the gains are not at anyone else's expense.

In sum, the main trouble for commercial banks in the post-oil boom has not been one of attracting funds but of finding good borrowers. Total assets and liabilities from the commercial banks in 1974–1975, for example, went up by 55 percent, and the money supply increased by 40 percent. With the government responsible for about 80 percent of domestic spending, the banks have not so far played a big part in medium or longer-term project finance. Their main role is still import financing and providing loans for construction. But as the pace of economic development increases, there are signs that some of the liquidity is being mopped up. Deposits in commercial banks rose by 55 percent in 1974–1975, while loans and advances to the private sector soared by 90 percent.

Specialized Banks

The specialized banks have been mentioned several times earlier. Their importance is two-fold. First, they are primarily a conduit for fiscal policy and are therefore essentially government agencies. Second, they are complementary to the commercial banks in that they provide long-term financing. Short-term financing, the essence of banking, is left to the commercial banks.

The function of the government-funded credit institutions is to provide long-term financing to certain sectors of the economy given a high priority by the government. Many projects funded by these institutions are not economically justified and, therefore, would not have been undertaken without the concessionary financing terms. It is significant that in 1978–1979 alone, these institutions disbursed approximately SR 17 billion, or just slightly less than the SR 20 billion total loans outstanding of all commercial banks in the kingdom.

Islamic Banks

Granted that private initiative will provide the dynamic element in an Islamic growth model, the central question arises: what specific policies should the government adopt to encourage investment? Furthermore, given the value of investment required to produce preassigned levels of output, the next fundamental question is how should the savings be generated to sustain such investment?

The process of savings formation can essentially take two forms: (1) the government can directly generate the requisite funds (through oil revenues as in Saudi Arabia's case), encourage private savings, and make these funds available to investors through the capital market; or (2) alternatively, the government can encourage corporate savings. In the latter case, savings are generated within the private sector by a combination of fiscal, price, and wage policies, all tending to increase undistributed corporate profits (which are then assumed to be reinvested). In this method the investors are also the savers. Because the first of these two policies relies on interest rates, these may be incompatible with the Islamic view of basic economic processes.

The dilemma for Saudi policymakers arises from the fact that the first policy, although relying on the interest rate to mobilize private savings, results in a more equitable distribution of income than the second. The second policy deliberately fosters extreme inequalities of income on wealth on the assumption that only the rich save and invest. Islam prohibits the payment and receipt of interest but it also refuses to tolerate glaring inequalities of income and wealth, and thus the dilemma.

An innovative way of reconciling this problem has been through the creation of a new type of bank—the Islamic bank run on the principles of *Shari'a* law.

The new Islamic Development Bank, headquartered in Jeddah and capitalized in great part with Saudi money, is an example of this innovation in banking. Its director indicated on occasion that only 20 percent of its future business will be in interest-free loans. The remainder is likely to be in the form of free or limited partnerships. If a lender becomes a partner, he or it can legitimately under *Shari'a* law accept part of the profits of the enterprise. This procedure circumvents the interest restriction.

Among the other activities of the Islamic Development Bank are:

1. Participating in capital projects.
2. Extending loans to institutions and productive projects in member countries.
3. Extending financial assistance in various forms for economic growth and social progress.
4. Helping in international trade between member countries and in the production of commodities.
5. Extending technical assistance, particularly in training personnel, economic development, research, banking, and other economic activities in accordance with the *Shari'a*.[22]

Broadly speaking, Islamic banks maintain three types of accounts: (1) nonprofit accounts with a very small minimum deposit from which withdrawal can be made at any time; (2) profit-sharing deposit accounts with a modest minimum balance from which withdrawal can be made annually (or at shorter intervals), and (3) social services funds, consisting of gifts from which payments are made in emergencies such as accidents involving participants. The profit made by these is said to be enormous for both profit-sharing depositors and stockholders.

Traditionalists who aspire to restore Islam to its original purity and to escape from alien influences have cited Islamic banks as proof of the suitability and adaptability of the Islamic doctrine to the needs of modern times. The sponsors of these banks argue that the Islamic banks are not much different from the familiar Western banks. The only difference is that they are not based on fixed rates of interest on loans or on deposits, which from their point of view are usurious under the *Shari'a* law. They argue that the regular banks not only deal in money but also invest in agricultrual, industrial, commercial, and human projects. They point out that Islamic banks can deal and invest in such projects but without the use of usurious interest rates.[23]

Effect of Monetary Policy

Throughout the postwar period there has been a growing awareness of the importance of monetary policy in the progress of economic growth. This awareness has been stimulated by research and debates concerning the role and effectiveness of money and monetary policy. While the issues have been discussed at length, at both the university and governmental levels, the role that monetary policy can play remains a subject of dispute among academicians and policymakers.[24]

Although the issues concerning the influence of monetary aggregates on production, employment, and economic growth has not been settled to everyone's satisfaction, all parties at least agree that the monetary and real sectors of an economy are invariably interconnected. In nations in which the economic activities are built upon the revenue of a single commodity such as oil, and in which all revenues accrue to the government, the need to disburse the huge revenues renders the entire economy dependent on governmental budgetary policies. As a result, both monetary and fiscal policies determine the level of production, consumption, and investment in such economies. As is the case in most surplus-funds countries, the monetary and fiscal policies of Saudi Arabia are so closely related that they can be taken as one and the same thing, for the flow of money into the economic system depends on the extent to which the Saudi Arabian government spends from its oil revenues.

With regard to countries like Saudi Arabia whose money and capital markets are extremely limited and in the process of evolution, the debate is not much concerned with the intricacies of the transmission process, but rather tends to be more policy oriented. Here primary concern is more with the manner in which monetary policy can be used to achieve economic objectives; in this connection there is also disagreement as to the extent to which these policies can be effective, given the prevailing economic conditions. In general, there has been a tendency to attribute a low importance to monetary policy in Saudi Arabia because the public sector so dominates economic activity. Largely because of inflation, there has been renewed interest in developing a more active role for monetary policy in the kingdom.

Obviously, given the institutional setting of SAMA, the question immediately arises as to whether the agency has enough tools at its disposal to perform the normal tasks involved in an activist monetary policy. For example, in the usual situation, if a central bank determines that it should tighten or raise interest rates and thereby slow the economic growth of the country, it has three major actions available. First, it can raise reserve requirements. Second, it can raise the interest rate for borrowing from the discount window. Third, it can conduct open-market operations by selling (and purchasing) government securities, and thereby decrease (and increase) the cash in the system as the securities are paid for (sold) and money transferred to (from) the government.

As noted, SAMA has evolved to the point where it performs many of the traditional central bank functions, such as serving as the government's fiscal agent, managing the country's foreign-exchange reserves, and supervising the commercial banks. Nominal money is created primarily by government spending (government consumption is paid for in cash) and to a lesser extent through the creation of excess commercial bank reserves (which may lead to additional lending).

Some important restrictions on SAMA remain, however. The agency may not extend credit to the government or to private entities (including banks), and because it may not contravene Islamic laws, it may not use the discount rate as an instrument of monetary policy.

These restrictions obviously place limitations on SAMA's ability to implement monetary policy. They also cast some doubt as to the capability of the country under certain circumstances of being able to achieve its major economic objectives. The seriousness one attaches to this problem depends in large part on the empirical relationships in the kingdom between government spending, the money supply, and macroeconomic aggregates—an area in which there is considerable controversy.

Because SAMA is not a lender of last resort in the traditional sense (it will not discount commercial paper), reserve requirements are the only major tool at its disposal. Clearly, this has restricted the agency's ability to stabilize the economy. It is not clear, however, that given the fact that it can inject funds into the system by placing government funds in its deposits at commercial banks, it is unable to pursue some sort of activist policy. SAMA can also regulate the money supply through modifying capital flows in and out of the kingdom.

In this regard Saudi monetary policy, because of the unregulated domestic interest rate, has much more flexibility than that of most other Gulf states. In particular Kuwait and the UAE governments have tended to regulate domestic interest rates quite arbitrarily at very low levels. With international rates much higher, arbitrage has resulted in a large exodus of capital from these countries and continues to be a major problem. Saudi Arabians' strong feelings against interest rates seem to moderate the outflow from the kingdom. In addition, the government, by regulating its expenditures, has controlled the growth of the money supply more tightly than the other Gulf centers. The result has been that SAMA has been able to control capital outflows somewhat, and in fact, uses them as a policy tool. For example, one simple way that SAMA reduces the domestic money supply is to let capital outflows occur when inflationary pressures are building up. With these flows, the money supply can be contracted simply by not putting any more money into the system and relying on the outflow to continue.

Despite the controlled capital-flow innovation, SAMA has relied by far on changes in reserve requirements as its major monetary tool. Changes in reserve requirements influences the currency issue indirectly; that is, an increase in reserve requirements causes commercial banks to increase their demand for reserves and thus sterilizes the effects of any increase in government spending. In this situation a reduction in government deposits is matched by an increase in bank deposits at SAMA leaving the amount of currency unchanged.

While reserve requirement changes are effective, there may be limits on its use. By the late 1970s, for example, de facto reserve requirements were between 40 and 50 percent. At these levels any significant increase might weaken the banking system and prevent it from playing a significant role in the economy. There are, however, several possible innovations in SAMA's policy that are consistent with Islamic law and at the same time capable of stimulating growth without inflation. For example:[25]

1. Set a target growth of currency equal to the real growth of the economy.
2. Control its spending so that it conforms with the targets established for currency growth.
3. Encourage private purchases of foreign assets in amounts which are consistent with the economy's domestic financial needs through the development of a new riyal-denominated certificate.

These certificates could be developed and managed along the following lines:

1. SAMA would establish a special account to which it could transfer a certain share of its foreign assets;

2. SAMA was prepared to sell the riyal-denominated certificates in an amount equal to the local currency value of the foreign assets in the special account. If these certificates were purchased by the government, they would be paid for by a reduction in government deposits at SAMA with no initial effect on reserve money or currency. If the certificates were purchased by the public, they would be paid for by both currency and checks that, via a reduction in bank reserves, would reduce the amount of reserve money and currency in the hands of the public.

3. These certificates would not pay interest directly, but would simply pass through the income received by SAMA on the foreign assets in its special account. In addition, because the certificates are denominated in local currency, there would be no foreign-exchange risk to the purchaser. These characteristics would make holding pass-through certificates desirable to the public.

4. Government purchases of the certificates would not immediately affect the level of reserve money, because the reduction in government deposits at SAMA would be matched by an equal and opposite increase in the number of certificates which SAMA would maintain for the government. However, in the event that the government runs a budget deficit at some future time, the certificates would provide a method of financing other than through SAMA. The government could sell the certificates to the public in an amount equal to its deficit. This would be noninflationary because the funds which the government would put into the economy would be matched by funds withdrawn via public purchase of certificates from the government. This procedure can be contrasted with the current situation whereby any government budget deficit would be financed by a simple reduction in government deposits at SAMA—financed in effect, by a money-creation process that would represent a net increase in public liquidity in the form of reserve money. Thus the current procedure potentially could be far more inflationary than the certificate plan.

Conclusions

In spite of its growth, the banking system remains less sophisticated than the market it serves. There is little computerization, no secondary market for money-market instruments, and a still somewhat passive monetary authority. This environment has led to wide and dangerous swings in the system's liquidity. There are signs, however, that the industry is addressing these issues. In particular, SAMA while not yet assuming all of the traditional functions of a central bank is nevertheless beginning to play a more active role in managing the kingdom's monetary affairs. In addition it seems clear that Islamic practices do not place any particular insurmountable constraints on the financial system.

Given Saudi Arabia's high growth rates, and relatively tranquil social and political atmosphere, one must come to the conclusion that at a minimum there is nothing aparently adverse associated with the Islamic growth model. At best it might be possible to attribute considerable amounts of the kingdom's economic success to the application of this model. Other Middle Eastern countries should be cautious, however, before seriously considering the adoption of some of the kingdom's Islamic-based economic policies.

Moslem scholars argue that the Islamic economic system is uniquely designed to minimize if not eliminate built-in contradictions and inequalities such as those characteristic of both capitalist and communist economic systems. In this regard the internal social and political stability of the kingdom appears to stem from the fact that through both the foresight of its leaders and their ability to combat inequality through programs made possible by oil revenues, they have already made genuine accommodations between the country's societal institutions whereby people live and function with cultural and religious values that give life meaning and worth.

Islamic scriptures are not explicit as far as the economic foundations of Islam are concerned. A reading of these sources provides some principles for behavior and a few constraints on human action. They more resemble a code of moral than economic behavior. Saudi Arabia's economic system and its Islamic growth model are unique to that country's history and institutions. Adaptation of the system by other countries might lead to an internally inconsistent conglomeration of economic policies. Any attempts to arti- ficially telescope the evolutionary process involved in framing rules of the game in a real-life Islamic society is fraught with great dangers. A sensible government will have to exercise utmost caution in forming economic policies for the simple reason that they undoubtedly do not have as many degrees of freedom as the Saudis.

Notes

1. Syed Nawab Haider Naqui, "Islamic Economic System: Funda- mental Issues," *Islamic Studies* (Winter 1977): 335.

2. For an excellent summary of these positions, see Syed Nawab Haider Naqui, "Ethical Foundations of Islamic Economics," *Islamic Studies* (Summer 1978): 105–136.

3. This description of the early banking practices is largely based on Michael Edo, "Currency Arrangements and Banking Legislation in the Arabian Peninsula," International Monetary Fund, *Staff Papers* (July

1975), pp. 510–538; and Arthur Yong, "Saudi Arabian Currency and Finance," *Middle East Journal* (Summer 1953): 361–380 and (Autumn 1953): 539–556.

4. Raymond Mikesell, "Monetary Problems of Saudi Arabia," *Middle East Journal* (Spring 1947): 172–173.

5. Yusif Sayigh, *The Economies of the Arab World* (New York: St. Martin's Press, 1978), p. 167.

6. See Anwar Ali, *The Role of the Saudi Arabian Monetary Agency* (Jidda: SAMA, 1971), ch. 1.

7. Banker Research Unit, *Banking Structures and Sources of Finance in the Middle East*, 2nd ed. (London: The Financial Times Business Publishing, Ltd., 1980), pp. 2–3.

8. Anwar Ali, *Monetary Agency,* pp. 16–17.

9. A good summary of SAMA's monetary tools is given in Michael Keran and Ahmed Abdullah Al Malik, "Monetary Sources of Inflation in Saudi Arabia," Federal Reserve Bank of San Franciso, *Economic Review* (Winter 1979): 17–19.

10. Saudi Arabian Monetary Agency, *Annual Report 1399* (1979), (Jeddah: SAMA, 1980), pp. 34–35.

11. R.J.A. Wilson, "The Evolution of the Saudi Banking System and Its Relationship with Bahrain," mimeographed (1980), pp. 14–15.

12. Nigel Harvey, "Money Changers: Serving the Public Without Rules," *Saudi Business and Arab Economic Report* (July 25, 1980): 20–25.

13. Mohammad Mohsin, "Feasibility of Commercial Banking without Rate of Interest and Its Socioeconomic Significance," *Islamic quarterly* (December 1978): 151.

14. Ibid., p. 152.

15. The following figures on bank oprations are from SAMA, *Annual Report*, pp. 25–41.

16. J. Tripp Howe, "Saudi Banking," *Saudi Business and Arab Economic Report* (June 6, 1980): 22–29.

17. John Whelan, "Al-Bank Al-Saudi Al-Fransi: Fully Committed to Saudiisation," *Middle East Economic Digest* (July 1980—Special Report): 69–70.

18. J. Tripp Howe, "The Riyad Bank," *Saudi Business and Arab Economic Report* (May 9, 1980): 20–21.

19. Howe, "The Riyad Bank," pp. 20–21.

20. Ibid.

21. Ibid.

22. Adel Bishtawi, "Arab Banking Survey," *Saudi Business and Arab Economic Report* (October 5, 1979): 13–15.

23. Mohsin, "Feasibility of Commercial Banking," p. 157.

24. For a good summary of this debate, see Tom Cargill, *Money, the Financial system and Monetary Policy* (Englewood Cliffs, N.J.: Prentice Hall, 1979), ch. 17.

25. The following is based on Michael Keran and Ahmed al Malik, "Monetary Sources of Inflation," pp. 21–22.

6 Macroeconomic Patterns of Growth and Development

No country of the world has seen as much development in the last two decades as Saudi Arabia. In fact during the 1960–1980 period, Saudi Arabia experienced what is likely to be recorded by future economic historians as one of the most rapid and most fundamental socioeconomic transformations in modern times. A fortuitous combination of farsighted leadership, internal political stability, improved development planning, increasingly educated people, newly discovered and better utilized natural resources, and the indispensable rise in oil revenues has helped the country reach its present stage of development.

Macroeconomic Growth Patterns

Saudi Arabia's recent growth record is particularly outstanding in view of the initial obstacles that the country has had to surmount: a severely underdeveloped infrastructure, a serious shortage of managerial and technical know-how, inadequacy of skilled and semiskilled labor, a low ratio of oil resources to population, and a rapidly rising population.

Thus the Saudi Arabian experience, if not completely unique in the contemporary world, is certainly a most interesting one. It can be misleading, therefore, to apply to Saudi Arabia many of the generalizations drawn in the literature from the experience of other developing countries. This is particularly true of the conventional diagnoses of the sources of growth and constraints on the growth of developing countries. As is pointed out numerous times in the chapters that follow, the most constraining factor in the kingdom's growth has been the availability of labor rather than (as has usually been the case for developing countries) new investment.[1]

Yet the kingdom, like all developing countries, must have new investments to transform itself and eventually overcome its labor shortages. The significance of the relative labor shortages that exist are in part best seen as constraints on the rate of investment. The rates of domestic investment actually achieved, therefore, should still provide one of the most significant indicators of success in achieving the transformations necessary in the course of development.[2]

Growth in Income

The systematic collection of data for computing the national accounts is a fairly recent occurrence in Saudi Arabia. The International Monetary Fund data began with 1967, but there are several sources containing reconstructed figures back to 1960.[3] The official figures show that over the last two decades Saudi Arabia has been witness to a tremendous change in its economic and social structure.[4] Indeed even a very cursory examination of national income figures is sufficient to gain an appreciation for the rapid progress made since 1960. Less obvious, but in many ways more interesting, is the fact that the post-1960 period can be divided into two quite distinct subperiods, 1960–1972 and 1972–1978 (see table 6–1), each with its own particular set of distinguishing characteristics. Thus while nonoil GDP growth was 10.62 percent for the 1960–1978 period, growth nearly doubled after 1972, increasing from an average annual rate of 8.32 during 1960–1972 to 15.38 between 1972–1978.

Consumption and Investment

The allocation of resources into private and public consumption also provides revealing insights into the country's growth process. Public consumption includes a wide variety of expenditures, some of which are the public services essential for individual welfare. Many of the important components of individual consumption are provided directly by the government or subsidized by the government. Expenditures on military manpower and equipment are also included in public consumption (see table 6–2) and have been a rapidly increasing use of resources.

Total resources—private consumption, public consumption, and investment—are calculated by adding imports and returns from factor services abroad to the gross domestic product and subtracting exports and payments to factor services abroad. The result is the net real resources available for satisfying the various types of demands within the kingdom. Because the country has been a capital exporter for some time, the net flow of exports and factor payments abroad makes the real resources that are used less than the gross domestic product.

One of the striking features of the pattern of expenditures is the very high proportion of total resources allocated to investment. Investment as a percent of GDP has reached 37.30 percent by 1978. Note that for most developing countries the proportion of investment in total use of resources almost never reaches 25 percent, and more typically is closer to 20 percent. Certainly, the current high proportion of investment reflects the relatively high per-capita

Table 6–1
Saudi Arabia: Macroeconomic Trends

	Constant 1970 Prices (billions of Ryals)			Average Annual Growth			Percent of Nonoil GDP		
	1960	1972	1978	1960–72	1972–1978	1960–1978	1960	1972	1978
Government consumption (GCNP)	0.757	4.005	10.738	14.89	17.87	15.88	23.1	46.9	53.3
Private consumption (PCNP)	3.007	6.463	10.646	6.40	8.67	7.28	91.9	75.7	52.8
Government investment (GINP)	0.031	1.349	9.243	36.95	37.82	37.24	0.9	15.8	45.9
Private nonoil investment (PINP)	0.435	1.206	4.246	8.87	23.34	13.49	13.3	14.1	21.1
Total investment (IINP)	0.838	3.269	15.532	12.01	29.66	17.61	25.6	38.3	77.1
Domestic absorption (DANP)	4.602	13.737	36.916	9.51	17.91	12.26	140.6	160.9	183.3
Exports of goods and service (FEXPTNA)	3.317	14.934	20.953	13.36	5.81	10.78	101.3	174.9	104.0
Imports of goods and service (ZNAMP)	1.009	5.480	16.228	15.14	19.83	16.69	30.8	64.2	80.6
Aggregate supply (ADNP)	7.919	28.671	57.869	11.32	12.42	11.68	241.9	335.8	287.3
Savings (SND)	1.749	9.194	18.634	14.83	12.50	14.05	53.4	107.7	92.5
Gross national product (GNPNP)	5.513	19.662	40.018	11.18	12.57	11.64	168.4	230.3	198.7
Gross domestic product (GDPNP)	6.910	23.191	41.641	10.62	10.25	10.49	211.1	280.1	206.7
Oil gross domestic product (OGDNP)	3.637	14.653	21.497	12.31	6.60	10.37	111.1	171.6	106.7
Nonoil gross domestic product (NOXNP)	3.273	8.538	20.144	8.32	15.38	10.62	100.0	100.0	100.0
Private expenditure (PENANP)	3.442	7.669	14.892	6.90	11.70	8.48	105.2	89.8	73.9
Public expenditure (GRNANP)	0.788	5.354	19.981	17.31	24.54	19.08	24.1	62.8	99.2
		8.532	20.144					8.532	20.144

Source: Compiled from Saudi Arabian Monetary Agency *Annual Report*, various issues; International Monetary Fund, *International Financial Statistics*, various issues; Faisal al-Bashir, *Structural Econometric Model of the Saudi Arabian Economy, 1960–1970*.

Note: The symbols after each variable are those used in the econometric model developed in later chapters.

Table 6-2
Saudi Arabia: Relation of Government Expendutures to Gross Domestic Product
(*Billions of riyals*)

	1960	1961	1962	1963	1964	1965	1966	1967	1968	1969
Government consumption	0.627	0.743	0.887	1.244	1.430	1.654	1.915	2.674	2.747	3.026
Defense expenditure	0.456	0.516	0.583	0.660	0.772	1.017	1.145	1.366	1.449	1.615
Nondefense expenditure	0.171	0.227	0.304	0.584	0.658	0.637	0.770	0.908	1.298	1.411
Nonoil GDP	2.710	3.028	3.373	3.792	4.306	4.769	5.378	5.909	6.382	7.180
Defense/nonoil GDP	0.168	0.170	0.173	0.174	0.179	0.213	0.213	0.231	0.227	0.225
Non Defense/nonoil GDP	0.063	0.075	0.090	0.154	0.153	0.134	0.143	0.154	0.203	0.197
Defense/total government consumption	0.727	0.694	0.657	0.531	0.540	0.615	0.598	0.511	0.527	0.534

	1970	1971	1972	1973	1974	1975	1976	1977	1978
Government consumption	3.421	3.798	4.285	5.335	9.864	15.911	28.883	41.003	47.034
Defense expenditure	1.678	1.805	2.145	2.533	3.490	4.990	8.271	10.613	16.538
Nondefense expenditure	1.743	1.993	2.140	2.802	6.374	10.921	10.612	30.390	30.496
Nonoil GDP	7.488	8.253	9.184	11.403	15.430	28.123	47.323	67.694	88.229
Defense/nonoil GDP	0.224	0.219	0.234	0.222	0.226	0.177	0.175	0.157	0.187
Nondefense/nonoil GDP	0.233	0.241	0.233	0.246	0.413	0.388	0.436	0.449	0.346
Defense/total government consumption	0.490	0.475	0.501	0.475	−0.354	0.314	0.286	0.259	0.352

Source: Compiled from data in Saudi Arabian Monetary Agency, *Annual Report*, various issues.

income of the country and its ability to satisfy public- and private-consumption demands while maintaining high investment rates.

Another important pattern has been the change in the proportion of resources going to investment over time. There has been a clear tendency for this proportion to increase—from 12.13 percent in 1960 to 14.10 in 1970, and finally reaching 37.30 percent in 1978. These increases reflect the substantial growth in resources available after the oil prices increases of 1973–1974. To some extent, however, they also reflect the growing ability of the country to absorb and make use of its expanding resources.

This impression of a growing absorptive capacity is also confirmed by the high growth rates in investment—12.10 from 1960–1972, and a 29.66 average annual rate between 1972–1978—and the size of the absolute increases in investment as compared to increases in the other categories of demand. While the growth rates of investment have been accelerating, the growth rates of private consumption have been much lower and were nearly the same in the two subperiods as was government consumption (see table 6–1). This is all the more significant when one notes that private investment also accelerated to an average annual rate of 8.87 percent during 1960–1972, and to 23.34 between 1972–1978.

Clearly, the pattern is one of growing absorptive capacity as investment shares, and absolute magnitudes of investment have expanded relatively consistently. Correspondingly, private and public consumption have not grown to nearly the same extent. The patterns within the consumption and investment categories also imply several interesting trends.

Private Nonoil Investment

The most significant trends are associated with private nonoil investment and are as follows:

1. It has grown considerably slower than government investment over the entire period—13.49 percent, in contrast to the government's 37.24 percent.

2. Despite its falling share in total investment, private investment increased its share of nonoil GDP from 13.3 to 21.2 percent.

Private Consumption

High overall growth has facilitated increased consumption. Given the lack of data on personal incomes or income distribution, trends in private consumption probably provide the best indication of the changes in the country's standard of living. These trends indicate the following:

1. Real private consumption expenditure grew at an average annual rate of 8.67 percent during 1972–1978, compared with 6.40 for the 1960–1972

period. In both periods this was somewhat lower than the growth rate achieved by nonoil GDP.

2. As a result of its relatively slow growth, the ratio of consumption to nonoil GDP has fallen since 1960.

3. The fall in the ratio of private consumption to nonoil GDP has been particularly sharp in recent years, and in those years when the money supply and consumer prices were increasing together at an accelerating rate.

4. The fall in private consumption cannot be attributed to increases in taxes, because if anything there was a reduction in the tax rate during this period. Also ruled out is the possibility that income was redistributed away from wage and salary incomes in favor of operating surplus. Over the period 1971 to 1976, for example, wages and salaries remained stable at around 52 percent of total-factor incomes.

These figures tend to suggest that the kingdom's high-growth rates are not necessarily benefitting all segments of the population. Yet there is no real way, given the available data, of verifying this hypothesis. One method might be to estimate the amount of revenue from each barrel of oil lifted that is being plowed back into the country.[5] As an example, in fiscal 1975–1976, gross fixed-capital formation was 35,075 million SR. Oil revenues that year were SR 95,040 million (from 2,837 million barrels of oil produced, and at an average price of $10.70). From each barrel of oil, therefore, (by rough calculation) Saudi Arabia obtained $9.50 in revenue, of which $3.50 ended up as fixed-capital formation. In terms of the selling price of oil, 32.7 percent was added to the country's fixed assets. In fiscal 1976–1977 this figure went up to 45.2 percent, and by fiscal 1977–1978 it was nearly 60 percent.

While interesting, these figures by themselves (as with the consumption figures) provide few insights into the determination of the benefits an average Saudi is deriving from the oil sector. Gross fixed-capital formation is measured in terms of construction, transport, machinery, and equipment. This figure is at best only a rough guide to the value of what is being put into the country. It is even less insightful as to the level of improvement that the average Saudi is experiencing in his own standard of living. The gross capital formation figures (whose high value, of course, in part is a reflection of the low levels of consumption growth) do not include government expenditures for investment in manpower, education, medical staff, or the general up-grading of social and administrative services. Improvements in these services are adding to the quality of the average Saudi's life just as much or perhaps more so than higher levels of consumption might.

Government Consumption

Government consumption expenditures also rose rapidly during this period, increasing from 0.8 billion SR in 1960 to 10.7 billion in 1978 (at constant

1970 prices). Of particular interest is that:

1. The ratio of government consumption expenditures to nonoil GDP increased from 23.1 percent in 1960 to 55.3 percent in 1978.

2. The average rate of increase in these expenditures was quite high for both subperiods (14.89 and 17.87).

3. Government consumption consists of both defense and nondefense expenditures. In general, demand for civil services of government was related to the behavior of the nonoil sector. Defense expenditures, on the other hand, were more related to GDP in the oil sector.

4. The relationship between nondefense and nonoil GDP has been very stable, averaging about 25 percent in the 1970s.

5. Government expenditures' patterns have undergone a marked change in the 1972–1978 period compared with the earlier 1960–1972 period. The major patterns observed in government consumption patterns before the 1973 (1960–1972 oil price increases were that:[6]

a. Appropriations tended to rise proportionate to increases in revenues.

b. Expenditures for development tended to be less than appropriations, and often unspent allocations were transferred to consumption appropriations and expenditures.

c. Expenditures for development tended to rise as a percentage of appropriated amounts.

d. Revenues fluctuated considerably over the 1960–1972 period which helps to explain why expenditures often diverged considerably from appropriations.

e. Appropriations for consumption increased steadily, averaging about 16 percent over the 1960–1972 period. Consumption expenditures fluctuated more than appropriations.

Since 1973 these patterns have been modified somewhat in that:

1. Appropriations have tended to lag a bit behind increases in revenues (especially in 1974 and 1979–1980).

2. Expenditures for development have increasingly been closer to appropriations. For the first 4 years of the Second Development Plan (1976–1979), actual expenditures were greater than budgeted expenditures (463,270 million SR budgeted, 495,484 million SR actually spent).

3. Expenditures for development tended to fall even faster as a proportion of government expenditures.

4. Revenues tended to be more stable than previously (after the initial 1973–1974 price increase).

5. Consumption appropriations, while increasing steadily, have tended to fluctuate less than in the previous period.

The two patterns indicate that the government is gaining greater control over the budgetary process, increasing its ability to implement projects, using its past investments as a means of smoothing out year to year expenditures, and in general gaining greater control over the economy in terms of the budgetary process.

Inflation

Prices on the other hand remained remarkably stable during the first period, but have shown a much higher increase (see table 6–3) after 1972. Again, the same two subperiods can be discerned in terms of a rather abrupt break in the historical trend. The oil-price increases and with them the introduction of the government's ambitious development programs exerted great pressure upon available domestic resources. While the rate of domestic savings and the capacity to import increased rapidly, absorptive capacity appears to have been pushed to its limits giving rise to persistent inflationary pressures. Achieved rates of growth in real product as reflected in the expansion of commodity production and ancillary sectors are comparable to those of the most rapidly growing economies elsewhere in the world at any time in history. Though production capacity has expanded at an unprecedented rate in response to rapidly increasing fixed-capital formation, the expansion of aggregate demand has persistently outpaced the expansion of real output.

Saudi Arabia's recent inflationary experience could conceivably differ from that experienced in the late 1950s to early 1960s for two reasons:

Table 6–3
Saudi Arabia: Cost-of-Living Index
1963 (1382/83) = 100.0

Year	Food	Housing	Clothing	Miscellaneous	General Index
1964	103.9	103.6	102.0	100.1	102.8
1965	104.2	106.7	96.2	100.5	103.2
1966	106.0	109.7	97.9	100.5	104.8
1967	111.4	112.1	96.2	100.9	107.0
1968	110.0	118.2	89.6	104.2	108.7
1969	116.0	120.7	96.7	104.3	112.5
1970	114.6	112.2	96.1	105.5	112.7
1971	117.7	136.2	102.9	106.2	118.2
1972	119.7	148.5	113.2	108.5	123.2
1973	138.7	166.4	129.7	135.9	143.1
1974	163.3	231.2	146.8	145.7	173.8
1975	195.9	406.7	149.1	163.4	233.9
1976	241.0	586.3	185.0	201.5	307.7
1977	309.2	602.5	210.0	228.8	353.1
1978	298.8	548.6	234.1	80.7	346.4

Source: Saudi Arabian Monetary Agency, *Annual Report 1399* (1979), p. 161.

1. Given that the operation of the economy can be described by a system of relationships (see chapter 15) with certain variables exogenous (such as the money supply, the exchange rate, and the levels of export and import prices), changes from one inflationary episode to another in the relative magnitudes of these variables may well be different. The result of this differential change in the environment could, for instance, mean that one inflationary period would be largely characterized as stemming from world price increases, while another period of price increases could be attributed largely to domestic budgetary policy.

2. The structural equations through which the exogenous influences work may have undergone change over time.

For example, Saudis might have become more responsive to inflation in the sense that because of adverse past experiences (1960), they tried harder in 1978 to anticipate and offset the effects of inflation on their activities. Apart from this expectational aspect, the economy's underlying inflationary mechanisms may alter for other reasons, including:

1. Changes in the composition of output.
2. Different types of activity.
3. Modifications of institutions that may cause shifts in the type and responsiveness of the markets which make up the economy.

Several features of Saudi Arabia have tended to shape the character of its inflations:

1. The economy is quite open to international economic influences. In 1960 the ratio of imports to nonoil GDP was 33.9. By 1978 this had increased to 92.8 percent (see table 6-4). The expansion of imports was mainly in the areas of food and manufactured products for both producer and consumer use. Saudi Arabia's world-market share for most of these products is relatively small. It is reasonable and customary to assume that export and import prices are essentially determined abroad.

2. The marginal import aggregate demand ratio has increased over time from 0.129 in 1961 to 1.201 in 1978. Presumably, this reflects the results of increased expenditures combined with the gradual elimination of domestic excess capacity.

3. The average capital output ratio has gradually increased, reflecting the growth of capital at rates faster than those of supportive productive factors of production and the capital intensive nature of the country's development strategy.

4. The marginal capital output ratio has fluctuated somewhat, reflecting more changes in investment than changes in income. Its long-run increasing trend is indicative of the falling short-run productivity of capital in the kingdom due to bottlenecks, the need for massive infrastructural investments,

Table 6–4
Saudi Arabia: Macroeconomic Trends, 1970–1978
(Billions of riyals)

	1970	1971	1972	1973	1974	1975	1976	1977	1978
Domestic absorption	12.086	12.936	14.696	18.811	28.926	52.397	87.106	127.435	166.060
External absorption	5.313	9.984	13.562	21.740	70.389	87.203	77.420	77.621	57.687
Total absorption	17.399	22.920	28.258	40.551	99.315	139.600	164.526	205.056	223.747
Aggregate demand supply balance	22.388	28.125	34.558	48.823	114.608	166.858	207.390	267.756	305.604
Private expenditure	6.915	7.562	8.205	9.564	12.178	24.709	34.530	50.896	69.594
Government expenditure	4.635	5.008	5.728	7.320	13.280	23.281	46.374	68.385	87.518
Private–government expenditure elasticity	0.610	0.86	1.692	1.678	2.979	0.732	2.495	1.001	0.762
Average capital output ratio	0.303	0.285	0.298	0.320	0.374	0.504	0.598	0.651	0.670
Marginal capital output ratio	0.919	−0.026	0.090	0.171	0.229	0.166	0.440	0.692	0.770
Average savings rate (savings–GNP)	0.333	0.465	0.504	0.587	0.612	0.541	0.461	0.463	0.471
Marginal savings rate	0.212	0.821	0.716	0.786	0.665	0.384	0.214	0.467	0.497
Import—domestic absorption ratio	0.413	0.402	0.429	0.440	0.529	0.520	0.492	0.492	0.493
Import—nonoil income ratio	0.666	0.631	0.686	0.725	0.991	0.969	0.906	0.926	0.928
Import—aggregate demand ratio	0.223	0.185	0.182	0.169	0.133	0.163	0.207	0.234	0.268
Marginal import aggregate demand ratio	0.727	0.904	0.541	0.284	0.284	0.439	0.590	0.701	1.201

Source: Computed from data contained in Saudi Arabian Monetary Agency, *Annual Report*, various issues.

the long gestation period of much investment in manufacturing, and the shortages of skilled workers.

Each of these ratios is reflective of changes in the structure of the Saudi Arabian economy. Movements in these ratios will ultimately determine the degree to which the economy will be able to attain a stable price-growth path.

At this point it suffices to say that the Saudi Arabian economy is confronted with a dual challenge; on the one hand, to employ the country's oil revenue for development of the economy and diversification of its sources of income; and on the other hand, to minimize the inflationary pressures that are an indispensable concomitant of accelerated spending. This is not an easy task in an economy where government domestic spending not only generates a direct demand for goods and services, but also has an expansionary effect on private-sector liquidity.

In fact it is now well-known both inside and outside of Saudi Arabia that at a relatively less rapid rate of expansion in aggregate demand, accompanied by fewer, milder shortages and bottlenecks, the intensity of inflationary pressures could have been diminished, and the task of controlling and further moderating inflation made less formidable. It is argued that with less rapid inflation there would have been fewer acute shortages and fewer distortions among prices and costs, and in commodity flows. It follows that a significant reduction in the rate of growth of aggregate expenditure, and in particular public-sector expenditure, could have resulted in equally rapid but possibly more uniform expansion of the various sectors.

The basic policy problems to be concerned with here involve determining:

1. Precisely to what degree does high growth (sustained annual rates of growth of 10 percent or more) in real nonoil GDP necessarily generate large inflationary pressures?
2. Must growth in the future necessarily be reduced to eliminate or reduce inflation?
3. Can the inflation in the 1972–1978 period be attributed to factors other than growth, and if so, what are they?
4. To what extent should the authorities attempt to maintain high rates of growth, and for how long?

Sectoral Transformation

The transformations that occur in the process of development are widespread, affecting society as well as the economy. The most important economic transformations that normally take place with development are in the importance of the various producing sectors in production, the methods used in each sector, the structure and functioning of markets, and the role and function of government.

This is not to assert that traditional values cannot be maintained, or that the transformations and new patterns must be uniform across countries. The great variety that advanced countries show in important social and economic dimensions is prima facie evidence that the developing countries can also be expected to generate their own somewhat unique patterns of development. Thus every country will have its optimum pattern of change, the identification of which is one of the major concerns of economic planning.

Although development does require transformation of the economic structure, it is not possible to make easy association between such transformations and progress toward development. This is especially true in Saudi Arabia's case, where the petroleum-producing sector has virtually retained (in current prices) its relative position in the rapidly growing economy. Although agriculture and manufacturing have grown, their growth rates have not in general been as rapid as the economy as a whole, so that in absolute terms their relative importance has been declining slightly (see table 6–5).

The other relative changes in the Saudi Arabian economy have also been modest. The share of construction activity in the total economy has, as might be expected, increased fairly rapidly since 1973. On the other hand, the share of public administration and defense in total gross domestic product has, somewhat surprisingly, grown only moderately. The sectorial patterns of the Saudi Arabian economy do not, therefore, give an unambiguous picture of the fulfillment of the major transformations which might be expected in the course of diversified development.

Thus a review of the sector information for the country yields one to conclude that the kingdom does not yet show a clear transition to a pattern of diversified growth that is generally associated with development. Although the dependence on petroleum production has tended to fall, it has not been made up, as one would hope, by improvements in agriculture or manufacturing (though rapid growth has occurred in these sectors). The compensating changes have tended, on the other hand, to be concentrated in the construction and trade sectors. However, it is possible that the investment programs which are reflected in the relative growth in construction in the country, and which have often generated more than proportionate growth in the infrastructure sector, may at some point in the future yield a more diversified production base.

The following observations are relevant to the economic and social development of the economy:

1. The petroleum and natural gas sector dominate GDP with nearly half of GDP accounted for by these sectors (see table 6–6).

2. The growth of the agricultural sector was substantially less than that of the other sectors throughout the period with a very uniform rate of growth of around 3.5–4.0 percent. Of particular interest is its relatively low share of GDP, as is also the case for manufacturing (see table 6–6).

Table 6-5
Saudi Arabia: Sectorial Output, 1960–1969
(Billions of 1970 riyals)

	1960	1961	1962	1963	1964	1965	1966	1967	1968	1969
Agriculture	0.855 (12.4)	0.867	0.919	0.978	0.998	0.948	0.924	0.885	0.925	0.957 (6.0)
Oil	3.273 (47.4)	3.623	3.939	4.181	4.191	4.122	5.155	6.216	6.786	7.150 (45.0)
Manufacturing	0.564 (8.2)	0.626	0.696	0.773	0.833	0.997	1.037	1.089	1.265	1.410 (8.9)
Construction	0.271 (3.9)	0.295	0.322	0.351	0.404	0.775	0.888	0.847	0.916	1.028 (6.5)
Electricity	0.075 (1.1)	0.086	0.099	0.114	0.124	0.140	0.174	0.198	0.219	0.217 (1.4)
Transportation	0.419 (6.1)	0.474	0.536	0.606	0.695	0.712	0.814	0.919	1.013	1.114 (7.0)
Trade	0.410 (5.9)	0.450	0.505	0.630	0.712	0.923	1.017	1.044	1.174	1.302 (8.2)
Public administration and defense	0.488 (7.1)	0.562	0.647	0.747	0.848	1.233	1.320	1.475	1.516	1.647 (10.4)
Other sectors	0.555 (8.0)	0.599	0.647	0.699	0.755	0.815	0.877	0.891	0.959	1.049 (6.6)
Gross domestic product	6.910	7.582	8.310	9.079	9.560	10.665	12.206	13.564	14.773	15.904

Table 6–5 (continued)

	1970	1971	1972	1973	1974	1975	1976	1977	1978
Agriculture	0.984	1.018	1.051	1.089 (3.9)	1.130	1.174	1.221	1.272	1.359 (3.3)
Oil	8.154	10.084	12.710	16.409 (58.0)	17.857	16.629	16.750	18.246	17.534 (42.1)
Manufacturing	1.672	1.840	1.847	1.978 (7.0)	2.082	2.040	2.187	2.475	2.596 (6.2)
Construction	0.934	0.957	1.053	1.396 (4.9)	1.737	2.189	2.846	3.813	4.214 (10.1)
Electricity	0.273	0.298	0.329	0.381 (1.3)	0.417	0.459	0.538	0.655	0.864 (2.1)
Transportation	1.243	1.468	1.544	1.849 (6.5)	2.224	2.721	3.388	4.212	5.168 (12.4)
Trade	1.362	1.412	1.523	1.795 (6.3)	2.097	2.469	2.942	3.605	4.448 (10.7)
Public administration and defense	1.678	1.722	1.834	1.981 (7.0)	2.177	2.438	2.757	3.140	3.296 (7.9)
Other sectors	1.099	1.223	1.300	1.395 (4.9)	1.525	1.420	1.623	1.900	2.162 (5.2)
Gross domestic product	17.399	20.022	23.191	28.273	31.246	31.539	34.250	39.318	41.641

Source: Computed from data contained in Ministry of Finance and National Economy, *National Accounts of Saudi Arabia*, various issues; Saudi Arabian Monetary Agency, *Annual Report*, various issues; The World Bank, *World Bank Tables*, 1976; The World Bank, *World Bank Tables*, 1980.

Note: Numbers in parenthises indicate percentage of Gross Domestic Product.

Table 6-6
Saudi Arabia: Nonoil GDP Sectorial Output Elasticities
(*Constant 1389-1390 prices, millions of riyals*)

	Estimated Coefficients		Output Elasticities			
Sector	Nonoil GDP	Lagged Sector Valve	Short Run	Long Run	r^2	F
Agriculture	0.0551	0.8472	0.0551	0.3606	0.99	2,985.66
	(76.5)	(10.6)				
Mining	0.9342	0.5341	0.9342	2.0052	0.98	157.98
	(17.7)	(1.6)				
Manufacturing	0.1086	0.9094	0.1086	1.1987	0.99	5,950.70
	(107.3)	(19.7)				
Petroleum refining	0.0104	0.6032	0.0104	0.0262	0.83	16.82
	(4.6)	(3.5)				
Electricity, gas, and water	0.4406	0.6445	0.4406	1.2394	0.99	1,171.59
	(14.2)	(4.7)				
Construction	0.6839	0.7004	0.6839	2.2827	0.98	147.00
	(16.9)	(2.5)				
Commerce	1.2297	0.0615	1.2297	1.3103	0.99	1,036.65
	(45.4)	(3.7)				
Transportation	1.0735	0.3189	1.0735	1.5761	0.99	1,272.80
	(50.4)	(1.2)				
Finance	0.7278	0.1402	0.7278	0.8465	0.99	259.00
	(22.7)	(0.4)				
Ownership of dwellings	0.5746	0.3613	0.5746	1.1116	0.99	1,133.16
Community, social & personal services	0.3107	0.6298	0.3107	0.8393	0.99	1,276.70
	(50.2)	(6.2)				
Imputed bank services	0.2123	0.5864	0.2123	0.5133	0.81	15.1
	(5.2)	(1.7)				
Other government services	0.5772	0.2790	0.5772	0.8006	0.99	818.48
	(40.5)	(0.8)				

Source: Computed from data in table 6-5.

Note: See text for structural form of estimated equation.
( ) — t value

3. Services have shown a good steady growth, but their output elasticity is in general less than one (see table 6-6). Usually the services sector lags behind the industrial if the strategy of economic development is aimed at promoting balanced growth. This is because the service sector operates on a derived demand basis, with backward linkages from the strictly output-oriented agricultural and industrial sectors.

4. There has been a leveling-off in crude petroleum output, and with the stabilization of world oil prices, the end result has been that the sector's share of GDP has fallen in recent years.

The dominance of the oil sector, the longer-term expansion of the construction, transportation, and the services sectors, together with the decline in the importance of agriculture, combine to give the kingdom an economy that does not deviate significantly from one usually associated with its per capita income and population, yet is somewhat unique among other oil producers (see table 6–7).

It is still too early to assess the effects of the high rates on investment that have in general prevailed since 1973. Some but by no means all of the permanent effects can already be discerned. The investments in infrastructure, housing, schools, roads, and hospitals will undoubtedly generate quite widespread improvements in the standards of living. What is more questionable is the rate at which the investments in agriculture and industry will result in increases in output in these sectors.

The uncertainty surrounding investment and sectorial value added was confirmed by a number of econometric equations. These were estimated in the context of the macroeconomic forecasting model developed in chapter 15. There were only three sectors—Public Administration (DDP), Agriculture (DAGP), and Electricity (DEP)—for which statistically significant relationships could be found (see table 6–8), where at constant 1970 prices:

$$CONP = \text{construction GDP}$$

$$MANP = \text{manufacturing GDP}$$

$$DP = \text{public administration and defense GDP}$$

$$TP = \text{transport and communication GDP}$$

$$EP = \text{electricity, gas, water GDP}$$

$$TDP = \text{trade GDP}$$

$$AGP = \text{agriculture GDP}$$

$$DEP = \text{change in electricity, gas, and water}$$

$$DAG = \text{change in agriculture GDP}$$

$$DDP = \text{change in public administration and defense GDP}$$

$$NOXNP = \text{nonoil GDP}$$

$$ICONNP = \text{construction investment}$$

$$ICONNPL = \text{construction investment previous years}$$

$$POP = \text{population}$$

$$GENANP = \text{government expenditure}$$

$$IONP = \text{other investment}$$

$$DNOXNP = \text{change in nonoil GDP}$$

$$DPOP = \text{change in population}$$

Table 6–7
Oil-Producing Countries: Actual and Normal Sectorial Output Levels, 1970
(Percentage)

Sectors	Saudi Arabia		Iran		Iraq		Libya		Kuwait		Venezuela	
	Normal	*Actual*	*Normal*	*Actual*	*Normal*	*Actual*	*Normal*	*Actual*	*Normal*	*Actual*	*Normal*	*Actual*
Agriculture	16.0	10.0	19.0	18.0	25.0	23.0	4.0	6.0	11.0	1.0	10.0	9.0
Manufacturing	28.0	18.0	29.0	13.0	22.0	13.0	4.0	30.0	9.0	37.0	20.0	
Construction	6.0	10.0	5.0	5.0	7.0	4.0	8.0	17.0	8.0	8.0	6.0	5.0
Transportation	9.0	15.0	7.0	5.0	7.0	8.0	12.0	8.0	14.0	9.0	9.0	12.0
Services	41.0	47.0	40.0	59.0	40.0	52.0	45.0	49.0	37.0	73.0	38.0	54.0

Source: Computed from data contained in World Bank, *World Bank Tables*, 1980; and equations in Hollis Cheney "Patterns of Industrial Growth," *American Economic Review* (September 1960).

Table 6-8
Saudi Arabia: Macroeconomic Model Sectorial Submodel
(*Two-stage least-squares estimates*)

Variable	Estimated Equation	r^2	F
CONP	$= 0.13NOXNP + 0.18ICONNPL - 0.25$ (3.29) (2.88)	0.9852	433.32
MANP	$= 0.17ICONNPL + 1.14$ (5.82) (9.59)	0.7073	33.83
DP	$= 0.54POP + 0.05GENANP - 1.91$ (6.25) (3.86)	0.9806	329.40
TP	$= 0.29NOXNP - 0.84$ (43.16) (-12.09)	0.9925	1862.64
EP	$= 0.05NOXNP - 0.10$ (22.04) (-4.43)	0.9720	485.61
TDP	$= 0.34ICONNPL + 0.23IONPL - 0.55$ (22.97) (4.10) (8.01)	0.9829	353.04
AGP	$= 0.03NOXNP + 0.79$ (12.29) (33.25)	0.9151	150.93
DEP	$= 0.50DNOXNP - 0.01$ (3.26) (-0.23)	0.4320	10.65
DAGP	$= 0.62DPOP - 0.08$ (2.92) (-2.15)		
DDP	$= 0.09DNOXNP + 0.08$ (2.92) (2.02)	0.3791	8.55

In no cases were changes in investment associated with changes in sectorial value added. In terms of the level of value added in construction (*CONP*), it was found to be correlated with the previous year's investment in construction (*ICONNPL*), as were manufacturing (*MANP*) and trade (*TDP*). For the other sectors, investment was not statistically significant when regressed on value added, either lagged or for the current year. Of course, only broad investment figures—investment in machinery, investment in construction, and other investment—were used due to the lack of sectorial investment figures. Had these been available, it is possible that better results would have been obtained.

We do know that investment in primary and processing industries has been undertaken on a large scale, although as noted there is no systematic collection on the sectoral allocation of investment. The high cost and possible wastage of much of this investment has been noted elsewhere.[7] Since the gestation periods of the industrial investment are 3 to 5 years, it is only within the next few years that the effects of many of the ambitious investment programs will be forthcoming.

It is reasonable to expect that most of the investments will be profitable, if not to the extent originally expected, than at least to some degree. However, the degree is important and it would be dangerous to make predictions without more evidence and close scrutiny. There are many examples of large projects in other developing countries that were based on inadequate analysis and as a result have added relatively little growth. Unfortunately, several (confidential) reports that are available suggest that some of the investments undertaken in the kingdom may not have been the result of careful investigations and decision processes that would help assure the returns projected for them.

The basic policy questions coming to mind with respect to future sectoral growth are

1. What is the growth potential of the agricultural sector over the next twenty years? If we assume rising incomes and consequently rising demand from the products of agriculture, can the country achieve a certain amount of self-sufficiency in this lagging sector, or does the country definitely not have any comparative advantage in the production of agricultural commodities. What specific policies should be adopted vis à vis agriculture within a comprehensive strategy of economic and social development?

2. Is it safe to assume that (given the assumption of more or less constant real-oil prices) the future growth potential rests on the performance of the industrial and service sectors? Does the country really have a comparative advantage in petroleum-based industrial products?

3. What kind of revenues can the country expect from the oil sector over the next two decades? How should the planners use these revenues to finance the growth of other sectors? What sectors should have priority on what criteria?

Balance of Payments

The stimulus for the acceleration of growth of the economy after 1973 came, of course, from the large increase in the revenues from oil. This expansion is discussed at length in chapter 10. It suffices to say here that subsequently a decline in real export earnings because of world inflation and the fall of the dollar did take place.

Despite the fall in the purchasing power of oil revenues (see table 6–9), the country has been able to increase its imports at a faster rate than had been anticipated even immediately after the increase in oil prices in 1973–1974. The growth of oil revenues from 1973 to 1974 was greatly overshadowed by

Table 6–9
The Sources of Percentage Change in OPEC's Terms of Trade

Year	Terms of Trade	Price of Oil	Inflation	Dollar's Fluctuation
1971	16.52	25.14	−3.99	−4.49
1972	2.908	8.66	−3.77	−2.51
1973	72.54	96.9	−14.83	−9.52
1974	106.52	130.46	−26.58	2.63
1975	10.22	10.27	−1.69	1.64
1976	−7.90	−9.93	2.76	
1977	−6.165	2.98	−2.43	−6.717
Annual average	27.80	39.097	−9.032	−2.31
Relative contribution	(100.00)	(140.63)	(−32.48)	(−8.30)

Source: Mansoor Dailami, "The Choice f an Optimal Currency for Determining the Price of Oil," MIT Energy Laboratory *Working Paper No. MIT EL 78-026WP*, rev. February 1979.

the growth in imports during that period. The resulting expansion in imports has been quite high and continuous.

Another interesting pattern is the close relationship between the balance-of-payments current account and the government surplus or deficit (see table 6–10). For example, in 1968 the government had a deficit and the current account was also negative, but by 1975 was running a budget surplus of SR 6 billion, and the current account was in surplus by SR 49 billion.

The ratio of the balance-of-trade account to imports suggests further important current trends. The country has had general surpluses on trade account, but these are typically larger than those on the current account because of net payments on services and outflows of unrequited transfers. The trends in the trade account surpluses have been downward in recent years, reflecting increasing import capacity, slower increases, or absolute declines in exports of oil and movements in the terms of trade against the country.

Imports

Imports continue to play a major role in the kingdom's development strategy. Modern technology in the form of know-how and machinery as well as new products can only be introduced via imports. There are no real purely indigenous mechanisms within Saudi Arabia to produce the requirements for growth and modernization in the country. That imports have played an essential role in the country's growth is evidenced by the fact that:

1. Total imports rose faster than nonoil GDP over the entire period, rising from 30.8 percent of nonoil GDP in 1960 to 80.6 percent in 1979.

2. Imports of machinery were particularly rapid during this period, far outpacing the increase in food imports (see table 6–11). The relative importance of this component in total imports indicates the sustained pattern of import substitution in the country during this period.

The most important aggregate policy problems in the import sector to be faced by Saudi Arabia in the coming years are

1. Is it realistic to expect the country to lessen its dependence on imports over the next twenty years? Will the economy continually require a large import component even in the more advanced stages of industrialization?

2. What will be (or should be) the composition of imports over the next twenty years? Should consumer goods be restricted to encourage local producers, and in line with this policy how much protection should be given to infant industries being set up and to those who have already operated for some years? How long should the Saudi planners protect inefficient industries on the basis that they must be given time to learn how to operate efficiently?

3. Is it reasonable to expect the kingdom to reduce its dependence on food imports, or must it be forever a large net importer of nearly all of its basic food items?

How much emphasis must be placed on importing technology and skills if the latter could presumably be given Saudis through increased expenditures on education?

Public–Private Expenditures

Although oil revenues have obviously contributed more significantly to the growth of the public sector than the private sector, its impact on the latter has by no means been negligible. That is to say, the public sector has been dynamic enough to engender very substantial increases in the private-sector aggregates. These through their linkages have in turn had a substantial positive feedback on the growth rates of the nonoil GDP.

The previously cited figures for consumption and investment suggest that a major structural change in the role of the public sector in the economy has taken place. The rate of growth of both government investment and government consumption has been over double that of its private counterparts. Private expenditure has in fact declined from 105.2 percent of nonoil GDP (in 1960) to 73.9 percent (in 1978). Between 1960 and 1978, government expenditure increased from 24.1 percent of nonoil GDP to 99.2 percent. These increases can be traced back to the increasing economic role of the public sector as a result of the very rapid increases in oil revenues during this period, and the fact that the government is the sole recipient of these revenues. The government has, therefore, been in the position of having the

Table 6–10
Saudi Arabia: Balance of Payments, Monetary Sector, Fiscal Survey Relationships, 1961–1969
(Billions of riyals)

	1961	1962	1963	1964	1965	1966	1967	1968	1969
Balance of payments									
Private direct investment	-0.068	-0.149	0.576	-0.072	0.338	0.194	0.432	0.063	-0.167
Other private long term	0.009	0.005	0.009	0.041		0.005	-0.005	0.540	0.189
Other private short term	-0.306	-0.185	-0.216	-0.329	-0.428	-0.590	-0.414	0.203	0.041
Government (net)	-0.225	-0.437		0.014		0.252	0.014	0.045	
Monetary movements	-0.392	-0.045	-1.238	-0.464	-0.509	-0.437	-0.486	-0.306	0.527
Errors and omissions	—	—	—	—	—	—	—	—	—
Current account balance	0.981	0.810	0.868	0.810	0.599	0.576	0.441	-0.441	-0.387
Asset movements									
Current account balance	0.981	0.810	0.868	0.810	0.599	0.576	0.441	-0.414	-0.387
Δ Net foreign liabilities banks	-0.120	0.050	-0.150	-0.030	0.120	0.070	-0.120	-0.030	-0.080
Δ SAMA foreign assets	0.240	0.130	1.150	0.330	0.720	0.260	0.580	-0.330	0.390
Δ Net government foreign liabilities	-0.621	-0.230	0.432	-0.450	0.001	-0.386	-0.269	0.114	0.857
Government fiscal balance									
Δ Net governemnt foreign assets	0.621	0.730	-0.432	0.450	-0.001	0.386	-0.269	-0.114	-0.857
Government revenues	1.898	2.164	2.491	2.583	3.644	4.358	4.823	5.137	4.957
Government expenditures	1.898	1.654	2.203	2.402	3.389	4.325	4.510	5.374	5.602
Government domestic assets	-0.298	-0.220	0.720	-0.269	0.256	-0.353	0.522	-0.123	0.212
Surplus (+) or deficit (−)	0.323	0.510	0.288	0.181	0.255	0.033	0.253	-0.237	-0.645

	1970	1971	1972	1973	1974	1975	1976	1977	1978
Balance of payments									
Private direct investment	0.090	−0.500	0.144	−2.577	−15.869	6.599	−1.300	2.897	
Other private long term	0.378	−0.036	0.099	−0.013	−0.137	−3.801	−4.601	−0.099	
Other private short term	−0.261	0.198	−0.671	0.605	−1.870	0.696	−0.807	−8.301	
Government (net)	−0.050	−0.104	0.009			−21.299	−26.489	−34.398	
Monetary movements	−0.392	−3.573	−4.919	−6.045	−63.477	−30.699	−13.702	−2.799	
Errors and omissions	−0.086	−0.068	−0.768	−0.123	−0.320	−0.500	−1.797	−2.394	
Current account balance	0.320	4.082	6.101	8.154	81.674	49.001	48.706	45.095	
Asset movements									
Current account balance	0.320	4.082	6.101	8.154	81.674	49.001	48.706	45.095	
Δ Net foreign liabilities of banks	−0.120	−0.070	−0.740	0.050	0.290	−1.070	−1.790	−3.320	
Δ SAMA foreign assets	0.490	2.930	5.040	5.000	53.720	66.270	43.860	27.430	
Δ Net government liabilities	0.290	−1.082	−0.321	−3.204	−28.244	18.399	−3.056	−14.345	
Government fiscal balance									
net goverment assets	−0.290	1.082	0.321	3.204	28.244	−18.399	3.056	14.345	
Government revenues	5.668	7.954	11.116	15.325	41.705	100.103	103.383	135.957	130.659
Government expenditures	6.079	6.418	8.303	10.148	18.595	32.038	81.784	128.273	138.027
Government domestic assets	0.121	0.454	2.552	1.973	−5.134	86.464	18.543	−6.481	
Surplus (+) or deficit (−)	−0.411	1.536	2.873	5.177	23.110	68.065	21.599	7.864	−7.368

Source: Computed from data contained in Saudi Arabian Monetary Agency, *Annual Report*, various issues.

Table 6–11
Saudi Arabia: Composition of Imports
(Millions of riyals)

	1968	1969	1970	1971	1972	1973	1974	1975	1976	1977	Average Annual Rate 1969–1977
Foodstuffs	796 (30.9)	926 (27.4)	1,011 (31.6)	1,097 (29.9)	1,222 (26.0)	1,875 (26.1)	2,023 (19.9)	2,301 (15.5)	3,536 (11.5)	5,365 (10.4)	23.6
Live animal and animal products	268	236	230	250	310	441	442	642	925	1,465	20.8
Vegetable products	375	466	501	500	496	661	911	934	1,478	1,647	17.9
Animal & vegetable fats and oils	41	35	42	74	61	58	72	100	147	224	20.8
prepared foodstuffs	112	189	239	273	354	526	598	625	986	2,029	38.0
Building materials (11.8)	303 (12.7)	429 (12.0)	384 (13.8)	463 (10.2)	480 (7.4)	534 (9.5)	968 (11.3)	1,676 (10.9)	3,332 (11.0)	5,702	38.6
Textiles and clothing	153 (5.9)	172 (5.1)	142 (4.4)	203 (5.5)	344 (7.3)	696 (9.7)	955 (9.4)	1,291 (8.7)	2,170 (7.1)	3,496 (6.8)	41.6
Machinery, electric appliances, and transport equipment	846 (32.8)	1,084 (32.1)	1,018 (31.8)	1,100 (30.0)	1,685 (35.8)	2,535 (35.2)	3,686 (36.3)	5,946 (40.1)	13,086 (42.6)	20,568 (39.8)	42.6
Chemical products	137 (5.3)	259 (7.7)	180 (5.6)	240 (7.1)	244 (5.2)	399 (5.5)	442 (4.4)	668 (4.5)	900 (2.9)	1,739 (3.4)	32.6
Miscellaneous	343 (13.3)	507 (15.0)	462 (14.5)	565 (15.4)	732 (15.5)	1,366 (19.1)	2,075 (20.4)	2,941 (19.8)	7,667 (25.0)	14,792 (28.6)	
Total	2,578	3,377	3,197	3,667	4,708	7,197	10,149	14,823	30,691	91,662	39.6

Source: Saudi Arabian Monetary Agency, *Annual Report*, 1398, 1396.
Note: Numbers in parentheses indicate percentage of total.

means and inclination for promoting a genuine "take-off" in the Saudi Arabian economy.

It must be understood, however, that these very rapid growth rates as well as the decreasing percentages of private sector activity in the total are not a reflection of lack of dynamism on the part of entrepreneurs, but rather, a result of both the rapid increases in oil revenues and the institutional aspects associated with the introduction of these revenues in the country's economic and social mainstream.

That the oil revenues find their way to the economy via government institutions means that increases in government consumption, in government investment and in the percentage share of each in GDP are a function of the increases in such revenues. Were oil or other similar revenues to begin to taper off, we would expect a decrease in public sector growth and in the share of government consumption to GDP, as well as in government investment to GDP. Under such conditions, and because the government intends to maintain the mixed (private and public) nature of Saudi Arabia's economy, the private sector would then be relied upon to stimulate growth.

It is at least arguable that a less-ambitious effort to develop the economy, particularly during the 1972–1980 period, might have proved at least equally effective. Less-rapid expansion of government expenditures for development might well have permitted (given appropriately restricture monetary measures) at least as rapid a rate of growth in real product at a somewhat lower rate of inflation. By permitting a more gradual process of adaptation through manpower development and skill formation, and the augmentation and upgrading of infrastructural facilities, a more moderate rate of expansion might well have avoided the creation of bottlenecks and created less-acute shortages.

Some of the pressing policy problems that the Saudi Arabian planners need to consider in this area from a long-term perspective are

1. In the light of abundant albeit depleting oil resources, how long can the kingdom maintain its oil-dependent economy?
2. What should be the role of the public and private sectors in the economy of Saudi Arabia, say 20 years from now? What are the possible alternatives?
3. How can the kingdom ensure that with the possible tapering-off of its oil-based windfall gains, it will be left with a viable economic structure capable of generating its own savings, investment, and growth?
4. Can private consumption expenditure ever replace oil-based government revenues as the engine of growth?

Conclusions

Since the country is for the most part still in the early stages of its development, the patterns of its structure have not been clearly established. It is clear, however, that the period since 1973 has been one of growth accelerated from the long-run trend. Increased resources have contributed to a rapid expansion of investment and to a lesser extent consumption. It is the latter on which the modernization and diversification of the economy must ultimately depend.

From all indications, this propitious atmosphere is going to continue to prevail, although numerous socioeconomic problems will undoubtedly develop and threaten the country's progress.

A number of questions were raised in this chapter concerning the likely nature of some future trends and other macroeconomic developments. In large part, these issues will be addressed in the following chapters, especially in constructing the macroeconomic model presented in chapter 14.

In general the results of that model, and the analysis underlying its formulation, stress the critical importance of continued high levels of oil revenues. The key to continued expansion will be determined to a large extent by the degree to which improvements in the country's planning and plan formulation process take place. Saudi Arabia's political philosophy of state assistance and guidance to the private sector, as well as significant direct state involvement in many areas of the economy, calls for a bureaucracy of better-than-average competence and efficiency. It is necessary that the state be able to do it well.

Whether growth can be sustained will also depend on the country's ability to solve new problems as fast as they are created by the solutions already at hand. Economic development has always been a race between answers found and new questions raised. Saudi Arabia is not likely to be an exception to this rule. So far, in addition to their phenomenal good luck, Saudi planners have avoided politicoeconomic crises by staying ahead of them. The same feat has to be achieved in the socioeconomic area if the past trend is to become self-sustaining.

There is one final point that is worth emphasizing. The country has been the recipient of a large number of immigrant workers. These to a considerable extent have been absorbed in the investment and the service sectors rather than in processing industries. That is the case simply because there is yet relatively little in the way of processing-industry capacity that could absorb labor. In the future, as investments in the processing industries mature the demand for labor in these industries will expand. The kingdom will then be faced with the immediate reality of whether the increases in output on balance will benefit their own nationals more than the immigrant workers who are such a large fraction of the labor force.

Notes

1. Darvin Wassink, "Eonomic Development with Unlimited Finances: Foreign Exchange Surpluses in OPEC Countries," *Rivista Internationale di Scienze Economichee e Commerciali* (December 1978): 1086.

2. M. Ali Fekrat, "Growth of OPEC Type Economics: A Preliminary Theoretical Inquiry," *Economia Internazionale* (February 1979): 82.

3. International Monetary Fund, *International Financial Statistics* (May 1980): 96. See Fisal S. Al-Bashir, *A Structural Econometric Model of the Saudi Arabian Economy: 1960–1970* (New York: John Wiley, 1977), statistical appendix.

4. All macroeconomic data unless otherwise specified are from the Saudi Arabian Monetary Agency, *Annual Report* (various issues).

5. Example is from David Shirreff, "IMF Encourages Saudis to be Big Spenders," *Middle East Economic Digest* (October 1979): 6–7.

6. As first noted by Donald Wells, *Saudi Arabian Revenues and Expenditures* (Baltimore: Johns Hopkins Press, 1974), p. 14.

7. For example Arthur Smithies, *The Economic Potential of the Arab Countries* (Santa Monica: Rand, 1978).

7 Economic Planning and Performance

Because of the mixed nature of the Saudi Arabian economy where both public and private sectors have separate but significant roles to play, development planning in the kingdom has been what is often referred to in the planning literature as "perspective" for the public sector, but only "indicative" for the private sector.[1] Accordingly, state planning has attempted to encourage the growth of both public and private sectors in a pragmatic fashion by: (1) earmarking a large proportion of oil revenues for direct public domestic investment, and (2) pointing the way for private investment in other fields through conducive information, projection and incentives.

Thus in addition to certain strategic, infrastructural and defense-related operations that universally lie within the public domain, the government has as a matter of policy undertaken other activities that were unattractive to the private sector by virtue of their capital needs, technological know-how, or risks. As such, the government has adopted the role of traditional entrepreneur; that is, the risk bearer, the innovator, and the pacesetter. At the same time to encourage as much as possible private activity, the five-year development plans have been supplemented (as noted in chapter 5) by a comprehensive set of orthodox policy instruments including tax incentives, subsidies, and trade policies.

In the choice of development objectives, the focus of policy has been laid mainly on rapid growth, supplemented by a growing array of social welfare policies. Because of the vast oil revenues and a relatively small population, the government's overall preference for attaining high growth rates has not created the familiar dilemma of choosing between capital-using, output-maximizing techniques or labor-using, employment-maximizing paths. In broad terms the overall aim of government involvement in the economy has been designed to bring capital and labor together, either directly by means of public investment or indirectly by acting as a catalyst in creating a stable environment in which private capital and labor could combine to maximize output. The government's main objective has been to increase output fast enough to provide for sustained growth of employment and improved standards of living, but no so fast as to create serious dislocation and social instability.

In sum, Saudi Arabia's development policy has involved a multifaceted approach aimed at grappling with the many problems and challenges inherent in the kingdom's late start at development. Its focus has been to build and expand on the resource endowments of the country while at the same time rectifying apparent shortages and spreading benefits of growth throughout the economy. While, of course, it is impossible to say precisely what the country's recent growth performance would have been without this involvement by the government, it is safe to assume, given the primitive state of the economy in the early 1960s, that in large part the macroeconomic trends and patterns examined in the previous chapter were the end product of government planning and implementation.

The Development of Planning

The conscious process of thinking ahead has become one of the three building blocks of modern planned economic policy. Indeed the first step in the planning activity consists of forming an idea of the future possibilities based on past trends. This extrapolation, which can be the result of either simply extending a line graph or of using more sophisticated models representing the interaction of social and economic forces, enables the decision maker to assess the possible variance of key planning parameters. This process began to gain some acceptance in Saudi Arabia in the 1950s, but it took King Faisal's foresight and persuasion to formally introduce economic planning in the kingdom.[2]

Initial Steps at Planning

The first step in the creation of a planning apparatus was taken in August 1958. Formal planning began in 1959 when the Prime Minister expanded what was then called the economic development committee. The committee was replaced in 1961 by the Supreme Planning Board whose functions were to design an economic development policy in cooperation with various ministries. The board and agencies were also charged with supervising the execution of development projects. In 1965 the board was in turn replaced by the Central Planning Organization (CPO), the head of which had direct contact with the king.[3]

Whereas Saudi economic policy prior to King Faisal was to some extent negative, in that it aimed at curing very short-run current economic and social ills, under Faisal it increasingly became regarded as an activity that fit closely into the whole economic process. It was aimed more at bringing about sound development than at solving immediate economic crises.

The general objectives of economic and social development policy have not fundamentally changed over three plan periods. They are to maintain its religious and moral values and to raise the living standards and welfare of its people, while providing for national security and maintaining economic and social stability. The means looked to for achieving these goals also have not significantly changed. They consist of:

1. Increasing the rate of growth of the gross domestic product.
2. Developing human resources so that the several elements of society will be able to contribute more effectively to production and participate fully in the process of development.
3. Diversifying sources of national income and reducing dependence on oil through increasing the share of other productive sectors in the gross domestic product.[4]

To carry these out, the functions of the CPO as defined in the Council of Ministers Resolution 430 in 1965 included:[5]

1. Writing periodic economic reports.
2. Formulating economic and social development plans in accordance with the needs and requirements of the various ministries.
3. Estimating the overall resources needed to implement the plan approved by the Council of Ministries.
4. Aiding ministries and government agencies in their economic planning.
5. Supplying the king with needed technical advice.
6. Assisting in the establishment of planning units in each ministry and public agency.
7. Monitoring planned projects and reporting to the Council of Ministers about the stage of the plan's execution.

One of the basic parameters of any planning exercise is the time horizon. While it is clear that the farther out in time from the base-year projections, the less reliable they are, it is also clear that some parameters of the planning process only vary over the longer run. If policymakers in Saudi Arabia had continued as was the case before Faisal to limit their activities to the near term (annual budget), it is now clear that they would have been abstracting from certain important and influential variables. While it is probably true that over the near and medium term these variables might have had little impact on most macroeconomic aggregates, the fact is that the government would have most certainly risked losing control of the kingdom's economic and social system. This is particularly true in the sense of not being able to efficiently aim and guide the country in the direction of becoming a wealthy and modern nation. To be sure if the kingdom had not begun formal planning in 1970, the country would have been simply overcome with the sudden affluence created in 1973–1974.

At that time the CPO consisted of four departments:

1. The Planning Department whose function it was to design economic development plans and prepare economic reports.
2. The Research Department charged with collecting and analyzing economic information.
3. The Follow-up Department that monitored and reported on program implementation.
4. The General Administration Department in charge of administering and controlling the daily work of the organization.[6]

On October 13, 1975, by Royal Order No. A326, the CPO was elevated to the Ministry of Planning. By then, however, the country was prepared to assimilate efficiently the vast increase in oil revenues.

The First Development Plan (1970–1975)

In 1970 the CPO had introduced the First Five-Year Development Plan (1970–1975).[7] The plan covered all aspects of economic life in Saudi Arabia and included an articulation of the policies, programs, and projects deemed necessary to meet the country's major objectives. The plan targets were by present standards fairly modest, consisting largely of increasing gross domestic product and the amount of available human resources. The basic philosophy underlying it was that only through increases in their stock of human capital would the country's citizens be able to have a real opportunity of contributing more efficiently to production and participating fully in the process of development. The plan emphasized diversification of economic resources as the best means of lightening the burden placed on the petroleum sector for financing government expenditures. At the same time its goal was to increase the share of other productive sectors in gross domestic product in preparation for the substitution of alternative sources of national income when oil becomes depleted.

The First Plan projections of revenues ranged from a conservative figure of SR 33.8 billion to a more optimistic one of SR 37.4 billion. Both total planned outlays were set at SR 41.3 billion—SR 22.9 billion for recurrent outlays and SR 18.4 billion for projects. A deficit was thus forecast with real gross domestic product anticipated to increase at an average annual rate of 9.8 percent.

Actual government revenues, however, turned out to be approximately SR 180.6 billion and actual expenditures, including a substantial amount of foreign aid, at around SR 86.5 billion.

Initially, therefore, the entire increase in revenues were not directly incorporated into the domestic budget. Over time, budget adjustments regarding the newly available revenues have been made. Apparently the magnitude of the surplus funds relative to past income and the assessment made of the performance of such revenues have influenced their ultimate allocation.

This spending pattern is not unlike that usually observed for an individual immediately after the initial receipt of part of a large windfall gain whose precise extent is now known with certainty.[8]

It is likely that without the existing planning framework and machinery, most of the newfound riches would have been squandered, or at least allocated to dubious areas of consumption and questionable investment projects. Because of the existence of a planning apparatus and outlook, the government was able to rationally contemplate the implications of and alternatives presented by the kingdom's sudden affluence.

Options for Dealing with Sudden Affluence

Given the small, closed family nature of the Saudi government, there is no reason why a line of analysis and reasoning similar to that of an individual might not be used to explain the action of the Saudi government following its windfall gain. In a sense the 1973–1974 oil-price and revenue increases accruing to the Saudi government were not fundamentally different than a sudden shift in an individual's income. It is difficult to think of a similar situation occurring in modern times whereby a country was in a position free of both political and resource constraints, thus enabling it to adopt what is essentially individual estate planning.

Economists have dealt with the problem of sudden affluence in attempting to explain consumer behavior.[9] In general, the economic theory they have hypothesized is predicated on the assumption that individual households base their consumption on expected average income over future years (rather than on actual realized income during any particular period). Economic theory would, therefore, predict that households will save a larger proportion of windfall gains (that is, unanticipated increases in income) than of their normal income. Further, the theory predicts that the proportion of windfall gains actually spent is not allocated according to the normal consumption pattern. Instead, it is used selectively for discretionary spending on such items as consumer durables. The theory's logical conclusion is that it is only when increases in income are expected to continue into the future that households begin to incorporate such income into their general consumption pattern. Presumably then, the individual, although living in a changing and uncertain world, is still capable of acting rationally in the pursuit of his long-run welfare objectives.

In developing a long-run strategy for allocating the post-1973–1974 surplus revenues, at least four very broad options merited the Saudi Arabian planners' consideration.[10]

Option 1: Invest in Foreign Assets. The most easily implemented option for the country would have been to invest most of its additional post-1973 earnings in foreign assets. Purchase of large foreign securities and the maintenance of deposits in foreign banks could have provided a convenient form for holding excess funds. On the other hand, large-scale direct investment of large sums abroad would have been more demanding in terms of managerial efforts required but at the same time more lucrative in terms of potential return.

The very magnitude of the kingdom's surplus meant that the prices of foreign assets might have become very inflated if most of the oil revenues were placed outside of the kingdom. In addition, the prospect of devaluation of the dollar would have represented a real threat to the value of these potential assets. In addition, Western governments often place restrictions on the type and amount of foreign assets that may be purchased. There was, of course, always the fear of confiscation of potential Saudi investments.

Finally, the purchase of foreign assets was not seen as very efficient with regard to dealing with the existing low level of domestic development or in addressing the problems associated with the country's long-term development. This was particularly the criticism made by some Saudi leaders of investments in securities or in interest-bearing deposits. While these types of investments are the least risky in terms of their effect on domestic development, they produce results not unlike a policy of economic imperialism—domestic resources are exploited with the earnings being invested (geographically) outside of the domestic economy.

The ultimate decision made regarding the proportion of surplus funds allocated for foreign assets was that it be based on criteria that take into account the magnitude of the surplus relative to domestic needs, and on their opportunity cost measured in terms of domestic options foregone.

Option 2: Provide Foreign Assistance. A second option considered as a means of utilizing the kingdom's surplus funds was the provision of massive amounts of foreign assistance (in the form of unilateral or multilateral aid and/or soft loans). It was not easy, however, given the primitive state of the domestic economy to develop a good case for giving to this extent. It was also acknowledged that the administration of an aid program on this scale would require a number of individuals with a high level of professional skills. These skills were generally quite scarce in Saudi Arabia as well as in most of the potential recipient countries (with Egypt as a notable exception).[11]

Option 3: Increase Government Services. As was to be expected, the mere recognition that a fiscal surplus existed generated strong domestic political pressures to increase the scope and magnitude of government services. This was to a certain extent also an attractive alternative to the authorities since some tended to view it as the best means of redistributing income and raising living standards.

With this strategy the government would also presumably assume the role of employer of last resort. The provision of increases in publicly provided and subsidized services (health, education, transportation, and so on) would also be a key role in this strategy. The main problem associated with this option would be the increase in wages, real property values, rents, and the prices of locally produced raw materials if government consumption accelerated significantly. As noted in chapter 5, the authorities have rejected on philosophical (and religious) grounds any plans to increase government's role as employer of last resort—or develop a Kuwaiti-type welfare state. Acting along these lines was seen as reducing productivity in the public sector and limiting entrepreneurial incentives, thus making long-term development more difficult.

Option 4: Domestic Investment. Finally a broad development strategy built on a massive expansion of the physical stock of domestic capital was considered. Economic theory gives high priority to domestic investment as a causal factor in initiating and sustaining rapid economic growth. In general, capital is viewed as a limiting factor in development, based on the observation that most less-developed countries have a surplus of labor and a shortage of capital. Much less attention had been given to situations such as Saudi Arabia's where labor was relatively scarce and capital abundant.[12] Most economic growth models in vogue at the time implied that if capital were abundant, the achievement of self-sustaining growth was largely a matter of implementing an appropriate investment policy.[13]

The types of capital investment required for development are generally divided into two categories: social overhead capital and directly productive capital. Social overhead capital includes those types of facilities and resources required to support productive growth; that is direct support facilities in such areas as transportation, communications and utilities, and nondirect support facilities such as schools, hospitals, and so on. These types of investments were viewed by most economists both within and outside of Saudi Arabia as creating the conditions necessary for directly productive private investment to flourish.[14]

A good deal of the discussion in Saudi Arabia surrounding this strategy centered on the respective merits of balanced versus unbalanced growth. Advocates of balanced growth tended to favor a development policy for the kingdom based on simultaneous investment in a number of mutually supporting lines of production on the grounds that a massive effort of this type is required to: (1) offset a number of individualities (for example, capital lumpiness) and (2) take advantage of consumption complementarities (for example, external economies).

The case of unbalanced growth made by a number of leading officials stemmed from their feeling that: (1) capital and other resources—in particular managerial skill and organizational abilities required for implementing a policy of balanced growth—were in scarce supply in the kingdom, and (2) while the country's ultimate development objective might be the attainment of a balanced economy, given the initial imbalances found in the kingdom, a balanced structure was most likely to be achieved through a policy of investing in strategic sectors, particularly those having strong forward and backward linkages. Thus advocates of unbalanced growth tended to emphasize the sequencing of domestic investments over the next several decades.

Economic theory aside, the most tempting option for the authorities when faced with the large inflow of new revenue was to devote the great bulk into social overhead capital-type projects. To be sure, large sums derived from the post 1973–1974 oil price increases have flowed out of the country into foreign aid and financial assets. The government has also expanded its consumption. Still, of the four options outlined earlier, the last one stressing social overhead capital and unbalanced growth comes closest to depicting the strategy ultimately adopted.

The projects associated with it have been highly visible and have tended to raise the prestige of the state .At the same time, projects of this type have been very attractive to the authorities since they can be acomplished on a turn-key basis (where the contactor uses imported labor, raw, materials, and management.)

As with the other strategies, the fourth option has its limitations. While investment in social overhead capital has the potential to stimulate the kingdom's growth by supporting the development of directly productive activities, construction of facilities, and so on, these investments in and of themselves may not contribute significantly to the economy's long-run economic growth. The development of excess capacity in supplying sectors will not necessarily induce investment in directly productive activities. This is particularly true in an economy like Saudi Arabia's, where there are relatively few entrepreneurs. In addition, the linkage between the creation of social overhead capital and inducement or productive investment is not necessarily axiomatic, nor is the direction of causation always one-way.

A more fundamental criticism often given by those outside the kingdom is that the government's determination to go ahead with its massive domestic investment program does not make much economic sense, but simply reflects the regime's conviction of its mission to create a viable and modern Islamic industrial state. Syranians and Egyptians among others often point out that pure economic logic dictates massive capital transfers to places where infrastructure, human resources, industrial base, and local markets already exist; in other words, their countries. Starting from scratch in a waterless desert is seen by them as an irresponsible waste of what should be considered a regional resource. And in that wastage, they feel that Saudi Arabia is risking undermining the only opportunity many of the oil-deficient capital-starved states of the area will ever have of breaking out of their underdevelopment.[15]

Although overstated, there is an element of truth in these arguments. Clearly, the Saudis decided to take a number of calculated risks when they finally released their Second Development Plan.

The Second Development Plan (1975–1980)

On May 21, 1975, the Council of Ministers approved the kingdom's Second Development Plan covering the period from 1975–1980. Total plan expenditure for the public sector was set at SR 498.2 billion, with the amount allocated for economic, manpower, and social development at approximately 64 percent of the total outlay (see tables 7–1 and 7–2).[16]

The preponderant theme of the plan was to increase the absorbing capacity of the economy that, because of its vast size and long history of low rates of capital formation, was seen by the planners as requiring a large volume of investment. The basic strategy of the plan was to improve and expand the country's physical and social infrastructure while minimizing bottlenecks; the objective was one of diversifying the economy through the harnessing of the country's agricultural, mining and industrial potential. The ultimate goal was to increase opportunities for gainful employment, raise the standard of living and welfare of all sectors of the population, diversify the sources of income and foreign-exchange earnings, and to reduce the country's dependence on imports (for a major part of its basic needs of life).

The size of the investments of the plan intrigued businessmen all over the world. Along with the government's planned financial allocations of approximately US $142 billion, an additional amount of private investment was planned. The financial size of the plan was increased several times as it became clear that oil revenues would stabilize at their new level. The final investment figure is likely to be more than double the figure with which the planners began. The planners acknowledged and seemed resigned to the fact that investments of this magnitude would create bottlenecks, shortfalls in

Table 7-1

Distribution of Finance Allocations for the Second Five-Year Plan

(in millions of riyals)

Economic resource development	92,135.0
Human resources development	80,123.9
Social development	33,212.8
Physical infrastructure development	112,944.6
Subtotal, development	318,416.3
Administration	38,179.2
Defense	78,156.5
External assistance, emergency funds, food subsidies, and general reserve	63,478.2
Subtotal, other	179,813.9
Total	498,230.2

Source: Ministry of Development, *Second Development Plan*, 1975–1980 (Riyadh: Ministry of Planning, 1976).

Table 7-2

Allocations for Major Programs—Second Five-Year Plan

(in millions of riyals)

Sector	Amount
Water and desalination	34,065
Agriculture	4,685
Electricity	6,240
Manufacturing and minerals	45,058
Education	74,161
Health	17,302
Social programs and youth welfare	14,649
Roads, ports, and railroads	21,283
Civil aviation and Saudi airline	14,845
Telecommunications and post	4,225
Municipalities	53,328
Housing	14,263
Holy cities and the Hajj	5,000
Total	309,104
Other development	9,312
Subtotal development	318,416
Defense	78,157
General administration	38,179
Funds	63,478
Subtotal other	179,814
Total plan	498,230

Source: Ministry of Development, *Second Development Plan 1975–1980* (Riyadh: Ministry of Planning, 1976), p. 530.

actual spending, and other problems, because the financial portion of the plan was not closely integrated with the actions of the private sector. In addition the growth rate anticipated for the oil sector was 9.7 percent, whereas the actual growth rate was 4.4—5.3 percent less than the plan target.

The Actual Growth Path

Nevertheless, the kingdom's growth path during the Second Five-Year Plan has been nearly on target with the actual plan targets (see table 7–3). Before the 1979 price increases, however, GDP growth had fallen a bit below the Second Plan projections, reflecting the several years when the oil sector had low or negative growth rates. The shortfall in GDP can, therefore, be attributed almost exclusively to exogenous developments in the world oil market and do not in any way reflect domestic production problems.

The 1979 price increases enabled GDP to grow at 9 percent in 1979 or at an average annual rate of 9.6 for the Second Plan period. Given the Second Plan target of 10 percent, the kingdom's overall performance was quite satisfactory.

Growth of the nonoil sector probably provides a better measure of the economy's performance relative to the Second Plan projections. Real nonoil GDP has in fact grown somewhat faster than GDP, decelerating from around 14 percent in 1979. While figures of components of the nonoil private sector have not been released for 1398–1399 there is evidence suggesting that several sectors (agriculture, transport, communications, and storage) have grown at rates higher than their targets, while manufacturing and construction grew at rates somewhat below.

The government sector has held even closer to projections, with the growth in 1398–1399 being identical with the plan target. The economy is clearly past the hectic post-1973 oil boom stage and is set on a more tempered course. There is no reason to believe that targets similar to those in the Second Plan could not be met during the Third Plan period if the government so wished.

Several other trends of significance stand out for the first four years of the Second Plan:

1. Before the recent price increases, the export surplus had declined all through the Second Plan period with its share in total gross national expenditures falling from 62.15 percent in 1975 to 25.8 percent in 1978. The 1979 price increases completely altered this trend (see table 7–4).
2. The share of export surplus has been taken over by consumption and gross capital formation—the share of the former has risen from 24.2 percent in 1975 to 43.8 percent in 1978, and of the latter from 13.3 percent to 30.4 percent.

Table 7-3
Saudi Arabia: Second Plan Growth Rates
(average annual growth)

	Average Annual Plan Projections	1395–1396 First Year Actual Growth	1396–1397 Second Year Actual Growth	1397–1398 Third Year Actual Growth	1398–1399 Fourth Year Actual Growth
Gross domestic product	10.2	8.6	14.8	5.9	7.6
Oil sector	9.7	1.1	13.2	0.5	1.8
Nonoil private sector	13.4	17.8	18.9	13.9	14.1
Agriculture	4.0	4.0	5.0	6.0	—
Manufacturing	14.0	8.2	13.6	8.7	—
Construction	15.0	34.5	25.3	10.5	—
Transport	15.0	22.6	22.1	22.7	—
Government sector	12.9	23.9	12.9	13.5	12.9

Source: Saudi Arabian Monetary Agency, *Annual Report 1399 (1979)*, p. 60.

3. The share of gross capital formation in gross domestic expenditures is estimated to have risen further in 1979 to more than one-third of that total.
4. Within total consumption, the share of government final consumption has tended to decline because of the public sector's conscious policy of reducing the pressure of its demand on available supplies.
5. The share of private consumption expenditures has, however, increased because of rising personal incomes and standards of living.
6. In contrast with consumption, the share of government in gross capital formation has been steadily rising through the plan period because of the government's controlled level of expenditures.

There have also been some significant trends in the oil sector. Oil production was 3,038 million barrels (8.32 million barrels per day) in 1978 compared with 3,335 million barrels (9.20 million barrels per day) in 1977. This decline has been officially attributed to technical factors, presumably because production levels had risen sharply from 7.07 million barrels per day (b/d) in 1975 to 8.75 million b/d in 1976 and further to 9.2 million b/d in 1977. Field pressures were reduced, thus necessitating lower production. Monthly data for 1978 indicate that production declined with minor fluctuations from 7.79 million b/d in January to 7.18 million b/d in August. Thereafter, it increased substantially to 9.31 million b/d in October, 10.26 million b/d in November, and 10.40 million b/d in December. These changes were undertaken largely to offset shortfalls in world supply due to the Iranian revolution.

With the resumption of Iranian supplies, the kingdom's production levels were adjusted downward to 9.77 million b/d in March and further to 8.79 million b/d in April 1979.

In terms of revenues, the kingdom's revenues from oil exports totaled $32,234 million in 1978, compared with $36,540 million in 1977, registering a decline of $4,306 million or 11.8 percent. Because of the increase in oil prices and the government decision to raise production levels, the kingdom's oil revenues greatly accelerated in 1979 (see table 7-4).

Because oil prices have more than doubled in the 18 months prior to January 1979, Saudi Arabia has been able to stave off a balance of payment deficit. Saudi production in late 1980 was running about 9.5 to 10.0 million b/d—a rate somewhat above the official 8.5 million b/d ceiling. Saudi authorities are apparently reluctant to go on producing at levels greatly in excess of those dictated by the country's financial needs. Plans to expand capacity to about 15 million b/d by the mid-1980s have, however, been discussed. Whether this capacity is being created for sustained production increases or only to strengthen its power with OPEC to influence prices is not clear.

Table 7–4
Saudi Arabia: Foreign Exchange Cash Flow, 1979–1980
($US million)

	1979	1980
Revenue	69,657	100,780
Exports or goods and services	69,657	100,780
Oil only	(59,242)	100,480
Transfers (net)	(−)	(−)
Expenditure	55,722	73,860
Imports of goods and services	54,652	72,140
Goods only	(27,736)	(36,920)
Transfers (net)	1,070	1,720
Net foreign exchange revenue	13,935	36,920
Asset movement (net)[a]	−13,935	36,920
SAMA	−73	n.a.
Commercial Banks	1,533	n.a.
Other[b]	12,329	n.a.

Source: Computed from International Monetary Fund, *International Financial Statistics*; various issues.

Notes: n.a. = not available.

[a]Positive sign indicates a decrease in assets.
[b]Includes all other unallocated assets/liabilities.

Implications for the Third Plan

The rapid increase in oil prices meant that the kingdom had to give up its official policy of balancing its budget. The admission by the authorities that money is being allocated to a general state reserve will undoubtedly strengthen the hand of those arguing for a decrease in production.

Another reason that the kingdom might reduce its domestic expenditures and a level of production is the inflationary pressures that have lingered on since the 1974–1975 period. There seems no way that these pressures can be eliminated without some sort of downward adjustment in demand. Those who argue the kingdom will reduce oil production also cite the facts that:

1. There is an inherent conflict between Islam and rapid modernization demonstrated by the events in Iran and the seige at the Great Mosque in Mecca. Both events apparently have had a profound psychological impact on

the government and weakened the supremacy of the modernists within the royal family.

2. The oil-price rises of 1979 took place even though they quite possibly hurt the Western economies. The Saudis had until this time tried to take the economic wealth of the West more into account on its oil policy.

3. If spending on infrastructural and industrial projects continues as planned in 1980, it will create a demand for 500,000 to 1,000,000 more foreign workers in the next five years (in addition to the 1.75 to 2.0 million who have arrived in the past five years). For a country with an indigenous population of only 4 to 6 million, the presence of 2 to 3 million foreign workers is in many respects rather risky politically, not to mention inviting criticism as to the wisdom of the kingdom's development strategy.

4. The growth under the 1975–1980 Five-Year Plan has possibly created some dangerous economic and social tensions. These stresses are inevitable in an environment dominated by massive projects manned largely by foreign workers. The stagflation of 1976 and 1977 led to almost excessive anxieties on the part of local businessmen concerning the return of spiraling costs. The mild acceleration of inflation in 1979 has tended to confirm their fears, and resulted in their placing pressures on the authorities to reduce expenditures.

5. The fact is that a relatively primitive absorptive capacity can no longer be relied on to moderate and discipline domestic economic activity. This is evidenced by the rate of implementation of government spending plans rising from 74 percent in 1975–1976 to over 95 percent in 1979.

Despite these reservations, however, it is undoubtedly safe to conclude that:

1. The GDP targets as defined in the Second Plan are likely to be reached (largely because of the recent oil price increases).
2. The government (because of built up foreign exchange reserves) appears to be in a position to smooth its expenditure from year to year, alleviating the previous pattern of gearing expenditure to current revenues.
3. The economy's expansion is rather broad based. The relatively slow growth in manufacturing is due in part to the long gestation period involved in many of the larger projects.
4. The kingdom has come a long way in controlling domestic inflation, but it has not been completely successful in achieving its target rate of inflation.

Several other developments are pertinent and apparently were instrumental in influencing the final form of the Third Development Plan:

1. It is clear that ultimately inflationary pressures in Saudi Arabia are caused by both domestic and foreign factors with the government largely determining the amount of domestic liquidity (through its expenditures),

while the commercial banks can expand liquidity through their loans to the private sector.

2. There seems (see table 7–5) to be an acceleration in the private sector balance of payments deficit (undoubtedly reducing somewhat domestic inflationary pressures).

3. The growth of the money supply seems to be decelerating somewhat from the rapid expansion years of 1974–1976, indicative perhaps of the government's increased control over the money supply.

4. The net result of closing the inflationary gap (the gap between aggregate demand and supply, or more correctly money or nonoil income) has been the observed deceleration in inflation (measured by the GDP deflator) to a little less than 10 percent.

5. In addition to the decline in the inflationary gap, removal of bottlenecks, the freer flow of goods because of infrastructure improvements, and greater competition in markets have apparently helped reduce the rate of domestic price increase.

6. Despite the many encouraging developments during the Second Plan period, many observers predicted that the period of rapid growth would be replaced by one of strong fiscal controls and deflation. The mild cutback in real spending in the 1978–1979 budget that called for an actual expenditure increase of one-half the rate envisaged in the previous budget was interpreted by these observers as a retreat from excessive growth.

Concerns along these lines were largely reduced by the figures contained in the 1400–1401 (1980) budget. The final release of the Third Plan document has put these fears to rest.

The Third Development Plan (1980–1985)

The expected expenditures of the Third Plan,[17] beginning in May 1980, amount to SR 782.8 billion and are allocated as follows:[18]

1. *Agriculture (SR 7.9 billion)*: The goals set for this sector are an increase in domestic food production, reclamation of land and irrigation projects, and development of large farms (agricultural estates).

2. *Water (SR 13.2 billion)*: The goals of this sector are an increase in the amount of potable water by 816,000 cubic meters during the next 5 years.

3. *Silos and Flour Corporation (SR 4.8 billion)*: In this sector there will be expansion or construction of grain silos and flour mills in Kizan, Khmamis-Mushayt, Qasim, and elsewhere.

4. *Electricity (SR 52.6 billion)*: The objectives are 15,230 milliwatts to be

Table 7–5
Saudi Arabia: Factors Affecting Changes in Money and Quasi-money

	1394–1395	1395–1396	1396–1397	1397–1398	1398–1399
Increase in gross private sector liquidity	20.1	46.2	60.7	98.9	109.4
Cash flows through government	17.9	43.1	60.8	96.1	101.0
Loans disbursed by government-sponsored credit institutions	(0.8)	(5.8)	(15.7)	(19.6)	(17.3)
Commercial bank claims on private sector	2.2	3.1	−0.1	2.8	8.5
Net private sector balance of payments deficit	− 14.8	−35.8	−47.8	−82.6	−101.6
Increase in net private sector liquidity	5.3	10.4	12.9	16.3	7.8
Money	(4.1)	(8.9)	(11.7)	(14.1)	(5.2)
Quasi-money	(1.2)	(1.5)	(1.2)	(2.2)	(2.6)

Source: Saudi Arabian Monetary Agency, *Annual Report 1399* (1979), p. 3.

added, 25 percent annual growth in installed capacity, and installation of transmission lines throughout the kingdom. Power generated from desalination plants alone will add 2,400 milliwatts in the next 4 years.

5. *Education (SR 100 billion)*: There will be continued construction at the universities of Riyadh, Mecca, Medina, and Imam Muhammed al-Saul University in Riyadh, construction of more than 560 elementary and secondary schools during the next 5 years. The number of enrolled students at all levels, male and female, is to increase by nearly 2 million students.

6. *Health (SR 34.4 billion)*: There will be construction of major health centers in Riyadh and Jeddah, and small and medium sized hospital construction in cities and towns. The number of hospital beds is to increase by nearly 25,000.

7. *Ports (SR 23.7 billion)*: The capacity of Saudi ports will increase to 46.8 million tons (compared to 24.3 million tons handled in 1979), and the number of berths at most ports will be increased. There will be new container terminals at Jizan and Yenbo, computerization, new navigation aids, and an emphasis on maintenance and repair.

8. *Roads (SR 37.7 billion)*: Construction is projected for 28.085 kilometers of roads.

9. *Communications (SR 28.9 billion)*: The plan will increase the number of telephones by 1,177,000 and the number of telephone circuits by 800,000.

10. *Municipalities (SR 68.1 billion)*: There will be improvements and development of towns and cities kingdomwide.
11. *Housing (SR 21.2 billion)*: Construction is projected for 35,853 houses, primarily in urban areas.
12. *Social Welfare and Affairs (SR 3.5 billion)*.
13. *Youth Welfare (SR 4.5 billion)*.
14. *Civil Aviation, Airports, and National Airlines (SR 44.4 billion)*: Expansion and construction of airport facilities is planned to handle 26.5 million passengers annually by 1985. There will be fifty-four aircrafts added to the national airline fleet.
15. *Petromin (SR 27.6 billion)*: Allocations are projected for construction of refineries, storage tanks, and oil pipelines, for continued development of petroleum and mineral sectors.
16. *SABIC (SR 25.5 billion)*: There will be construction of industrial complexes, primarily at Jubail and Yenbo, for development of the petrochemical industry.
17. *Industry (SR 200 billion)*: Allocations are projected for the continued development and expansion of the industrial base via light industry, located in cities and towns throughout the kingdom, as well as heavy industry, primarily at Jubail and Yenbo.

While a more detailed analysis of the growth targets and their implications is made in the context of the forecasts presented in chapter 15, several observations concerning the Third Plan are in order.

The Third Development Plan Period—
Initial Observations

Given the overall social and economic development strategy just noted, as well as the lessons for the Third Plan period derived from the experience of the Second Plan, it is possible to speculate as to the likely growth path the Third (and probably Fourth) Plan will follow. In this regard, it is best to view the Third Plan as both a transition period and an important building block for the future. More specifically:

1. While the First and Second Development Plans often have been characterized as infrastructure building, the Third Development Plan will be noted more for industry building and a period of initial consolidation, the elimination of most physical infrastructure bottlenecks, and the initiation of a more comprehensive data collection and planning process.

2. The Third Plan represents a continuation of the strategy initiated in the Second Plan. In addition it will remain totally dependent on oil revenues for its implementation.

3. The core of the Third Plan, given the obvious conflicting current and future needs of the kingdom, consists of building a strong industrial foundation. This will be accomplished largely through creation of heavy industries by public sector ventures. Other areas of industrial production will be reserved for private sector initiatives.

4. The first Third Plan budget (1980–1981) (see table 7–6) gives some insights as to the likely magnitude and course that the plan will actually take. Two aspects of the budget stand out: (a) it is larger than anticipated; (b) the official public statements preceding its release stressed its orientation more toward investment in human capital and away from physical infrastructure projects. This shift in priorities is not reflected all that much in the actual budget figures.

5. Government expenditures are expected to increase during the fiscal 1980–1981 year by 53 percent over the original expenditure budget for 1979–1980 of SR 160 billion ($48 billion), by 13 percent over the final figure for appropriations of SR 216 billion ($64.9 billion), and 27 percent over actual expenditure of SR 193 billion ($57.6 billion).

6. Actual expenditure in 1979–1980 rose by 31.3 percent over expenditure in 1978–1979. It seems then that expenditure in the 1980–1981 fiscal year will continue at about the same rate of increase as in the previous year.

7. Because the impact of the final oil-price increases was largely

Table 7–6
Saudi Arabia: Budget Estimates, 1980–1981
(millions of riyals)

Sector	1980–1981 Budgeted	(%)	1979–1980 Actual	(%)
Education and training	22,604	(9.95)	18,288	(11.50)
Transport and communications	32,097	(14.12)	24,447	(15.37)
Development of economic resources	19,370	(8.52)	14,761	(9.28)
Social development and health	12,334	(5.43)	9,838	(6.19)
Infrastructure	11,764	(5.78)	6,679	(4.20)
Municipal services	19,745	(8.69)	12,725	(8.00)
Defense and security	68,945	(30.34)	59,207	(37.23)
Public administration	15,799	(6.95)	13,099	(8.24)
Local subsidies	5,100	(2.24)	n.a.	
Internal government loans	19,500	(8.58)	n.a.	
Total	227,258		159,044	

Source: Ministry of Finance.

Note: n.a. = not available.

unanticipated, the kingdom entered the Third Plan period with a budget surplus of at least SR 23 billion in 1979.

8. Some of the more significant aspects of the Third Plan budget are:

a. On the surface there seems to be a 75 percent increase in infrastructure expenditure. This is probably not indicative of the overall orientation of the Third Plan, however, because much of this expenditure is likely to take place earlier rather than later in the plan. There should be a fairly large reduction in this type of expenditure when Jubail and Yenbo are completed.

b. Transport, communications, and economic resource developments all have an increase of about 30 percent in expenditures, while the allocations to municipal services rose by almost 55 percent.

c. Manpower, social, and health expenditures have somewhat lower rates of increase at 25 percent, while the bureaucracy/public administration sector has only a 20 percent increase.

d. While defense allocations rose by only 18 percent, that sector still has 28 percent of the budget.

e. Most significantly, if the same level of spending were continued throughout the five years of the plan, a total expenditure of SR 1,225 billion would be undertaken. This is 56 percent above the base figure of SR 782.8 billion that was originally announced.

9. The document gives little detailed attention to inflation. Upon release in the latter part of 1980, the plan's financial implications for the last 4 years of the plan had apparently not been worked out in detail. In its official statement at the time of release, however, the government seemed confident of its ability to contain prices to a target rate of 7 percent a year. It also, however, acknowledged the possibility of renewed hyperinflation stemming from labor shortages.

10. Implicit in the plan is that labor shortages are to be overcome by big increases in productivity. Skilled Saudi labor will be spread further as a result. However, no details are given of how productivity is to rise by the target 27.2 percent by 1985.

Conclusions

During the Second Five-Year Plan the Saudi Arabian economy pushed ahead with a quantum leap forward. This remarkable achievement was made possible by an upsurge in oil revenues at the beginning and end of the planning period. Still the very benefits of increased oil revenues have been mitigated by some of the negative aspects of the very rapid transition to a new and significantly higher growth path. While many observers felt that these developments would mean the Third Plan would usher a new phase of consolidation of past gains and a bridge to the Fourth Plan, early indications indicate that the Third Plan will be simply an extension of the Second Plan. It is possible, of course, that the initial years of the Third Plan will simply reflect expenditure levels associated with completing the Second Plan commitments, and that the final years of the plan will be more indicative of an increasing awareness on the part of Saudi leaders of the hazards entailed with a continuation of the growth and expenditure rates of the 1970s.

Based on the considerations just outlined, one might argue that the kingdom's policy of rapid industrialization geared toward export-oriented production on an efficient basis is sufficient to assure the creation of a viable self-sustaining economy in the year 2000. It will probably be necessary, however, for the authorities to specify more clearly the eventual foreign manpower requirements and spatial configuration associated with the implementation of such a policy.

It is becoming apparent, for example, that the kingdom's macroeconomic and macrosocial planning cannot be conceptualized solely on sectoral terms. In the final analysis all plans must translate themselves into specific physical and geographical actions. For example, the foreign worker and spatial dimension aspects need to be integrated at the national level of policymaking with the more macroeconomic and macrosocial aspects of the strategy. Given the resistance of Saudis to engage in many types of industrial activity currently planned for the future, it is clear that the current strategy, while correct in principle, contains a number of important contradictions that unless addressed soon may eventually undermine the transition to a self-sustained nonoil growth.

Beyond this, one must ponder the likely social and political consequences of the massive social overhead investments on the Saudi society. Most of the Saudi population has not been involved, in an occupational sense, in the oil boom. Social services, education, and some money have trickled down to the Bedouin. The service of some people in the army have exposed them to the paraphernalia of a modern state. The real Saudi participants in the oil-based economy have been the small royal and urban bourgeoisie elites that make up the highest echelons of the government apparatus, the officers' corps, and the small (but rich) trading and business sector. The oil industry itself is not a big employer, and the market for unskilled and semiskilled labor has been filled mostly by Omanis and Yemenis, not Saudis. Of the estimated 50,000 people employed in industry, more than half are foreign and 60 percent are illiterate.[19]

For better or worse, the Saudi development strategy was irreversibly set with the release of the Third Plan. A logical first step in arriving at an ultimate assessment of the likelihood of its success is an analysis of the kingdom's demographic patterns.

Notes

1. For a description of this general type of economic system, see Jahangir Amuzegar, *Comparative Economics: National Priorities, Policies and Performance* (Cambridge, Mass.: Winthrop Publishers, 1981), ch. 4.

2. A fascinating account of King Faisal's insights into the country's development process is given in Savad Abdul-Salam Al-Farsy, "King Faisal and the First Five -Year Development Plan," in Willard A. Beling, ed., *King Faisal and the Modernisation of Saudi Arabia* (Boulder: Westview 1980), pp. 58–71.

3. Yusif A. Sayiah, *The Economies of the Arab World* (New York: St. Martin's Press, 1978), pp. 177–178.

4. Ibid.

5. Ramon Knaverhase, *The Saudi Arabian Economy* (New York: Praeger Publishers, 1975), pp. 316–320.

6. Ibid.

7. See Central Planning Organization, *Development Plan, 1390 A.H.* (Riyadh: CPO, n.d.).

8. See Milton Friedman, *A Theory of the Consumption Function* (Princeton: National Bureau of Economic Research, 1958), and F. Modigliani, "The Life-Cycle Hypothesis of Saving, The Demand for Wealth, and the Supply of Capital," *Social Research* (Summer 1966): 160–217.

9. Ibid.

10. A similar but somewhat different interpretation of the strategies open to the government is given by Jean Paul Cleron. See his *Saudi Arabia 2000* (New York: St. Martin's Press, 1978), ch. 8.

11. Hossein Askari and John Cummings, *Oil, OECD and the Third World: A Viscious Triangle?* (Austin: Center for Middle East Studies, 1978), ap. II.

12. Jahangir Amuzegar, "Atypical Backwardness and Investment Criteria," *Economica Internazionale* (August 1960).

13. Hollis Chenery, "The Application of Investment Criteria," *Quarterly Journal of Economics* (February 1953): 78.

14. A.O. Hirschman, *The Strategy of Economic Development* (New Haven: Yale University Press, 1958), pp. 297–300.

15. An excellent account of this issue is given in Malcolm Kerr et al., *Inter-Arab Conflict Contingencies and the Gap Between the Arab Rich and Poor* (Santa Monica: Rand, 1978), pp. 1–4.

16. Ministry of Planning, *The Second Development Plan 1975–1980* (Riyadh: Ministry of Planning, 1976).

17. Ministry of Planning, *Third Development Plan, 1400–1405 A.H.* (Riyadh: Ministry of Planning, 1980).

18. Ibid.

19. Ministry of Planning, *The Construction Industry in Saudi Arabia* (Riyadh: Ministry of Planning, 1977), pp. 23–25.

8 Demographic Patterns

Until recently, development was widely regarded as a largely economic phenomenon. As a result, the main quantitative indicator of a country's development status was its gross domestic product. While this index does measure one of the key aspects of development—the accumulation of wealth and productive power—it is inadequate as an indicator of the country's social and institutional characteristics and level of evolvement. In particular, pure economic measures of development are often quite weakly connected to some of the demographic determinants of fertility and mortality, themselves presumed to be a function a well as determinant of economic growth.[1] Nowhere is the discrepancy between per-capita income and the normal patterns of demographic change more obvious than in Saudi Arabia.

Since the publicly available demographic statistics for Saudi Arabia are notoriously incomplete, it is not possible to construct a totally accurate picture of the country's population dynamics. What data that is available do indicate some patterns, however, and can be made to serve most of the purposes of the study. The methodology used here is to hypothesize on the basis of general knowledge, demographic movements likely to be taking place in the kingdom.

Population Size

The actual size of Saudi Arabia's population has been the subject of controversy for some years, but in particular since 1974 when the first national census was undertaken and the detailed results were never released.

The motivation for official glibness concerning the first official census in unclear. Apparently the results are seen as embarrassing by the Saudi government. One rumor has it that the original census listed the Saudi population at near 4 million, while a summary report released by the government in 1976 estimates the country's population at 7,012,642. Most independent observers, however, feel that the official figure is highly inflated, and that a more reasonable estimate is around 5.6 million.[2] Several observers feel confident that there may be as few as 3 to 4 million Saudis[3] (see table 8–1).

While there is some doubt as to the size of Saudi Arabia's population, there is little question that the total is growing very rapidly. This expansion is

Table 8–1
Saudi Arabia: Population Estimates (Millions)

	IMF ILO	UN	Japan Center	U.S. Census	Birks– Sinclair
1960	5.98				
1961	6.12	1962	6.26		
1963	6.42				3.31
1964	6.58				
1965	6.75				
1966	6.93				
1967	7.12				
1968	7.33	5.89			
1969	7.53	6.07			3.88
1970	7.74	6.25			
1971	7.97	6.43			
1972	8.21	6.62			
1973	8.45	6.81			4.33
1974	8.71	7.01			4.56
1975	8.97	7.21	3.90	6.2	4.59
1976	9.24	7.43			
1977	9.52				

Sources: International Monetary Fund, *International Financial Statistics* (1979) pp. 358–359; International Labor Organization, *Labor Force 1960–2000, Estimated Projections* (Geneva, 1977), p. 45; UN, Population Division, Economic Commission for Western Asia, *Estimates and Projections of Population, Vital Rates, and Economic Acuity for Members of the Economic Commission for Western Asia* (June 1978), p. 68; Japan Co-operation Center for the Middle East, *Analysis of Demand and Supply of Manpower in the Arabian Gulf Countries* (Tokyo, 1976), p. 13; United States Bureau of Census, Department of Commerce, Washington, D.C.; T.S. Birks and C.A. Sinclair, *The International Migration Project, Country Case Study, the Kingdom of Saudi Arabia* (University of Durham, 1978), p. 15.

taking place through the stepped-up immigration and a relatively high natural growth of indigenous Saudis. Again, however, the good statistics on the country's population size, structure, and number of births and deaths leaves the magnitude of a number of important demographic trends in doubt. On the other hand, there is substantial evidence that several of the Arab countries in the region with fairly good demographic data are likely to have similar demographic patterns. In-depth analysis of the demographic dynamics of these countries, particularly Jordan and Kuwait, has identified a number of common elements bearing on several key parameters.[4] Using what Saudi data is available, and making comparisons with these neighboring countries, one can, based on expected levels of birth and death rates, indirectly infer the natural growth of the kingdom's population.

General Arab Demographic Patterns

The Arab countries as a group have certain economic and demographic characteristics that distinguish them from countries in other geographic areas.[5] Saudi Arabia and most of the other oil-exporting countries are in large part still in the early stages of development and demographic transition; that is, large families are the norm rather than the exception. In addition, even though experiencing severe labor shortages, they maintain a number of restrictions on female participation in all parts of society. In general, the less affluent Arab countries while capital-deficient have at least until very recently had abundant labor. These countries are also more liberal concerning female participation in the labor force. Several countries (Egypt in particular) in this group have introduced family-planning programs (Saudi Arabia has strictly forbidden the introduction of any contraceptive measures into the kingdom to check the increase in population). The two groups of countries complement each other in several ways. In particular a considerable flow of capital and human resources takes place within the region proving highly beneficial to both groups.[6]

With several notable exceptions, Saudi Arabia's demographic patterns show a marked similarity to those experienced in the region as a whole. The average rate of population growth in both Saudi Arabia and the Arab region is approximately 3 percent a year, and in both instances fertility rates are high. The demographic structure of these countries is characterized by the youthfulness of the population; in most of the Arab countries, the proportion aged 15 years or under acounts for over 48 percent of the population. The rate of economically active population is very low, ranging from 22 percent to 32 percent of the total population, with the female participation rate varying from 3.5 percent to 18.5 percent. In the nonagricultural sector, the average activity rate of women (over the age of 15) usually does not exceed 6 percent.[7]

Arab countries are also characterized by their high infant-mortality rates. In 1975 these ranged from 60 to 200 per thousand.[8] Illiteracy rates for the group as a whole are also high, and they are significantly higher among women than among men. In 1975 the illiteracy rate for the Arab countries as a whole averaged approximately 47 percent for males over 15 years old; it exceeded 70 percent for females in this age group. In nearly all of these countries, there has been increasing concern over the amount and quality of education received by women. The result has been that special attention is currently being directed toward girls education.[9] This is reflected in the increased proportion of girls (ages 6 to 24) enrolled at various educational levels. For the Arab countries as a whole, this proportion rose from approximately 14.3 percent in 1960 to approximately 25 percent in 1975.

In spite of the progress, female illiteracy rates in Arab countries are still among the highest in the world, two and one-half times higher than in Latin America, for instance, and half again as much as in the Far East.

When it comes to participating in the work force, Arab women tend to be concentrated in agriculture. In Saudi Arabia, Syria, Tunisia, and the two Yemens, for example, rural female activity rates for women are about twice as high as in the urban areas. Female employment in these countries is apparently acceptable as long as it is confined to family farms. When families move to the city, however, females seem forced for one reason or another out of the labor force.[10]

Educational levels, customs, traditions, and social obligations (among other socioeconomic factors) all have been used to explain the rather unique pattern of labor participation rates exhibited by Arab women. Like Saudi Arabia, many countries in the region adhere strictly to the Islamic law and code of behavior. One discovers, however, that it is mainly conservative interpretations of Islamic teaching (as in Saudi Arabia) rather than the *Qu'ranic* law itself that prohibits Moslem women from participating to a greater extent in political, religious, social, and economic life. As a matter of fact, the *Qu'ran* generally deplores negative treatment of women and calls for giving women educational opportunities equal to those of men.[11]

Whatever the reason, Arab families have emphasized early marriage for girls, and female education has historically been viewed by many in these countries as a waste of time. The high value of children in Arab culture has contributed to fertility levels that are very high by international standards, and has restricted women to household activities and childrearing.

General Determinants of Fertility

Most of the recent empirical work on fertility patterns in both developing and developed regions of the world rests on the asumption that couples act rationally to maximize their welfare.[12] At the household level, this concept relates to pertinent household decision making where families are confronted with many interrelated options such as adjustments in fertility, whether the wife can work, and whether the children can have many or few years of formal education.

At the national level, the assumption relates to a situation that can be accepted as the broader and more comprehensive representative representation of the household. The theory is, therefore, extended to relate socioeconomic and demographic conditions through a system of simultaneous relationships.[13]

Whether rationality and economic calculations of this sort permeate the typical Arab household is a matter of great controversy. Because of skepticism over the applicability of rational behavior models to the Arab household, very little empirical research was, until quite recently, carried out to analyze and test these socioeconomic determinants of fertility and female labor-force participation. Despite stepped-up empirical work, many of the cause and effect relationships in this area between fertility and female labor-force participation are still unknown. Recent findings have begun to fill significant gaps in our knowledge about Arab family and female behavior, however.[14]

Arab Fertility Patterns

Fertility studies for specific countries in the region have all found a strong correlation between the fertility rate and level of education. These results confirm the important finding, documented in other developing areas, that fertility declines as the level of education of women rises. While the overall education-fertility pattern is now well established, it appears that a certain level of eductional attainment is necessary before a noticeable drop in fertility rates can occur.

In summarizing research carried out on Arab fertility, most studies found the major variables correlated with fertility to be[15]

1. Levels of infant mortality. Fertility tends to vary directly with this figure.
2. The degree of urbanization. This is almost always inversely related to levels of fertility.
3. Level of education or literacy and female labor-force participation. For most countries, these are negatively related to levels of fertility.
4. The level of per-capita income or standard of living and fertility. Here the relationship tends to vary from country to country.
5. Social status of females.

It should be noted that most of these variables, while significant for individual Arab countries, have not been shown to be correlated with fertility for the region as a whole. The relationship with per-capita income illustrates the problem of generalizing about demographic patterns in the area. Apparently increasing per-capita income causes many Arab families to emphasize a better quality of living and increased education for their children. Thus the tendency is to opt for fewer children, who will be sure of receiving the material requisites of life. On the other hand, an increasing level of family income seems to generate a tendency for Arab families to consume more of everything in general, including having more children. These two effects may or may not offset each other when considered simultaneously.

Saudi Fertility Patterns

What we know about Saudi fertility patterns comes largely from a multi-purpose survey conducted by the Saudi Arabian Central Department of Statistics during 1976 and 1977. From that survey a live birth rate of 54.2 per 1,000 was calculated for the Saudi population.[16] This is somewhat above the U.S. figure of 49.5 for the country and over the average for Arab countries of 46.6 for 1975 (see table 8–2).

According to the multipurpose survey, live birth rates for Saudis vary considerably from town to village. Live births were 41 per 1,000 in the six

Table 8–2
Demographic Variables Bearing on Fertility: Saudi Arabia and Arab Countries, 1970

Variable	Saudi Arabia	Arab Countries
Crude birth rate	49.5	46.6
Infant mortality rate	152	121
Labor force participation rate—women aged 15–44	6.83	9.94
Secondary-school enrollment rate	9.00	22.03
Per-capita income	495.00	762.44
Percentage illiterate adult male and female population	81.32	66.52
Percentage illiterate adult female population	98.00	82.12
Education attainment of female	10	25
Percentage of labor force in agriculture	40.40	43.80

Source: Compiled from Henry Azzam, "Analysis of Fertility and Labor Force Differentials in the Arab World," United Nations Economic Commission for Western Asia, *Population Bulletin* (June 1979): 36.

Note: Arab Countries include Algeria, Buhran, Democratic Yemen, Egypt, Iraq, Jordan, Kuwait, Lebanon, Libya, Morocco, Oman, Qatar, Saudi Arabia, Sudan, Syria, Tunesia, UAR, and Yemen.

largest municipalities, 54 per 1,000 in the smaller municipalities, and an extremely high 61 per 1,000 in villages and other rural areas.

Several factors have been cited for these patterns:

1. Many Saudi men live and work in urban areas where wages are high, while their families remain in rural areas where housing is more readily available and less expensive.
2. Women who have accompanied their husbands to urban areas often return to the parental home for the birth of a child.
3. Traditionally, family size is larger in rural areas of the kingdom.

These seem plausible enough, and given the rather limited education of Saudi women, their exclusion from the work force, and the government's ban on the importation of contraceptives, it is fairly safe to argue that no major reduction is likely to occur at least through the 1980s.

Finally, one of the questions asked on the survey was how many children each married Saudi woman had borne in her lifetime. Thirty-two percent of the women 15 years and over had at least seven children in their lifetime. Only 12 percent had never had a child. Many of these childless women (37 percent) were under age 20. The survey also indicated that the average size of a completed family was 7.2. The women:child ratio was 8 to 1, again one of the highest in the world.

Mortality—General Considerations

The decline in mortality is an integral component of the process of socio-economic development and modernization. In part, its role in modernization is definitional and results from its preeminent position as a social indicator; no country would qualify as modern in the standard sense of the term if it failed to significantly reduce its death rate from its historical levels.

A number of important relationships tend to exist between mortality and other growth-inducing variables. For example, a decline in death rates contributes to the return to many forms of investment that are necessary to achieve high levels of economic production. Most obvious among these are investments in one's personal economic future such as schooling and training. Presumably, the longer the period over which one expects the benefits to accrue, the greater the expected value of such investments as improvements in other factors of production, such as irrigation or land reclamation.[17]

From the purely macroeconomic point of view, it seems clear that the major consequence of mortality change is in its effects on population growth rates. There is now abundant evidence that mortality decline should not be expected to induce an equally large reduction in fertility (usually for at least several generations). Population growth therefore tends to accelerate for an extended period following declines in mortality.

The effects of accelerated population growth on economic progress is controversial. On the one hand a main line of argument suggests that more population retards the growth of output per worker. The overwhelmingly important element in the theory is Malthusian diminishing returns to labor, and the stock of capital (including land) does not increase in the same proportion as does labor.

Another important theoretical element is the dependency effect, which suggests that saving is more difficult for households when there are more children, and that higher fertility causes social investment funds to be diverted away from high productivity uses. Combined in simulation models these elements suggest that relatively high fertility and positive population growth have a negative effect on output per worker. These models assume a closed system, where resources are fixed, diminishing returns occur, savings rates fall, and stagnation sets in.[18] As such the models have no applicability to Saudi Arabia, where outside resources in the form of oil revenues are continually augmenting domestic resources.

On the other hand, there is some evidence that population growth may actually stimulate development. Conlisk and Huddle, for example, regressed the output growth rate on the savings rate and the rate of population growth over roughly 1950–1963 across the twenty-five less-developed countries that received AID (an external source of funds).[19] The coefficient of the population growth was 0.692 and was statistically significant, suggesting that an increment of population has, ceteris paribus, a positive effect on per-capita income.

Less controversial is the link between economic growth and mortality decline. Prior to the era when the knowledge of cheap and effective public health intervention was developed, there is evidence to suggest that improvements in general living standards were the dominant source of mortality decline. Since that time many new factors have come to the fore. Although economic factors remain very important in differentiating among nations' mortality levels, pure economic growth now appears to be an inefficient method of reducing mortality.[20]

Diverting a dollar of income toward improved literacy appears to offer a far greater change for mortality reduction than allowing that money to either consumption or investment. Nations that have structured development in such a way as to increase levels of literacy and to spread public health and nutritional programs widely among the population have achieved remarkable advances in lengthening life.[21]

Mortality in the Middle East

This pattern observed in numerous less-developed countries seems to hold for the Middle East. The four fastest growing economies in Western Asia during 1970–1975 were Bahrain, Iraq, Saudi Arabia, and Yeman. Mortality decline in these countries, however, has been quite modest. In no country for any given year during this period did the rate of gain in life expectancy increase as much as a year (as a contrast there was a gain of 11.2 years in Sri Lanka between 1946 and 1948). The observed Middle East pattern is, however, quite consistent with other cross-sectional studies which indicate that on the average a 0.05 increment in life expectancy should accompany each percent increase in per capita GNP. Thus while the mortality picture probably did not change radically for Saudi Arabia during this period, it is changing about as fast as could be expected.

It is likely that mortality will not significantly decline in the kingdom until past income gains have been translated into social and health programs. If in fact the direct effect of this type of expenditure on mortality is much greater per dollar than that of income growth, and given the massive expenditure during the Second and Third Five Year Plan periods, there should be a fairly swift reduction of mortality in the kingdom during the 1980s.

Mortality in Saudi Arabia

In this regard there is plenty of room for improvement. According to the aforementioned multipurpose survey, the mortality rate for the Saudi population is 14.1 per 1,000. This rate is very close to the average of fourteen countries in Western South Asia (1974), but nearly double the Kuwaiti rate of 7.2. As with the birth rate, the crude death rate is related to the degree of urbanization, increasing from 6 per 1,000 in the kingdom's six largest municipalities, to 16 per 1,000 in the smaller municipalities, and finally to 18 per 1,000 in the country's villages and other rural areas.

Some of the more important factors that may contribute to this urban/ rural differential are the availability of hospitals, clinics, and other types of health-care facilities. Higher education levels and the higher proportion of the younger age groups in the urban areas undoubtedly reinforce this pattern.

Saudi Arabian Population Growth

If we accept the birth and death rates indicated by the multipurpose survey, then it is safe to conclude the kingdom's population is growing at a national rate of 3 percent or more per year.

The youthfulness (see table 8–3) of the population and the large numbers of women who will be entering the fertile age group (ages 15 to 44) over the next decade means that the process of demographic transition and the attainment of a stable population will require several generations. Even if fertility begins to decline, the country can be expected to maintain a high rate of natural population growth well into the next century (see table 8–4).

Immigration

Superimposed on the high natural rates of population increase is extensive immigration into the kingdom.[22] Migrants are drawn in because wage rates in their own countries are significantly below those offered in Saudi Arabia. Their duration of stay is limited (almost always less than 3 years). The typical expatriate worker is young (20 to 40 years old), single, works exclusively on a job he was hired for prior to arrival, transfers a large amount of his earnings to his home country, and does not plan to establish permanent residence in the kindgom.

In 1975 there were approximately 773,000 foreign workers in the kingdom. While no official figures exist as to the increase in immigrants since that time, several unofficial estimates place the 1980 foreign work force in the kingdom at around 2 million.

The post-1973 oil boom was by no means the beginning of Saudi Arabia's increasing dependence on foreign manpower. Ever since a modern state structure began to emerge under King Abdul Aziz Ibn Saud in the 1930s or 1940s, skilled advisors and technicians have been brought in from the outside to run large areas of adminstration and industry. The most

Table 8–3
Saudi Arabia: Percentage Distribution of Total Population, by Age and Sex, 1395 and 1400

	1395					1400				
Age	Male	Female	Total	%Age Male By Age Group	%Age Female By Age Group	Male	Female	Total	%Age Male By Age Group	%Age Female By Age Group
Under 5	15.9	17.1	16.5	50.3	49.7	16.4	17.5	16.9	50.6	49.4
5–9	13.8	15.0	14.4	50.2	49.8	13.1	14.0	13.5	50.6	49.4
10–14	12.8	13.2	12.9	51.5	48.5	11.8	12.4	12.1	51.0	49.0
15–19	11.2	10.9	11.1	53.0	47.0	11.2	11.4	11.3	52.0	48.0
20–24	9.7	8.4	9.1	55.9	44.1	10.5	9.5	10.0	54.8	45.2
25–29	7.3	5.9	6.6	57.5	42.5	9.0	7.3	8.2	57.6	42.4
30–34	5.5	5.2	5.3	53.8	46.2	6.0	4.9	5.5	57.3	42.7
35–39	4.8	5.0	4.9	51.5	48.5	4.5	4.3	4.4	53.2	46.8
40–44	4.4	4.6	4.5	50.9	49.1	3.8	3.8	3.7	52.2	49.8
45–49	3.7	3.8	3.8	51.5	48.5	3.5	3.8	3.7	52.2	49.8
50–54	3.1	3.1	3.1	52.8	47.2	3.0	3.2	3.1	50.9	49.1
55–59	3.1	3.2	3.2	51.8	48.2	2.4	2.5	2.4	51.2	48.8
60 +	4.6	4.6	4.6	52.4	47.6	4.8	4.8	5.1	51.0	49.0
Total:	100.000	100.0	100.0	52.3	47.7	100.0	100.0	100.0	52.3	47.7

Source: Ministry of Planning, Quantitative Economic Unit, "Estimated Population-Manpower Statistics" (Riyadh, 1395).

Table 8–4
ILO Forecast of Saudi Arabian Population, by Age Group, 1975–2000
(Thousands)

Age Group	Males					Females				
	1975	1980	1985	1990	2000	1975	1980	1985	1990	2000
0–9	1,494	1,753	2,024	2,307	2,788	1,449	1,698	1,960	2,232	2,695
10–14	542	641	768	898	1,185	525	622	745	871	1,149
15–19	461	533	631	759	1,031	444	516	613	736	1,001
20–24	393	450	521	620	876	379	434	506	603	853
25–44	1,050	1,203	1,385	1,602	2,225	1,016	1,167	1,344	1,558	2,176
45–54	297	341	394	455	615	294	339	391	454	613
55–64	184	213	247	287	392	193	222	258	300	410
65+	115	135	160	191	273	131	156	185	221	319
Total	4,534	5,269	6,130	7,119	9,385	4,431	5,154	6,002	6,976	9,215

Source: International Labor Office, *Labor Force: 1950–2000, vol. I, Asia* (Geneva: International Labor Office, 1977).

obvious is ARAMCO, the American oil operation consortium, but until very recently the majority of the immigrants came from the Arab world. Since 1975 the picture has begun to change radically; more and more unskilled workers are being imported from Asia and the proportion is gradually shifting over to Asian preeminence.

Since nearly all construction workers in the kingdom are foreigners, an appreciation of the magnitude of this inflow can be obtained from the various estimates made of the manpower requirements implied for this sector if it were to meet the targets set for it by the country's Second Five-Year Development Plan (1975–1980).

When the required number of indirect laborers are added, over 2 million construction workers, or about 25.7 percent of the total population, are forecast for 1980. This implies that to meet plan targets, an increase of 1.8 million foreign workers from the 1394 base of 220,000 would have to take place over the five-year period. If productivity increases continue, the full capacity construction labor force is forecast to peak around 1986 at a total of 2.25 million foreign workers. From the mid-1980s on, the foreign work force is expected to slowly decline as increases in productivity accompany changes in technology and a general tapering off of construction.

Projections of the construction labor force usually start with the assumption of 400,000 workers directly related to the construction industry in 1395. As such these workers represented about 5.6 percent of the natural population. Counting the supervisors and clerical workers to support the direct workers, this would have been about 6.1 percent of the natural population. Projections made in 1975 using the conservative set of assumptions (see Table 8–5) about increases in labor productivity forecast 1,832,000 direct construction laborers in the kingdom by 1980 (assuming construction industry is operating at the capacity required to meet the goals of the Second Development Plan).

To see the implications of these forecasts, note that even if only half the construction capacity is used, there would still be over 800,000 non-Yemeni, non-Saudi construction laborers in the kingdom in 1980. On the other hand, if only half of the 1974 labor base, largely Yemenis, are replaced by foreigners, there will still be over 900,000 non-Yemini, non-Saudi foreign construction laborers, supervisors, and support personnel in the kingdom by 1980. These workers would account for roughly 13 percent of the projected natural population of the kingdom for that year.

And this is not the full extent of the problem. Construction workers, especially supervisors and managers, often bring their households with them. For the sake of estimation, if we assume from past experience that all of the supervisors of the administration personnel and 20 percent of the direct workers (all listed in table 8–5) brought their households with them, and each of these households added 1.5 more persons, then an additional 76,000

Table 8–5
Saudi Arabia: Projections of Construction Activity

	Stanford Research Institute			SCET								
	Square Meters (Thousands)	Productivity Square meter/ Man Year	Man Years	Square Meters (Thousands)	Productivity Square Meter/ Man Year		Man Years		Square Meters	Productivity Square Meter/ Man Year	
					Low	High	Low	High		Low	High
1395	7,008	17.56 (4.5)	399	8,776	43.88	45.88	200.00	200	5,586.00	27.93	27.93
1396	11,737	18.37 (4.6)	639	12,988	49.35	47.95	270.84	263.18	9,048.76	37.50	37.61
1397	16,305	19.18 (4.4)	850	19,220	52.40	55.61	366.77	346.32	14,658.09	50.36	50.64
1398	25,090	20.77 (8.3)	1,208	28,444	57.26	62.43	496.68	455.72	23,747.64	67.62	68.19
1399	40,013	23.96 (15.4)	1,670	42,095	62.58	70.21	672.61	599.68	38,463.84	90.81	91.81
1400	49,755	27.16 (13.4)	1,832	62,303	68.39	78.96	911.00	789.00	62,301.00	121.92	123.62
1401	58,412	30.34 (11.7)	1,925								
1402	63,153	31.59 (4.1)	1,999								
1403	64,387	32.58 (3.1)	1,976								
1404	65,793	33.23 (2.0)	1,980								
1405	67,607	33.90 (2.0)	1,994								
1406	68,524	34.57	1,992								
1407	68,847	35.27	1,952								
1408	67,725	35.93	1,885								
1409	66,109	36.69	1,802								
1410	64,482	37.42	1,723								

Source: Ministry of Planning, *The Construction Industry in Saudi Arabia* (Riyadh, 1977), p. 24.
Note: Numbers in parentheses indicate average annual rate of growth.
SCET = Societé Civile d'Étude Technique.

foreigners would be in the country in 1976. By 1980 that figure would increase to 217,000. Given these assumptions as to the number of dependents together with those concerning the size of the full-capacity plan workforce, there would be approximately 798,000 construction workers and their families in the kingdom in 1976 increasing to 2,287,000 by 1980.

In addition, the spin-off effects of these construction jobs must be taken into account for a complete estimate of the likely foreign work force. Based on international experience, an extremely conservative estimate would be one job created for every five construction workers. A more liberal, but still plausible assumption is that one job is created for every two construction workers.

Using the conservative figure (but not including the family dependents discussed above), the Ministry of Planning has estimated that in 1976, 144,000 jobs were generated by employment in the construction sector. Adding these to the estimated 722,000 employees in the construction sector gives 12 percent of the kingdom's natural population in 1976 as either engaged in construction or serving workers engaged in that activity.

The more liberal assumptions concerning construction-induced employment imply that there would be 1,083,000 construction and construction-related jobs in 1976. This would be 15 percent of the present natural Saudi population. Projecting the conservative figure to 1980 indicates that by that date 2,484,000 persons or 31 percent of the natural population of the kingdom would be working on or serving the construction population.

Note that construction accounts for over 52 percent of all development plan expenditures. If the total economy reflects this distribution of construction/nonconstruction expenditures and if the capitalization ratio of the average nonconstruction sector job is equal to or less than the construction sector, there could be as many nonconstruction foreign laborers as there are construction sector foreign laborers.

Saudis are more likely to be a part of the labor force of the nonconstruction sector, so not as many foreigners are likely to come to serve all other economic sectors as presently serve in the construction sector. But the percentage would be high in any case. For example, even if there were only half as many foreigners in the nonconstruction sector as in the construction sector, the foreign work force would still be approximately 37 percent of the natural (Saudi) population.

It may be some time before we learn if these figures were reached. Even if they were not, the actual inflow of foreign workers probably occurred on a scale unprecedented in modern history.

Changing Geographic Composition of the Workforce

In 1975 the vast majority of foreign workers in Saudi Arabia were from the regional Arab countries. Most of these were employed as unskilled laborers, with the largest group by far coming from North Yemen. The latter are still the only group permitted to obtain residence permits untied to specific labor contracts, making them the only legal floating reservoir of workers in the kingdom. Increasingly, however, the Saudis have been adopting the practice of controlled labor contracts whereby foreign workers are brought into the kingdom for stipulated periods of time on specific jobs under block visas. As a result the Yemenis are on specific jobs under block visas and are increasing as a percentage of the foreign work force.[23]

Indeed, the proportion of Arab immigrant labor to the kingdom is going steadily down. Several authorities feel that the share of Arab foreign labor in Saudi Arabia will drop about 90 percent in 1975 to below 50 percent by 1985. Several reasons are given for this pattern:

1. The rapid increase in the rate of development after 1973 found the traditional Arab-exporting countries increasingly unable to send more workers abroad. Jordan, for instance, has nearly one-third of its labor force outside the country. Thus, the Saudis were obliged to link increasingly elsewhere. Shortages of available Arab labor forced the Saudis to tap other labor pools.

2. The massive increases in foreign workers made the Saudis apprehensive over the political and social implications stemming from the imbalance between indigenous and foreign labor. The creation of a fast-growing population of effectively second-class citizens (the Saudis are extremely reluctant to grant citizenship to immigrants) was felt to be too risky in terms of possible social strains and political turbulence.

3. The Saudis apparently felt that immigrants from radicalized Arab states presented a particular menace—hence the Saudi preference in the latter half of the 1970s for immigrants effectively isolated from the indigenous population by their inability to speak Arabic or engage in religious activities.[24]

The substitution of Asians for Yemenies has been the major change in geographic composition since 1975, with the proportion of immigrant laborers brought in from the Far East and the Indian subcontinent growing from less than 5 percent in 1975 to about 30 percent by 1980. The growth in Korean workers from 4,000 in 1975 to approximately 40,000 in 1980 was especially dramatic.[25]

Although importing labor to operate the economy has created a certain kind of dependency, it is a dependency envied by most other less-developed countries. Also there are certain advantages to utilizing a foreign work force. Given the nature of the international system and the established conventions of a nation's perogatives over nonnationals, for example, foreign manpower is controllable in a way that indigenous labor is not. It can be brought in and sent out at the will of the government. The world market contains a vast pool of manpower with all qualifications, ready and willing to contract themselves for short or long periods. Moreover, complete work forces can with modern technology be mobilized in the countries of origin and imported for a particular job and then exported en masse. While there, they can also be effectively isolated from the local population (who in any case would probably be unwilling or unable to engage in the tasks performed).

Despite the attractiveness of foreign workers, the government began steps in 1978 (presumably for security reasons) to control the flow of migrant workers into the country. Previously, official documents required for work in Saudi Arabia were easy to obtain and often never asked for by the Saudi authorities. This was particularly true for groups like the Yemenis who at one time traveled to Saudi Arabia without passports or visas. By imposing the responsibilities of correct documentation on employees, the government gained a degree of control over its migrant work force unknown previously.[26]

Third Plan Targets

Apparently, the Saudis have come to feel that their dependence on foreign workers is no longer desirable. The projected increase in the size of the civilian labor force over the Third Plan period (1980–1985) is 155,000.[27] This represents an annual growth rate of 1.2 percent and corresponds to the difference between the new civilian employment opportunities (310,000) and the estimated number of people leaving agriculture (70,000) and construction (85,000). The growth of expatriate workers is limited to over 9,000. This figure represents a net balance comprising 74,000 new jobs and 65,000 phased-out positions.

Officially, the Saudi Arabian government has stated that development in the kingdom has reached the point whereby most jobs can be effectively manned with Saudi workers. To compensate for the foreign workers and still attain the Third Plan targets, the level of productivity must increase by 27.2 percent by the end of the Third Plan period. This is an average annual rate of approximately 5 percent.

Conclusions

The population of Saudi Arabia, like the population of most of the Arab oil-exporting countries along the Arabian Gulf, has grown very rapidly since oil exporting began. This increase stems both from international immigration and rapid rates of natural increase for both the indigenous and the immigrant populations. Unfortunately, the quality of the country's demographic data does not allow us to ask a number of interesting questions. For example, while both a rapid decline in mortality and the passing of the main wave of immigration are likely to take place in the 1980s, an unpredictable feature is the level of fertility.

There are clear indications of urban–rural fertility differentials. Slight changes in the age pattern of fertility may also have occurred. Both factors indicate that the situation is not entirely static. On the other hand, the preference of Saudi Arabians for large families seems unlikely to change very quickly. As evidence of the slow pace of social change and thus more or less constant fertility rates, we can cite the still modest levels of female education and the small number of Saudi women working outside the home.

Defining development as the complex process of social, institutional, and economic change leading to sustained improvements in the quality of human life, an examination of Saudi Arabian demographic history leads to several somewhat different conclusions. One is that development as defined has simply not occurred in the kingdom. This conclusion runs against the commonly held view that the physical changes that have taken place in the country over the last 30 or so years are immense, and must therefore have had some bearing on social attitudes and behavior.

In view of the poor quality of the data, the lack of statistics for the pre-1970 period and the weak connection between some selected demographic parameters and measures of economic growth, we should be cautious about accepting this line of argument until we know much more about the structure and change in Saudi family life.

An alternative conclusion is that in the case of Saudi Arabian development, even development defined in the broadest social terms is unconnected with the country's pattern of demographic change. If true, this phenomena would make Saudi Arabia a remarkable exception to a significant body of knowledge that indicates countries follow a number of fairly normal demographic patterns with increasing levels of income. Since there is no real intuitive reason why Saudi Arabia should deviate from these patterns, this explanation is unacceptable.

A better conclusion, and one supported by what we know about the kingdom's economy (industrial development in particular), is that development is a very recent phenomenon in the country, beginning as late as 1970.[28] Given that much of the demographic information we have on the kingdom comes from the 1974 census (and several sample surveys taken soon after), it is likely that the country's rapid advancement was not yet reflected in the observed demographic patterns.

The constraint of a small indigenous Saudi population on the growth of the country is particularly emphasized by the increasing reluctance of the government to rely on foreign manpower. This is compounded by the authority's extreme reluctance to allow women to work. Only 1 percent of the female population is actively employed in the modern sector; they are not permitted to work in proximity to men, and the government is making further efforts to restrict opportunities for viable female labor.

New decrees were issued in 1979 forbidding women to trade in gold or to run their own commerical affairs. As a result Saudi Arabia has a very low rate of participation by the total population in the work force—one of the world's lowest rates of participation by women. In following this line of action, the country is neglecting a vast potential reservoir of labor in an economy that is already overextended.

Despite its vast natural wealth, its high natural rate of population growth, and its admirable policies of becoming less dependent on foreign labor, the kingdom is a very small country and thus at a distinct disadvantage in several important areas.[29] Economically, a sparse population implies that potential economies of scale in a number of important industrial activities will probably never be taken advantage of. Thus, the small size of the domestic market may, ceteris paribus, retard the long-run development of the nonoil sector and thus per capita income.

More important perhaps are the implications for the kingdom's security of a sparse population. Given the need for ever-increased defense expenditure, a potentially unstable and hostile regional environment, and the Saudi authorities reluctance to be totally dependent on the United States for its security, the kingdom's small population may not be able to be compensated for by other resources. The basis for this conclusion is simple: it is not the size of the country but the size of possible opponents that must govern the kingdom's response.

As a tentative hypothesis, we may conclude that all other conditions being equal, the relative magnitude of the possible emergency reflected in the eyes of would-be opponents increases as the gap widens between population size in the kingdom and in its would-be adversaries. While not strictly an economic consideration, the issue of the kingdom's population and its relation to the country's long-run security is too important a topic to be completely disregarded.

Notes

1. I. Adelman and C.T. Morris, "A Factor Analysis of the Interrelationship between Social and Political Variables and Per-Capita Gross National Product," *Quarterly Journal of Economics* (November 1965): 558–560.

2. J. Hoagland, "Saudi Arabians Push $100 Billion Development Plan," *The Washington Post* (April 13, 1975).

3. Japan Cooperation Center for the Middle East, *Analysis of Demand and Supply of Manpower in the Arabian Gulf Countries—An Excerpt* (Tokyo: JCCME, 1976), p. 13; J.S. Birks and C.A. Sinclair, *The International Migration Project, Country Case Study: Saudi Arabia* (Durham, Great Britain: University of Durham International Migration Project, 1978), p. 8.

4. For an example using this approach see the Royal Commission for Jubail and Yenbo, Directorate General for Jubail Region, *Community Programming: Permanent Community for Jubail Industrial Complex* (London: Colin Buchanan and Partners, 1977), ch. 1.

5. As Chovcri notes, however, one must still recognize that there is great heterogeneity with regard to many demographic features in the region. See Nazli Chovcri, "Demographic Changes in the Middle Ease," in Joint Economic Committee, Congress of the United States, *The Political Economy of the Middle East: 1973–1978* (Washington: U.S. Government Printing Office, 1980), p. 26.

6. J.S. Birks and C.A. Sinclair, "International Labor Migration in the Arab Middle East," *Third World Quarterly* (April 1979): 87–88.

7. Population Division of ECWA, "Demographic and Socio-Economic Situation in Countries of the ECWA Region, 1975," *Population Bulletin of the United Nations Economic Commission for Western Asia* January 1977): 3–11.

8. Unless otherwise specified, comparative population figures on the Middle East are taken from the ECWA, *Population Bulletins.*

9. Baha Abu-Laban and Sharon Abu-Laban, "Education and Development in the Arab World," *Journal of Developing Areas* (April 1976): 285–304

10. Henry Azzam, "Analysis of Fertility and Labor Force Differentials in the Arab World," *Population Bulletin of the United Nations economic Commission for Western Asia* (June 1979): 45.

11. William Rugh, "Emergence of a New Middle Class in Saudi Arabia," *The Middle East Journal* (Winter 1973): 18–19.

12. For an excellent summary of this literature see Pan Yotopoulos and Jeffrey Nugent, *Economics of Development: Empirical Investigations* (New York: Harper & Row, 1976), ch. 13.

13. This follows the approach of T. Paul Schultz, "Fertility Patterns and Their Determinants in the Middle East," in Charles Cooper et al., *Economic Development and Population Growth in the Middle East* (New York: American Elsevier, 1972), pp. 400–447.

14. See Riad Tabbarah et al., "Population Research and Research Gaps in the Arab Countries," *Population Bulletin of The United Nations Economic Commission for Western Asia* (December 1978): 3–32, for a survey of these studies.

15. Ibid.

16. As reported in Ali Rashid and Robert Casady, "Methods and Preliminary Estimates from the Saudi Arabian Multipurpose Survey," paper presented at the *41st Session of the International Statistical Institute*, New Delhi (December 5–15, 1977), pp. 1–7.

17. Yotopoulous and Nugent, *Economics of Development*, ch. 11.

18. J.D. Pitchford, *Population in Economic Growth* (New York: American Elsevier, 1974), ch. 4.

19. J. Conlisk and D. Huddle, "Allocating Foreign Aid: An Appraisal of a Self-Help Model," *Journal of Development Studies* (July 1969): 245–251.

20. Julian Simon, "Population Growth May Be Good for the LCDs in the Long Run: A Richer Simulation Model," *Economic Development and Cultural Change* (January 1976): 309–337.

21. Samual Preston, "Mortality, Morbidity, and Development," *Population Bulletin of the United Nationa Economic Commission for Western Asia* (December 1978): 68–69.

22. The following draws heavily on data presented in Ministry of Planning, *The Construction Industry in Saudi Arabia*, pp. 21–34. Also see R. Paul Shaw, "Migration and Employment in the Arab World: Construction as a Key Policy Variable," *International Labor Review* (September–October 1979): 589–605.

23. Fred Halliday, "Migration and the Labor Force in the Oil Producing States of the Middle East," *Development and Cultural Change* (July 1977): 263–292.

24. See J.S. Birks and C.A. Sinclair, *International Migration and Development in the Arab Region* (Geneva: International Labor Office, 1980), pp. 75–78, for a general discussion of these issues.

25. S. Sidahmed, "The Lost Labor," *Saudi Business and Arab Economic Report* (January 9, 1981): 22–24.

26. David Shierreff, "Strict Society Keeps Rein on Growing Work Force," Special Report on Saudi Arabia, Middle East Economic Digest (June 1979): 7–8.

27. Ministry of Planning, *Third Development Plan 1400–1405 A.H.* (Riyadh: MOP, 1980), pp. 97–101.

28. See Yusif Sayigh, "Problems and Prospects in the Arabian Peninsula," *International Journal of Middle East Studies* (February 1970): 51–56.

29. A skeptical view of this goal is given in "Foreign Labor Dominates Key Sectors—And Some Will Remain Indefinitely," Special Report on Saudi Arabia, *Middle East Economic Digest* 53–54.

9 Agriculture

A whole chapter devoted to the role of agriculture in Saudi Arabia's future development may seem somewhat surprising when set against a background of relatively slow growth in farming production, the immensely negative resource endowment of so much of the kingdom, and the chronic manpower shortage that affects not only the economy in general, but agriculture in particular. And yet evidence now clearly points to the 1980s as a decade of quickly accelerating agricultural transformation—this following the decade of the 1960s, characterized by progressive stagnation, and the 1970s' slow gathering of momentum.

Curiously despite rural depopulation, inefficient farming, poor land use, lack of training centers, and official neglect, agriculture has turned in a respectable growth rate over the 5 years of the Second Plan. While the average growth rate of 4 percent in the kingdom's agricultural sector is higher than that of other developing countries, its share of Saudi Arabia's nonoil gross domestic product has, however, dropped from 12.1 percent in 1970 to 2.4 percent in 1978.[1] With perhaps 30 percent of Saudis engaged in farming, it is clear that there is room for improvement.

The economic development potential of agriculture in Saudi Arabia, the problems involved, and the measures required to achieve that potential are herein considered. Several major assumptions underlie the analysis:

1. While declining, agriculture will continue to be the source of employment for a large proportion of the total population. This should be the case for at least another generation, even if industrialization and other economic development proceed rapidly.

2. The traditional main inputs into agricultural production—climate, soil, and water—will continue to remain highly important, although breakthroughs in technology may result in their being used in new ways or combinations in the future.

3. Breakthroughs in technology are not, however, likely to result in hydroponics becoming established in a scale sufficient to significantly displace growing crops on the land. Chemical synthesis of food supplements will continue to expand, but to augment rather than replace reliance upon soil.[2]

4. Agricultural technology throughout the world is likely to advance slowly in the future, no matter what public or private measures are taken. The rate of development and of adoption of agricultural technologies new to the

141

kingdom is, however, capable of accelerating sufficiently enough to bring about a virtual agricultural revolution within a generation.[3]

Major Characteristics

Agriculture continues to play an important part in the economic activity of the country. It is characterized by the fact that:[4]

1. In 1970 there were 7,805 agricultural villages in the country, with a total area of holdings amounting to 1.4 million hectares.
2. Only about 525,000 hectares—or about 0.2 to 0.3 percent—of the total land area is under cultivation.
3. Of the area under cultivation, 121,000 hectares are irrigated and 404,000 are rain-fed.
4. The total of about 525,000 hectares of cultivated land is shared among 181,000 holdings, the average size of which is under 8 hectares.
5. The average area of irrigated land per holding is less than 1 hectare.
6. The number of agricultural villages declined sharply to 3,084 villages in 1975. The main cause was low real income in agriculture and increasing opportunities for well-paid employment in other sectors of the economy.
7. The total number of Saudis engaged in agriculture was assumed in the Second Development Plan to have declined from 40.4 percent of total Saudi employment in 1970 to 28.0 percent in 1975.
8. The sector's average annual growth did not exceed 1.6 percent at constant prices between 1961 and 1971. Over the first five-year plan this average annual rate rose to an estimated 3.6 percent, compared with the plan target of 4.6 percent.
9. While growing at approximately 4 percent for the 1970s as a whole, the share of agriculture in nonoil GDP dropped from 12.1 percent in 1970 to 2.4 percent in 1978.
10. Net imports accounted for 45 percent of total food requirements in 1971. By 1979 the kingdom imported 4.98 million tons of food by sea alone or about 60 percent of its food requirements. Sugar, rice, oils and fats are almost entirely imported, while less than half the total consumption of wheat and flour, milk, meat, and eggs are produced domestically.
11. Development of agriculture and water resources has recently received high priority in government policies and programs as is reflected in the more than six-fold rise in budgetary allocations for these sectors, from SR 1.40 billion in 1975 to SR 8.25 billion in 1979 and 8.67 billion in 1980.

Reasons for Renewed Interest in Agriculture

Increased government allocations to agriculture have been made possible by the fact that there does not appear to be any strong sentiment within the government against reversing the decline of the agricultural sector. On the contrary, there are many in the country who believe that rural activity had been unduly neglected for a long time and that the government had a moral responsibility to use part of its oil revenues to revive and modernize the sector.[5]

In addition the stress on agricultural development now accorded by the kingdom's planners stems from the increased importance placed by Saudi leadership on: (1) reducing the country's dependence on food imports; (2) reforestation as a means of modifying the country's climate, and (3) perhaps most important, using agriculture as an acceptable means of settlement of the Bedouin nomads.

Four subsequent events have been primarily responsible for this renewed interest in the sector: (1) an emerging food shortage over the world;[6] (2) the possibility of physical bottlenecks to the inflow of imports even if foreign exchange were no obstacle; (3) the more sobering realization that the kingdom might be isolated from its major trading partners during a period of international conflict, and (4) the reality that fast growth concentrated exclusively in the nonagricultural sector might, as in the case of Iran, create social tensions so severe as to undermine the country's entire development effort.

More specifically, the rapid increase in world commodity prices in the 1970s and the inability of the country to currently produce food for any reasonable level of self-sufficiency was the initial stimulus to accelerating growth of the agricultural sector. The world food price index, for example, increased from 100 in 1970 to 278 in 1974.[7]

As in other parts of the world, there is growing concern about the food situation in Saudi Arabia. The present world food crisis is not simply a cyclical phenomenon, nor has it come about suddenly. It has wrought its way gradually and imperceptibly since the existence of huge surpluses with the large food exporters, until the early 1970s obscured the fact that the supply–demand relationship has been worsening continuously over the previous two decades, with the result that world food production had been barely keeping pace with population growth.[8]

While the kingdom's oil revenues place the country in the enviable position of being able to easily import all of its food requirements even if world food prices increase drastically, a feeling of increased vulnerability is evident in the kingdom. Policymakers in Saudi Arabia are increasingly inclined to believe that food has become a strategic commodity that can, over the long run, be as potent a foreign policy weapon as oil. There is also concern that food imports will become the basis for a new economic dependence that is not only likely to undermine ambitious development plans, but will sap the economic assertiveness and compromise political independence.[9]

Finally by the mid-1970s, a better appreciation of the limits of technological and social change has emerged within the kingdom. Without abandoning ambitions for industrial growth, the government has given higher priority to rural society in overall development. Industrialization has proved a far more illusive goal than was conceived earlier. Efforts to induce rapid change caused strong inflationary pressures and other strains on the domestic economy. Worker productivity has proved low as a result of both poor skills and motivation. Industrial goods are thus uncompetitive in international markets, and the domestic demand is too weak to absorb most of the finished products. Social problems have emerged out of the concentration of transplanted labor in the cities while income disparities between urban and rural areas have increased social tensions.

Patterns of Food Consumption

Of immediate cause for concern is the fact that the high rates of economic growth achieved during the last decade have dramatically increased the kingdom's demand for food and food products. This, together with lagging rates of production, has caused agricultural imports to grow at an average annual rate of 23.6 percent a year between 1968 and 1977. Between 1973 and 1977 when incomes were accelerating, imports of cereals, vegetables, and fruits more than tripled, while that of meat more than tripled.

Clearly if the government wishes to attain any sort of self-sufficiency in food, it must identify the current consumption patterns as well as possible trends in individual items.

The best source of information on household consumption patterns is the Central Department of Statistics consumer surveys of 1969–1970 and 1977.[10] The most significant difference in household consumption patterns during the 7 years between surveys would seem to be the decline in the proportion of food in total household budgets.

The decline in the importance of food in budgets with increased incomes is also apparent when comparisons are made between Saudi and non-Saudis. In the survey Saudi households reported average total expenditures of SR 5,927, of which SR 1,596 or 27 percent was allocated to food. In contrast non-Saudi household expenditures were SR 3,050 of which SR 1,129 or 37 percent was spent for food.

Finally, of the five cities comprising the survey (Riyadh, Jeddah, Dammam, Burayadh, and Abha) Riyadh showed by far the lowest proportion of total expenditure (23 percent) for food. Given Riyadh's relative affluence, the fact that the pattern of food as a proportion of expenditures declined with increases in income is confirmed. With regard to the composition of consumption of food purchases, meat and poultry were the most important, followed by fresh fruits, then vegetables. There was surprisingly little variation among cities in the proportion of total expenditures allocated to fresh fruits and vegetables (averaging about 29 percent) or meat and poultry (where the average is about 28 percent).

Overall the expenditure elasticity of food is 0.5881 (see table 9–1); that is, a 1 percent increase in expenditure results in a little over a 0.5 percent increase in the demand for food. Meat (0.6872) has a particularly high elasticity undoubtedly accounting for the rapid increase in imports of this item.[11] These results imply that:

1. The rapid rise in food demand was due to an increase in income and not an increasing proportion of incomes spent on food.
2. Future needs for all agricultural products will be very dependent on the magnitude of population growth.

Table 9–1
Saudi Arabia: Elasticity Coefficients of Demand for Major Food Groups

Food Group	Income Elasticity Demand	r^2	t	Asfour Figure
Cereals	0.4315	0.9743	15.07	0.2
Meat	0.6872	0.9791	16.76	0.4
Fish	0.3196	0.9611	12.17	
Eggs	0.4731	0.9508	7.48	
Dairy products	0.4498	0.9055	7.55	1.2
Oils and fats	0.5129	0.9359	9.33	0.5
Fresh vegetables	0.4782	0.9269	8.72	0.6
Preserved vegetables	0.6255	0.8872	6.86	
Fresh fruits	0.5746	0.9226	8.43	0.6
Preserved fruits	0.6001	0.4367	9.38	
Sugar	0.6181	0.8787	6.56	0.5
All food	0.5881	0.9722	14.46	0.44

Source: Computed from data in table 7, Central Department of Statistics, *Consumer Expenditure Survey*.

Note: See Edmond Asfour, *Saudi Arabia Long-Term Projections of Supply and Demand for Agricultural Products* (Beirut, 1965), p. 19, for information about the Asfour figure.

3. The standard of living will undoubtedly rise for all income groups as better access to nutritional information is made possible by higher degrees of literacy, government campaigns, and so on. Changing eating habits and improved diets will therefore modify the consumption patterns for each income group.

Constraints on Agricultural Development

In addition to the diverse climatic conditions, the constraints on agricultural development in Saudi Arabia are the limited supplies of cultivable land, water, and labor. Within the Saudi Arabian context agricultural development has differed from that experienced by many other developing countries in two important respects: (1) in general the degree of inelasticity of the factors listed previously is far greater in Saudi Arabia, and thus the constraints on agricultural development are more severe, and (2) the elasticity of the supply of capital which facilitates the flow of technology needed to overcome the constraints mentioned is greater in Saudi Arabia.

Soils

The soils of Saudi Arabia are not yet well-known. They have, however, been under intensive study in recent years. Preliminary findings confirm that the country's low and variable precipitation, its high temperatures (which quickly burn up any organic matter that does grow), and its sparse natural vegetation have all combined to prevent the development of mature soils. The soils that have potential for irrigated agriculture are for the most part found at the wadi bottoms or outlets. These soils consist mainly of clay and silt, and have been brought to these depressions by flood waters. Thus they have better physical properties for plant growth under irrigated agriculture than do the dominantly sandier soils of the higher-lying ground from which they were washed. Because they are alluvial soils, soluble salts are usually present and must be washed out before most crops can be produced profitably.

Since a large proportion of these alluvial soils are in closed depressions in desert areas, ultimate disposal of drainage water from irrigated areas presents a problem. Indeed, many oases have large areas of poorly drained land where salt accumulations are already unusually high. In many cases drainage will be necessary before cultivation can be undertaken on a profitable basis. However, because of the relatively large area of arable soils in relation to available water and the very high evaporation rates in most areas, the capacity of a number of natural depressions to serve as salt sinks may be adequate for the amount of irrigation likely to be undertaken in the near future.

For many oases, however, the amount of water available is insufficient for flushing salts from the soil. Cropping has often been carried out too near the low point of the natural basins, so that salts accumulated in the farmed areas. In the future croppings may have to be moved to higher ground, and the bottoms of the basins converted to salt sinks.

Drainage

Drainage is therefore becoming a major problem for Saudi Arabian agriculture. By being something of a late developer, the kingdom can benefit by mistakes previously made in other countries in the Middle East.[12] Experience in countries such as Iraq have demonstrated conclusively that drainage is a collective good, and as such it is difficult to link rewards to effort invested. Most Middle Eastern countries have eventually found that drainage is best provided under state control and through some special organization, and that it cannot be left, at least initially, to local initiative.

Based on Middle Eastern experience, the best solution to Saudi Arabia's existing drainage problem would seem to require a mix of physical drainage facilities and improved irrigation management. Overirrigation has been a particular problem in some of the Eastern Province oases, and has occurred because:[13]

1. Water is underpriced.
2. Farmers are without control over water supplies and face unpredictable fluctuations in water availability.
3. There are no provisions for some sort of water sharing in times of scarcity.

Under these circumstances overwatering is a rational response. Ultimately it will require greater understanding and cooperation among farmers and/or the imposition of penalties by the authorities to bring this practice to a halt.

Water

More than 75 percent of the arable land in Saudi Arabia is rainfed. Irrigation water is quite limited and often of low quality. Because of their access to water, the coastal fringes of the kingdom offer the best prospects for expanded food production. In the Asir, next to North Yemen, the mountains rise to 10,000 feet and precipitation is fairly abundant, thus permitting the practice of rainfed agriculture using terracing techniques. Along both the east and west coasts, areas of natural springs and shallow water tables along the wadis probably offer the country's best prospects for agricultural development. Even in the huge central Saudi plateau, some cultivation is possible in the oases near Riyadh, Aqsim, Buraydah, and Hail.

Most authorities agree that water will continue to be the major physical constraint on expanding Saudi agriculture. There are no perennial streams, and despite several technical innovations, desalinated water is still expensive. A spin-off from oil exploration has been the discovery of a number of huge acquifers of fossil water, but effective utilization has proved slow and expensive. In any case the long-run potential of underground water must be considered limited. Moreover water consumption by urban and industrial centers has expanded rapidly.

With the kingdom's soaring water needs to meet the requirements of agriculture, as well as the ever expanding urban population and the demands of its industrial development projects, there is no viable alternative to desalination at the moment. Since 1965 desalination plants have been constructed with a total capacity of 12.7 million gallons of water a day. The cost of the kingdom's long run desalination program is estimated at $50 billion, with $15 billion to be spent during the Second Plan (1975–1980). In all likelihood, actual investment will, however, be far less than planned. Most of the actual expansion of water production will be consumed by urban and industrial centers. It is unrealistic, therefore, to expect sufficient water for significant agricultural expansion.

Jeddah, for example, requires 25 million gallons a day. Of this 20 million comes from wells in the nearby Wadi Fatima and Wadi Khylys. A further 2 million gallons a day is to be extracted from Wadi Khylys where 11 kilometers of pipeline are being laid. The water table in both wadis has been dropping rapidly over the past few years with the city's growth and increasing needs. As a result deeper wells and more powerful pumps are now needed to support agriculture in the wadis. Cultivation of plants with a high water consumption has been discontinued and in some places whole farms have been abandoned.

The city is expected to need to rely on the water resources of the wadis for several years to come, and extraction from these sources must increase. Water needs are calculated on a basis of 250 liters per person per day. Taking the 1974 population figures of 600,000 inhabitants, this would put the city's needs at 40 million gallons per day. By 1979, however, the population had risen to nearly 800,000.[14]

Desalination can relieve some of the water shortage, but not enough to significantly aid local agriculture's requirements. In 1977, Jeddah received 15 million gallons per day from its first desalination plant. Another plant which will add an extra 20 million gallons per day will not be completed until 1979–1980.

Riyadh, another city with large water requirements, is fortunately situated in a region of vast underground aquifers which flow eastward from below the western face of the Tuwaiq Escarpment. The main water supplies so far have been drawn from very deep wells in and around the town (some of the deepest operational water wells in the world), and from the Minjur aquifer which outcrops about 100 km. to the west of the city. The Upper Minjur is from 1200 to 1500 meters below ground and water brought up from it is hotter than can be conveniently used. It has to be cooled from 52 degrees C. to 30 degrees C. before being fed into the network.

Riyadh already consumes nearly 40 million gallons of water per day for its population of 750,000. Consumption is currently 200 liters per capita per day. With the rapid expansion of the city and its increasing beautification with gardens and parks in addition to industrial developments, the needs are expected to rise to around 145 million gallons per day (530,000 cubic meters) by 1981.

During the next few years, the Ministry of Agriculture and Water will be exploiting other aquifers in the Riyadh district to provide for the rapidly rising needs of the city. In 1977 an additional 8 million gallons a day were brought from Kharj Road and Wadi Guddaih; in 1978 water became available from the large Salbukh field 60 kilometers north of Riyadh. This source provides 22 to 23 million gallons per day. In 1980, a similar amount will be brought from Buwaybiyat, 60 kilometers northeast of the city.

By the mid-1980s, it is hoped that water will be available from the vast Wasia aquifer 110 kilometers to the east of the city. British consultants have carried out a study for the use of this aquifer and were commissioned in October 1976 to design a system for exploiting it. The total cost of the project will be about SR 2 billion and the amount of water supplied will be some 55 million gallons (200,000 cubic meters) per day.

The aquifers are so vast that it is unlikely that they will be exhausted in the foreseeable future. The recharge rate, however, is low and as water is extracted the water table drops. This process is visible in the oasis of Al Kharj, southeast of Riyadh where surface rock strata have collapsed. This water is extracted for agriculture and the water level can be seen to have dropped 4 or 5 meters in the past 10 years.

A further problem is that the salinity of the water increases with extraction. The salinity of Wasia, for example, is expected to rise to 1,250 parts per million in a little over 20 years. It will, therefore, be necessary to desalinate this geological water to bring it within the range of 500 to 700 parts per million salinity stipulated for Riyadh's future water needs. Riyadh's present water supply is treated in three separate treatment plants, and two others, using reverse osmosis, are under construction.

Because of rapid urbanization, the difficulties of providing expanded water supplies to the cities and increased water usage for agricultural purposes will be permitted only if it is clearly in the long-term public interest. A National Water Policy with provisions for the enforcement of a National Water Code and National Water Standards is being developed. Public awareness must be improved so that ground water management can be implemented and conservation practiced throughout the kingdom.

Labor

Shortages of labor are also an important constraint on agricultural output, but unlike water the magnitude of the problem is not one that can be treated in very precise terms.

The structure of rural employment differs somewhat among the regions, but the main outlines are clear. It consists of self-employed peasants, family members, workers with contractual or personal obligations to the landowner, free wage labor (most of whom own small pieces of land), and Saudi and non-Saudi migrant workers. There are 7.6 persons per rural household, 19.57 *dunums* (4.89 acres) of cultivated land per household, and 11.47 *dunums* (2.87 acres) of cultivated land per worker.[15]

The females in the rural labor force hold a unique position. While women contribute to output in the agricultural sector, they are only part of the rural labor pool. If the family moved into the city, the women would drop out of the labor force, because under no circumstances would women be allowed to work in an urban area outside the house.[16]

The labor force in agriculture is declining by 0.9 percent annually; a decline reflected in abandoned farmland and partly depopulated villages, particularly in the southwestern region. The main factors responsible for these trends are low real incomes in agriculture and increasing opportunities for well-paid employment in other sectors.

Policies for Agricultural Development

The government has a number of policy options that show some promise in correcting some of the difficulties currently facing the agriculture sector. Given that the objective of the government is to maximize the long-run wealth of the kingdom, it is argued here that one step toward achieving this objective is to continue to transfer a relatively small, but larger part of the country's oil revenues into agriculture. An increase in the public resources allocated to the agricultural sector is needed not only to develop agricultural infrastructure, both physical and organizational, but also to assist in the development of new inputs and techniques to stimulate their adoption, and thus to contribute to the sector's modernization.

The scope for future agricultural development in Saudi Arabia includes both the horizontal and vertical expansion of cultivation. Given the constraints of water, land, climate, and labor, it seems that the scope of horizontal expansion in Saudi Arabia is limited in the short and medium terms, but that considerable increases in agricultural production can be achieved through vertical expansion. Thus, the medium-term objectives of agricultural development should concentrate on increasing agricultural productivity within the existing land and resource limitations. Long-run objectives should focus on a gradual horizontal expansion.

Policy for Water Use

Development of water resources should continue to be accorded a high priority among governmental activites. Despite the great scarcity of water resources, water is not efficiently used. In addition, annual extraction has greatly exceeded replenishment. Water policy, therefore, should aim at achieving both a proper balance and an optimum use. Achieving water balance is necessary to prevent or reduce water salinity and sustain the level of ground water (thus preventing its replacement by sea water).

Government-provided irrigation water is, for all practical purposes, furnished free. The government bears the cost of digging wells as well as their operating fuel cost. This practice has resulted in excessive and uneconomic use of water, which in turn increases the salinity of both land and water.

While the tendency to use excessive amounts of irrigation water in the kingdom seems to be strong and difficult to overcome, there are several measures that may contribute to reducing this practice. One method is the establishment of an efficient water management system which regulates and scientifically coordinates the use and construction of water pumps in accordance with land and water topography. The other is through institutional reorganization.

Institutional Reorganization

Several important institutional changes are needed in the medium term. One is the reorganization of the Minstry of Agriculture and Water, and redefinition of its functions. The functions of the new ministry should focus primarily on the total task of creating a modern agriculture and would include:[17]

1. Agricultural research.
2. Provision of farm inputs.

3. Rural agri-support infrastructure.
4. Farmer's incentives and agricultural prices.
5. Land development and management.
6. Agricultural manpower training.
7. Water development management.

Thus, the Saudi Arabian Ministry of Agriculture should be reorganized in seven major divisions, each of which is responsible for one of these seven elements that form the components of creating a modern agriculture in the kingdom. In addition to these major divisions, three offices are needed to provide the required cooperation and coordination among these divisions—statistical services, integrated projects, and planning. These major divisions and offices would provide the framework of an organization focused primarily on creating the necessary conditions of agricultural development.

Factor Substitution and Labor Policy

A severe labor shortage currently exists in agriculture. The situation is aggravated by the high rate of turnover because of immigration of farm labor to the cities, where wages are higher and living conditions are better. The situation is worsened by the fact that most of the rural workers lack experience in modern agricultural methods. This forms one of the principal barriers to the country's agricultural development. One way of overcoming the shortage of workers is through factor substitution. Unlike the situation in many developing countries, where capital is scarce and agricultural labor is abundant, Saudi Arabia's factor endowment suggests the possibility of efficiently substituting capital for labor.

In 1981, however, the precise value for the elasticity of substitution of one factor for the other is still uncertain.[18] What evidence that does exist suggests that the elasticity of substitution between capital and labor is greater than unity and is close to 1.5. If these estimates are correct, they indicate that a relatively wide range of alternative agricultural techniques can be adopted under various conditions. In Saudi Arabia, the needs range from simple agricultural tools to sophisticated farm machinery. There are several problems involved in introducing such types of capital intensive technology into Saudi Arabia.

A second problem is that farmers have resented to a certain extent the introduction of such machinery because it has changed their accustomed patterns of work. However, this problem is being overcome as farmers recognize the new technology's benefits in the form of increased productivity and higher incomes.

The policy of substituting capital for labor in Saudi Arabian agriculture seems to be consistent with the general worldwide trend in agricultural development strategy. Differences in technical inputs and human capital apparently account for a very substantial share of the agricultural productivity gap among countries; and even within the resource endowments category, internal capital accumulation appears to be relatively important compared to land.[20] Recent results indicate that output per worker in several developing countries can be increased by several times, while land per worker remains constant or even declines slightly.[21] To achieve levels of labor productivity comparable to the levels achieved in the developed countries, however, it will at some stage be necessary to complement those technical changes designed to increase output per unit area with technologies that reduce the labor input per unit area.

The mechanization of farms not only reduces the labor input per unit area, but also contributes to retaining farm labor in the agricultural sector. To discourage labor migration to the cities, wages must be increased, and new services, similar to those available in the cities, must be introduced in agricultural areas. The introduction of machinery will raise labor productivity, which in turn will permit the increase in wages needed to provide incentives to farmers to stay on the farms.

However, to be successful, the introduction of capital intensive technologies will require several measures. These include the following:

1. Farm specialization will be needed to make the use of machinery economical.
2. Effective servicing centers must be established.
3. Training centers will be needed to provide the required training in the new type of technology.

First, a large amount of capital is needed. The government certainly has the resources to assist in solving this problem, however. In fact it has made a start in this direction through the Saudi Arabian Agricultural Bank (SAAB) which provides funds at rates partly subsidizing the cost of this new technology. In addition, SAAB provides for: (1) raising, storage, and marketing of crops, livestock, poultry, fish, and forestry products; (2) the reclamation of land; and (3) making available the facilities to find water. The bank has greatly expanded its lending capacity in recent years.

Implications for Policy

It is difficult to determine with precision the likely overall impact of these policies. While the kingdom already has one of the largest agricultural development programs in the world (on a per capita basis) and is expanding it rapidly, it is pointless to generalize on a macro level as to the effectiveness of even the expenditures currently under way.

Development of agriculture in the Eastern Province has been given a high priority by the government, and an examination of this area's experience provides some useful insights into the problems and prospects facing the agricultural sector.

Agricultural Development in the Eastern Region—
A Case Study

The Eastern Region of Saudi Arabia comprises the area along the Arabian Gulf and inland for some distance. Because of large variations in the area's socioeconomic structure, the region is often divided into three zones— Northern, Coastal, and Southern. The populated coastal areas of Qatif, Dammam, and Al Khobar are in the coastal zone which also reaches westward to Ayn Dar; Abqaya also forms part of the Coastal Zone, as does Hofuf.[22]

The coastal belt oases of Al Hasa and Haradh are the major centers of irrigated agriculture in the Eastern Region. In the rest of the region (the Wadi al Batin, Qaryat al Uliyah, the Wadi al Miyah, Judah, Mutalah and Yabrin), irrigated agriculture is only of minor importance because there is either insufficient suitable water available or little interest in settled farming.

Cropping Patterns. Date palms occupy by far the major part of the net cultivable area in the Eastern Region. By the 1970s there were over 1.8 million date trees under cultivation; however, 40 to 50 percent of these were in die-back state. Total date production has been declining from about 54,000 tons in 1967 to less than 36,000 tons in 1979. Reduced yields are the major cause of the decrease, with average yields per bearing tree falling rather continuously during this period. Declining demand is also a factor tending to reduce production by decreasing profitability of date growing. The result of both factors has been a deterioration of the trees that are no longer replaced, and/or insufficient attention paid to the quality of dates.

There are four types of animal production in the region:

1. Settled stock raising in the oases.
2. Nomadic stock raising.
3. Large-scale sheep breeding and fattening at the King Faisal Settlement Project Organization in Haradh.
4. Relatively large-scale poultry production around the major urban centers.

Nomadic stock raising is by far the most important element of animal husbandry in the Eastern Region. The herds of the bedouin nomads, however, are prone to sharp fluctuations since they fluctuate with periods of drought and abundant rainfall. The number of bedouin families has declined appreciably since the mid-1960s.

The total number of farms in the region is around 6,000, with 1,500 to 2,000 in the coastal belt oases and 4,000 to 4,500 in al Hasa. The settled male labor force is about 13,000 and is engaged in crop production and settled animal production in the region, while the male labor force of the bedouin nomads amounts to approximately 11,000.[23]

The net present value of crop production and settled stock raising amounted to SR 580 per capita of agriculture population or to SR 3,600 per male worker in 1973. These amounts, however, are by no means indicative of the income position of the agricultural workers. First, a yearly land rent (either in cash or in kind) or some SR 2 million is paid to nonagricultural landlords. Second, the expenditure on hired labor in 1973 aggregated to about 15 (SR 20/man-day). Third, income distribution in the agricultural sector is rather skewed; the comparatively small group of vegetable growers and poultry producers may earn as much as SR 20 to 40 per day, while date growers seldom earn more than SR 5 to 8 per day.[24]

Qatif is the other large oasis in the Eastern Region. Over the last several decades more than 900 shallow wells have been drilled in the area. Irrigation from these wells has raised the water table and markedly increased soil salinity. To improve the situation, a drainage system discharging directly into the gulf has been constructed but the results have been somewhat unsatisfactory. Further land reclamation experiments have been conducted and a 100 hectares experimental farm has been established.[25]

King Faisal Settlement Project. The King Faisal Settlement Project Organization at Haradh is another major agricultural center in the region. The original aim of the project (which was approved in the early 1960s) was to settle around 1,000 bedouin families. The feasibility study recommended concentration on the production of vegetables in rotation with alfalfa. Subsequently, the objectives were reformulated; the current aim is to establish a commercial enterprise where:

1. Sheep are produced economically.
2. Job opportunities are provided to bedouin nomads.
3. Bedouin nomads are intensively trained in farming to prepare them for taking over the project.
4. The ultimate target to be attained by the early 1980s is to have a herd of 150,000 Black Hajd ewes producing over 200,000 lambs per year.

By the end of 1973 the construction of the irrigation and drainage system was completed while 2,000 to 2,500 hectares of the 3,500 hectares target of cultivable acreage had been achieved. The irrigation system was designed on the basis of the original objective of the project; that is, settlement of bedouin nomads. The capacity of this system, however, was too small for mechanized, intensive fodder production.

The Al Hasa Reclamation Project. Al Hasa is an ancient oasis with age-old irrigated agriculture. In 1964, a West German consulting firm approached the Agriculture and Water Ministry with a plan to add 12,000 irrigated hectares to the 8,000 hectares being cultivated. The contract was approved and work on the plan began in December 1966.[26] In large part the project involved taking water from the 34 most productive artesian springs and distributing it over 16,000 hectares through 1,500 kilometers of concrete canals. Some 4,000 hectares were on higher ground, so three pumping stations were needed to supply them. Essential to the plan was discharging the used irrigation water, so that it would not contaminate the water table. Three areas outside Al Hasa were designated as evaporation lakes for the discharged water. The irrigation system was completed in 1972 with little trouble.

The Al Hasa Irrigation and Drainage Authority (HIDA) was set up to be responsible for providing the water for irrigation. HIDA also advises farmers on new crops and gives instruction in the use of fertilizers, insecticides, and in new growing methods.

In addition to HIDA, farmers at Al Hasa get a great deal of financial and technical assistance from both the Agriculture and Water Ministry and the Agricultural Bank. Through these agencies farmers can buy equipment on credit and, provided they keep up with their payments for the first 2 years, are only required to pay 35 percent of their costs. In addition a farmer new to the area can request up to 50 hectares, get credit to farm it, and if cultivation succeeds within three years take legal possession.[27]

While in general the project has been successful on the production side, a number of problems have developed. A major difficulty surrounds the patterns of land ownership and water usage. Before the government's irrigation scheme, well owners and farmers with water rights paid for the labor by making their water available. Islamic laws mandate that estates are divided up between the surviving sons, and that has meant that the size of farms has steadily diminished. Water rights have also been extremely complex.

Many areas remain uncultivated simply because no one has been able to prove ownership. To make the irrigation scheme's water freer to every farmer, compensation had to be paid to well owners, but again conflicting land ownership claims have held up the expansion of irrigation.

In 1981 water use is still far from optimum because:

1. The layout of fields and crops has not been modernized; dates, vegetables, alfalfa, and rice are grown in small plots at different locations in the oasis, thus requiring far more water than would be the case if cultivation were in large blocks.

2. Most of the farmers are still new to optimum water application. So far the existing extension services have paid little or no attention to advising farmers on improved water use.

3. A large number of wells and springs are privately owned. Therefore, the project authority does not have complete control of the use of irrigation water.[28]

The Al Hasa experience illustrates the potential of the country to further develop its agricultural sector, and the difficulties that are likely to be encountered in doing so.

A further difficulty has been created by the fact that the local population will not accept newcomers. Depopulation is a further problem. Few young Saudis want to become farmers or to carry on the family tradition of farming. The lure of the urban areas with their promise of a good income, even as a taxi driver, is more enticing than farm work. In 1966, 2,500 Saudis worked as laborers on the irrigation scheme. Today, not a single Saudi works as a laborer for HIDA.

The problem lies not so much in Saudi reluctance to work—they are extremely industrious farmers on their own land. The wages that HIDA can offer, however, are simply too low to attract Saudi labor. As a result most of HIDA's workers are Yemenis and Palestinians.

Lack of interest on the part of Saudis for agriculture was demonstrated when the Eastern Province's King Faisal University opened an agricultural and veterinary faculty in Hofuf in 1975. Nearly two-thirds of its 200 students come from neighboring gulf states. Only one-third are Saudi.

In addition to the need to increase its attractiveness to Saudi farmers, Al Hasa's long-term future depends on overcoming a number of ecological problems. A team of 250 people is working on sand stabilization. The government has planted about 5 million assorted trees—tamariks, acacia, oleander, and eucalyptus. The latest idea is to plant trees that can be used commercially (such as for match wood). While the stabilization program may halt the desert from advancing further, there is no sure way of predicting the effects of prolonged irrigation.

Strategy for Further Development. As noted the first objective for agricultural development mentioned in the Second Development Plan was to improve living conditions of the agricultural population by increasing their incomes through: (1) the application of economic efficiency criterion for the allocation of scarce water resources between various categories of use; and (2) the development of strategies of self-sufficiency in important food and fiber commodities.

Since the scope for agricultural development in the Coastal and Al Hasa oasis is determined by the availability of irrigation water, optimum use should be made of these water resources.[29] This calls for cropping patterns yielding maximum net production values per unit of irrigation water, as far as technical conditions allow.

Crops that can be grown in the Al Hasa oasis can be compared (see table 9-2) in terms of their potential yield figures (GPU) and net production values (NPU). Vegetables appear to generate by far the highest NPU per unit of water; that is, SR $0.55/m^3$.

Farmers, however, plant crops based on their private (micro) profitability, and this does not necessarily result in the same ranking as with the GPU or NPU macro measures. In general farmers will base their priorities on the net production value per unit of labor. Vegetables rank highest by both the macro and micro criteria. When using the labor ranking, however, other perennial fodders replace cotton and sugar beets as the next most attractive crops. Whereas alfalfa is lowest ranked by the water criteria, sugar beets followed by cotton are the lowest ranked by the labor criterion.

The combination of objectives as mentioned earlier should determine the government strategy for agricultural development in the Eastern Region. Water is the scarcest resource. Therefore, agriculture development should be pursued along the line of water-use optimization. This need not conflict with cropping patterns based on private profitability or the goals of raising the income of the farming population and achieving self-sufficiency in important food and fiber commodities. Optimization of water use would, however, necessitate thorough changes of the cropping patterns in Al Hasa; that is, area in alfalfa would have to be reduced, and the cultivation of vegetables and fodder increased.

To obtain optimization of water use, farmers may need substantial financial support. Construction of drainage provisions and land reclamation are investments which the average farmer cannot make. This situation may provide the government with an important tool to regulate farmers' incomes; that is, the authorities can decide to lease the farmer the entire NPU generated per cubic meter of water, but it can also charge him for the costs of the irrigation and drainage system, land reclamation, and so on, by imposing water duties. It seems, however, not advisable to impose such duties in view of the still-limited NPU labor day and the wish to provide the workers in agriculture with incomes comparable to those in other sectors.

Subsidies will, therefore, have to be given to channel production into the most efficient areas. The Al Hasa experience indicates that despite the difficult problems which hinder the country's agricultural development, there are in principle a number of ways these problems can be overcome. Success in this

Table 9–2
Al Hasa: Potential Gross and Net Values of Irrigated Crop Production

Crop	Yields (Tons/Ha)	Ofo-farm Price (SR/Ton)	GPV (SR/Ha)	Nonfactory Costs (SR/Ha)	NPV (SR/Ha)
Alfalfa	100.0	35	3,500	850	2,650
Other perennial fodders	140.0	25	3,500	800	2,700
Animal fodder crops	90.0	30	2,700	700	2,000
Vegetables	22.0	400	8,800	2,200	6,600
Cotton	3.0	1,000	3,300	900	2,100
Sugar Beets	45.0	45	2,400	1,250	1,150

Crop	Gross Water Requirements (m^3/Ha)	Labor Requirements (Days/Ha)	NPV/Vats of Water (SR/m^3)	NPV per Labor Day (SR/Day)
Alfalfa	35,000	85	0.08	31.20
Other perennial fodders	27,500	75	0.10	36.00
Animal fodder crops	20,000	70	0.10	28.60
Vegetables	12,000	145	0.55	45.50
Cotton	18,000	100	0.12	21.00
Sugar Beets	10,000	100	0.12	11.50

Source: Central Planning Organization, *Socio-Economic Development Plan for the Eastern Region of Saudi Arabia, vol. II, Main Report* (1974), p. 110.

Note: NPV = net present value; GPV = gross present value; ha = hectare area will depend to a great extent on the innovative activities of the government sector and on the availability of technological assistance from international organizations and foreign firms. The role of the public sector is emphasized also because Saudi Arabian agriculture is characterized by small producers that cannot afford either the investment or the risk involved in such aspects of agricultural development as technological change.

Summary and Conclusions

Despite the many constraints confronting Saudi agricultural development, favorable opportunities for agricultural development exist. Oil revenues can provide the means to overcome directly or indirectly some of the major constraints. Since the government controls these resources, its policies will ultimately determine the direction the sector will take. To date, however, most of the government's resources have been used for expanding the industrial sector. Transferring a small (but larger than previously) part of government resources into agriculture, along the lines suggested, would contribute greatly to the transformation of Saudi agriculture into the type of modern agriculture that is needed to contribute to the economic development of the country.

The kingdom does not, nor should it have a set policy of trying to achieve self-sufficiency in foodstuffs. With at least half a century of continually rising revenues from oil ahead, Saudi Arabia cannot fear an inability to meet her import bills. Nevertheless, it cannot feel comfortable at its continued immense dependence on imports and, therefore, on the availability of agricultural produce in a world in which protectionism grows and politico-economic stability is declining.

Notes

1. Saudi Arabian Monetary Agency, *Annual Report 1399 (1979)* (Riyadh: SAMA, 1980), pp. 65–70.
2. See E. Barton Worthington, "Water, Science and Technology in the Middle East," in A.B. Zahlan, *Technology Transfer and Change in the Arab World* (New York: Pergamon Press, 1978), pp. 223–235.
3. Ibid.
4. Based on information in Richard Nyrop et al., *Area Handbook for Saudi Arabia*, 3rd ed., (Washington: Superintendent of Documents, 1977), ch. 13.
5. Thimothy Sisley, "Farming in the 1980s," *Saudi Business and Arab Economic Report* (Jan. 11, 1980): 30–31.

6. See Radha Sinha, "The World Food Problem: Consensus and Conflict," *World Development* (May–June 1977): 371–382.

7. Lyle Schertzad Byron Berntson, "The New Politics of Food," *World Development* (May–June 1977): 627–628.

8. Thomas Poleman, "World Food: Myth and Reality," *World Development* (May–June 1977): 384.

9. Marvin Weinbaum, "Political Risks in Agricultural Development and Food Policy in the Middle East," *Policy Studies Journal* (Spring 1980): 735–738.

10. See Central Department of Statistics, *Consumer Expenditure Survey in Five Cities of Saudi Arabia, 1397/1977* (Riyadh: Ministry of Finance and National Economy, 1979); and Central Department of Statistics, *Consumption Expenditure Survey in Rural Areas of Saudi Arabia, 1397/1977* (Riyadh: Ministry of Finance and National Economy, 1979).

11. For other empirical estimates see Nassar Saad, "Agricultural Demand, Supply and Prices with Special Reference to Arab Countries," *L'Egypte Contemporaine* (October 1976): 39–64. The results presented in the text are in conformity with those estimated by Asfour for the 1950s. See Edmond Asfour et al., *Saudi Arabia: Long-Term Projection of Supply and Demand for Agricultural Products* (Beirut: Economic Research Institute of American University, 1965).

12. An excellent account of Middle East problems is given in A.A. El-Sherbini, "Problems of Arid Agriculture in West Asia," *World Development* (May–June 1977): 441–446.

13. Frederico Vidal, "Development of the Eastern Province: A Case Study of Al Hasa Oasis," in Willard Beling, ed., *King Faisal and the Modernization of Saudi Arabia* (Boulder: Westview Press, 1980), pp. 90–91.

14. These figures are from Jamie Buchan, "Water Supplies," *Financial Times* (April 17, 1978), p. 21.

15. Ministry of Agriculture and Water, *A Guide to Agricultural Investment in Saudi Arabia* (Riyadh: MAW, 1979), pp. 9–10.

16. Ramon Knaverhase, "Social Factors and Labor Market Structure in Saudi Arabia," Yale Economic Growth Center, *Discussion Paper No. 247* (May 1976), p. 15.

17. See A.T. Mosher, *Creating a Progressive Rural Structure* (New York: Agricultural Development Council, 1969), for thoughts along these lines.

18. Elasticity being defined as the percent change in the capital labor ratio that would result from a 1 percent change in the ratio of interest-to-wage rate. See C.E. Ferguson, *The Neoclassical Theory of Production and Distribution* (London: Cambridge University Press, 1971), p. 41.

19. T.D. Liano, "The Relative Share of Labor in United States Agricul-

ture," *American Journal of Agricultural Economics* (August 1971).

20. Yujiro Hayami and Vernon Ruttan, *Agricultural Development: An International Perspective* (Baltimore: Johns Hopkins Press, 1971), p. 101.

21. Ibid.

22. These delineations are usually made by the government in planning for the region. See Central Planning Organization, *Socio-Economic Development Plan for the Eastern Region of Saudi Arabia (1975/76–1979/80)* (Riyadh: Ilaco Consultants, 1975).

23. Population figures are from the 1974 census.

24. *Socio-Economic Development Plan,* Agricultural Appendix.

25. Scott Pendleton, "Developing Qatif," *Saudi Business and Arab Economic Report* (October 17, 1980), pp. 22–25.

26. A fascinating account of the origin and development of the project is given in H. Dequin, *The Challenge of Saudi Arabia* (Singapore: Eurasia Press, 1976), especially ch. 2.

27. David Shirreff, "Reclamation Scheme Flourishes at Al-Hassa Oasis," *Middle East Economic Digest* (January 26, 1979): 7.

28. Ibid.

29. James Buchanan, "Farming in the Eastern Province," *Saudi Business and Arab Economic Report* (November 23, 1979): 34–38.

10 Industrial Development and Policies— the Private Sector

In almost every country, industry is the glamour sector of economic development. People look to industrial development to provide much-needed employment, generate higher individual and national incomes, relieve balance-of-payments constraints through import substitution, open up markets for primary products such as those from the mining and fishing sectors, give the country greater economic independence, generate new tax revenues, and furnish an important source of national pride.[1] By and large, these hoped-for benefits of industrialization are sensible and realistic—provided a country makes sensible choices.

The problem facing Saudi Arabia is well known. The kingdom has to invest its current oil revenues to develop a viable economic structure for the day when its oil will have been depleted. Industrialization is one apparently attractive strategy open to the government—but this is an option which needs careful analysis.

First, industrialization does not inevitably lead to sustainable, long-term growth. Based on the Iranian case, this appears to be particularly the case if the process is largely initiated by expatriate companies and individuals with no permanent commitment to the welfare of the country. Industry is of no use if it forms a symbolically modern sector of the economy without developing ever expanding linkages with the indigenous economy and culture.

Second, development economists often price industrialization for its employment-generating effects. Yet this should not be a high priority for the country, given its small population. In the long run, nonoil related jobs will obviously be needed. In the short run though, there may be no point in creating jobs that can only be filled by foreigners.[2]

Given such doubts, is it possible to identify an industrial strategy that is particularly suited to the special circumstances of the country? And how does the existing industrial strategy measure up to this ideal?

Industrial Strategy

Industrialization in the kingdom is carried out by both the public and private sectors. Because the country adheres to the concept of a free economy, the government has intervened in the industrial development of the country only when it has felt it to be essential for the welfare of the people. The

163

government has been continuously encouraging the private sector to under-take industrial and other investments as a means of diversifying the economy. When the size of the investment has been large and beyond the capacity of the private individuals, however, the government itself has undertaken the capital investment. A number of organizations have been established by the government to develop the basic industries in the kingdom.[3]

The Saudi Arabian government's approach to industrialization seems to have been guided by five major objectives:[4]

1. To assure the availability of essential consumer goods, free of the disruptions caused by international events.
2. To lay the basis for a greatly broadened pattern of industrialization by starting the domestic production of iron and steel.
3. To assure the availability of construction materials.
4. To demonstrate to private investors the feasibility of certain industrial and mining projects by making initial investments in industries not previously carried on in the country.
5. To assist private investment by giving suggestions, technical assistance, and credit or credit guarantees.

The primary objective for industrialization is certainly the eventual establishment of an industrial production base that will reduce the country's heavy dependence on oil as the main source of income.

Diversification is aimed at developing those industries that will maintain their economic viability over the long term and includes the development of hydrocarbon-based industries and those contributing to national security and social prosperity. To attain this goal, the government wishes to establish a complex of export-oriented heavy industries in collaboration with foreign and domestic enterprise based on hydrocarbons and minerals, with a view to exploiting the country's potential comparative advantage in this field. On the other hand, it wishes to provide incentives and external economies to the private sector to establish a number of industries supplying the basic consumer and development needs of the economy, thus reducing the country's dependence on imports.[5]

These basic considerations underly most of the government's specific industrial objectives, which include:[6]

1. Increasing the economy's capacity to produce at competitive costs as wide a range of products as possible for domestic as well as for export markets.
2. The industrial exploitation of the substantial comparative advantages arising from low-cost energy, raw materials from hydrocarbon-related industry, minerals, agricultural, and fishery resources.

3. Widening and deepening the kingdom's access to modern technology.
4. Achieving fuller capacity utilization in the private manufacturing sector.
5. Developing a regionally balanced industrial sector.
6. Increasing productivity through closer approach to optimal size of plants.
7. Reducing dependency on expatriate workers by national skill creation, through the development of general and technical education and on-the-job training of national workers.
8. Promoting interlinkage among industries.

The main principles of the government's industrial policy include:[7]

1. The encouragement of manufacturing industries, including agricultural industries that can effectively contribute to increasing the national income, raising the standard of liviing and of employment, and diversifying the economy. To diversify the economy, the government will work toward the adoption of plans that in addition to increasing the national income, will reduce the effect of outside economic disturbances and diversify the opportunities open to Saudi workers.

2. The principle that the economy of the kingdom is based on competition between the private commercial and industrial enterprises. In practice this implies that the government realizes that the objectives of industrial development may be more effectively attained if the business community bears (in the long run) the responsibility of implementing industrial projects.

3. The assurance that businessmen who are prepared to take the risks of success and failure motivated by prospects of profits will enjoy the full support of the government during all stages of preparation, establishment, and operation of industrial projects (which are beneficial to the kingdom).

4. The philosophy that competition serving the interests of local consumers is the best means of influencing the business community in the industrial field.

5. The belief that the imposition of quantitative restrictions or of control on prices as a means for implementing the industrial policy will be avoided if at all possible; that is, the government does not intend to impose restrictions except in the cases in which competition cannot have an effective role (as in the case of commodities, which by their nature are characterized by monopoly).

6. The right of the business community in the industrial field to select, use, and manage the economic resources, including industrial workers, insofar as this does not conflict with statutes in force.

7. The attraction of foreign capital as well as foreign expertise, and foreign participation in the industrial development projects in cooperation with Saudi businessmen.

8. Assurances to foreign capital that there will be no restrictions on the entry and exit of money to and from the kingdom, and that the government

shall continue its policy based on the respect of private ownership based on Islamic law.

9. The provision that in addition the government will attempt to promote the growth of all economic sectors to make available for the producers suitable local resources in sufficient quantities. It will also aim to increase purchasing power to consumers within the framework of an ever-growing national economy.

Early Attempts at Industrialization

In view of the country's almost total lack of modern infrastructure in the early 1950s, the government's first programs were devoted, in the main, to updating and expanding existing facilities, with little emphasis on new industrial investments. This period saw the rapid expansion of new road and rail networks, construction of desalination plants for drinking and industrial use, and the setting up of the foundations for a modern communications system.[8]

In 1954 Saudi Arabia made an unsuccessful effort to incorporate the oil industry into its economy through an agreement with Aristotle Onassis, whereby all Saudi Arabian oil that was not transported by tankers directly owned by the concession companies would be transported by a joint government–Onassis tanker line. The concession companies protested this action, since most of their oil was transported by chartered ships. Eventually in 1958, the shipping agreement was declared a violation of the 1933 concession agreement by a three-member arbitration board.[9]

Based on this experience, the government felt that little progress could be made in utiliziing the oil sector as an instrument through which it could diversify the economy. As an alternative the government established its own national oil company, Petromin, in 1962 to try to attain these goals on its own.

Petromin

The General Petroleum and Minerals Organization—Petromin—was established by the government largely to develop industries based on petroleum, natural gas, and minerals. Besides prospecting, exploration, and drilling, Petromin has undertaken a number of activities in the field of oil, such as oil production, refining, transportation, distribution, and marketing. Petromin has initiated a number of studies to establish various hydrocarbon-based industries, and since its inception has been active in many sectors of the economy.

In general Petromin has been active in three main areas:

1. Development of local industry through exploration, production, purchase, sale, transportation, distribution, and marketing of petroleum and minerals.
2. Ventures with other companies and/or participation in their capital so as to enter in all areas of industry as stated in the preceding item of this list.
3. Additional power to import any oil products or minerals as needed by Saudi Arabia.

During most of the 1960s and into the 1970s, there was a surplus of oil in the world market. Lacking foreign markets or a substantial crude supply, the company concentrated on the development of the local market.[10]

Development by the Early 1970s

Despite these initial efforts, little progress had been made toward building up an industrial base by the late 1960s. This is evidenced by the results of several surveys beginning with the 1962 Industrial Census.[11] Unfortunately, these early surveys and census are not strictly comparable because of differences in comprehensiveness. Nevertheless, a fairly consistent picture emerges.

By the early 1970s, industry was still dominated by firms in services, trade, and commerce. In general industry was characterized by the small number of employees per establishment, the lead that construction had in large establishments, and the high percentage of manufacturing establishments employing only one to four persons (about 90 percent).

Of particular significance was the apparent relative increase between 1967 and 1971 in the number of establishments employing one to four persons, and the drop in the number of establishments employing 100 and over during the same period. While the industrial surveys for these years may have been incomplete in their coverage, there was in any case no clear evidence that larger establishments were becoming more predominant. In fact, the average number of workers per establishment actually dropped from 3.09 for 1967 to 2.4 for 1971. (However this drop is probably the result of the much wider coverage of cities and establishments in the 1971 census that undoubtedly resulted in biasing results in favor of establishments with small employment.)

Several other features are of interest. First, the average capita-to-output ratio (based on the 1969 census) was about 1:1. Second, wages represented 20 percent of total product, while raw materials represented 36 percent. Third, food and beverages, and cement and nonferrous metal products accounted for 50 percent of total product. Together with transport equipment and wood and furniture, these branches accounted for just a little less than 75 percent of total manufacturing product. In terms of employment, these branches employed 73 percent of the country's industrial workers. However, cement and nonferrous metal products had by far the largest size per average establishment in terms of capital invested, value of raw materials, wages, value added, and total product. Only in terms of workers per establishment does cement and nonferrous metal products fall behind the three other branches.

Both the 1967 and 1971 census, therefore, paint a consistent picture of a very primitive industrial structure. In addition, several commentators on the period have noted that industry was still beset by a number of difficulties including: (1) a shortage of national industrial entrepreneurialship, as well as managerial, technical, supervisory, and skilled manpower, and (2) certain cultural influences pertaining to attitudes toward work, work intensity, incentives, and the like, tended to depress productivity, especially at the lower skill levels.

In 1970 a survey of 294 manufacturing establishments from the largest, such as ARAMCO's refinery, to most of those hiring only ten people provided the first glimpse at the structure of large scale industry.

Because the large ARAMCO refinery was included, the Eastern Province had nearly 70 percent of the capital, but employed only 34 percent of the work force. The Western Region employed nearly 24 percent of the capital and 45 percent of the work force. The Central Region employed 7 percent of the capital and 20 percent of the workers. Other areas had almost no large industry even when the category required only ten workers in a plant to qualify.

The 1970 survey found that most of the plants operated substantially below capacity. Underutilization averaged 64 percent for the plants surveyed. The reason the plants failed to operate near full capacity was not given, but presumably included shortages of skilled manpower and materials, competition from imports, and limited domestic markets. The underutilization of capacity continued into the mid-1970s for some of the important industries.

The 1971 industrial survey shows a similar pattern for that year:[12]

1. About 66 percent of all firms were engaged in commerce. Manufacturing was a poor second at 16 percent, followed by services at 4 percent.
2. While the largest number of manufacturing establishments were located in the Western Province, 32 percent of all persons employed in these firms were unpaid family workers. This percentage rose to 45 percent for firms engaged in commerce. Also for that year, one-person establishments, and those with less than ten workers represented 98 percent of all establishments in the kingdom. In contrast, firms in the oil sector, while few in number, employed more than fifty persons each.

In 1972 a survey showed a similar pattern in that:

1. About 65 percent of all firms operated in food and textile activities. These firms were found to be small family undertakings.
2. Less than 0.5 percent of these firms employed more than fifty persons.
3. The relative contribution to the GDP of large and small firms was inverse to their sizes.

The picture of Saudi manufacturing in the early 1970s is, therefore, one dominated by small firms. In 1971 nearly 95 percent employed fewer than five persons. These firms were essentially handicraft shops and accounted for nearly one-half of the employment in all of the manufacturing sector. Presumably most of these firms were smiths (working with gold, silver, brass, and iron), carpenters (making carved screens, panels, and doors), and handloom weavers (weaving products like the famous wool cloaks from Hufuf). Food processing was the final area of activity.

A second group of small-scale manufacturing establishments, which numbered 746, employed between five and nine workers. These shops probably had a little more but still simple equipment. The range of activities probably included bookbinding and perhaps some printing, producing bricks and other building materials, repairing by small machine shops, food processing, and wood and metal forming.

More than one-half of the small-scale industry was located in the Kejaz and northern Asir. A little over one-quarter of the manufacturing was in the central area, reflecting the growing urbanization around Riyadh and some of the oases of the Najd. The Eastern Province contained less than one-fifth of the establishments, and the Northern and Southern Regions, the remainder.

In general, by 1971 the major difficulties in industry were as they had been a decade earlier:

1. Insufficient clarity in industrial policy and insufficiency of legislation concerning incentives, commercial codes and contractual relations.
2. Slowness in government departments and the proliferation of agencies dealing with industrial establishments.
3. Costliness of labor and the need to rely on expatriates whose visas and residence permits took an inordinately long time to obtain.
4. Costliness of imported raw materials and irregularity in their flow.
5. The large volume of capital investment required generally, owing to the inability of most establishments to enjoy large-scale protection, which is in turn at least partially due to the preference for imported goods in the market.
6. The inadequacy of certain public facilities such as electricity, roads and means of communication, and studies by the competent government agencies.

Recent Initiatives

Since the early 1970s, the basic structure of industry has changed dramatically and is beginning to take on a more modern form. This process has been brought about by three major factors:

1. The use of formal economic planning for the development of both the public and private sectors, beginning with the First Five-Year Plan (1970–1975).
2. The decrees, regulations, and incentives that the government uses to solicit the participation of the Saudi and foreign private entrepreneur.
3. The tremendous economic power that the government derives from its increased oil revenues.

Before the First Plan was crystallized, certain priorities were assigned to the role of industry in the country's development. These involved:

1. The conscious decision that, wherever possible, private investment should be encouraged, and furthermore, supported by the supply of certain essential services by the government.
2. An impetus to move government-sector investment into a number of basic heavy industries.
3. The creation of industrial estates to facilitate industrialization and at the same time try to minimize heavy concentrations of industry and population, thus avoiding an overload on existing urban locations.

The sharp increase in oil revenues in the mid-1970s had removed the financial constraint on industrial development. Money was available to finance any project thought desirable. The Second Development Plan (1975–1980) was prepared in this setting. Planned industrial investments amounted to the equivalent of nearly $15 billion over the plan period (excluding projects in electricity and transportation). It was anticipated that private investment would also add sufficiently to industrial investment.

Incentives for the Private Sector

Because of some hesitancy on the part of Saudi entrepreneurs to invest in manufacturing, the government has increasingly been involved in the economy through enacting a series of incentives designed to increase the profitability of this type of investment and/or reduce the uncertainty of that investment.[13]

Tariffs Exchange Rates and Excise Taxes

The government is committed to the preservation of free trade, to a fixed exchange rate, and to no restriction on exchange and remittance of net earnings. In August 1974 tariffs were reduced significantly as a measure to control the cost of living. Foods, medicine, raw materials, and machinery are tariff free, but again, the tariff could reach 20 percent if it were to protect domestic industry.

Subsidies in Cash

In 1974 the government abolished taxes on fuels leading to a substantial cost reduction for business users. In addition to what might be the lowest fuel cost in the world, the government has reduced the electricity rate to SR 0.05 per kilowatt hour for industrial uses. The electric generating firms are, however, privately owned. To guarantee a fair rate of return to them, a subsidy program was initiated in 1974. The problem arose largely because the power stations are small and costs are high. Costs could be reduced by enlarging capacity, but demand is not sufficient. Guaranteeing a fair return to enlarged power stations in this case led to the company's claims for some sort of subsidy.

In recognition of the effect of the rising cost of construction on the willingness and ability of private investors to undertake new projects or expand existing ones, the government took it upon itself to subsidize building materials. As of 1980 cement was the only subsidized material, but producers in several other areas had requested subsidies.

To enlarge expansion of farm output and improvement of farm productivity, the government administers one of the country's oldest subsidy programs. Subsidies cover a substantial portion of the cost of fertilizers and farm machinery.

The government discriminates in favor of Saudi producers of government supplies by accepting their bids, even though their prices may be up to 10 percent higher than the similar imported supplies.

In 1973, the government began subsidizing the importation of basic food items such as wheat, flour, sugar, and rice in an effort to reduce the cost of living. Appropriations in the first year of the program totaled SR 300 million. During 1974–1975, more commodities such as milk, milk products, and vegetables were added to the list of subsidized food items. The budget appropriations have increased accordingly to SR 800 million. In addition to cement and fertilizers, those subsidized products provide the only examples of price control in Saudi Arabia.

Financial Assistance

The Saudi Industrial Development Fund was established in 1974 to finance new industrial ventures on concessionary terms. Medium to long-term loans (average 7 years) are granted to companies. The fund's program to date had taken on a specific orientation:

1. Loans are made to companies able to demonstrate a likelihood of their products being financially and economically viable and fitting the government's development criteria.
2. Capital and energy intensive projects are encouraged; labor-intensive projects are looked on with less favor.
3. Funds covering up to 50 percent of a project's capital requirements are lent at a cost of approximately 2 percent a year.
4. The government is reluctant to impose new tariffs although in special cases it does grant protection up to 20 percent.
5. Incentives and subsidies in the form of low interest rates, low utility rates, and low tax rates are the preferred methods of channeling funds, into the industrial sector.

During the period 1974–1975 to 1978–1979, the fund approved 506 industrial loans involving a total amount of SR 5,416 million. The loans disbursed during 1978–1979 amounted to SR 1,117 million, thus raising the total loan disbursements to SR 3,414 million.

To support the activities of SIDF, the Industrial Studies Development Center (ISDC) has undertaken a number of feasibility studies to identify projects likely to be attractive to the private sector.[14]

The criteria used to determine likely candidates for investment are based on ISDC's perception of the inclinations of Saudi entrepreneurs. ISDC's view of investor preferences is that:

1. Demonstration of existing demand plays a fundamental role of assuring investors of the absence of risk. Because Saudi businessmen are conservative by nature and tradition, it is logical that they would prefer import substitution-type industries.

2. In responding to the government's incentives, projects that display linkages on both the supply and demand side would be favored by the private sector.

3. Saudi entrepreneurs are profit maximizers. It is thus assumed by ISDC that throughout the massive program of government assistance and expenditure, private investors will find that an expected yield of at least 20 percent rate of return on investment is sufficient inducement. This rate is assumed to be fair in comparison with returns on conventional alternative uses such as commerce.

A second important financial development has been the establishment of the Public Investment Fund (PIF). This organization was established in 1971 to meet the credit requirements of public corporations engaged in commercial or industrial activities, especially Petromin and SABIC. Cumulative loan disbursements by the fund between 1972–1973 and 1978–1979 reached SR 10,812 million, while domestic and foreign investments stood at SR 4,750 million and SR 973 million, respectively.

Industrial Estates

One of the most constructive facilities provided by government to the private sector to encourage industrial expansion has been the establishment of industrial estates, which besides allocating land plots at nominal rates are also equipped with utilities, workshops, transportation facilities, communications channels, banks, and other necessities. The Riyadh, Jeddah, and Dammam estates have witnessed considerable expansion. The area of the Riyadh estate has been expanded from 451,028 to 21,000,000 square meters; that of the Jeddah estate from 1,044,008 to 9,100,000 square meters; and that of the Dammam estate from 994,653 to 24,000,000 square meters. Work is in progress for setting up industry in Mecca, Qasim, Hafuf, Medinah, and Abha.

Subsidies in Kind

The ambitious government programs to develop the country's social and economic infrastructure are evident from the size of government expenditure. These programs lower business cost significantly.

The government has established industrial parks in major industrial.and trading zones of the country. These estates are planned to provide all basic infrastructures essential to business firms; that is, water, electricity, telephone, banking, post office, police, and fire protection services. Lots of these industrial parks are available to prospective users at a nominal rent.

Several institutions provide research, consulting, and training services to the business sector either free or at a nominal cost. ISDC vocational-training institutions and agricultural extension services are part of this effort.

Licensing

Licensing is obligatory for new or joint industrial projects. Saudi firms who expect to seek government protection and assistance must also be licensed. Government licensing assures prior to undertaking of feasibility studies that the projects will contribute to plan fulfillment.

Taxes

As noted in chapter 5, Saudi business firms pay a tax called *zakat* at a rate of 2.5 percent.[15] Except for that, there are no property, income, or sales taxes on Saudi firms. In view of the fact that most small businessmen do not keep accurate records and in view of the difficulty of auditing on the part of the tax authorities, most of these firms end up paying little or no tax. The light burden of this tax and the absence of other taxes makes business an attractive activity which seems to be in line with Moslem tradition.

Nonoil foreign businesses, however, pay income tax at a rate of 25 to 45 percent on net income. Oil companies are taxed at a higher rate of 55 percent on net-operating income. Joint ventures, with at least a 25 percent Saudi share, are granted a tax holiday for 5 years commencing from the production date. Qualifying joint ventures, according to the foreign investment law, enjoy all "other" advantages granted to Saudi firms.

It is apparent that taxes paid by the Saudis are a highly ineffective instrument for changing the pattern of resource allocation. It is perhaps for that reason that the government relies more heavily on negative taxes rather than subsidies in its effort to increase the nonoil GDP. As for foreign business firms, the tax breaks that they are entitled to are highly conducive for those firms with Saudi participation. Currently, there is an effort under way to reform taxation of foreign companies to accelerate their participation in development projects.

Other Incentives

In addition ARAMCO has perceived the need for support industries.[16] That company has identified opportunities and assisted prospective entrepreneurs in establishing enterprises in construction, mechanical and maintenance contracting, transport, offshore servicing, catering, and many other fields related primarily to the company's own needs.[17]

Finally, after 1973, the enormous investment in government revenues rapidly disseminated to the populace encouraged a boom in construction and consumer goods, and thus created a market sufficiently substantial to interest local merchants in establishing import-substitution industries.

Industrial Growth

Encouraged by the government which provided services, plots in industrial estates, cheap power, and inexpensive finance and benefitting from the appalling delays in landing goods in 1976–1977 because of port congestion, private Saudi firms responded with an unprecedented wave of activity. In the 1974–1977 period alone, over 600 new industrial plants were initiated and in the implementation stage (see table 10–1).

As a result of this growth, Saudi Arabia is now virtually self-sufficient in the principal building materials: production of cement, clay concrete and sand-lime bricks, tiles, aggregate, precast concrete and prefabrication systems, doors, windows, and a number of other items. The same applies to screws, steel, scaffolding and reinforcing mesh, fencing, insulation materials, air conditioning, and desert coolers. Because of their high ratio of volume and weight to value, many of these items were obvious choices for local production. More recently, emphasis has been placed on consumer goods. Foodstuffs (represented by modern dairies, bakeries, soft drink plants, date-packing, and meat-processing facilities), household goods (plastic bags, containers, detergents, insecticides, and other chemicals, furniture and furnishings), and household appliances (such as refrigerators) all contribute to lessen the dependence for importation items of consumption.

Conclusions

The future, although very bright for the private sector, will not take care of itself. Certain difficulties and numerous obstacles to change exist. The most serious difficulties center around the fact that:

Table 10–1
Industrial Licenses Implemented during 1974–1977

Activity	Number of Licenses	Capital[a] Paid Up	Authorized	Employment
Food and beverages	111	524.1	1,793.3	5,213
Textile, clothing, and leather products	11	46.7	132.8	1,144
Wood products	16	73.8	160.7	1,365
Paper products & printing	23	73.0	185.5	1,303
Chemical products, including petrochemicals, rubber & plastics	78	316.5	738.3	2,318
Construction materials, china ceramics, & glassware	262	2,509.3	5,685.1	16,634
Metal products	147	515.9	1,354.6	7,502
Other products	2	12.4	17.8	102
Total	650	4,071.7	10,068.1	35,581
National	(467)	(3,009.7)	(7,201.1)	(22,859)
Joint venture	(183)	(1,062.0)	(2,867.0)	(12,722)

[a] In millions of riyals.

1.   Reliable statistics on current output, investment, employment, and industrial capacity are not available. While there have been several census of manufactures, these census are out of date and the new ones are kept confidential.

2.   Governmental machinery operates weakly, with occasional good individuals presiding over a cumbersome and inexperienced administrative apparatus.

3.   Private businessmen have not yet learned to operate effectively with the government as government laws and incentives change rapidly.

4.   Few government people are familiar with the characteristics and problems of industry.

5.   Nearly all planning activity is centralized in Riyadh with a consequent limiting effect on the planners' perspectives. Overcentralization is not a fault of the planners' approach to their task; it simply reflects the historical policy of not allowing local government and private interest groups to become strong.

6.   And finally, the limited size of the market makes it difficult to foresee a long vigorous growth in import substitution projects, since many of the available sectors, particularly in building materials, are now in a supply-demand equilibrium. In foodstuffs, plastics, chemicals, and metal working, opportunities still undoubtedly exist. But (as seen in the following chapter) increasingly attention must be focused on export possibilities using feedstock from the large petrochemical plants planned for Yenbo and Jubail. The extent to which downstream export factories will be erected depends on the government's approach. By maintaining a cheap capital and energy supply, and by subsidizing the necessary raw materials, many possibilities will undoubtedly present themselves.

Notes

1. Ali M. Jaidah, "Downstream Operations and the Development of OPEC Member Countries," *Journal of Energy and Development* (Spring 1979): 305.

2. Points clearly articulated by Louis Terner. See his "Industrial Development Strategies in the Arab Gulf States," in May Ziwar-Daftari, ed., *Issues in Development: The Arab Gulf States* (London: MD Research Services Limited, 1980), p. 210.

3. Industrial Studies and Development Centre, *A Guide to Industrial Investment in Saudi Arabia,* 5th ed. (Riyadh: ISDC, 1977), p. 35.

4. Ibid.

5. See "Saudi Arabia Moves to Diversify Economy: Industrial Development Has Priority," *Arab Economist* (August 1977): 24–29.

6. Industrial Studies and Development Center, *Industrial Investment,* pp. 35–36.

7. Ibid.

8. Ramon Knaverhase, "Saudi Arabia's Economy at the Beginning of the 1970s," *The Middle East Journal* (Spring 1974): 126–127.

9. Fariborz Ghadar, *The Evolution of OPEC Strategy* (Lexington, Mass.: Lexington Books, D.C. Heath and Company, 1977), p. 108.

10. Ramon Knaverhase, *The Saudi Arabian Economy* (New York: Praeger Publishers, 1975), p. 144.

11. The results of the early census may be found in Central Department of Statistics, *Statistical Year Book,* various issues.

12. Ibid.

13. The following list of incentives is based largely on information contained in: Saudi Arabian Monetary Agency, *Annual Report,* various issues: Industrial Studies and Development Center, *Industrial Investment*; *Non-Oil Manufacturing in the Private Sector: Present Conditions and Projections for the Second Plan* (Riyadh: ISDC, 1974).

14. A.M. Sharshar, "Oil , Religion and Mercantilism: A Study of Saudi Arabia's Economic System," *Studies in Comparative International Development* (Fall 1977): 54.

15. Details are spelled out in: Zakat and Income Tax Department, *Regulations for Income Tax, Road Tax, and Zakat* (Riyadh, Ministry of Finance and National Economy, 1978).

16. Joseph Malone, "Building a Constituency: NonPetroleum Activities and Programs of the Arabian American Oil Company," paper presented at Center for Arab Gulf Studies, University of Exeter, State, *Economy and Power in Saudi Arabia* (Symposium, July 4–7, 1980), pp. 18–19.

17. Through ARAMCO's Local Industrial Development Department, see Emid Hill, "Saudi Labor and Industrialization Policy in Saudi Arabia," paper presented at Center for Arab Gulf States, University of Exeter, *State, Economy and Power in Saudi Arabia* (Symposium, July 4–7, 1980), p. 25.

11 The Government's Industrialization Program

While stressing the desirability of private sector involvement in the economy, Saudi Arabian officials do not have any clear ideological approach to industrialization. Instead the country's planners tacitly accept that industrialization is one way of diversifying away from oil. However, there is as yet no clear perception on their part as to precisely the type of industry that will best meet the kingdom's long-run development needs.

In fact, one of the most intriguing questions concerning the kingdom's development strategy centers around the country's plans for industrialization. A steel plant, fertilizer plants, domestic and export-oriented refineries, and four major ethylene-based petrochemical complexes (methanol plants) have been built (in the case of the domestic refineries and a fertilizer plant), are in the process of construction, or have reached the stage where it is virtually certain that they will be completed during the 1980s. What is the rationalization for this strategy and is all this too ambitious for a country with virtually no industrial experience?[1]

Comparative Advantage

The existence of underexploited gas reserves in the kingdom has been one of the strongest arguments for developing gas-based heavy industries. Gas—especially the dry gases (methane and ethane, for example)—is an expensive product to transport, thus making it sensible to look for more productive uses for its exploitation.

International trade theory is capable of rationalizing a gas-based industrialization strategy. For example, according to the Heckscher-Ohlin theory of international trade, a country tends to have lower comparative costs in the commodity that uses the largest amount of the relatively cheapest factor in its economy. These considerations provide the fundamental rationale for specialization.[2] In general, the theory indicates that Saudi Arabia should establish and promote industries based primarily on natural gas and/or oil, which are the industries that are most likely to be efficient and successful. Fortunately for the Saudis, these industries are not only energy intensive but also capital intensive. Thus, they tend to utilize its abundant financial surplus as well as gas and oil.

Once gas has been used optimally as oil substituted within the domestic economy, there is an excellent theoretical argument for developing gas intensive industries around it. These can either be chemical industries, which use the gas as a feedstock for conversion into higher value and more easily transportable chemical products, or they can be energy intensive industries such as steel or aluminum production, which can use the gas as a reasonably cheap source of energy.

Few observers would quibble with these general observations. The planners' task in identifying precisely those industries best suited for the kingdom has not been as easy as it might appear at first sight, however.

Because the country had virtually no heavy industry or industrial experience to speak of in the early 1970s, the Heckscher-Ohlin predicted pattern of trade had not been established and the price system had not developed to the point where it was capable of giving the planners the correct signals about the best areas of investment. In addition, a number of less-obvious considerations surrounding the introduction of heavy industry into the country have made it extremely difficult to design procedures capable of identifying the most effective methods of allocating the country's resources. Although financial capital may not be a constraint, especially in the short term, the kingdom has to face other constraints to industrial development. Physical bottlenecks, manpower shortages, and inflation have proved to be real impediments to the absorptive capacity of the economy. In particular the impact of these negative factors has often been most severe in the very developmental activities intrinsic to a successful diversification policy.

Government Investment in Industry

A number of potentially profitable projects have been identified by the government for its investment program. These are industries that conform to the Heckscher-Ohlin theory of trade by using relatively large amounts of the kingdom's relatively abundant factors of production, oil, natural gas, and capital. These industries appear attractive because not only do they mesh into the present structure of the economy, but also should logically fit the next phase of development by providing competitive exports with which to pay for future imports.

Because the capital costs of these industries are immense, the private sector is unable to undertake investment in them at this time. Instead, the Saudi Basic Industries Corporation (SABIC) was founded by the government to initiate development of the kingdom's heavy industries.

SABIC was incorporated in 1976 with an initial capital of SR 10 billion to establish these hydrocarbon-based industries. For these projects, the government has designated two industrial sites at Jubail on the Arabian Gulf and at Yenbo on the Red Sea. The program includes four petrochemical complexes at Jubail and one complex at Yenbo, each complex producing

500,000 tons of ethylene annually. Other planned projects are: four fertilizer plants (producing ammonia and urea), two methanol plants, an animal feed (petroproteins) plant, and a steel rolling mill at Jubail.[3] There are four ethylene complexes at Jubail that have been completed. Total investment in these four complexes, scheduled to start operations during 1980–1983, is estimated to be $4,600 million.

Studies are being prepared for the establishment of two fertilizer plants, each having an annual capacity of 330,000 tons of ammonia. Total cost of the two plants is estimated to be $600 million. The two methanol plants to be constructed by SABIC will have an annual capacity of 660,000 tons each and will cost a total of $500 million. The steel plant at Jubail is planned to have an initial annual capacity of 800,000 tons. Jubail will also be the location of a 200,000 tons per year plant at a total cost of $1,100 million. SABIC projects expected to be concluded in 1980 include:[4]

Petrochemical Projects

SABIC/Shell Project. This project is to be located at Jubail and will produce 656,000 metric tons of ethylene, 295,000 metric tons of styrene, 454,000 metric tons of ethylene dichloride, 281,000 metric tons of crude industrial ethanol, and 355,000 metric tons of caustic soda annually.

SABIC/Mobil Project. This project is to be set up at Yenbo and will produce 450,000 metric tons of ethylene glycol, and 91,000 metric tons of high-density polyethlene annually.

SABIC/Dow Project. The purpose of this project is to construct a petrochemical complex at Jubail in collaboration with Dow Chemical Company. It will produce 440,000 metric tons of ethylene, 200,000 metric tons of low-density ethylene, and 300,000 metric tons of ethylene glycol annually.

SABIC/Exxon Project. This project is to be set up at Jubail in collaboration with Exxon Corporation, and will produce 240,000 metric tons of low-density polyethylene annually.

SABIC/Japanese Consortium Project. The purpose of this project is to set up a methanol project at Jubail in association with a group of Japanese companies. It will produce 600,000 metric tons of chemical-grade methanol per annum.

SABIC/Celanese–Texas Eastern. This project is to be set up at Jubail in collaboration with two American companies, and will produce 700,000 metric tons of methanol annually.

Other Petrochemical Projects under Study. The SABIC/Mitsubishi project will have an annual production of 450,000 metric tons of ethylene equivalent.

Metallurgical Projects

SABIC/Korb Iron and Steel Project. This project will produce 800,000 metric tons of sponge iron, 850,000 metric tons each of steel billets, reinforced iron bars, and wire rods.

SABIC/Aluminum Smelting Project. The purpose of this project is to establish a joint-venture aluminum smelting plant having a capacity to produce 225,000 metric tons of aluminum ingots per annum, and other secondary products.

Fertilizer Projects

SABIC/Taiwan (TFC). An interim agreement was due to be signed between SABIC and Taiwan Fertilizer Company to study the feasibility of a joint-venture project to produce 500,000 metric tons of urea annually for export.

SABIC/Urea. SABIC is currently engaged in negotiations with other companies for the establishment of another urea project with an annual production capacity of 500,000 tons.

The basic responsibilities of SABIC are project preparation and evaluation along with the joint ventures, partnerships, financing, and successful implementation of these projects.

The Case for Petrochemicals

In addition to the availability of gas, several additional characteristics associated with petrochemicals have made investment in this industry especially attractive to the Saudi Arabian government.[5]

Capital Intensity

This industry enjoys one of the highest capital-to-labor ratios in the world. In fact, investment per new job created is estimated at $20,000 to $100,000.

Also, larger amounts of investment are required as the stage of production advances from basic products to intermediaries, to finished products, and finally to the consumer stage. In fact the investment required for the transformation of finished products into consumer or industrial products (third manufacturing phase) is two to three times higher than that necessary for the production of intermediate products (second manufacturing phase), and five times higher than that necessary for the production of basic products (first manufacturing phase).

Economies of Scale

Investments do not vary in proportion to the capacity, but rather according to a power factor generally lying between 0.6 and 0.85. This is the reason why it is advantageous to build large-capacity units that cost proportionately less than small- or medium-capacity units. Manpower as well as general and plant overhead also appear to have proportionately lower expenditures with larger plant size.

Given Saudi Arabia's abundant endowments of both the raw materials and capital needed to finance large-scale investments, petrochemicals seem to be an ideal sector around which the country could build its industrialization program.

Issues in Industrialization

Several general conclusions have emerged from Saudi Arabia's initial attempts at industrialization. The most important is that there is no industrial option open, even including petrochemicals, to the country that gives anywhere near the kind of returns provided by successful investments in the oil sector. This implies that while the country may be choosing to restrict production levels for the benefit of future generations, it is still not absolved from the responsibility of ensuring that oil is produced as efficiently as possible. That means ensuring that existing oil fields are exploited with the best techniques, with growing attention to enhanced recovery and to the exploration necessary to replace declining production in existing fields.

In countries like Saudi Arabia, prudence may dictate the building of pipelines designed to give greater commercial flexibility. With oil prices so far above oil production costs, the country's planners would be extremely unwise not to start by ensuring that they are getting the optimal returns from the oil sector before turning their attention to diversification strategies.[6]

Second, it appears that there is not a very strong case for investing in export-oriented refining capacity. The bulk transportation of crude oil will always remain cheaper than transporting oil products, so the best that the kingdom can do is to maximize the efficiency of its refineries. However, the comparatively greater cost of transporting oil products rather than crude is still very small in comparison to the final market price of oil. It is, therefore, perhaps at least possible to defend the decision to increase refining capacity.

Third, before utilizing gas in industry, Saudi planners should first ensure that they have used it as productively as possible in prolonging the life of oil fields (through gas injection) or in substitution for oil in the domestic economy (thus releasing high-value crude for export). The returns from exporting oil are so much more than exporting gas or its derivatives that there is an overwhelming logic in substituting gas for oil in such areas as electricity-generating, powering oil refineries, and desalination.

Fourth, simple generalizations about the comparative economics of petrochemicals are difficult to make because a project that may make economic sense in a tight market may be unjustifiable if its products are in global oversupply. However, it appears that the creation of gas-based industries in the kingdom make sense if the relative cheapness of the country's gas can be used to overcome some comparative disadvantages which the country currently faces:

1. Construction costs are high in Saudi Arabia for the current generation of plants under consideration. Costs may be at least 25 percent more expensive than in the United States or Western Europe. The country simply does not yet have the industrial infrastructure permitting the most efficient construction practices (though this will change over the next decade or two).

2. The country is a long way from the richest world markets (North American, Japan, and West Europe). Its export-oriented industries will thus have to be particularly competitive if they are to break into these established markets. The alternative strategy is to aim for markets in Africa and Asia, where the kingdom may be closer as a supplier than the established competition in the advanced industrial countries. However, there are limits to how far the country can concentrate solely on third-world markets, which are by definition relatively poor and unsuitable for the more-sophisticated chemical products.[7]

Fifth, it must be emphasized that regional cooperation is essential, not only as a means for securing access to the wider regional market for the growing petrochemical industries, but also as a vehicle for coordination and harmonization with the other oil producer's plans for the development of petrochemicals and various energy and capital-intensive industries. This type of cooperation is particularly necessary to prevent duplication, waste, and harmful competition.[8]

Finally, a number of different factors have combined to form a bias against the conversion of oil revenues into productive industrial output and employment. It has been much easier to create direct government employment than industrial employment. To develop public sector jobs, it is only necessary to build a room and put a desk in it; to develop a job in the modern industrial sector involves importing machinery and finding a skilled work force. The easiest activity for the government to promote has been construction, and the authorities have been notably successful in this area. Most of the jobs in this sector, however, have gone to foreigners.

The underlying reasons accounting for so few Saudis employed in modern industries are, in addition to those mentioned earlier, numerous, complex, and interwoven. They include:

1. The great distances between regions and the poor communications connecting many parts of the kingdom.
2. Many government programs—loans and grants to small farmers with the objective of aiding their mechanization and modernization of farming are not spent on farming activity, but instead are considered additional income by recipients and spent on consumer goods—the result is to raise the opportunity cost of leaving the rural sector.[9]
3. The high value that rural men in Saudi Arabia place on leisure, reinforced by the utilization of women in activities not permissible in urban areas.
4. Various government payments for social welfare contribute significantly to rural incomes.
5. Supplemental incomes earned by many in agriculture from patronage, traditional obligations, loyalties, and rents from family properties and land.
6. The high financial and social costs of moving into cities: rents are high and properties are difficult to acquire.
7. Conditions in towns are relatively poor, meaning that average life in the cities for lower and middle-income Saudis is lower than in rural areas.
8. Women see their lives in the cities as more constrained.
9. The low level of educational attainment, work experience, and skill-level results in few jobs for migrants in their preferred job areas.
10. Even at the unskilled manual level at which Saudi nationals are reluctant to work, foreign labor that is most cost effective is easily available.

Given the virtually unlimited amount of financial resources, the existence of large amounts of low or underemployment in Saudi Arabia is somewhat surprising. It has been shown, however, that this condition is the direct result of a complex mix of economic and social factors. One additional factor is the phenomenon of socially induced voluntary underemployment because Saudi workers have a bias against types of work that they consider socially inferior.[10]

Labor theory suggests that the unwillingness to accept socially undesirable employment can be overcome by payment of a premium over the wages in the more desirable occupations. The market equilibrium wage would then be established by the simultaneous interaction between the strength of demand and the distribution of tastes. It appears, however, that in Saudi Arabia the social factors are so strong that, given the limited size of internal markets and the inefficiency of labor and capital in the modern industrializaed sector, the wage gap is not large enough to draw Saudi workers into the formal sector. The extended family, subsidized loans, and the existence of the informal sector enabling occasional work to supplement other incomes allow Saudi workers to set a high reservation wage.[11]

There should be a positive compensating wage differential large enough to overcome the Saudis' reluctance to accept socially inferior jobs. It appears, however, that in Saudi Arabia, because the income incentive is so weak, even excessively high wages are not sufficient to elicit Saudi workers into the industrial labor force.

As a result of this interaction of economic and social factors, numerous Saudi workers have not gained appreciably from economic development. In most cases their move from country to city involves a horizontal move from one low-productivity job to another equally low-producitivity job. Under-employment continues to exist because the planners have failed to provide the right types of employment opportunities given the existing cultural environment. Again, in time this problem may be overcome. It is hard to predict at this point, however, whether Saudis will be more inclined to join the industrial work force. The outcome may depend on how successful technology transfer to the kingdom is during the next decade.

Transfer of Technology

Within the framework of Saudi Arabia's industrial strategy, attention is being closely paid to the selection of new technology and the means of innovating the existing technology. The concept of technology transfer used here is expanded to apply to the transfer of technological knowhow internally between various industries and scientific research and development organizations, and also internationally from similar institutions in other countries.

True industrialization is achieved not only through production, but also through the development of national design and application capability so that an increasing number of products can be conceptualized and realized in Saudi Arabia. There are presently many areas where such capability has already been developed; progress is being made with acquired maturity.

It may be opportune to point out that the course of the transfer of technology has never been a smooth one. Among the major obstacles that the Saudis have had to overcome in their attempt to absorb new technology are

1. Lack of industrial infrastructure and an industrial tradition.
2. Lack of skilled manpower, particularly on operational levels (for example, skilled workers and technicians).
3. The reluctance of many foreign companies to cooperate sincerely in the transfer of technology.

In the past decade the Saudis have begun to adopt a cohesive effort to tackle the issue of technology transfer. The most important measures which have been taken are the following:[12]

1. Inroducing advanced technical subjects in vocational schools and universities.
2. Establishing contact with technical and scientific organizations of international repute.
3. Sending many students and researchers to institutions of higher education abroad in the various branches of science and technology.

It is recognized that sustained growth of the technological base is almost directly correlated to the quantity and quality of research and development work being carried out. Therefore, the Saudi Arabian government has been investing heavily in its institutions of higher learning, and at the same time establishing the real data base that indigenous research requires.

The government is currently offering incentives and developing programs to encourage research and development by the private sector. In the past year, 0.36 percent of GNP was given to research; 10 percent of this figure as taken up by research in universities, and the rest by industrial research.[13] This figure by itself is not impressive, but that it exists in a measurable quantity is a cause for some satisfaction.

Conclusions

It is still too early to say with much certainty what success the kingdom will have in its industrialization effort. The country is still going through an experimental period in which it is finding out exactly what future its oil and gas sector has and which kinds of industrial diversification make the most sense for its society. One lesson that will probably emerge is that it is pointless to push ahead too fast with such a diversification.[14] It takes time to build up an industrial culture, and there may be no point in developing industries that have to be run by more expatriates than the indigenous society can tolerate. At the same time, we really do not know if the Saudi workers will choose to dedicate themselves to mastering manufacturing skills. It may well be that they will prefer to continue settling for desk jobs, in which case the kingdom's strategy should continue to be to develop a limited range of capital intensive hydrocarbon-processing industries, firmly leaving the labor-intensive operations for other countries.

Based on its factor endowments, the private sector in conjunction with government guidance has been wise in selecting techniques of production that make maximum use of available energy and/or capital resources. Government investment in petrochemicals, cement, and steel are examples of energy and capital intensive industries. In other industries catering primarily to the local markets, such as the building materials industry, capital-intensive techniques of production must be chosen to combat acute labor shortages prevalent in most of these countries. Unlike labor surplus economies unable to draw extensively on existing modern foreign technology because it is labor saving, Western technology is particularly suited to the factor endowment of the kingdom. The employment of capital-intensive and sophisticated techniques of production requires, however, skilled and scientifically trained manpower. Thus the upgrading of human resources will become a critical factor in expanding the capital-absorptive capacity of the economy.

Few other countries would consider or could afford to consider the industrial program taking place in Saudi Arabia. There is a genuine concern for the educational, social, and ethical development of the Saudi citizen, from a current low base. Much has been accomplished in the last 10 years, but standards are still not high. Much more will be done in the coming decade. But without satisfying employment prospects, a contradiction between talents and expectations on the one hand and opportunities on the other must inevitably arise.

Notes

1. A question also asked by Louis Turner, "Industrial Development Strategies in the Arab Gulf States," in May Ziwar-Daftari, ed., *Issues in Development: The Arab Gulf States* (London: M.D. Research Services Limited, 1980, pp. 210–211, 213.

2. J.L. Ford, *The Ohlin-Heckscher Theory of the Basis and Effects of Commodity Trade* (New York: Acia Publishing House, 1965), ch. 1.

3. See Saudi Arabian Monetary Agency, *Annual Report*, various issues.

4. Ibid.

5. See Louis Turner and James M. Bedore, *Middle East Industrialization* (Farnborough: Saxon House, 1979), ch. 6, for an excellent elaboration of these and other related issues.

6. Turner, "Industrial Development Strategies," pp. 215–219.

7. Ibid.

8. Based on questions of economies of scale and efficiency of plant size;

see M.M. Metwally, "Market Limitation and Industrialization in Arab Countries," mimeographed, 1979.

9. J.S. Birks and C.A. Sinclair, "The Domestic Political Economy of Development in Saudi Arabia," in Centre for Arab Gulf Studies University of Exeter, *State, Economy and Power in Saudi Arabia* (Symposium, July 4–7, 1980), p. 7.

10. See Ramon Knaverhase, "Social Factors and Labor Market Structure in Saudi Arabia," Yale University Economic Growth Center, *Discussion Paper No. 247* (May 1976), for an elaboration of this thesis.

11. Ibid.

12. See Joseph Szyliowicz, "The Prospects for Scientific and Technological Development in Saudi Arabia," *International Journal of Middle East Studies* (August 1979): 355–372, for a discussion of these issues.

13. Ibid.

14. Turner, "Industrial Development Strategies," p. 219.

12 Considerations in Forecasting the Saudi Arabian Economy

Based on the events of the last decade, but in particular the escalation in oil revenues following the Tehran agreements in December 1973, the major revisions of the Saudi Arabian Second Five-Year Plan (1975–1980) in the summer of 1974, the oil price increases in 1979, and finally the country's experience during the 1974–1980 period in utilizing its greatly augmented revenues for domestic development, it is now apparent that much of the direction of the Saudi Arabian economy in the 1980s and 1990s will depend on the policies used to implement both the Third (1980–1985) and Fourth (1985–1990) Economic Development Plans.

This is particularly the case given that Saudi Arabia's economy is in 1981 at something of a watershed, having reached the completion stage of many of the massive construction and infrastructure projects begun in the mid-1970s.

Several economic-forecasting linear-programming optimization models are developed in the following chapters. These are used to make a number of projections of the main macroeconomic variables. The intent is to identify a feasible set of production opportunities that will be open to the economy in the 1980s and 1990s, and at the same time be consistent with the Saudi leaders preference for a reduced foreign work force and a low rate of inflation.

Econometric Models

Despite their limitations, econometric models are increasingly being used by planners in developing countries for two basic purposes: simulation and policy analysis.[1] Simulation can be performed simply by forecasting values of the exogenous variables over the desired horizons, introducing them into the model, and obtaining the values for the key macrovariables.[2] Yet simple forecasts are not the only uses of the models. Indeed, forecasts under alternative conditions with respect to the exogenous variables and policy instruments are invaluable. This is where the structural analysis of the economy that an econometric model involves makes it superior to other forecasting techniques. Aside from the alternative results, one can check other sensitivity of the key macrovariables to particular exogenous variables and/or policy instruments.

Treatment of Government Activity

While it is possible to construct economic models that abstract from the role of the government, just as it is possible to focus on the activities of a highly centralized, all-pervasive government, neither approach seems appropriate because of the nature of Saudi Arabia's capitalistic economic system and rapidly growing (and largely unregulated) private sector.

The general problem of economic policy, on the other hand, is to determine what government policy package will maximize its welfare function (long-run goals or objectives) subject to the constraints represented by the econometric model.[3]

The first major task in using the econometric technique to forecast an economy such as Saudi Arabia's is to determine the best manner in which to treat government activity.

Saudi Arabia's public sector, while very activist, still responds to various social, political, and military influences.[4] Incorporating these types of qualitative influences into a quantitative forecasting framework is always difficult, but the task is generally easier if it is possible to trace the effect of the variables through the system as an aid in evaluating their consistency.

In addition, adjustments for likely changes in government expenditure patterns can be based on economic theory, historical patterns of other countries at a similar stage of development, and from very recent information about conditions in the kingdom. Granted that an attempt should be made to apply informed judgment as to likely changes in the government's pattern of allocation, there still remains the general problem of depicting that expenditure pattern. The range of issues influencing government behavior must be restricted, but the choice of restrictions is difficult because on the surface, at least, so few constraints seem to be present and also capable of constricting the authorities in a particular direction. The only practical solution is in attempting to narrow the range of choice to that consistent with the government's most likely development strategy, and to consider only the important influences on government expenditures within that context.

Steps in Forecasting the Economy

With these points in mind, the steps in the analysis comprising the remainder of the study consist of:

1. Determining, through an examination of the discussion in chapter 6, the growth options open to the kingdom.
2. Selecting, given the general preferences of the Saudi authorities, the growth strategy that will be likely to characterize the country's pattern of economic development over the next two decades.

3. Identifying the manner in which oil revenues empirically effect the economy, as a necessary first step in constructing a realistic econometric model capable of assessing the feasibility of the economy staying on the forecasted growth path. This step entails quantifying the mechanisms largely responsible for Saudi Arabian growth.
4. Estimating the structural relationships hypothesized by the model.
5. Projecting on a preliminary basis the major macroeconomic variables for the 1980–1990 period, with an eye to extending these into the Fifth (1990–1995) and Sixth (1995–2000) Plan periods.
6. Drawing on the analysis in previous chapters to identify any possible side effects associated with this growth path.
7. Prioritizing the macroeconomic constraints [identified in (6)], given the kingdom's social, philosophical, and institutional system.
8. Analyzing in light of the Third Plan targets an optimal Third Plan growth path and its concomitant policy requirements.
9. Examining the implications of that analysis for an oil production strategy that is compatible with the kingdom's long-run interests, given its economic and social constraints.

The remainder of the chapter is concerned largely with the first two tasks.

Probable Development Strategy

The cornerstone of Saudi Arabia's strategy of development is now well established and is unlikely to fundamentally change between now and the end of the century. In essence the strategy consists of the timed channeling of resources earned by the petroleum sector into expanding the nonoil production base. This in turn involves anticipating several likely eventualities.

1. An expanding economy requires an increasing flow of resources to maintain its momentum. Given:

a. Estimates of known oil reserves;
b. The likely expansion of needs for domestic energy sources; and
c. The plans to supply the petrochemical industry and refineries with enough crude oil and gas to meet domestic and export requirements.

2. Because oil reserves are not infinite, the kingdom will have to prepare for the day when its hydrocarbons have been economically depleted. Saudi Arabia still has by far the largest reserves of crude petroleum in the world— more than six times that of the United States. While there are probably about 530,000 million barrels of oil remaining in the kingdom's fields, with current technology only about half of this is economically recoverable (that is,

possible reserves). The proved reserves are currently (1981) estimated at 163,350 million barrels. About 50 percent of this oil consists of light crude [340 API (American Petroleum Institute)]. In addition the kingdom's natural gas reserves, estimated at 93.23 trillion cubic feet, are very substantial by world standards. Yet even these vast amounts of hydrocarbons are finite. If the present rate of extraction of oil is maintained, the four main producing fields—Ghawar, Abquiq, Berri and Safaniyah—will start to decline in production in the late 1980s and early 1990s. Considerable new investment will then be required to develop new fields if the overall level of output is not to decline. On the assumption that this investment is made, production should be capable of being maintained until the middle of the next century. In 2050, therefore, the overall level of petroleum production will gradually begin falling off.[5] Long before then, the investment requirements needed to maintain production will have resulted in an end to the present pattern of relatively easy growth (probably at the end of this century).

3. The longer-term problem of economic diversification is intimately tied with the kingdom's strategy of economic development and the possibilities for developing an international comparative advantage in the production of certain commodities. Of the productive sectors—agriculture, industry and mines, and services—only certain industrial and mining activities (given the kingdom's high wage structure and distance from markets) offer even the slightest possibility of becoming significant earners of foreign exchange.

The possibilities for growth in agriculture and livestock, the most traditional sectors (as noted in chapter 9) are extremely limited not only because of the shortages of water and arable land, but perhaps more important because of an insufficient number of Saudis willing to pursue a career in farming. Economies of scale (as noted in chapters 10 and 11) also preclude the kingdom from undertaking an efficient, comprehensive import substitution program. Pending a major breakthrough in tehcnology, local production will continue to meet only a small proportion of domestic needs. In fact, if anything, the gap between domestic production and consumption will likely increase over time.

The kingdom will have had to adjust to an environment where growth will have become every more dependent on the mobilization of domestic resources and alternative (noncrude based) taxes. That is, the public sector will have to have diversified its revenue sources, and the private sector will have had to reach a level of sophistication capable of generating a larger proportion of its own investment funds. Simply put, the elimination of oil as an adequate and easy source of savings will necessitate improvements in productive efficiency and a more-rational allocation of domestic investment than is currently taking place.

4. Given the limited number of linkages in its productive structure, expansion of the kingdom's gross domestic product requires increased

imports to maintain the economy's growth momentum. Thus, by 2005–2010, the kingdom will have had to develop a number of new and viable export industries, capable of earning foreign exchange adequate to meet import needs. While this situation is generally true of all nonrenewable resource exporters, it is especially true for Saudi Arabia; its small domestic market, the limited nonpetroleum resource base, and shortages of Saudi workers preclude developing a number of industries capable of assuring the kingdom greater domestic self-sufficiency. This applies particularly to the establishment of a group of capital goods industries capable of enabling domestic entrepeneurs to channel their domestic savings into investment in plant and capacity irrespective of possible foreign-exchange shortages.[6]

Whether oil will enable the kingdom to cope with these eventualities will at least in the long run depend almost entirely on the government's expenditure strategy and the response of the private sector. As noted in chapter 7, there are several options open to the government, each of which would seem to have certain strong and weak points.

With regard to addressing the previously stated problems, the strategies consist of increased oil conservation, proportion of investment in foreign assets, foreign aid, government consumption, and domestic investment.

Increased Conservation

Today any country endowed with easily accessible energy resources, given the present state of technology, is generally assumed to be capable of maintaining an acceptable rate of growth. But a country such as Saudi Arabia, at an early stage of industrialization, does not currently need large quantities of energy. As noted in chapter 7, the logical strategy for the kingdom is undoubtedly one of conserving its energy resources for as long as possible. This would assure that they would still be available locally at low cost when its industrial sector had matured to the point where it required large quantities of energy to operate.

As of 1981 Saudi Arabia is not following this path. During recent years, its exports have varied between 8 and 10 million barrels a day. Given the relatively low-absorptive capacity of the economy, it is doubful that the kingdom's future domestic needs are best served by this level of production. This is particularly evident, given the relatively high rate of population growth and the anticipated level of future domestic demand. In fact producing at such a high rate today may mean considerable difficulties early next century in providing cheap energy for local industrial and agricultural needs. Thus the kingdom might be losing one of its best opportunities for development in the next century; that is, relatively inexpensive energy resources with which it could build up an efficient and competitive industrial sector capable of penetrating foreign markets and earning an alternative source of foreign exchange. Yet, it is clear this strategy is not followed because of pressure from the consuming countries.

Increased Proportion of Investment in Foreign Assets

As in the recent past, the major problems with this strategy would likely involve: (1) continued devaluation of the dollar and the subsequent erosion of value of Saudi Arabia's dollar-demanded foreign portfolio; (2) the limited amount of high-yield nondenominated assets in which to diversify; (3) restrictions on the type and amount of foreign assets that may be purchased, and (4) the ever-present possibility of confiscation of Saudi investments.[7]

Clearly, the ultimate decision here regarding the proportion of surplus funds allocated to the purchase of foreign assets must be made by somehow taking into account the magnitude of the surplus funds relative to domestic needs and on their opportunity cost, measured in terms of the consequences of eventually facing the problems outlined here.

Increased Foreign Assistance

The kingdom's surplus funds could be increasingly channeled into foreign assistance in the form of unilateral or multilateral aid and soft loans.[8] It is not easy for any country to develop a rationale for giving aid, and even more difficult to justify its increase over time—witness the more than 20 years of debate in the United States on the merits of its foreign aid programs.

Increased Government Consumption

While it is always desirable to increase the scope and magnitude of the government's services (health, education, transportation, and so on) a point is often reached beyond which the costs of doing so begin to outweigh the benefits obtained. As seen in the previous chapters, expansion of government services has often tended to aggravate many of the kingdom's short-term economic problems. Furthermore, expenditure of this type, particularly in the military area, may not contribute significantly to long-term economic development.

In short the major limitations inherent with this strategy as in the past are likely to be increased inflationary pressures, such as rising wages, increased land prices, expensive urban housing and rentals, and continued advances in the prices of most locally produced (nontraded) goods. Along similar lines, increased involvement of the government acting as an employer of last resort may reduce productivity in the public sector and limit entrepreneurial incentives.

Increased Investment

The most tempting option for the authorities when faced with the large inflow of new revenue was to devote the great bulk into social overhead capital-type projects. These have been highly visible investments that have tended to raise the prestige of the state and give the impression that development is taking place. At the same time many projects of this type have been very attractive to the authorities because they can be accomplished on a turn-key basis (where the contractor uses imported labor, raw materials, and management).

While investment in social-overhead capital has the potential to stimulate the kingdom's growth by supporting such projects as the development of directly productive activities and the construction of facilities, these investments in and of themselves may not contribute significantly to the economy's long-run economic growth. The development of excess capacity in supplying sectors will not necessarily induce investment in directly productive activities. This is particularly true in an economy like Saudi Arabia's where there are relatively few industrial entrepreneurs. In addition, the linkage between the creation of social-overhead capital and inducement or productive investment is not necessarily axiomatic, nor is the direction of causation always one-way.

Beyond this, the fact remains that a large proportion of the Saudi population have not taken the jobs created by this type of investment. The real Saudi beneficiaries of the post-1973 government boom have been the small royal and urban bourgeoisie elites that make up the highest echelons of the government apparatus, the officers' corps, and the small (but rich) trading and business sector. Of the estimated 50,000 people employed in industry, more than 50 percent are foreign and 60 percent are illiterate.[9]

In addition this strategy implies a continuation of massive transfers of technology from industrialized countries to Saudi Arabia. Saudi concern with foreign technology has stressed that:

1. Several UNCTAD studies have shown the importance of additional costs that less-developed countries in general have to bear when dealing with transnational firms.[10] The practice of overpricing imports of intermediate products is apparently becoming wider and wider.

2. In addition to these costs, one should take into account specific engineering and research and development costs linked with solving unexpected problems, the need to adapt or modify the technology to Saudi conditions, prestart-up training costs, and excess manufacturing costs during the initial

phases of production. Data based on a sample of twenty-six fairly recent cases of international transfers of technology in petrochemicals and machinery showed that on the average these extra costs amounted to 19 percent of total project costs (with a range from 2 to 59 percent).[11]

3. The present mechanism of technology transfer—either in the form of turn-key contracts or joint ventures—is not only a source of increased technical dependency on foreign firms, but is also retarding the emergence of local engineering capacities.

The Likely Strategy

Despite the limitations of each of the previous strategies, it is difficult to conceive that Saudi Arabia could implement a strategy that would completely avoid some element of each. One such strategy might be a policy of reducing oil exports and optimizing available energy resources locally within the framework of a long-term strategy over, say, the next 50 years of self-sustained inward-oriented industrialization and agricultural modernization. This is probably the only strategy that could almost totally avoid the problems inherent in the alternative strategies. Its chances for selection would seem highly unlikely, if for no other reason than that the pressures from the industrialized countries would become unbearable if there were a dramatic reduction in the kingdom's exports.

Other strategies, such as developing into a major exporter of services, are precluded because of: (1) a disinclination of Saudis to engage in activities of this sort, and (2) religious considerations preclude developing financial activities along the line such as those being established in Bahrain.

One is therefore left with a strategy that is essentially an amalgmation of the ones just outlined and stressing the selective development of industrial activities, particularly capital-intensive industry, capable of compensating for domestic manpower shortages as the only potential efficient (that is, nonsubsidized) earner of foreign exchange. The number of realistic development options available to the Saudi Arabian authorities and planners is surprisingly limited.

In essence the role of the government during the forecast period will likely continue to be constrained along the lines established during the Fifth Plan period:

1. Designing a domestic infrastructure network capable of supporting a modern industrial apparatus.
2. Implementing health, welfare, and education policies necessary for maintaining the human element in the development process, while at the same time contributing to improvements in labor and managerial quality.

3. Investing in selected heavy industries into which the private sector is reluctant to venture.
4. Guiding the future spatial configuration of population and economic activity through locational investment decisions.

The continued increasing role of government in the economy is simply a logical consequence of the development strategy already adopted by the government and the constraints facing Saudi planners. Government activity will continue to be directed toward economic activities that the private sector will be reluctant to enter because of the risk involved or size of the investment required.

In essence the government will continue to face the basic problem of utilizing its petroleum revenues to support consumption while ensuring that eventual self-sustained growth is achieved. This perception of the kingdom's growth process will be incorporated in the forecasting model through the separation of the petroleum sector from the remainder of the economy. As noted, linkages (forward and backward) between the petroleum industry and other sectors of the economy are minimal. Consequently the influence on the economy on the petroleum sector is negligible, as is the direct influence of that sector on the rest of the economy.

Finally, the model is structured to anticipate both high levels of government investment and government consumption reflecting the government's desire to:

1. Diversify the economy in preparation for the ultimate depletion of their oil reserves.
2. Employ the revenues to improve immediately the standards of living of Saudis.
3. Minimize the risk and uncertainty surrounding the level of petroleum revenues in the short run and the number of periods during which the revenues will be available in the long run.

Mechanisms of Growth

The manner in which exports act as a leading sector and the determinants of the overall impact of changes in exports on national economies has been discussed in the literature for some time.[12] The consensus among economists seems to be that exports can contribute to economic growth (through their direct contribution to gross domestic product), because they are included as part of GDP, and indirectly through linkages created with nonoil sectors in a sequence of multipier–accelerator mechanisms. Theoretically, these indirect contributions to the economy may continue to operate long after a particular change in exports has occurred.[13]

Thus while the petroleum sector may not participate directly in the buying and selling of goods in the domestic market as was historically the case of the leading export growth sectors, it may still act as they did in providing an engine of growth for the economy, rather than a direct effect through large backward and forward linkages. The mechanism may be one of a series of demand responses that result once the sector's revenues begin to interact with the rest of the economy.

In śum the overall effect of a change in exports will depend on changes in technology that result, the propensity to import, the extent to which investment opportunities are generated, the ability to attract foreign factors, and other nonquantitative effects. Obviously, neither the exhibited or relative sizes of exports' direct and indirect contributions to the growth of the economy need to be fixed and could conceivably vary between our and different time periods. Clearly, if the opportunities generated by the growth of the export sector are exploited, then a pattern of economic growth will evolve and be characterized as a process of diversification about an export base.[14]

While the relationship between the growth of oil exports and GDP over time is central to an export-based model of growth, the literature has never been specific as to the operational nature of this relationship; that is, exactly what the time period or pattern changes in exports should have on income. The problem of determining the time lag between oil export growth and economic growth in Saudi Arabia must therefore be central to any econometric investigation that attempts to forecast the economy's likely growth path.

More precisely, to have any credibility at all a forecasting model of the Saudi Arabian economy must identify to what extent demand-increasing effects stemming from petroleum revenues have induced movements in the country's indigenous (nonoil) income. As a first step in constructing an econometric model of the economy, therefore, an attempt was made to statistically estimate the manner in which the oil sector has interacted with the rest of the economy.

Empirical Formulation of the Export Base Theory

It is quite likely that because the government does not need to spend the oil revenues immediately after they accrue, but instead build up a foreign portfolio to sustain expenditures during years of falling revenues, oil exports will effect GDP over time rather than instantaneously. One formulation would be to specify GDP in the current period as depending not on exports that period (year), but also on the series. This formulation implies that the effect of exports goes back a specific number of years in the past; that is,

$$GDPN = b0EXPTNA + b1EXPTNAL + b2EXPTNAL2 \ldots \qquad (12.1)$$

where *GDNP* is GDP (current price), *EXPTNA* is nominal exports, *EXPTNAL* is exports lagged 1 year, *EXPTNAL2* is exports lagged 2 years, and so on.

In this form there are an indefinitely large number of parameters to be estimated—*b0*, *b1*, *b2*.... This is clearly impractical, if not statistically impossible. It is therefore necessary to make some simplifying assumptions. A priori, the most reasonable would be to assume that the effect on current GDP of previous exports declines exponentially; that is, exports in period *a* has an effect *b* on GDP in period *s*, but only affect *ba* in period *t* + 1, *ba*2 in period *t* + 2, and so on. This formulation implies that the effect of exports on GDP would decline over time in a systematic manner.

Using this framework equation 12.1 can be written as:[15]

$$GDNP = bEXPTNA + baEXPTNAL + ba2EXPTNAL2 \ldots \qquad (12.2)$$

which can be simplified to a form easily estimated:[16]

$$GDNP = d(1 - a) + bEXPTNA + aGDPNL \qquad (12.3)$$

The value of *c* can be obtained from the estimated value of the intercept and *a* from the *GDPNL* term, where *GDNP* = GDP, *GDPNL* = GDP lagged 1 year.

In addition to estimating the value of *a* by using equation 12.3, we can measure the effect on GDP because of a change in exports for both short- and long-term analysis. The effect multiplier measuring the instantaneous effect of a change in exports on GDP is calculated by using *b*. It can be shown that the equilibrium multiplier or long-run multiplier measuring the change in equilibrium value of GDP because of a change in exports is calculated by[17]

$$b/(1 - a) \qquad (12.4)$$

The relationship of oil to GDP was calculated using this framework. For a number of theoretical reasons both GDP and exports were calculated as the percent rate of change from year to year. Theoretically this function makes sense because:[18] (1) the spread effects include acceleration effects, and thus proper specification requires some concept of change; (2) because we would not expect exports to have a constant impact on the economy over time (as the economy undergoes structural changes). The percent annual change was approximated by taking the natural logarithm of the change from one year to the next in each variable.

The results for GDP for the period 1960–1978 were:

$$\text{Ln}(GDPN2/GDPN21) = 0.7424\text{Ln}(FEXPTNA/FEXPTNAL)$$
$$(194.76)$$

$$+ 0.1369\text{Ln}(GDPN2L/GDPNL2) + 0.0248 \qquad\qquad (12.5)$$
$$(3.5710)$$

$$r^2 = 0.9341 \qquad F = 99.1676$$

where ( ) = partial F values, and Ln = natual logarithm.

$$\text{Ln}(NOXN/NOXNL) = 0.1817\text{Ln}(FEXPTNA/FEXPTNAL)$$
$$(1.5926)$$

$$+ 0.8196\text{Ln}(NOXN/NOXNL2) \;\; + 0.0015 \qquad\qquad (12.6)$$
$$(29.8601)$$

$$r^2 = .6920 \qquad F = 15.7264$$

$NOXN$ = nonoil GDP for 1960–1978.

For equation 12.5, $b = 0.7424$ and $a = 0.1369$, yielding a long-run multiplier of 0.8602. For equation 12.6, $b = 0.1817$ and $a = 0.8196$, yielding a long-run multiplier of 1.0072; that is, for each dollar increase of oil exports, there is in the long run a corresponding 1.0072 dollar increase in nonoil GDP.

Note that in equation 12.5 the second term depicting the effect of past exports yielding the equation 12.6 multiplier is just barely significant at the 90 percent level by the partial F test.[19]

These results indicate that current exports are extremely important in determining GDP. The spread effects, however, are questionable. Perhaps a more meaningful result is that obtained when nonoil GDP is used in place of GDP. Nonoil GDP is highly significant by the F test in the regression equation, thus indicating that spread effects were in fact very important in the kingdom during the period and that investment opportunities generated by the oil revenues were being exploited to advantage.

For the pre-1973 price-increase period (1960–1973), the results were:

$$\text{Ln}(GDPN/GDPNL) = 0.6194\text{Ln}(FEXPTNA/FEXPTNAL)$$
$$(22.4272)$$

$$+ 0.1009\text{Ln}(GDPNL/GDPNL2) + 0.0369 \qquad\qquad (12.7)$$
$$(0.1412)$$

$$r^2 = 0.7149 \qquad F = 11.2842$$

With the lagged export effect insignificant and for nonoil GDP:

$$\text{Ln}(NOXN/NOXNL) = 0.2015\text{Ln}(FEXPTNA/FEXPTNAL)$$
$$(4.1966)$$

$$-0.0463\text{Ln}(NOXNL/NOXNL2) + 0.0761 \tag{12.8}$$
$$(0.0142)$$

$$r^2 = 0.3187 \qquad F = 2.1054$$

For the pre-OPEC price increase period, the spread effects of oil exports were statistically insignificant, even taking a negative sign in equation 12.8. Apparently the country since 1973 has become much more efficient in channeling export-drived revenues into productive investment.

To examine the hypothesis that exports stimulate the Saudi Arabian economy through a spread effect that takes place over a rather long period of time (as opposed to a very transitory stimulus), the export–income relationship was specified as:

$$\text{Ln}(NOXNP) = b1 + b2\text{Ln}(E/EL) + b3\text{Ln}(EL/ELS) + b4\text{Ln}(EL2/EL3)$$
$$+ b5\text{Ln}(EL3/EL4) \tag{12.9}$$

where $E = EXPTNA2 =$ current price exports deflated by the import price index. The advantage of this formulation is that it makes no presumption about the pattern of weights used to determine the effect of past exports on real nonoil GDP ($NOXNP$).

Results of regressing both constant and current price nonoil GDP on lagged exports confirm the general results obtained above (see table 12–1). For the constant-price case, exports do not have a significant effect until 2 years out; then they are significant for three- and four-year lags, but are insignificant for a lag of 5 years. Exports also decline in stength with lags of 2, 3, and 4 years (see equation 5, table 12–1).

For the current-price case a similar pattern emerges, although exports have a significant impact on income after only a one-year lag.

Also the evidence of declining weights of past exports is not as strong as in the constant-price case; that is, exports lagged by 1, 2, and 3 years have fairly similar coefficients (see equation 10, table 12–1).

A somewhat different picture emerges, however, when exports are regressed on individual sector (such as agriculture) output. In this formulation exports were not significant in any of the equations using sectoral value added as the dependent variable.

This indicates weak direct linkages, and means that these sectors' growth pattern is independent of fluctuations in exports. Manufacturing output, for

Table 12–1
Saudi Arabia: Effect of Exports on Nonoil Gross Domestic Products

	$Ln(E/EL)$	Ln $(EL/EL2)$	Ln $(EL2/EL3)$	Ln $(EL3/EL4)$	Ln $(EL4/EL5)$	Ln $(EL5/EL6)$	Interest	r^2	F
Constant Prices									
$Ln(NOXNP/NOXNPL)$ =	0.0166 (0.01294)						0.1001	0.0076	0.1294
$Ln(NOXNP/NOXNPL)$ =	0.0242 (0.3052)	0.0254 (0.2036)					0.923	0.0351	0.2544
$Ln(NOXNP/NOXNPL)$ =	0.0218 (0.3175)	0.0064 (0.3981)	0.1289 (9.1792)				0.0774	0.4519	3.2983
$Ln(NOXNP/NOXNPL)$ =	0.0095 (0.5173)	0.0206 (0.7189)	0.1131 (14.6695)	0.1036 (9.0429)			0.0602	0.7139	6.2371
$Ln(NOXNP/NOXNPL)$ =	0.0532 (0.6945)	0.0001 (0.9812)	0.1275 (20.3886)	0.0843 (12.4363)	0.0835 (5.5538)		0.0421	0.8375	8.0109
$Ln(NOXNP/NOXNPL)$ =	0.0929 (0.0009)	0.0381 (0.5027)	0.0463 (13.5029)	0.0620 (10.7391)	0.1140 (15.6837)	0.2960 (1.4533)	0.0068	0.8747	6.9804
Current Prices									
$Ln(NOXN/NOXNL)$ =	0.1259 (0.5913)						0.1672	0.0356	.5913
$Ln(NOXN/NOXWL)$ =	−0.0507 (0.9878)	0.5014 (13.2038)					0.0950	0.5034	7.0958
$Ln(NOXN/NOXNL)$ =	−0.0330 (1.4875)	0.3554 (27.4154)	0.3734 (15.2600)				0.0476	0.7863	14.7210
$Ln(NOXN/NOXNL)$ =	−0.0765 (4.8957)	0.4020 (100.7798)	0.2434 (63.2990)	0.3496 (50.3375)			−0.0009	0.9564	54.820

Note: $NOXNP$ = real nonoil GDP; $NOXNPL$ = real nonoil GDP lagged 1 year; $NOXNPL2$ = real nonoil GDP lagged 2 years, etc.; $NOXN$ = current price nonoil GDP; E = exports. Real nonoil GDP is regressed on exports deflated by the import price index; current price nonoil GDP is regressed on undeflated exports.

example, may be largely of the import substitution variety, and thus responds to the general level of domestic demand. These findings may also indicate that export's full potential in stimulating an expansion of manufacturing output has not been fully exploited, perhaps because of insufficient domestic market size. An alternative explanation is that the overall results (using nonoil GDP) are significant, while that for the sectors (whose values add up to the nonoil GDP total) are not significant simply because the lag structure is complex and somewhat staggered over time.

Again, at the aggregate level an analysis of capital stock and investment patterns shows a clear relationship to export changes over time.

$$\text{Ln}(FKP/FKPL) = 0.1495\text{Ln}(E/EL) + 0.7467\text{Ln}(FKPL/FKPL2)$$
$$\quad\quad\quad (0.6210) \quad\quad\quad\quad\quad (15.0174)$$

$$+\ 0.0224 \quad\quad\quad\quad\quad\quad\quad\quad\quad\quad (12.10)$$

$$r^2 = 0.5658 \quad\quad F = 7{,}8192$$

where FKP = real capital stock (defined as the sum of total investment in year t + investment in the previous 2 years); E and EL = real exports (nominal exports deflated by the import price index) and lagged real exports, respectively. The ( ) terms are the partial F values.

$$\text{Ln}(FTINP/FTINPL) = 0.1905\text{Ln}(E/EL)$$
$$\quad\quad\quad\quad\quad (1.7497)$$

$$+\ 0.4251\text{Ln}(FTINP/FTINPL2) \quad\quad (12.11)$$
$$(3.4428)$$

$$r^2 = 0.2705 \quad\quad F = 2.5963$$

where $FTINP$ = real investment.

Current-period exports are not significant determinants of either capital stock or investment, while the lagged export term is highly significant for the capital stock, but only significant at the 90 percent level for investment. Apparently, expansion of current exports is not necessary for the growth of capital and may indicate that the country has enough reserves to finance its current investment needs; that is, that short-run fluctuations in export earnings need not impair the country's development plans.

These results also suggest that much of the kingdom's capital accumulation takes place in industries whose output does not depend significantly on growth in exports (for example, infrastructure and/or investment in import substitutes for which demand is readily available). From what we know of the economy, it is also apparent that the results simply reflect the fact that much of the country's investment is in projects with very long gestation periods, such as those being undertaken at Jubail. Again there is always the possibility that some imported capital goods may not be fully utilized because of domestic market limitations. Clearly for many industries even a massive expansion of exports would not be enough to give the required volume of sales or to create enough demand to justify the economic establishment of a large number of manufacturing industries.

It is possible that because these results were derived from current-price data, they may exhibit an inflationary bias. To suppress the inflationary effect, the relationship between exports and both GDP and nonoil GDP was tested in constant prices (but allowing for improvements in the terms of trade).[20] Thus GDP was deflated with the GDP deflator (1970 = 100), and exports by an index of import prices. Deflating exports in this manner is preferable to using an index of export prices, since any rise in the price of exports relative to that of imports (that is, an import bent in the terms of trade) reflects a true gain to the economy.[21]

For nonoil GDP, the results are similar to those above. For 1960–1978:

$$\text{Ln}(NOXNP/NOXNPL) = 0.0392\text{Ln}(FEXPTNA2/FEXPTNA2L) + (0.3959)$$

$$0.4950\text{Ln}(NOXNPL/NOXNPL2) + 0.0452$$
$$(4.4270)$$

$$r^2 = 0.2562 \qquad F = 2.4114 \qquad\qquad (12.12)$$

and for 1960–1973:

$$\text{Ln}(NOXNP/NOXNPL) = 0.0807\text{Ln}(FEXPTNA2/FEXPTNA2L)$$
$$(1.7736)$$

$$-0.1419\text{Ln}(NOXNPL/NOXNPL2) + 0.0825$$
$$(0.1203)$$

$$r^2 = 0.1171 \qquad F = 0.5907 \qquad\qquad (12.13)$$

with $NOXNP$ = real nonoil GDP, $FEXPTNAR$ = real exports.

Again, the results are strikingly different, indicating that for real nonoil GDP (but non total GDP) the spread effects are quite significant. As with the current-price case, this pattern appears to be a fairly recent phenomenon. If the 1960–1973 period is examined separately, the spread effect is not significant (the sign of the lagged nonoil income term is in fact negative).

Conclusions

Do the empirical tests prove that the country's oil revenues have created numerous incentives for the nonoil sector, and that that sector has responded in a manner generating spread and linkage effects through the economy? As is well-known, statistical anaysis can only be used to reject a hypothesis. Analysis of the sort presented here can never prove a hypothesis to be correct.[22] As such, the empirical results just examined do much to disprove the idea that the Saudi Arabian petroleum sector has had only a transitory stimulating effect on the domestic economy, and that the country has not taken advantage of at least some of the investment possibilities made possible by the revenues generated by this sector. It appears that changes in the level of exports have a number of effects on the nonoil sector of the economy that take time to be fully felt. The identification of the precise nature of these mechanisms occupy, to a large extent, the remaining chapters of this book.

Notes

1. Excellent critiques are given in Raymond Vernon, "Comprehensive Model Building in the Planning Process: The Case of the Less-Developed Economies," *Economic Journal* (March 1966): 57–69; and Aron Shourie, "The Use of Macroeconomic Regression Models of Developing Countries for Forecasts and Policy Prescription," *Oxford Economic Papers* (March 1972): 1–35.

2. Jere Behrman and L. Klein, "Econometric Growth Models for the Developing Economy," in W.A. Eltis, et al., *Induction, Growth and Trade, Essays in Honour of Sir Roy Harrod* (London: Oxford University Press, 1970), p. 169.

3. Hollis Chenery, "Comparative Advantage and Development Policy," *American Economic Review* (March 1961): 28–31.

4. A point made by Timothy Sisley, "Saudi Arabia: The Contemporary Political Scene," in Centre for Arab Gulf Studies, University of Exeter, *State, Economy and Power in Saudi Arabia* (A Symposium, July 4–7, 1980), p. 5.

5. See H.G. Hambleton, "The Saudi Arabian Petrochemical Industry: Its Rationale and Effectiveness and the Social Political Inplications," in Centre for Arab Gulf States, University of Exeter, *State Economy and Power in Saudi Arabia* (A Symposium, July 4–7, 1980), p. 1, for documentation on these forecasts.

6. To avoid the implications of the foreign exchange constraint on growth as described in Hollis Chenery and Alan Strout, "Foreign Economic Assistance and Economic Development," *American Economic Review* (September 1966): 679–733.

7. Sheikh Ahmed Abdullatif, "A Strategy for Investing the OPEC Surplus," *Euromoney* (August 1980): 23–24.

8. Of course, much does go for aid. See Ragaei Mallakh, "Where Does OPEC Money Go?" *The Wharton Magazine* (Winter 1980): 34–39.

9. J.S. Birks and C.A. Sinclair, "The Domestic Political Economy of Development in Saudi Arabia," in Centre for Arab Gulf Studies, University of Exeter, *State, Economy and Power in Saudi Arabia* (A Symposium, July 4–7, 1980), pp. 4–5.

10. UNCTAD, *Major Issues in Transfer of Technology: A Case Study of the Pharmaceutical Industry* (Geneva: UNCTAD, 1975); UNCTAD, *An International Code of Conduct of Transfer of Technology* (New York: UNCTAD, 1975).

11. D.J. Teece, "Technology Transfer by Multinational Firms: The Resource Cost of Transferring Technological Knowhow," *The Economic Journal* (June 1977): 242–261.

12. See, for example, G.W. Bertram, "The Relevance of the Canadian Wheat Boom in Canadian Economic Growth," *Canadian Journal of Economics* (August 1973); and R.E. Caves, "Export Lead Growth and the New Economic History," in J. Bhagwati, *Trade, Balance of Payments and Growth, Essays in Honor of Charles P. Kindieberger* (Amsterdam: North Holland, 1971), pp. 403–442.

13. Raymond Mikesell, "The Contribution of Petroleum and Mineral Resources to Economic Development," in Raymond Midesell, ed., *Foreign Investment in the Petroleum and Mineral Industries* (Baltimore: The Johns Hopkins Press, 1972), pp. 3–28.

14. An exhaustive analysis is given in G. Nankani, "Development Problems of Mineral-Exporting Countries," The World Bank, *World Bank Staff Working Paper No. 354* (August 1979).

15. From a general formulation elaborated on in M. Dutta, *Econometric Methods* (Cincinnati: South-Western Publishing Co., 1975), ch. 7.

16. As proved in L.M. Koyck, *Distributed Lags and Investment Analysis* (Amsterdam: NorthHolland, 1954).

17. Dutta, *Econometric Methods*, p. 189.

18. Following M.M. Metwally and H.V. Tamaschke, "Oil Exports and Economic Growth in the Middle East," *Kyklos*, no. 3 (1980): 499–521.

19. The use and significance of the partial F test is given in N.R. Draper and H. Smith, *Applied Regression Analysis* (New York: John Wiley, 1966), p. 71.

20. The following tests follow Metwally and Tamaschke, "Oil Exports and Economic Growth."

21. Y. Kurabayshi, "The Impact of Changes in Terms of Trade on a System of National Accounts: An Attampted Synthesis," *Review of Income and Wealth* (1971): 285–297.

22. See Paul Davidson, "Causality in Economies, A Review," *Journal of Post Keynesian Economics* (Summer 1980): 576–584, for an excellent discussion of this point.

13

An Econometric Model for Saudi Arabia— the Structural Equations for Consumption and Investment

As the Saudi Arabian government becomes more concerned with developing efficient policies to further the kingdom's economic development, it is likely that econometric models capable of depicting the main forces at work in the economy will be used as a major planning tool. Although the kingdom has lagged significantly in developing models of this type,[1] the increasing acceptance by high-level officials of the merits of economic planning has led to the initial attempts at developing an analytical framework capable of representing, through a system of structural relationships, the behavioral and institutional factors responsible for movements in the country's major macroeconomic aggregates.

While these models have not yet reached a level of sophistication capable of providing a significant input into the plans themselves, their attraction for eventual application into the country's planning process stems from the simple fact that the pursuit of national policy goals requires some sort of logical basis for studying alternatives.

In the absence of an econometric model of the economy—a general framework—within which to examine the problems associated with the country's economic growth, much of the discussion in Riyadh has taken place in a theoretical vacuum. As a result many planning decisions have been unsatisfactory both logically and practically.

Clearly an important gap exists in the country's planning process. The institutional characteristics and the historical background of Saudi Arabia that were presented in the earlier chapters provide the foundation for this task.

With the model's ultimate objectives and structure in mind and following the work of Theil[2] and Timbergen,[3] the following model is developed to aid in overcoming that deficiency. In its entirety the model consists of:

1. A characterization of the policy problem, specification of a preference function, the quantitative model, and the constraints or boundary problem facing Saudi planners.
2. The delection problem; that is, classification of variables by their properties (such as randomness, direct or indirect controllability, and time dependence).
3. The steering problem; that is, derivation of optimum decision rules in static and dynamic senses.

As formulated here the model consists of these basic ingredients:

1. A welfare function (W) representing the objectives of policy that is a function of the policy variables (zj) and the target variables (yi).
2. An empirical model (M) (in this case an econometric model) that expresses the empirical relationships between the target variables and the policy variables under specified boundary conditions.
3. The structural relations of the model that come in three groups: behavioristic, technical, and definitional. The most important are the behavioristic equations as they express quantitative hypotheses about economic and social behavior.
4. Boundary conditions on all the variables.

The key element in this framework is the model (M). The first task, therefore, in any attempt at rationalizing economic policy making in Saudi Arabia is to estimate the structural relationships that make up the model.[4]

The remainder of this chapter: (1) presents the estimated structural equations for the major macroeconomic variables—consumption and investment; (2) discusses several insights provided by these equations into the structure and operation of the economy, and (3) draws several implications for policy suggested by the equations. The remaining structural equations are discussed in the following chapter, while the welfare function, together with the policy variables, target variables, and projections to the year 2000 are presented in chapter 17.

Consumption

The Saudi Arabian national income accounts distinguish between private and public consumption.[5] Private domestic consumption consists of fourteen categories: (1) food, (2) beverages, (3) tobacco, (4) clothing, footwear, and other personal effects, (5) rent and water charges, (6) fuel and light, (7) furniture, furnishings, and household equipment, (8) household operations, (9) personal care and health expenses, (10) transportation, (11) communications, (12) recreation and entertainment, (13) education, and (14) miscellaneous services.

Government final consumption expenditures, on the other hand, are calculated as the sum of compensation of employees plus current purchases, minus sales of goods and services. These figures are obtained from the government budget, and in general are considered more reliable than the figures on private consumption.

Since the composition of and factors determining the values of the two types of consumption were so different, each was estimated separately. More specifically, because the recent and sudden wealth of Saudi Arabia is derived from oil income, which in turn is owned exclusively by the government and foreign oil companies, construction of the consumption function must reflect the phenomenon that the public sector is wealthy, but that the majority of the population (at least until quite recently) is as poor as in most other developing countries. A consumption function that does not consider this dichotomy between private and public incomes will be of limited use and may at best yield uninformative results. Most likely, the results would be erroneous, particularly about the magnitude of the marginal propensity to consume.[6]

Ideally the consumption function should be estimated using disposable income. It would also be desirable to disaggregate consumption into durable and nondurables, with relative prices and possibly income distribution included as dependent variables.

In addition it would be desirable to estimate two consumption functions— one for the native Saudis, and a second for foreigners. Clearly , an aggregate consumption function estimated without regard for the high percentage of foreign workers in the total labor force cannot be claimed to be truly representaive of the country. An aggregate function, particularly if the marginal propensities to consume differ greatly between Saudis and foreigners, may give misleading forecasting results as the foreign labor force is reduced over time. Unfortunately, a distinction of consumption along these lines was not possible because neither foreign workers' income and their consumption, nor their total numbers, are known.

Since nonoil income, total private consumption, and the overall price deflators were the only figures available, analysis was, by necessity, confined to these relationships.

Because Saudi Arabia's wealth is characterized by its recent and sudden nature, the kingdom's liberal import policy, and the initial low level of development, one would expect the marginal propensity and the average propensity to be high. More specifically:

1. The country's dependence on imports in meeting its demands has introduced new goods and services very rapidly into the kingdom. The awareness of the existence and the availability of such new items in the local market means that the demonstration effect is an important inducement to spend more.

2. An illiterate individual who suddenly finds himself wealthy is more included to spend most of his income on consumption than an educated person who may be more aware of the importance of saving for investment purposes. Based on this shortsightedness and the knowledge that the Saudi Arabian population until quite recently was almost completely illiterate, the likelihood of finding a high marginal propensity to consume is very probable.

3. Satisfaction of consumption needs, if it is ever achieved, takes time to

materialize. Therefore starting from a primitive base of recent wealth and limited goods and services in a consumer's basket, it is to be expected that the country and its people would first indulge in high and rising consumption. Later more rational behavior may prevail and part of the resources may be diverted from conspicuous-type consumption to investment.[7]

Private Consumption

As noted in chapter 6, several patterns have tended to characterize the movement of private consumption over time, with the most interesting being its increase at a significantly slower rate than nonoil GDP. As predicted by the considerations listed here, the kingdom's average and marginal propensity to consume was quite high in the early 1960s. Since then, the average private propensity to consume nonoil GDP has been from 91.9 percent in 1960 to 52.8 percent in 1978. This decline was especially sharp during the early 1970s (see table 13–1).

It has become common practice to assume that effects on demand due to changes in prices or income are distributed over time, rather than being felt instantaneously.[8] In the case of the permanent-income hypothesis, for example, permanent income is approximated by a weighted average of all past observed incomes.[9] The distribution is assumed known, the weights declining geometrically.

Under a stock adjustment model the distributed lag is only incidentally implied and pertains to a dynamic model of consumer behavior.[10] If several assumptions are made, the so-called Nerlove model can be derived and estimated as a special case of the stock adjustment model.

Since there was no a priori basis for assigning weights to reflect the importance of past incomes in affecting the consumption decision, one of the equations tested utilized a modified version of the simple Keynesian function in which previous levels of consumption (in addition to nonoil income) were included as an explanatory variable:

$$PCNP = a + bNOXNP + cPCNPL \tag{13.1}$$

Equation 13.1 is sometimes referred to as the Brown-Klein consumption function.[11] Its main hypothesis is that consumers react to changes in income in a gradual manner trying to maintain the levels of consumption with which they are familiar. This relationship has been well established by both budget surveys and cross-country analyses in numerous countries, and there is no reason to believe that the kingdom is an exception to this pattern.

The regression results (equations 13.2 to 13.7) are interesting in that: (1) both the long-run and short-run propensities to consume are equal to 0.70

Table 13–1
Saudi Arabia: Consumption–Income Relationships (Billions of riyals)

Year	Private Consumption (PCNP)	Government Consumption (GCNP)	Nonoil GDP (NOXNP)	GDP (GDPNP)	PCNP NOXNP	PCNP GDPNP
1960	3.01	0.76	3.27	7.50	0.92	0.40
1961	3.02	0.85	3.67	8.15	0.82	0.37
1962	3.15	1.01	3.82	8.88	0.82	0.35
1963	3.10	1.40	4.28	9.79	0.72	0.32
1964	3.11	1.57	4.73	10.23	0.66	0.30
1965	3.18	1.81	5.21	11.37	0.61	0.28
1966	3.27	2.07	5.81	12.91	0.56	0.25
1967	4.22	2.82	6.23	13.86	0.68	0.30
1968	4.75	2.85	6.61	15.19	0.72	0.31
1969	5.37	3.03	7.19	16.01	0.75	0.34
1970	5.85	3.42	7.49	17.40	0.78	0.34
1971	6.29	3.72	8.09	22.47	0.78	0.34
1972	6.46	4.01	8.54	26.41	0.76	0.24
1973	6.75	4.56	9.75	34.66	0.69	0.19
1974	7.12	7.15	11.18	71.97	0.64	0.10
1975	8.03	7.14	12.61	62.60	0.64	0.13
1976	7.64	9.23	15.12	52.56	0.51	0.15
1977	8.97	10.71	17.68	53.54	0.51	0.17
1978	12.47	10.74	20.14	51.08	0.62	0.24
1979	13.26	11.82	22.88	51.86	0.53	0.26

Source: Calculated from data in Saudi Arabian Monetary Agency, *Annual Report*, various issues.

(equation 13.2). Usually the long-run function is somewhat greater than the short-run, unless of course some particular factor tends to systematically prevent the adjustment of consumption to increases over time in income.

Private Consumption

(Constant price)

$$PCNP = 0.21NOXNP + 0.70PCNPL + 0.15$$
$$\quad\quad (2.90) \quad\quad\quad (3.98) \quad\quad (0.39)$$

$$r^2 = 0.9611 \quad\quad F = 185.54 \quad\quad\quad (13.2)$$

$$PCNP = 0.32NOXNP + 0.68PCNPL - 1.67\Delta DPGDP - 0.37$$
$$\quad\quad (4.07) \quad\quad\quad (4.27) \quad\quad\quad (-2.53) \quad\quad (0.82)$$

$$r^2 = 0.9701 \quad\quad F = 132.94 \quad\quad\quad (13.3)$$

$$PCNP = 0.46NOXNP + 0.83PCP - 2.21\Delta DFGDP + 0.44$$
$$\quad\quad (5.38) \quad\quad\quad (1.80) \quad\quad\quad (-2.39) \quad\quad (0.90)$$

$$r^2 = 0.9446 \quad\quad F = 73.87 \quad\quad\quad\quad (13.4)$$

(Current price)

$$PCN = 0.23NOXN + 0.86PCNL - 0.42$$
$$\quad\quad (2.08) \quad\quad\quad (2.69) \quad\quad (-0.59)$$

$$r^2 = 0.9924 \quad\quad F = 844.56 \quad\quad\quad\quad (13.5)$$

$$PCN = 0.38NOXN + 0.63PC + 1.30$$
$$\quad\quad (6.43) \quad\quad\quad (1.89) \quad (3.81)$$

$$r^2 = 0.9904 \quad\quad F = 667.51 \quad\quad\quad\quad (13.6)$$

$$PCN = 0.83NOXN - 12.14DFGDP + 1.48PC + 8.94$$
$$\quad\quad (8.49) \quad\quad\quad (-4.16) \quad\quad (2.97) \quad (4.63)$$

$$r^2 = 0.9949 \quad\quad F = 787.28 \quad\quad\quad\quad (13.7)$$

Inflation may have inhibited that adjustment.[12] While the ratio of consumption to both GDP and nonoil GDP declined over the 1960–1978 period, the fall was particularly sharp in the early and mid 1970s. This period was characterized by money creation taking place at an accelerating rate, with a corresponding rise in the rate of consumer price increases. Thus a situation may have been created whereby inflation acted as an effective tax, causing real disposable incomes to slow down or even decline.

A somewhat similar explanation of the observed pattern of private consumption is that the government increased taxes during this period as part of an antiinflationary stablization program. Flexibility in altering taxes for this purpose is ruled out by the nature of the Islamic tax codes with their reliance on the flat rate of *zakat*.

Another possibility is that income was somehow redistributed from wage and salary recipients in favor of corporate-operating surpluses. This also does not seem to have happened ,however. Over the period 1971 to 1976, wages and salaries actually were remarkably stable (at about 52 percent of total factor incomes).[13]

Some sort of inflation induced reduction in consumption would, therefore, seem to be the only logical explanation remaining. A regression of the rate of inflation lagged 1 year on the ratio of private consumption to nonoil GDP yielded:

$$PCNP/NOXNP = \begin{array}{c} 0.72 \\ (6.73) \end{array} \begin{array}{c} - 0.0065INFL \\ (3.98) \end{array}$$

$$(\ ) = t \text{ test for significance} \qquad r^2 = 0.5144 \qquad (13.8)$$

thus indicating a statistically significant pattern where a little over half of the decline in consumption-income ratio was explained by inflation.

The change in the GDP deflator ($\Delta DFGDP$) was also statistically significant (with a negative sign) when introduced into the consumption equation (equations 13.3 and 13.4). Also, the GDP deflator was significant and negative in the current-price equation (equation 13.7).

The negative inflation–consumption pattern suggests some sort of forced savings mechanism was present in the 1970s.

Using the gross national product identify:

$$Y = C + I + X - M \qquad (13.9)$$

where C = (private and public) consumption; I = gross domestic capital formation; X = exports (including factor income from abroad); and M = imports (including factor payments to foreigners). It is possible to depict the IS (savings, investment) identify as:

$$I = S + F \qquad (13.10)$$

where F is foreign capital outflow (defined as: $F = M - X = I - S$).

Equations 13.9 and 13.10 should hold not only as ex-post identities, but also as equilibrium conditions. This assumes that commodity markets are cleared at equilibirium prices. If ex-ante or desired levels of investment exceed ex-ante savings at prices that prevailed in the preceding period.[14] However, the nature of this adjustment will depend on F or net capital outflow, which was positive during this period. If, for example, the capital outflow was elastically supplied to other countries, the initial adjustment problem would be mitigated since any excess of I over S would simply be filled by a negative F, thus relieving the excess domestic demand.

It is quite likely, however, that in the short run—especially after a sharp rise in oil revenues—a large component of F cannot be easily placed outside the kingdom at acceptable terms .

During periods of increasing oil revenues, therefore, F is unlikely to be of much help in relieving the aggregate supply–demand imbalance.

Also during these periods output is likely to be at full capacity or at least (because of deficiencies in infrastructure—bottlenecks) not capable of expanding and thus aiding in the equilibration process.

In other worlds if output were flexible and responded to demand stimulus in the short run (within the given period), then I and S could adjust to establish an equilibrium Y (given the exogenously determined level of F). For this Keynesian type of adjustment process to be effective, it is also necessary for the savings and investment functions to be responsive to changes in GNP (with movements that are in the right direction and magnitude). As noted during some years and particularly after a spurt in oil revenues, output may not be sufficiently responsive. Price changes may then have to assume a major role in macroeconomic adjustment; that is, aggregate price level increases would take place under the pressure of excess demand for goods (which is represented by the excess of ex-ante I over ex-ante $S + F$, both of which are evaluated at the previously prevailing price level). For inflation to eliminate the aggregate demand supply gap, the investment function and/or the savings function must shift.[15]

As noted in chapter 5, however, Islamic codes prevent interest rate changes from providing the adjustment mechanism of this type often found in the more-advanced countries; that is, for religious reasons, the government does not permit interest rates to move sufficiently to clear the financial markets.

Because the public sector's fiscal actions are more or less independent of movements in nonoil income, all the pressure for macroeconomic adjustment is placed on private savings. All this suggests that increases in private savings at the expense of consumption could account for the sharp decline in private consumption.

Government Consumption

Real government consumption expenditures (*GCNP*) consist of the government's purchases of goods and services to provide social, administrative, and military services, and are therefore not subject to the same type of behavioral constraints as private consumption. Even less is known about the behavior of public consumption in the kingdom than private consumption. A logical case could be made for treating them: (1) as autonomous, (2) disaggregated according to the type of factors purchased, or (3) as a function of revenues.

In the absence of disaggregated time-series data, government consumption was regressed on oil and nonoil revenues (nonoil revenues are direct and indirect, but mainly customs duties). Several formulations give good results (see equations 13.11 to 13.21), with equation 13.12 probably the most sound statistically.[16] In that equation real government consumption is a function of real oil revenues (*GORFSP*) and real exports (*FEXPTNARL*) in the previous year. While nonoil revenues (*GNORFSP*) are a significant determinant of government consumption (see equation 13.14), their very low level makes them somewhat suspect as a major determining factor of government consumption.

Other relationships of interest are:

1. If deviations from the past trend of real nonoil GDP ($\Delta TNOXL$) are statistically significant and have a negative sign (see equation 13.16), they apparently indicate some sort of stabilizing role on government expenditure; that is, government expenditure is reduced when the economy is straining productive capacity.[17]

2. Government consumption, also perhaps as part of countercyclical policy, appears to be reduced when inflationary pressures are present. In both equations 12 and 15, changes in the GDP deflator ($\Delta DFGDP$) are highly significant determinants of current price government consumption (GCN).

Government Consumption

(Constant Price)

$$GCNP = 0.22GORFSPL + 2.11$$
$$\quad\quad\quad (8.81) \quad\quad\quad (4.77)$$
$$r^2 = 0.847222 \quad\quad F = 77.65 \quad\quad\quad\quad (13.11)$$

$$GCNP = 0.03GORFSP + 0.31FEXPTNARL - 0.18$$
$$\quad\quad\quad (5.85) \quad\quad\quad\quad (8.23) \quad\quad\quad (0.49)$$
$$r^2 = 0.9748 \quad\quad F = 251.60 \quad\quad\quad\quad (13.12)$$

$$GCNP = 0.05GORFSPL + 0.45GCNPL + 0.36$$
$$\quad\quad\quad (6.27) \quad\quad\quad\quad (3.04) \quad\quad\quad (1.86)$$
$$r^2 = 0.9610 \quad\quad F = 160.36 \quad\quad\quad\quad (13.13)$$

$$GCNP = 0.11GORFSPL + 1.47GNORFSP + 1.11$$
$$\quad\quad\quad (2.07) \quad\quad\quad\quad (2.51) \quad\quad\quad (2.03)$$
$$r^2 = 0.8971 \quad\quad F = 56.70 \quad\quad\quad\quad (13.14)$$

$$GCNP = 0.34FEXPTNARL + 0.10GCNPL - 0.16$$
$$\quad\quad\quad (8.37) \quad\quad\quad\quad (4.63) \quad\quad\quad (-0.39)$$
$$r^2 = 0.9655 \quad\quad F = 181.95 \quad\quad\quad\quad (13.15)$$

$$GCNP = 0.83NOXNPL - 29.38\Delta TNOXL - 1.87$$
$$\quad\quad (10.59) \quad\quad\quad (-2.11) \quad\quad\quad (-2.94)$$

$$r^2 = 0.9455 \quad\quad F = 112.7 \quad\quad\quad\quad (13.16)$$

$$GCNP = 0.17GORFSP + 0.60\Delta GENANP + 1.73$$
$$\quad\quad (5.90) \quad\quad\quad\quad (2.55) \quad\quad\quad\quad (0.54)$$

$$r^2 = 0.8527 \quad\quad F = 37.62 \quad\quad\quad\quad (13.17)$$

$$GCNP = 0.06GORFSPL + 1.93GNORFSP + 0.95$$
$$\quad\quad (3.88) \quad\quad\quad\quad (2.60) \quad\quad\quad\quad (1.67)$$

$$r^2 = 0.9314 \quad\quad F = 88.28 \quad\quad\quad\quad (13.18)$$

(Current Price)

$$GCN = 0.45FEXPTNAL - 23.94\,\Delta\,DFGDP - 0.43 \quad\quad (13.19)$$
$$\quad\quad (22.59) \quad\quad\quad\quad (-8.20) \quad\quad\quad\quad (-0.57)$$

$$r^2 = 0.9911 \quad\quad F = 776.85$$

$$GCN = 0.13GORFS + 0.52NOXNL - 0.94 \quad\quad (13.20)$$
$$\quad\quad (7.68) \quad\quad\quad (12.52) \quad\quad\quad (-2.14)$$

$$r^2 = 0.9918 \quad\quad F = 849.33$$

$$GCN = 0.60FEXPTNAL - 38.90\,\Delta\,DFGDP + 0.05GCI - 1.40$$
$$\quad\quad (22.46) \quad\quad\quad\quad (-14.93) \quad\quad\quad\quad (2.47) \quad\quad (-4.77)$$

$$r^2 = 0.9971 \quad\quad F = 1260.12 \quad\quad\quad\quad (13.21)$$

Investment

Investment is defined as the sum of imported and domestically produced machinery and equipment together with expenditures for new structures and repair outlays. Imported capital is a significant part of total capital formation, and also represents a channel through which new technology from abroad may enter the system.[18]

Unfortunately, the investment data for Saudi Arabia is incomplete. The national income accounts present the figures: (1) by sector (which includes government, nonoil private, oil sector) and type (which includes construction, transport equipment, machinery, and other capital goods, and (2) change in stocks.[19]

Lacking is a breakdown by ownership (that is, private construction) or by sector (that is, investment in argriculture). Also lacking are figures on the capital stock. Despite these deficiencies several patterns as noted in chapter 6 are still identifiable.

From 1960 to 1979 total real investment grew at an annual compound rate of 16.90 percent. Between 1973 and 1979 its growth was at an annual rate of 22.30 percent, compared with 12.01 percent from 1960–1972. Thus for the whole 1960–1978 period, investment in contrast to consumption grew at a rate faster than the rate of growth of real nonoil GDP. As a result the share of investment in real GDP increased from just over 13 percent in 1960 to over 20 percent in 1978.

Investment in Saudi Arabia has, until the last several years, been characterized by two features:

1. At least 50 percent of the annual growth of fixed investment since 1960 has originated from the government budget. As expected, almost all government investment has been in social-overhead projects (roads, hospitals, and schools).

2. Most investment in the country (private as well as public) has been in construction (houses, roads). Only a small amount of total investment goes into the manufacturing sector.[20]

As with consumption, the empirical estimates that follow have divided capital formation in Saudi Arabia into that controlled by the government and that influenced (private investment) by market developments. Although the investments made directly by the government are not divorced from what happens in the market, the government at any time can decide to increase or reduce its capital spending.[21] Roads, for example, are constructed according to certain estimates of present and future needs, but the government can accelerate or retard the implementation of projects in response to macro-economic considerations. The same applies to most other public projects.

Based on the distinction between private and public investment, a distinctive pattern of the rapid increase in government investment's share of the total is immediately apparent. By 1978 government investment had increased to 60.52 percent from 3.70 in 1960. The major change in the pattern of government investment occurred between 1973 and 1978, when government investment grew by 40.81 percent in real terms, compared with 24.05 between 1961 and 1972.

Private investment was not stagnant during this period. It grew at an annual compound rate of 13.49 percent between 1960 and 1978. Since nonoil GDP grew by 16.62 percent, its share of this aggregate increased slightly from 13.3 percent in 1960 to 21.1 percent in 1978.

These latter trends are prima facie evidence as to the success of the government's strategy to encourage private enterprise. Through investing in a wide variety of physical infrastructure projects, providing incentives of various kinds, and by participating in the production process itself where necessary, the government has awakened the private sector to the possibilities of long-run gains through capital formation.

Government investment has thus helped to break down some of the discontinuities inherent in the early phases of the kingdom's development. Most importantly in this regard, it has helped create an environment in which economies of scale could be obtained for the first time in many areas by private entrepeneurs. Government investment has thus performed a dual role. The first has been to create an institutional, financial, and infrastructural environment that has been conducive to private enterprise and initiative. In this role it has complemented private investment by filling gaps in areas where the private sector was clearly unable to participate. The second and much less important role to date has been to serve as a signal to the private sector by inducing a flow of private resources into activities and regions that the planners perceive as having high social, but not necessarily private, profitability (areas with a payback period of over 3 years).[22]

The nature of capital formation as described makes construction of an investment function for total investment almost impossible if we follow traditional economic theory. The theory, and especially the empirical studies of industrial countries, usually specify that interest rates, profits, total income of a sector or the country, or mortgage rates should be used—selectively or in combination—as independent variables.[23] Even if statistics were available, most of these variables would not be considered the main factors explaining investment in Saudi Arabia, because they are largely irrelevant to government investment.[24]

Regressions for total investment clearly show the importance of government expenditure, which (see equation 13.22) accounts for over 98 percent of its fluctuations, compared with only slightly over 82 percent accounted for by lagged real exports (see equation 13.23). Investment in construction (see equation 13.24), transportation, and communications (see equation 13.25) seem to be jointly determined by public and private expenditure.

Total Investment (*Constant Prices*)

$$TINP = 0.80 GENANP - 0.75 \qquad (13.22)$$
$$(33.13) \qquad\qquad (-3.48)$$

$$r^2 = 0.9849 \qquad F = 392.12$$

$$TINP = 0.64 FEXPTNARL - 2.36 \qquad (13.23)$$
$$(8.54) \qquad\qquad (-2.40)$$

$$r^2 = 0.8292 \qquad F = 72.95$$

Investment in Construction (Constant Prices)

$$ICONP = 0.12TINP + 0.50 \qquad (13.24)$$
$$(3.88) \qquad (1.90)$$
$$r^2 = 0.5153 \qquad F = 15.06$$

Investment in Construction (Current Prices)

$$ICON = 0.30GIN + 1.89PIN - 0.43 \qquad (13.25)$$
$$(2.08) \qquad (7.96) \qquad (-1.25)$$
$$r^2 = 0.9930 \qquad F = 850.62$$

Investment in Transportation and Communications

$$ITRNP = 0.03GENANP + 0.08PENANP - 0.36 \ (13.26)$$
$$(2.59) \qquad (4.87) \qquad (-5.19)$$
$$r^2 = 0.9771 \qquad F = 276.91$$

Private Investment

Accepted theory on private investment tells us that its main determinants should be the stock of capital and output.[25] The model specification with this information usually revolves around the manner in which private investors close the gap between their actual and their perceived optimal or most profitable stock of capital. The absence of capital stock figures, however, rule out formulations along these lines. Instead, private real investment was regressed on various factors that are likely to have affected to one degree or another the profitability of investment.

Profitability (particularly that of investment in machinery and construction) is in turn generally considered to be reflected in certain lagged variables.[26] Decisions concerning investment not only take time to make but are also based on past experiences. The existence of a very definite lag structure found for investment behavior in most countries confirms this general formulation. Specification of the probable length of the lags for Saudi Arabia, however, is more difficult to assess.

The evidence for the United States suggests two separate lag sequences in investment decision. The first is the so-called administration lag, representing the time necessary to have plans approved by management committees and designs completed. This lag is usually relatively short, anywhere from 3 to 6 months. The second lag, the appropriations lag, is nearly always longer.[27]

Tom Mayer suggests on the basis of his exhaustive study of United States data, a fifteen-month interval between the start and completion of construction;[28] in an earlier study, it was suggested that during World War II and the Korean War this lag was about 10 months.[29] Also for the United States, Almond concluded that 3 to 4 quarters was a realistic estimate for the appropriations lag.[30] This combined with the usual three- to six-month administrative lag would yield a total lag of 18 months or 6 quarters.

There are several reasons, however, for believing that a six-quarter lag, while perhaps relevant for the U.S.-type environment, should be reduced to approximately 1 year in Saudi Arabia's case. First, Saudi Arabian entrepreneurs are (for reasons discussed in chapters 10 and 11) not yet capable of undertaking investments in heavy industry. Because this is obviously not the case in the United States, and given that it is quite likely that large, complex investments in heavy industry would have a larger than average appropriations lag, there is likely an upward bias in the U.S. figure. Second, because entrepreneurial ability to carry out detailed, in-depth cost-benefit analysis is limited and because of the general high profitability of investment, in Saudi Arabia, the administrative lag should be much lower than in the United States.

In addition, most investments consist of new activities, unrestrained by existing competition, and while not heavily protected by the current government policies, would undoubtedly receive aid if survival ever became a problem. Therefore, they are not subject to the risks and resulting committee and board meetings characteristic of U.S. business practice. Thus for a number of reasons all pointing in the same direction, we would expect the investment lag in Saudi Arabia to be shorter than in the United States. On the average, 4 quarters should be a realistic figure.

The one-year lags examined in the investment equations consisted of: (1) lagged total private expenditure (*PENANPL*), (2) private consumption (*PCNPL*), (3) money (*MIPL*), (4) private credit (*PCPL*), (5) exports (*FEXPTNARL*), (6) government expenditures (*GENANPL*), (7) private savings (*SPPL*), and (8) the change in private consumption (Δ *PCNPL*).

The inclusion of government expenditure is based on the underlying theory that this type of outlay is undertaken in part to unbalance the economy, thus raising the profitability of private investment. Changes in nonoil income (Δ *NOXNP*) should stimulate investment through an accelerator-type mechanism. As for private consumption, a good case could be made for either a positive effect by creating a direct demand for goods and services, or a negative effect by increasing the competition for financial resources.

Capital rationing, therefore, may be a problem as private consumers compete with businesses for funds. On paper financing business activity does not seem to be a problem. As noted in chapter 11, the Saudi Industrial Development Fund with its medium-term soft-term loans had managed (by early 1980) over the first 5 years of its operations to commit SR 5.5 billion, with SR 3.5 billion actually being disbursed. In early 1980, the Council of Ministers promised to add SR 2 billion to the fund's resources if they were needed.[31]

Although SIDF has issued only one report (in 1977), it is understood that it has committed money to 467 projects, of which 370 have started. In terms of commitments, joint ventures took SR 1.6 billion, 31 percent of lending by value, but by 24 percent by number. SIDF lending grew from SR 300 million in its first year to SR 800 million in 1976, SR 1.3 billion in 1977, and SR 2 billion in 1978. In 1979, however, it fell to SR 1 billion, and the volume of cash committed in 1980 was expected to be about the same. The decline in lending can be attributed to an overall slowing in economic activity, the investment saturation of several sectors, and an understanding that government-spending restraints apply equally to the fund.[32]

A recent government report on the performance of the private sector found shortcomings in the operation of the fund. The report's main criticism was that the fund could not cope with small loans; nearly 97 percent of all loans made available by mid-1979 were for amounts of over SR 2 million.[33] In addition, government had to assume responsibility for almost all investment lending beyond short-term financing because of commercial bank preference for other types of assets.

Some of the private-sector complaints, therefore, may have validity. A typical observation is that interest rates are too high and that adequate volumes of credit are unobtainable from the banks.

While we cannot be sure of the effect of interest or profit rates on private investment in Saudi Arabia, there is evidence that private savings may be an important factor in facilitating investment. After surveying almost all manufacturing establishments in the country in 1969, the Industrial Studies and Development Center found that most factories were managed and financed by the owner (usually a family);[34] 80 percent of invested capital in all surveyed factories belonged to the owner (that is, no borrowing).[35] On this basis, private savings was included as one of the independent variables in the regression equations.

The regression results were quite satisfactory for a number of alternative formulations. Inflationary expectation (captioned by Δ $DFGDP$) seem to be an important stimulant to investment (see equations 13.28, 13.29, 13.30). This may reflect a tendency in the kingdom for investment to flow into speculative areas such as inventories. Inflation plus the accelator (Δ

NOXNP) and lagged government expenditure (see equation 13.28) give one of the better statistical results and confirms the validity of our speculation about entrepreneurial behavior.

The statistical significance of lagged government expenditure indicates the important role that the government performs to create a favorable infrastructural and institutional environment conducive to the growth of private investment. The lag undoubtedly reflects the gestation period between government initiation and the private response.

Islamic banking practices appear to constrain changes in interest rather than their actual rate (or level) (which is surprisingly high on commercial bank loans to business). Thus, interest-rate changes (often an important link in the adjustment mechanism in other countries) are not very relevant to Saudi Arabia and were not included in the investment equations. It is unlikely that interest rates move sufficiently to clear the kingdom's financial markets. The monetary authorities have in fact tended to create new credit more or less independently of domestic savings, often in response to noneconomic factors.[36] Changes in the volume of real credit may, however, not influence the change in capital stock, because smaller firms in Saudi Arabia are generally more dependent on private savings rather than credit for financing their investments.

These factors probably explain the importance of money (*M2PL*) and private (*SPPL*) savings (see equation 13.31) in explaining private investment. Lagged private savings and private credit (*PCPL*) were also found to contribute independently to the investment function (see equation 13.32).

Government protection and expenditure made possible by increased real exports (*FEXPTNARL*) and an increase in the domestic price level vis à vis import prices (*ZITT*) undoubtedly combine to increase private profitability and thus investments (see equation 13.33).

Consumer competition for loans and the crowding out of small businesses from credit is evidenced by the negative sign of lagged private (*PCNPL*) consumption (see equations 13.29 and 13.30).

Private Investment

(Constant Prices)

$$PINP = 0.07NOXNP + 0.88PENANPL + 0.61 \quad (13.27)$$
$$(4.10) \qquad\qquad (7.92) \qquad\qquad (1.12)$$

$$r^2 = 0.9861 \qquad F = 461.00$$

$$PINP = 0.42\Delta NOXNP + 1.17\Delta DFGDP + 0.12GENANPL + 0.34$$
$$(2.22) \qquad\qquad (3.64) \qquad\qquad (5.08) \qquad\qquad (3.75)$$

$$r^2 = 0.9821 \qquad F = 219.78 \qquad (13.28)$$

$$PINP = -0.10PCNPL + 1.74\Delta DFGDP + 0.20GENANPL + 0.76$$
$$ (-1.87) \qquad (6.96) \qquad\qquad (8.52) \qquad\qquad (3.89)$$

$$r^2 = 0.9806 \qquad F = 219.10 \qquad\qquad (13.29)$$

$$PINP = 0.42\Delta NOXNP + 1.19\Delta DFGDP + 0.12GENANPL \qquad (13.30)$$
$$ (2.04) \qquad\qquad (4.12) \qquad\qquad (6.59)$$
$$- 0.19DPCNPL + 0.39$$
$$ (-1.75) \qquad\qquad (4.45)$$

$$r^2 = 0.9864 \qquad F = 199.56$$

$$PINP = 0.28M2PL + 0.05SPPL + 0.37 \qquad (13.31)$$
$$ (10.39) \qquad (4.74) \qquad (3.06)$$

$$r^2 = 0.9733 \qquad F = 236.56$$

$$PINP = 0.29M1PL + 0.04SPPL + 0.27PCPL + 0.14 \qquad (13.32)$$
$$ (6.08) \qquad\quad (3.83) \qquad\quad (1.87) \qquad\quad (0.75)$$

$$r^2 = 0.9766 \qquad F = 166.91$$

$$PINP = 0.14FEXPTNARL + 3.41ZITT - 3.66 \qquad (13.33)$$
$$ (12.07) \qquad\qquad (6.69) \qquad (-6.97)$$

$$r^2 = 0.9487 \qquad F = 138.70$$

Public Investment

From what one can glean from official statements, public investment depends largely on total revenue on the one hand, and the established target rate of nonoil GDP on the other.[37] Since oil revenues have been more than adequate for government needs in the past few years, it is the country's absorptive capacity and/or official fear of inflation that appears to set an upper limit on the amount that can be allocated to investment. The target growth rate specified in the kingdom's five-year development plans seems to act in setting a constraint on how much government investment can be cut back in periods of inflation or declining oil revenues.

The target growth rate is, of course, established by the planning authorities on the basis of realistic estimates of expected revenues from the oil sector. But given the price of oil, petroleum-derived revenues are determined mainly by world demand. The government does have some power, however, to ensure that adequate revenues will be forthcoming to meet planned expenditure levels. In the past the authorities have increased the compaines' tax rates and also obtained more favorable contractual arrangements with ARAMCO.[38]

The highly significant value observed for lagged oil revenues (*GORFSPL*) highlights once again the importance of petroleum in the Saudi Arabian economy. Clearly, oil has not only played a key element in raising both the magnitude and the tempo of capital formation, but the stability (in the sense of not declining significantly in the short run) of these revenues has also allowed the authorities to take a longer-run view of the development process than is normally possible in developing countries. This has allowed the government the comparative luxury of being able to pursue short-run stabilization programs without concern about undermining the economy's long-run growth path.

Short-run stabilization effects are evidenced by the negative sign for changes in the GDP deflator ($\Delta DFGDP$), and is indicative of the government's continued concern about inflation. Because of the country's banking structure and the lack of government debt through which central bank open-market operations normally implement monetary policy, government expenditure movements must assume the major role in stabilization.

Apparently (see equations 13.34 to 13.36, 13.38) increases in domestic ($\Delta DFGDP$) prices have provided signals to the authorities of the need to reduce investment to combat inflationary pressures.

Lagged deviations from the trend of real nonoil GDP ($\Delta TNOXL$) are also statistically significant, but positive. This pattern may be reflective of the long length of time often needed to complete major public-sector investment projects and the effectiveness of these projects in stimulating nonoil income; that is, an initial round of government investment increases nonoil GDP, but investment continues to take place over time as projects are completed.

Another interpretation of the positive value for $\Delta TNOXL$ is that the government responds to upturns in nonoil GDP with investment in anticipation of bottlenecks.

Government Investment

(Constant Prices)

$$GINP = 0.30 NOXNPL + 0.21 GORFSPL + 26.06 \Delta TNOXL \qquad (13.34)$$
$$(3.02) (3.41) (3.69)$$

$$- 7.25 \Delta DFGDP - 1.71$$
$$(-3.60) (-3.19)$$

$$r^2 = 0.9898 \qquad F = 86.5$$

$$GINP = 0.28NOXNPL + 0.06GORFSPL - 3.18\Delta DFGDP - 0.90$$
$$(5.23) (10.57) (-7.31) (-2.71)$$

$$r^2 = 0.9692 \qquad F = 386.36 \qquad\qquad (13.35)$$

(Current Prices)

$$GIN = 1.94\Delta NOXNL - 7.22\Delta DFGDP + 0.13 \qquad (13.36)$$
$$(16.78) (-3.00) (-0.22)$$

$$r^2 = 0.9742 \qquad F = 264.25$$

$$GIN = 0.22GORFS - 0.74 \qquad\qquad (13.37)$$
$$(6.37) (-0.40)$$

$$r^2 = 0.7300 \qquad F = 40.55$$

$$GIN = 0.48FEXPTNAL - 40.79\Delta DFGDP - 2.31 \qquad (13.38)$$
$$(19.74) (-13.32) (-7.10)$$

$$r^2 = 0.9871 \qquad F = 457.59$$

Government and Private Expenditures

Based on the previous analysis, there is little to add in discussing the determinants of total government expenditure (*GENANP*) and total private expenditure (*PENANP*). Both are the sum of their respective consumption and investment expenditures.

As might be expected one finds variables and patterns similar to those identified as significant determinants of one or both subcomponents (see equations 13.39 to 13.58). Again, oil revenues dominate the government expenditure decision-making process, and together with concern over stability (measured by $\Delta DFGDP$) account for nearly 90 percent of the observed fluctuations in *GENANP* (see equation 13.34). When lagged nonoil income reflecting the target growth rate and deviations of nonoil income $\Delta TNOXL$ are added to the regression (see equation 13.38), over 97 percent of the fluctuations in government expenditures are accounted for. Private expenditures on the other hand are clearly related to government expenditures, with over 96 percent of the fluctuation in *PENANP* determined by current and lagged government expenditures (see equation 13.54).

When the capital stock is defined as the sum of total real investment in the current year plus that of the past 3 years, the role of government expenditures in the country's development becomes apparent, with government expenditure accounting for nearly 95 percent of the variation in the figures in constant price value (see equation 13.56) and over 98 percent in current prices (see equation 13.58).

Total Government Expenditures

(Constant Prices)

$$GENANP = 0.07GORFSPL + 0.63GENANPL + 1.62 \qquad (13.39)$$
$$ (3.43) \qquad\qquad (3.69) \qquad\qquad (2.55)$$

$$r^2 = 0.9617 \qquad F = 163.26$$

$$GENANP = 0.85GORFSPL - 18.85\Delta DFGDP + 0.99 \qquad (13.40)$$
$$ (4.82) \qquad\qquad (-2.64)$$

$$r^2 = 0.8743 \qquad F = 48.69$$

$$GENANP = 2.81GNORFSP + 0.47FEXPTNARL - 2.62 \qquad (13.41)$$
$$ (3.58) \qquad\qquad (2.36) \qquad\qquad (-1.95)$$

$$r^2 = 0.9250 \qquad F = 80.18$$

$$GENANP = 16.54\Delta TNOXL + 1.00NOXNPL + 0.23GORFSPL \quad (13.42)$$
$$ (1.34) \qquad\qquad (5.79) \qquad\qquad (2.12)$$
$$- 5.85\Delta DFGDP - 3.09$$
$$(-3.42)$$

$$r^2 = 0.9795 \qquad F = 143.04$$

(Current Prices)

$$GENAN = 3.37GNORES + 0.46GENANL - 0.92 \qquad (13.43)$$
$$ (7.68) \qquad\qquad (3.73) \qquad\qquad (-1.20)$$

$$r^2 = 0.9916 \qquad F = 824.41$$

$$GENAN = 0.25GORFSL + 0.92NOXNL - 2.56 \qquad (13.44)$$
$$(7.25) \qquad\qquad (12.24) \qquad\quad (-4.80)$$

$$r^2 = 0.9967 \qquad F = 2100.2$$

$$GENAN = 0.90EXPTNAL - 61.60\Delta DFGDP - 2.51 \qquad (13.45)$$
$$(32.09) \qquad\qquad (-14.87) \qquad\qquad (-3.95)$$

$$r^2 = 0.9945 \qquad F = 1223.03$$

$$GENAN = 0.10GORFS + 1.31NOXNL - 4.54 \qquad (13.46)$$
$$(3.54) \qquad\qquad (13.28) \qquad\quad (-6.55)$$

$$r^2 = 0.9926 \qquad F = 809.64$$

$$GENAN = 1.21GNORFS - 6.90\Delta DFGDP + 0.85NOXN - 2.78$$
$$(1.71) \qquad\qquad (-3.28) \qquad\qquad (6.16) \qquad\quad (-5.35)$$

$$r^2 = 0.9974 \qquad F = 1674.65 \qquad\qquad (13.47)$$

Government Domestic Expenditure

$$GNDEX = 25.48DFGDP + 0.62NDEXL + 0.18DDC - 22.44$$
$$(7.02) \qquad\qquad (3.69) \qquad\qquad (2.76) \qquad (-7.16)$$

$$r^2 = 0.9910 \qquad F = 401.57 \qquad\qquad (13.48)$$

Private Expenditures
(Constant Prices)

$$PENANP = 0.07NOXNPL + 0.58PENANPL + 0.61 \qquad (13.49)$$
$$(4.10) \qquad\qquad (7.92) \qquad\qquad (1.12)$$

$$r^2 = 0.9861 \qquad F = 461.00$$

$$PENANP = 12.72GENANPL + 31.42PINPL - 9.69ZNANPL - 14.03$$
$$(3.68) \qquad\qquad (1.99) \qquad\qquad (-3.15) \qquad (-1.26)$$

$$r^2 = 0.7380 \qquad F = 11.27 \qquad\qquad (13.50)$$

$$PENANP = 0.11GORFSP + 0.05GORFSPL + 4.80 \quad (13.51)$$
$$\quad\quad\quad\quad (2.93) \quad\quad\quad (4.40) \quad\quad\quad\quad (10.56)$$

$$r^2 = 0.8792 \quad\quad F = 204.59$$

$$PENANP = 0.21FEXPTNARL + 0.48GENANPL + 2.37 \quad (13.52)$$
$$\quad\quad\quad\quad (6.95) \quad\quad\quad\quad (11.83) \quad\quad\quad\quad (12.06)$$

$$r^2 = 0.9917 \quad\quad F = 831.91$$

$$PENANP = 1.03GCNP - 1.21GINP + 0.26PENANPL + 2.51 \quad (13.53)$$
$$\quad\quad\quad (7.46) \quad\quad (-2.64) \quad\quad (3.24) \quad\quad\quad (6.70)$$

$$r^2 = 0.9694 \quad\quad F = 137.31$$

$$PENANP = 0.15GENANP + 0.56GENANPL + 3.35 \quad (13.54)$$
$$\quad\quad\quad\quad (1.31) \quad\quad\quad\quad (4.02) \quad\quad\quad\quad (12.65)$$

$$r^2 = 0.9669 \quad\quad F = 204.59$$

(Current Prices)

$$PENAN = 0.71GENAN + 3.49 \quad\quad\quad\quad (13.55)$$
$$\quad\quad\quad (21.76) \quad\quad\quad (4.79)$$

$$r^2 = 0.9733 \quad\quad F = 473.66$$

Capital Stock

(Constant Prices)

$$KP = 0.42GENANP + 1.05KPL - 1.29 \quad\quad (13.56)$$
$$\quad\quad\quad (3.09) \quad\quad\quad\quad (8.33) \quad\quad (-3.61)$$

$$r^2 = 0.9916 \quad\quad F = 767.69$$

$$KP = 0.41GENANP + 5.85 \quad\quad\quad\quad (13.57)$$
$$\quad\quad\quad (15.40) \quad\quad\quad (7.77)$$

$$r^2 = 0.9472 \quad\quad F = 269.08$$

(Current Prices)

$$K = 1.64GENAN - 0.13 \qquad (13.58)$$
$$\quad (33.33) \qquad (-0.09)$$

$$r^2 = 0.9867 \qquad F = 1110.80$$

Government Revenues

It is apparent from the previous analysis the extent to which the magnitude of government revenues ($GRFS$) plays a major role in Saudi Arabia's economy. Oil revenues, of course, dominate the government's receipts. Oil revenues ($GORFS$, nominal; and $GORFSP$, constant price) depend on oil exports ($EXPTNA$, nominal; and $FEXPTNAR$, constant price). An important factor not explicitly incorporated here is the effect of specific contractual arrangements entered into between the government and ARAMCO (and the other minor producers). These arrangements themselves are not important for estimation since for all practical purposes they are fixed (once they are agreed on). In this sense, revenues are directly linked to the total value of oil exports (see equations 13.59 to 13.63). Nonoil exports are ($GNORFS$) minor, and their determination is a straightforward relationship with nonoil income ($NOXN$) (see equation 13.64).

Government Revenue

$$GORFSP = 1.77FEXPTNAR - 9.16 \qquad (13.59)$$
$$\quad (7.79) \qquad\qquad (-2.96)$$

$$r^2 = 0.7912 \qquad F = 60.63$$

$$GNORFS = 0.22NOXN - 0.56 \qquad (13.60)$$
$$\quad (35.60) \qquad (-3.74)$$

$$r^2 = 0.9878 \qquad F = 1267.68$$

$$GRFS = 0.56FEXPTNA + 0.97NOXN - 6.79 \qquad (13.61)$$
$$\quad (6.18) \qquad\qquad (4.03) \qquad (-2.99)$$

$$r^2 = 0.9812 \qquad F = 312.88$$

$$GORFS = 0.42FEXPTNA + 0.47FEXPTNAL + 3.68 \qquad (13.62)$$
$$\qquad (4.53) \qquad\qquad (4.62) \qquad\qquad (-2.22)$$

$$r^2 = 0.9880 \qquad F = 575.40$$

$$GRFS = 0.91FEXPTNA - 4.90 \qquad\qquad (13.63)$$
$$\qquad (20.40) \qquad\qquad (-1.64)$$

$$r^2 = 0.9652 \qquad F = 415.99$$

$$GNORFS = 3.01\Delta FGDP + 0.07NOXN - 2.50 \qquad (13.64)$$
$$\qquad (3.22) \qquad\qquad (2.69) \qquad (-3.65)$$

$$r^2 = 0.9531 \qquad F = 72.98$$

Savings

The relationship between savings and income is one of the most critical aspects of development. Despite the theoretical and statistical attention that it has received, however, there is little agreement as to the causes of the variation in savings either among countries or over time.[39] Also in the context of OPEC countries, there is considerable doubt as to how domestic savings is affected by fluctuations in oil revenues.[40]

It is clear that savings rates are the result of many interrelated changes that take place as economies develop—in the structure of production, the type of income received, the inequality of income distribution, and so on. Historically, many of the these structural factors have been quite significant at income levels corresponding to those currently experienced in Saudi Arabia. Lack of available data on household savings, however, precludes any confirmation of this pattern for the kingdom. In place of household savings, aggregate savings figures were derived from national income relationships. Independent variables were selected for the regression equations on the basis of the theoretical considerations underlying the two-gap theory of development.[41]

As is well known using a national account framework, two resource gaps can be identified. The difference between exports and imports is the foreign gap, and (in the ex-post sense) the gap between savings and investment is the domestic gap. Both gaps are defined as equal and are identified here as F.

The savings equation $SNP = a + bGNPNP + cF$ in conjunction with an import equation of the type:

$$FZNANP = d + eGNPNP + fF$$

can be used to identify the historical constraints on growth. It can be shown that:[42]

1. If c is close to -1, with f not significantly different from 0, then trade gap has prevailed.
2. If c is close to 0 and f is significantly positive, then savings gap would have been binding.
3. When c is significantly negative but less than unity and f is significantly positive, then it is likely that there has been alternative periods of binding savings and trade gaps without clear dominance of either gap.

The results:

$$SNP = 0.46GNPNP - 0.43F - 1.50 \qquad (13.65)$$
$$(34.36) \qquad (-11.02)(-6.48)$$

$$r^2 = 0.9950 \qquad F = 1502.50$$

$$FZNANP = 1.06GNPNP + 1.63F - 4.43 \qquad (13.66)$$
$$(31.63) \qquad (16.57) \quad (-7.62)$$

$$r^2 = 0.9855 \qquad F = 511.08$$

indicate contrary to popular belief that foreign exchange has at one time been a constraint on the kingdom's growth. Undoubtedly, this would have occurred in the 1960s, but it is impossible given the limits of analysis to tell for certain.

Other formulations of the total, private, and government savings factors are straighforward, and in general confirm the importance of exports and government expenditure in determinging savings rates during the period under consideration (see equations 13.67 to 13.75).

Savings

(Constant Prices)

$$SNP = 0.69GENANP + 0.90FCAPFP - 0.20 \qquad (13.67)$$
$$(42.43) \qquad (38.44) \qquad (-1.14)$$

$$r^2 = 0.9973 \qquad F = 2420.96$$

$$SNP = 2.39GENANPL - 0.47PENANPL + 1.63 \qquad (13.68)$$
$$(3.11) \qquad\qquad (-1.75) \qquad\qquad (0.81)$$

$$r^2 = 0.6751 \qquad F = 13.51$$

$$SNP = -1.21ZNZNPL + 3.75NOXNPL - 12.34 \qquad (13.69)$$
$$(-4.10) \qquad\qquad (6.31) \qquad\qquad (-4.08)$$

$$r^2 = 0.8644 \qquad F = 41.44$$

$$SNP = 1.48FEXPTNARL - 0.78NOXNPL - 1.15 \qquad (13.70)$$
$$(9.56) \qquad\qquad (-1.97) \qquad\qquad (-0.91)$$

$$r^2 = 0.9165 \qquad F = 71.37$$

(Current Prices)

$$SN = 0.47FCAPF + 0.43GNPN - 1.35 \qquad (13.71)$$
$$(17.97) \qquad (90.40) \qquad (-6.62)$$

$$r^2 = 0.9993 \qquad F = 9153.72$$

Government Savings

(Constant Prices)

$$SGP = -33.27\Delta DFGDP + 1.48FEXPTNAR - 4.64$$
$$(-8.93) \qquad\qquad (7.63) \qquad\qquad (-2.21)$$

$$r^2 = 0.8619 \qquad F = 40.56 \qquad\qquad (13.72)$$

$$SGP = -52.37\Delta DFGDP + 1.08GENANP + 0.64GRFSP + 1.58$$
$$(-6.45) \qquad\qquad (3.64) \qquad\qquad (3.38) \qquad\qquad (0.93)$$

$$r^2 = 0.7899 \qquad F = 16.29 \qquad\qquad (13.73)$$

Private Savings

(Constant Prices)

$$SPP = -7.58DNOXNP + 0.40INF + 1.26SPPL + 2.68$$
$$(-2.23) \qquad\qquad (4.60) \qquad (4.57) \qquad (1.10)$$

$$r^2 = 0.9704 \qquad F = 130.94 \qquad\qquad (13.74)$$

$$SPP = 0.88SPPL - 3.31NOXNPL + 2.21FEXPTNARL + 2.08$$
$$(4.67)(-3.51)(4.35)(0.62)$$

$$r^2 = 0.8339 \qquad F = 20.08 \qquad\qquad (13.75)$$

Conclusions

The remaining structural equations that make up the forecasting model are presented in the chapter 14. The equations estimated previously have numerous implications, many of which are better discussed in the context of the forecasts made in the following chapter. Several general observations can be made, however:

1. The importance of the government in nearly all of the key macroeconomic relationships is perhaps the most significant—yet hardly surprising—result established in the regressions.

2. That the oil industry is under the control of the government makes it possible to clearly delineate the role of the public sector in the economy. Public-sector equations for consumption and investment indicate the strong effect that government expenditure has on the activity of the private sector and on key macroeconomic aggregates such as capital stock.

3. Most important, with regard to the private-sector expenditures on consumption and investment, the results indicate that despite great cultural differences, many of the sector's observed patterns are behavioristically similar to those observed in the developed countries.

At least in the Saudi Arabian case, Islamic institutions, while altering the manner in which economic activity is carried out, do not seem to have fundamentally affected the final relationships between the most important macroindicators of economic performance.

Notes

1. The pioneer and only published work in this area is the now somewhat outdated Faisal S. Al-Bashir, *A Structural Econometric Model of the Saudi Arabian Economy: 1960–1970* (New York: John Wiley, 1977).

2. H. Theil, "On the Theory of Economic Policy," *American Economic Review* (May 1956).

3. J. Timbergen, *On the Theory of Economic Policy* (Amsterdam: North Holland Publishing Co., 1952).

4. In terms of estimation procedures, ordinary least squares were used as a first screening of the numerous variables considered for each equation. When the model was essentially complete structurally, with each equation

limited to only a few possible expressions, the next logical step was undertaken: that of attempting to correct for the simultaneity biases. Since the number of exogenous variables did not exceed the number of observations, two-stage least-squares procedures were used for the final estimations. Unless otherwise indicated, the empirical regressions presented were estimated by this method.

5. See Central Department of Statistics, *National Accounts of Saudi Arabia 1386–1387 Through 1391–1392, A.H.* (Riyadh: Ministry of Finance and National Economy, 1973) for a detailed explanation of the items included and methods used to compile the country's national income statistics.

6. Bashir, *Structural Econometric Model*, p. 55.

7. Ibid.

8. Beeker, "A Theory of the Allocation of Time," *Economic Journal* (September 1965): 493–517.

9. See M. Friedman, *A Theory of the Consumption Function* (Princeton: National Bureau of Economic Research, 1957), for an explanation of the methods used.

10. Michael K. Evans, *Macroeconomic Activity: Theory Forecasting and Control* (New York: Harper & Row, 1969), pp. 23–24.

11. See Robert Ferber, "Consumer Economics: A Survey," *Journal of Economic Literature* (September 1973): 1303–1342.

12. A hypothesis originally proposed by Arthur Smithies, *The Economic Potential of the Arab Countries* (Santa Monica: Rand Corporation, 1978), p. 41.

13. Ibid., p. 42.

14. See Nathanial H. Leff and Kazvo Sato, "Macroeconomic Adjustment in Developing Countries: Instability, Short-run Growth and External Dependency," *The Review of Economics and Statistics* (May 1980): 170–179, for a detailed elaboration of this approach.

15. Ibid., p. 171.

16. A complete list of the model's variables and their symbols are presented in appendix A.

17. Deviations from the trend were used by Ichiro Otani to measure inflationary pressures in the Philippines. See his "Inflation in an Open Economy: A Case Study of the Philippines," *IMF Staff Papers* (1975), pp. 379–418. A criticism of this approach is given in Edmond Sheeley, "On the Measurement of Imported Inflation in Developing Countries," *Weltwirtschaftliches Archiv* (1979): 68–79.

18. Central Department of Statistics, *National Accounts of Saudi Arabia*, p. 32.

19. Ibid.

20. Bashir, *Structural Econometric Model*, p. 75.

21. As was done when inflationary pressures built up in 1976 and 1977, see "Deficits in Saudi Arabia: Their Meaning and Possible Implications," in Colin Legum, ed., *Middle East Contemporary Survey*, vol. II, *1977–1978* (New York: Holmes & Meier Publishers, 1979), p. 336.

22. Timothy Sisley, "The Evolution of the Private Sector," *Saudi Business and Arab Economic Report* (February 15, 1980): 24.

23. E. Kuh, *Capital Stock Growth: A Microeconometric Approach.* (Amsterdam: North-Holland, 1963).

24. Bashir, *Structural Econometric Model*, p. 75.

25. Edwin Kuhand, Richard Schmalensee, *An Introduction to Applied Macroeconomics* (Amsterdam: North Holland, 1973), p. 59.

26. E. Greenberg, "Fixed Investment," in David Heathfield, *Topics in Applied Macroeconomics* (New York: Academic Press, 1976), p. 97.

27. Evans, *Macroeconomic Activity*, pp. 100–101.

28. T. Mayer, "Plant and Equipment Lead Times," *Journal of Business* (April 1960): 127–132.

29. T. Mayer and S. Sonenblum, "Lead Times for Fixed Investment," *Review of Economics and Statistics* (August 1955): 300–304.

30. S. Almon, "The Distributed Lag Between Capital Appropriations and Expenditures," *Econometrica* (January 1965): 188.

31. Sisley, "Evolution of the Private Sector," p. 22.

32. Ibid.

33. Quoted in Sisley, "Evolution of the Private Sector," p. 22.

34. Quoted in Bashir, *Structural Econometric Model*, pp. 75–76.

35. Ibid.

36. Michael Keran and Ahmed Abdullah Al Malik, "Monetary Sources of Inflation in Saudi Arabia," Federal Reserve Bank of San Francisco, *Economic Review* (Winter 1979 Supplement): 14.

37. See Saudi Arabian Monetary Agency, *Annual Report*, various issues.

38. Farid Abolfathi et al., *The OPEC Market to 1985* (Lexington, Mass.: Lexington Books, D.C. Heath and Company, 1977), p. 240.

39. An outstanding review is given in Raymond Mikesell and James Zinser, "The Nature of the Savings Function in Developing Countries: A Survey of the Theoretical and Empirical Literature," *Journal of Economic Literature* (March 1973): 1–26.

40. Eprime Eshag, "Quantification of Disruptive Effects of Export Shortfalls," *Tahqiqate e Eqtesadi* (Winter 1971): 29–64.

41. Following the approach developed by H. Chenery and A. Strout,

"Foreign Assistance and Economic Development," *American Economic Review* (September 1966) 679–733.

42. See Louis Landau, "Savings Functions in Latin America," in Hollis Chenery, ed., *Studies in Development Planning* (Cambridge: Harvard University Press, 1971), pp. 299–321.

14

A Macroeconomic Model for Saudi Arabia—Foreign Trade and Production Equations

It is apparent from the previous chapter that despite a number of unique aspects characterizing the Saudi Arabian economy, many of the functional equations for consumption and investment are similar to those usually found in the more advanced Western countries. The same cannot be said for the relationships characterizing the foreign sector, however. Here all of the characteristics associated in its underdevelopment and an oil-dominated export pattern become fully apparent.

Exports

For all practical purposes, there are no nonoil exports to be concerned with in analyzing the kingdom's external position. The major issue when dealing with oil exports is, therefore, not one of proper disaggregation, but instead, whether it is more accurate to treat them as endogenous or exogenous variables.

Endogeneity of exports implies that they are determined within the planning system. The form and size of the country's plan are determined by factors such as absorptive capacity; that is, once the plan is set the rate of production would be determined according to the needs of the plan and its associated level of investment. The interaction of the two would simultaneously determine both variables: the rate of production and the levels of investment.

If we treat oil exports as endogenous, then considerations such as optimal depletion of the country's reserves become paramount. There are a wide range of alternative criteria that could be used as the basis for determining an optimal depletion pattern over time.

One approach is to determine the consumption pattern of oil strictly from a market behavior point of view.[1] Basically, the issue here is whether market-determined depletion rates are acceptable. It can be shown that under perfectly competitive commodity and capital markets, the optimal price of the resource would increase by the same rate as the interest rate. In theory one can argue that free market behavior (under certain conditions) will allocate the kingdom's oil reserves in an intertemporarily efficient manner.

One can come to a different conclusion by giving more prominence to the problem of achieving an equitable balance between present and future generations. Using the criterion of fairness, it is easy to argue that consumption per capita should be the same for all generations.[2] One study exploring the consequences of a straightforward application of the maximin principle to the intergenerational problem of capital accumulation (when there is a finite pool of exhaustible resources involved) has concluded that earlier generations are entitled to draw down the pool so long as they add to the stock of reproductible capital.[3]

This approach comes closest to the question often publicly posed by the Saudis when they discuss the issue of equality between generations and optimal planning. This is evidenced by the fact that whenever Saudi Arabia adjusts its rate of production, it must weigh the advantages of increased revenue against the resulting depletion of its oil reserves. In recent years, however, the kindgom has consistently produced more oil than it needed for revenue purposes. According to various estimates, the sector could probably generate sufficient income to meet the country's domestic economic needs by exporting around 5 million barrels per day (b/d).[4] Other observers have cited lower figures.[5] Domestic critics of the kingdom's production policies have noted that the country can only watch its growing foreign-exchange reserves lose value through inflation and currency fluctuations. Indeed some Saudi conservationists argue that oil may be worth more in the ground.[6]

The experiences of the 1970s has in fact demonstrated that the world oil market is extremely difficult to forecast using strictly economic factors.[7] Although the Organization of Petroleum Exporting Countries (OPEC) seems to have had the power to increase their prices steadily, each member country has nevertheless operated with a certain margin of the price agreed on by the cartel. Hence revenues from the sale of oil cannot be treated as endogenous. Oil revenues are simply not a variable that the kingdom can fully control over a prespecified time horizon, nor can the government determine in advance the magnitude of these payments with any sort of real precision.

There seem to be at least three major factors affecting Saudi oil policy:

1. The need to generate oil revenues at a level compatible with the country's total economic development.
2. The need to ensure regional and international political and economic stability.
3. The need to maintain a predominant influence over price-setting through the Organization of Petroleum Exporting Countries (OPEC).

In fact a close examination of the decision-making process in the kingdom reveals that at any given time the choice of whether to produce oil for exports is unlikely to be determined exclusively by internal economic planning. Rather the decision is very much influenced by political considerations both within the kingdom and in conjunction with other OPEC countries.

If the kingdom's oil policy were strictly under the control of the government with no outside factors influencing the production decision, then there is little doubt that an endogenous, intertemporal, optimizing criterion along the lines previously mentioned would be implemented. The fact is, however, that the rate of extraction is more determined by exogenous than endogenous forces.

Moreover, the endogeneity of the depletion rate is only meaningful when the country has the ability to determine its oil receipts over a certain length of time and can vary them to suit its requirements. Determination of the time path of its oil revenue in turn calls for the country's ability to determine and set its price of oil in each time period over the planning horizon. This has not been Saudi Arabia's experience as of 1981.

Several models have been proposed to illustrate the kingdom's dilemma and at the same time explain Saudi Arabia's strategy within OPEC. These include:

1. The conventional price-leadership model.[8]
2. A model emphasizing a concept of egalitarian leadership.[9]
3. Team models.[10]
4. Eclectic models composed of elements of the first three patterns.

Price Leadership Model

According to the price leadership model, OPEC decision making is highly centralized and under Saudi Arabian control. The attributes that permit the kingdom to assume this role consist of its possession of:

1. By far the largest reserves of any OPEC country.
2. A small population requiring less financial revenue than the larger countries.
3. Substantial excess production capacity.

The model has a strong and weak variation. The strong version contends that Saudi Arabia is the residual producer, allowing all other OPEC members to produce up to their capacity. At that point, the kingdom fills the gap between the aggregate export level and world demand. According to this view, Saudi Arabia in effect unilaterally sets the world price for oil. A weaker variant to the model hypothesizes that the country is more of a traditional price leader exploiting its own capability to expand production.[11] The kingdom might vary production in the short run either to reduce prices during periods of excessive demand or reduce production to increase revenues, thus enabling the country to build up its financial resources for the purpose of strengthening its ability to deal with potential cartel rivals.

There is some evidence consistent with the behavior predicted by this model. For example, Saudi Arabia doubled its market share between 1969 and 1974 and has continued to increase it ever since (though at a slower rate). This could be interpreted as building a base for a more firm leadership position. The data also show, however, that Venezuela, Kuwait, and Libya were reducing their production shares by roughly an equal aggregate percentage, presumably for conservation. The behavior of these three countries makes the stronger version of the price leadership model less convincing; that is, excess production capacity presumably existed throughout OPEC between 1974 and 1978, a period of generally slack petroleum demand, yet a number of members held off the market voluntarily rather than because they were incapable of exporting greater amounts.

Despite these shortcomings, the model is consistent with the commonly made observation that the kingdom is determined to keep OPEC strong and will absorb considerable economic costs to that end. Moreover, within OPEC the Saudis want to maintain their predominant position. In this regard their ability to cut production to maintain prices—without seriously affecting their economic development—is highly advantageous. They also have the capacity to increase production to keep prices from rising too rapidly.

Egalitarian Model

An interesting development in the trends of OPEC production since 1973 is that a more egalitarian (relative to reserve-size) pattern has developed. It seems that as decision making passed to OPEC in 1973, prior disparities in which the poorer states produced at low levels began to disappear; that is, that per capita income increasingly became correlated with the reserves to production ratio.[12]

While perhaps not the dominant trend over time, this pattern does show that OPEC production follows a pattern constrained by some commonly understood notions of equity.

With a current capacity of over 10.5 million b/d, the Saudis can easily increase production as demand picks up in the 1980s. The real question, however, is not about future production with current capacity limits, but about future capacity itself. How fast will the Saudis expand capacity to keep up with anticipated demand? Some recent studies have stated that Saudi capacity will have to reach 20 million b/d by 1990 to keep up with world needs, a figure the Saudis reject out of hand.[13]

Team Model

This model suggests that OPEC leadership evolves out of interchanges between coalitions within OPEC. The differences in these coalitions or teams ultimately boil down to diametrically opposed views as to price policy. The teams are identified through factor analysis, and seem to: (1) vary from four to five members; (2) change composition over time, and (3) be characterized by a single primary coalition headed by Saudi Arabia.[14] Each member of this dominant coalition has relatively large petroleum reserves, low capital absorption capability, and enormous financial surpluses. Hence each country in the dominant group has a vested interest in cartel stability (and following the 1973 price revolution, perpetuation of the commercial status quo).

In examining the model's results over time, it is apparent that Saudi Arabia was successful in coopting Iran—a potential commercial and military rival—into participation in the dominant coalition. The model's results are consistent with the view that Saudi Arabia has a fear of isolation, especially political isolation, and that as a result its government is not likely to adopt policies that would fundamentally threaten the unity of the dominant coalition (or inner cohesion circle).[15]

Eclectic Model

The team model seemed to predict well until the Iranian revolution, but the collapse of the Shah's regime and the resulting reduction in output has undermined the alliance between Iran and Saudi Arabia. It would seem the effect of these developments has been to leave the Saudi government much more vulnerable to pressures from the Arab left than either the leadership or egalitarian models would depict.

Saudi Arabia will now have to decide whether to yield to the price hawks inside OPEC (and thus keep its own production constant), or to the United States and consumer nations (thereby expanding its production to supplant the Iranian cutback). In the eclectic model, Saudi Arabia becomes a focal point for two sets of pressures: (1) those involving price escalation or price stability, and (2) those involving the security of the Saudi monarchy and the question of political unity within the Arab world.[16] The eclectic model clearly indicates, particularly in the aftermath of the Iranian revolution, that management of OPEC policies has become much more troublesome for Saudi Arabia.

Events over the last two decades, but particularly since 1973, indicate that there will be increased temptation for Saudi Arabia to yield to intra-OPEC pressure for price increases and/or expansion of capacity at a rate significantly lower than in the past. Presumably, compliance with this policy will enable the kingdom to avoid a further splitting of the dominant-governing coalition within the organization (and thus further isolating itself politically).

Even if the cartel were to break up, the kingdom (along with each of the other oil-exporting countries) would be facing a world price for oil that would be reached under conditions of competitive equilibrium in the international market. Again, this would be a situation that would inhibit Saudi planners from treating oil revenues as an endogenous variable capable of manipulation.

In light of the aforementioned considerations, it seems plausible to treat oil revenues as exogenous. This does not preclude investigations of the extent to which our model solutions are sensitive to variations in the time path of oil receipts. As a first step in this process, the relationship between exports and oil prices and production levels was identified. The two factors that determine the kingdom's oil exports—the price of oil (EUV) and the level of production (CPPDF)—were, therefore, taken as exogenous (see equations 14.1 to 14.4).

Exports

(Constant Prices)

$$FEXPTNAR = 0.13EUV + 7.37$$
$$\qquad\qquad (6.58) \qquad\quad (6.27)$$

$$r^2 = 0.9704 \qquad F = 130.93 \qquad\qquad (14.1)$$

$$FEXPTNAR = 0.01EUV + 14.98CPPDF + 1.81$$
$$\qquad\qquad (1.29) \qquad\quad (16.51) \qquad\qquad (4.25)$$

$$r^2 = 0.9889 \qquad F = 578.34 \qquad\qquad (14.2)$$

(Current Prices)

$$FEXPTNA = 0.95EUV + 0.34EUVL - 10.40$$
$$\qquad\qquad (14.47) \qquad\quad (4.64) \qquad\qquad (-7.07)$$

$$r^2 = 0.9945 \qquad F = 1263.59 \qquad\qquad (14.3)$$

$$FEXPTNA = 1.23EUV - 10.07$$
$$\qquad\qquad (32.53) \qquad\quad (-4.45)$$

$$r^2 = 0.9860 \qquad F = 1058.32 \qquad\qquad (14.4)$$

Both production (*CPPDF*) levels (actually a production index based on line 66aa of International Monetary Fund Financial Statistics) and crude petroleum (*EUV*) price (line 456 of IMF Financial Statistics) are significant in the regression equations (in particular, equation 14.2).

The model, therefore, treats *CPPDF* and *EUV* as exogenous. Ultimately, their fluctuations affect either directly or indirectly nearly all of the other macroeconomic variables.

Barring a major crisis such as the resumption of Arab–Israeli hostilities, it is both logical and likely that the Saudis will follow a middle of the road policy on oil for the foreseeable future. Yet there is still room for some flexibility. For example, with the development of excess world capacity in the late 1970s, conservationists in the Saudi government were able to succeed in effecting a policy of allowing the kingdom's oil production to fall without placing undue pressure on the world economy. In February 1978 the government placed a ceiling on production of light crude not to exceed 65 percent of total production. (The move was made to bring light-crude production into line with the estimated proportion of light-to-heavy crude oil in total Saudi reserves, as well as to ease the strain on the Ghawar field.) The effect of this decision was to reduce overall production in the late 1970s to roughly 1 million b/d less than the 1981 ceiling of 8.5 million b/d.[17]

In the meantime the Saudis will probably continue to exert a moderating force on prices within OPEC, though slightly less so than in the past. To avoid another energy crisis they will probably support a gradual rise in oil prices, slightly higher than the rise in global inflation.[18]

Imports

Imports play a crucial role in the Saudi Arabian economy. They provide a multitude of goods without which growth and expansion are not possible. As a developing, narrowly specialized country, Saudi Arabia exchanges oil for practically everything else. It imports heavy machinery and equipment as well as a wide range of consumer goods that includes medicine, cloth, and most important, food.

In addition, most of the country's imports are of a variety for which no domestic production exists. But even the limited range of imports for which there is domestic production, such as certain types of processed and unprocessed food, is still insignificant because local industries are too small to provide the market needs on a year-round basis.

Imports tend to be very closely related to movements in domestic aggregate economic activity, rising with booms and falling with recessions. There are at least two components to this mechanism. The first takes place during a boom, whereby increases in disposable income elicit increases in spending on consumer goods, most of which must in turn be imported. The second and more important component is the increased demand for productive capacity during a boom. Expanded aggregate demand leads to increased domestic investment and, concomitantly, increased imports of capital goods and raw materials.

The supply curve facing Saudi Arabia for most imported goods is likely to be infinitely elastic (in foreign prices times the effective exchange rate), and consequently in the short run the amount spent on imports is determined by domestic demand. In the longer run it might be argued that there is some influence on the domestic substitutes influenced by the real rate of exchange (the price ratio between tradables and nontradables), and therefore imports (which equal the quantity demanded less domestic production) are also affected by this rate. Because of the still limited volume of import substitution industries existing in the kingdom ,the short-run approach seemed more appropriate and was thus used in the estimations below.

In the actual formulation of individual import equations, the role of relative prices was assumed likely to be significant from two points of view. The first is that high import prices relative to domestic prices should induce import substitution if the factors (including managerial talent) are domestically available. The plausability of this expectation is increased by the government's active campaign to diversify the economy and to reduce the country's dependence on imports.

The second is the terms of trade effect; that is, high import prices relative to domestic prices could imply a reduced ability to import unless export prices have increased commensurately. The terms of trade was measured as the ratio of the price index for domestic goods to that of imported goods. Two indices were used: (1) the ratio of the domestic consumer price index to the price index of industrial country exports ($Z1TT$), and (2) the ratio of the GDP deflator to the price index of industrial country exports ($Z2TT$). The base year for all of the indices is 1970.

To summarize, based on the theory of demand it was assumed that Saudi Arabia's real imports ($ZNANP$) would be significantly related to changes in national income and the price of imported goods relative to domestic goods. In some of the equations, imports were disaggregated into three functional categories: (1) food (ZFP), (2) machinery (ZMP), and (3) other (mainly intermediate) goods (ZOP). Disaggregation of this type facilitates the analysis of trends. It also allows an investigation of structural change over time.

For example, it is apparent as shown by a decreasing share of some consumer goods and an increasing share of capital and intermediate goods in imports that the country is implementing its policy of diversification and industrialization. A related point is that disaggregation allows one to delineate between those imports associated with the increase in general well being, and those whose main purpose was to further industrial growth.

Imports

(Constant Prices)

$ZNZNP = 1.53GENANP + 10.72Z1TT - 12.74$
$\quad\quad (19.45) \quad\quad\quad (3.61) \quad\quad\quad (-4.37)$

$\quad\quad\quad\quad r^2 = 0.9816 \quad\quad F = 399.17 \quad\quad\quad\quad (14.5)$

$ZNANP = 1.29GENANP + 9.81Z2TT - 10.88$
$\quad\quad (24.64) \quad\quad\quad (9.81) \quad\quad\quad (-12.02)$

$\quad\quad\quad\quad r^2 = 0.9953 \quad\quad F = 1605.11 \quad\quad\quad\quad (14.6)$

$ZNANP = 0.97GENANP + 7.11Z2TT + 0.34ZNZNPL - 8.01$
$\quad\quad (16.09) \quad\quad\quad (10.15) \quad\quad (6.07) \quad\quad\quad (-11.78)$

$\quad\quad\quad\quad r^2 = 0.9987 \quad\quad F = 3643.42 \quad\quad\quad\quad (14.7)$

$ZNANP = 0.91GENANP + 12.11Z2TT + 0.72PCNP - 15.09$
$\quad\quad (8.27) \quad\quad\quad (12.53) \quad\quad (3.68) \quad\quad (6.09)$

$\quad\quad\quad\quad r^2 = 0.9976 \quad\quad F = 1972.90 \quad\quad\quad\quad (14.8)$

$ZNANP = 1.06GNPNP + 1.63FCAPFP - 4.43$
$\quad\quad (31.63) \quad\quad\quad (16.57) \quad\quad\quad (-7.62)$

$\quad\quad\quad\quad r^2 = 0.9855 \quad\quad F = 511.08 \quad\quad\quad\quad (14.9)$

$ZNANP = 0.92ZNANPL + 0.14MSFAPL + 0.14$
$\quad\quad (19.46) \quad\quad\quad (8.39) \quad\quad\quad (0.51)$

$\quad\quad\quad\quad r^2 = 0.9952 \quad\quad F+ = 1360.43 \quad\quad\quad\quad (14.10)$

$ZNANP = 0.89ZNANPL + 0.80NOZNPL - 3.78$
$\quad\quad (4.88) \quad\quad\quad (2.18) \quad\quad\quad (2.03)$

$\quad\quad\quad\quad r^2 = 0.9777 \quad\quad F = 284.61 \quad\quad\quad\quad (14.11)$

$$ZNANP = 1.14\Delta GENANP + 2.00\Delta PENANP - 0.79$$
$$(6.10) \qquad\qquad (5.15) \qquad\qquad (-1.63)$$

$$r^2 = 0.9962 \qquad F = 1038.37 \qquad\qquad (14.12)$$

$$FZP = 0.73GENANP + 0.40PCNP - 1.47$$
$$(10.46) \qquad\qquad (3.41) \qquad (-3.16)$$

$$r^2 = 0.9852 \qquad F = 432.44 \qquad\qquad (14.13)$$

$$ZMP = 0.34GENANP + 0.73TINPL - 1.52$$
$$(2.66) \qquad\qquad (2.99) \qquad\qquad (-4.54)$$

$$r^2 = 0.9608 \qquad F = 171.48 \qquad\qquad (14.14)$$

$$ZFP = 0.14PCNP + 0.01GORFSPL + 0.12$$
$$(3.54) \qquad (4.52) \qquad\qquad (0.60)$$

$$r^2 = 0.9373 \qquad F = 97.23 \qquad\qquad (14.15)$$

$$DZP = 0.41\Delta GENANP + 0.54\Delta PENANP + 0.14$$
$$(4.05) \qquad\qquad (2.57) \qquad\qquad (0.53)$$

$$r^2 = 0.6380 \qquad F = 11.46 \qquad\qquad (14.16)$$

$$FZOP = 0.39GENANP - 0.22$$
$$(19.46) \qquad\qquad (-1.21)$$

$$r^2 = 0.9644 \qquad F = 378.75 \qquad\qquad (14.17)$$

$$\Delta ZFP = 0.25\Delta GENANP + 0.60\Delta PENANP - 0.29$$
$$(4.97) \qquad\qquad (5.77) \qquad\qquad (-2.21)$$

$$r^2 = 0.8161 \qquad F = 21.84 \qquad\qquad (14.18)$$

$$\Delta ZOP = 0.15\Delta GENANP + 0.32\Delta PENANP - 0.002$$
$$(2.02) \qquad\qquad (2.14) \qquad\qquad (-0.01)$$

$$r^2 = 0.3989 \qquad F = 4.31 \qquad\qquad (14.19)$$

(Current Prices)

$$ZNAN = -0.03DC - 5.16Z1TT + 0.92NOXN + 3.17$$
$$\quad\quad (-4.68) \quad\quad (3.71) \quad\quad\quad (57.70) \quad\quad\quad (2.27)$$

$$r^2 = 0.9995 \quad\quad F = 8555.67 \quad\quad\quad\quad (14.20)$$

$$ZNAN = 0.90NOXN - 4.91Z1TT + 0.59PC + 2.36$$
$$\quad\quad (15.30) \quad\quad\quad (-2.33) \quad\quad (2.05) \quad (1.12)$$

$$r^2 = 0.9987 \quad\quad F = 2994.01 \quad\quad\quad\quad (14.21)$$

$$ZNAN = -0.04DC + 0.82NOXN - 1.60$$
$$\quad\quad (-4.11) \quad\quad (23.07) \quad\quad\quad (-5.93)$$

$$r^2 = 0.9985 \quad\quad F = 449.45 \quad\quad\quad\quad (14.22)$$

$$ZNAN = 1.19PENAN + 8.55Z1TT - 0.06\Delta DC - 11.58$$
$$\quad\quad (31.84) \quad\quad\quad (3.16) \quad\quad\quad (-3.28) \quad\quad (-4.40)$$

$$r^2 = 0.9983 \quad\quad F = 2216.40 \quad\quad\quad\quad (14.23)$$

$$ZNAN = 1.18PENAN + 8.56Z1TT - 0.06\Delta DC - 11.60$$
$$\quad\quad (31.82) \quad\quad\quad (3.16) \quad\quad\quad (-3.29) \quad\quad (-4.41)$$

$$r^2 = 0.9983 \quad\quad F = 2216.41 \quad\quad\quad\quad (14.24)$$

$$ZNAN = 1.21PENAN + 5.60Z1TT - 8.30$$
$$\quad\quad (49.58) \quad\quad\quad (1.90 \quad\quad\quad (-2.83)$$

$$r^2 = 0.9975 \quad\quad F = 2560.48 \quad\quad\quad\quad (14.25)$$

(Current Prices)

$$FZ = 0.57GENAN + 0.37PCN - 1.10$$
$$\quad (6.97) \quad\quad\quad (7.31) \quad\quad (-1.78)$$

$$r^2 = 0.9963 \quad\quad F = 1749.02 \quad\quad\quad\quad (14.26)$$

$$FZ = 0.44FZL + 0.55NOXN - 1.91$$
$$\quad (4.29) \quad\quad (10.03) \quad\quad (-4.45)$$

$$r^2 = 0.9967 \quad\quad F = 1965.42 \quad\quad\quad\quad (14.27)$$

$$FZM = 0.01DC + 0.39GENAN - 0.41$$
$$\quad\quad (2.24) \quad\quad (34.25) \quad\quad\quad (-2.65)$$

$$r^2 = 0.9976 \quad\quad F = 2757.88 \quad\quad\quad (14.28)$$

$$FZF = 0.04GORFS + 0.60$$
$$\quad\quad (7.47) \quad\quad\quad (2.04)$$

$$r^2 = 0.7992 \quad\quad F = 55.73 \quad\quad\quad (14.29)$$

$$FZF = 0.04GENAN + 0.05GENANL + 0.58$$
$$\quad\quad (3.07) \quad\quad\quad (2.73) \quad\quad\quad (6.99)$$

$$r^2 = 0.9830 \quad\quad F = 376.06 \quad\quad\quad (14.30)$$

$$FZO = 0.31GENAN - 0.16$$
$$\quad\quad (32.67) \quad\quad\quad (-0.53)$$

$$r^2 = 0.9871 \quad\quad F = 1067.15 \quad\quad\quad (14.31)$$

$$\Delta ZNAN = 0.42\Delta GENAN + 0.62\Delta PENAN + 0.22$$
$$\quad\quad (5.97) \quad\quad\quad (5.89) \quad\quad\quad (0.86)$$

$$r^2 = 0.9846 \quad\quad F = 383.98 \quad\quad\quad (14.32)$$

$$\Delta ZM = 0.29\Delta GENAN + 0.41\Delta PENAN - 0.12$$
$$\quad\quad (8.99) \quad\quad\quad (3.15) \quad\quad\quad (-0.64)$$

$$r^2 = 0.9741 \quad\quad F = 244.62 \quad\quad\quad (14.33)$$

$$\Delta ZF = 0.03\Delta GENAN + 0.06\Delta PENAN + 0.02$$
$$\quad\quad (1.99) \quad\quad\quad (2.82) \quad\quad\quad (0.24)$$

$$r^2 = 0.8529 \quad\quad F = 37.69 \quad\quad\quad (14.34)$$

$$\Delta ZO = 0.31\Delta GENAN + 0.03$$
$$\quad\quad (7.15) \quad\quad\quad (0.06)$$

$$r^2 = 0.7850 \quad\quad F = 51.13 \quad\quad\quad (14.35)$$

The results (see equations 14.5 to 14.35) are consistent with the general observations made earlier concerning the factors influencing the kingdom's imports.[19] Almost always the expenditure term was significant, together with some index of relative prices. In general government expenditures gave better results (see equations 14.5 to 14.8) than nonoil GDP (see equation 14.11). This is not surprising considering that Saudi Arabia is not only a developing country but one where many of the individual entrepreneurial decisions are in effect formed by definite government policy objectives and implemented directly by the authorities. Imports of machinery for example are more likely to be a function of the official policy of diversification aimed at furthering the industrial process. As such they are more likely to show a pattern of quantum jumps, rather than a steady incremental increase inherent in the unfettered supply and demand mechanism.

Consistent with this interpretation are the results showing that government expenditure gives much better results in the current period than when lagged (an alternative interpretation of this pattern is simply that government expenditures are really a proxy for available resources to import rather than a proxy for overall demand).

Apparently, despite that the world supply schedule for the country is likely to be infinitely elastic, the country is not able to import all it wishes within a given period. Equation 14.7, for example, indicates that the short-run marginal propensity to import is 0.97, but the long-run marginal propensity is 11.33.

A number of factors could explain this pattern in addition to the well-publicized port bottlenecks dramatized in the press during 1974–1975. Importers, for example, are required to go through certain time-consuming procedures to obtain licenses. Of course, the international transportation of goods takes time, as does the placing of foreign orders.

In sum, a mechanism that stresses that only a part of the desired level of imports have tended to arrive within a given period seems realistic. Changes in imports during any period can be viewed as a function of the gap between the desired level of imports in the current period and the actual level of imports in the previous period.

Finally, disaggregation into such areas as food and machinery did not yield a significantly different picture. Government programs and policies were also the dominant factors influencing the levels and changes in the values of these categories.

Production Function

Conceptually, output may be determined primarily by input (or productive capacity constraints) on the one hand, or demand factors on the other. On the basis of the discussion in previous chapters, it is reasonable to assume nonoil GDP constrained by a broad range on input factors. Supporting evidence for this may be found in the structure of the country's imports, which indicates that a significant part of domestic demand for agricultural and especially industrial products is still being met by imports.

Nonoil gross domestic product is assumed to be a simple linear function of the capital stock and employment. The employment variable is, of course, important from the point of view of the government's strategy to eliminate eventually the need for a large foreign work force. In equation form:

$$NOXNP = f(KP, EMPT, T), \text{ where } KP = \sum_{t=1}^{3} . TINP$$

Capital stock is in gross terms and is a three-year summation of total (private + government + oil sector) investment (*TINP*).

In the absence of any consistent time-series data on man/hours or unemployment, the total work force (*EMPT*) was used as a measure of labor input. The time trend (*T*) was initially included to capture any technological change not embodied in capital or labor. Preliminary tests indicated this effect was minimal, and therefore it was omitted from the analysis.

Best results were obtained with capital and employment (see equation 14.36). The significance of employment and the lack of any significant amount of disembodied technological change in the past mean that the government's foreign worker strategy is likely to present the economy with serious difficulties in the future. It is clear that nonoil GDP is largely determined by the economy's absorptive capacity (the demand for resources) and its import capacity (the supply of resources). Because of the growing industrial base and several years of emphasis on the establishment of infrastructure, absorptive capacity per se is unlikely to be a severe constraint in the future. Even if the import intensity of the industrialization effort increases, especially resulting in increased demand for intermediate goods, a shortage of foreign exchange is unlikely to develop. That means that only labor is a major constraint on growth. It is extremely difficult to see, therefore, how the country will be able to carry out its foreign worker policy and avoid severe manpower shortages and a reduced growth of the economy.

Finally, on the demand side, both domestic absorption and domestic supply (see equations 14.44 and 14.45) show again the pervasive nature of the government in the economy.

Gross Domestic Product

(Constant Prices)

$$NOXNP = 8.71EMPT + 0.21KP - 4.38$$
$$(8.16) \qquad (6.50) \qquad (-4.42)$$

$$r^2 = 0.9959 \qquad F = 1720.47 \qquad (14.36)$$

$NOXNP = 0.36GENANP + 1.49POP + 0.31GENANPL - 4.42$
　　　　(2.52)　　　　　(4.70)　　　(2.42)　　　　　(−2.62)

$$r^2 = 0.9924 \qquad F = 1559.55 \qquad\qquad (14.37)$$

$OGDPNP = 2.46FEXPTNAR - 11.25$
　　　　　(7.11)　　　　　　　(−2.27)

$$r^2 = 0.7832 \qquad F = 50.58 \qquad\qquad (14.38)$$

$\Delta NOXNP = 0.03\Delta KP + 8.60\Delta EMPT + 0.27$
　　　　　(1.89)　　　(2.09)　　　　(1.48)

$$r^2 = 0.8554 \qquad F = 35.44 \qquad\qquad (14.39)$$

(Current Prices)

$GDPN = 1.14OGDPN + 1.07GENANL + 1.67$
　　　(34.45)　　　　(7.86)　　　　(1.55)

$$r^2 = 0.9987 \qquad F = 30512.64 \qquad\qquad (14.40)$$

$OGDPN = 0.98FEXPTNA - 0.25$
　　　　(53.72)　　　　　(0.93)

$$r^2 = 0.9999 \qquad F = 371{,}739.70 \qquad\qquad (14.41)$$

$NOXN = 14.87EMPT + 0.49FK - 12.97$
　　　(3.53)　　　　(16.49)　(−2.72)

$$r^2 = 0.9949 \qquad F = 774.90 \qquad\qquad (14.42)$$

$\Delta NOXN = 105.70\Delta EMPT + 2.76\Delta TINP - 3.75$
　　　　(3.86)　　　　　(2.13)　　　　(−2.88)

$$r^2 = 0.8720 \qquad F = 44.28 \qquad\qquad (14.43)$$

Domestic Absorption

(Constant Prices)

$\Delta ANP = 0.83GENANP + 1.50PENANP - 1.43$
　　　(6.92)　　　　　(7.74)　　　　(−1.92)

$$r^2 = 0.9956 \qquad F = 1470.47 \qquad\qquad (14.44)$$

Domestic Supply

(Constant Prices)

$$ADNP = -9.69ZNANPL + 12.72GENANPL + 31.42PINPL - 14.03$$
$$(-3.15) \qquad (3.68) \qquad (1.99) \qquad (-1.26)$$

$$r^2 = 0.7380 \qquad F = 11.27 \qquad (14.45)$$

Conclusions

Econometric model building in Saudi Arabia appears to be a very feasible and desirable endeavor. The results presented in this chapter would tend to support such an assertion. The importance of this type of activity seems self-evident. It is difficult to see how the pursuit of national policy goals could not take place efficiently within the framework capable of examining the economic forces at work in the kingdom.

Notes

1. See M.C. Weinstein and R.J. Zeckhauser, "The Optimal Consumption of Depletable Natural Resources," *Quarterly Journal of Economics* (August 1975): 371–392.

2. The approach of R.M. Solow, "Intergenerational Equity and Exhaustible Resources," *Review of Economic Studies* (October 1974): 29–47.

3. Ibid.

4. Summarized in Theodore Morgan, *Oil Prices and the Future of OPEC* (Washington: Resources for the Future, 1978).

5. Ibid.

6. A rationale for this position is given in Angelos Pagoulatos and John Timmons, "Management Options in the Use of Exhaustible and Nonrenewable Natural Resources," *Rivista Internationale de Scienze Economiche e Commerciali* (June 1978): 489–507.

7. M.A. Adelman, "The World Oil Cartel: Scarcity, Economics and Politics," *Quarterly Review of Economics and Business* (Summer 1976): 7.

8. As developed for example in K.A. Tourk, "The OPEC Cartel: A Revival of the 'Dominant-Firm' Theory," *The Journal of Energy and Development* (Spring 1977): 321–328.

9. Charles Doran, "Three Models of OPEC Leadership and Policy in the Aftermath of Iran," *Journal of Policy Modeling* (September 1979): 415.

10. H. Chenery, "Restructuring the World Economy," *Foreign Affairs* (April 1975): 242–262.

11. Doran, "Three Models," p. 414.

12. ibid., p. 415.

13. David E. Long, "Saudi Oil Policy," *The Wilson Quarterly* (Winter 1979): 91.

14. By Doran, "Three Models," p. 415.

15. Ibid.

16. Ibid., p. 423.

17. Long, "Saudi Oil Policy," p. 90.

18. The broader factors underlying this strategy are given in Adeed Dawisha, "Internal Values and External Threats: The Making of Saudi Foreign Policy," *Orbis* (Spring 1979): 129–143.

19. Again, the reader unsure of the meaning of a symbol can find a complete listing in appendix A.

15 Macroeconomic Adjustment Mechanisms—the Supply and Demand for Money

Despite the kingdom's many unique economic institutions, macroeconomic equilibrium must be established there just as is the case for any more-developed (or underdeveloped) economy. The particular adjustment mechanisms that operate to eliminate disequilibrium are of special interest because alternative adjustment mechanisms may have different effects on the subsequent path of economic growth.

The final equations developed below should provide a new perspective on the growth mechanisms of the country. The adjustments of particular relevance for the forecasts made in chapter 17 include:

1. Portfolio adjustments (adjustments in the demand and supply of money).
2. External adjustments (the monetary measure of the balance of payments).
3. Internal supply–demand adjustments (inflation).

The monetary demand and supply adjustments are discussed in this chapter. The remaining two mechanisms are examined in chapter 16.

Demand for Money

Money is a stock, and since expectations play a role in portfolio adjustments of individuals (more specifically wealthy holders), the speed at which actual portfolios are adjusted to desired levels should determine variations in the kingdom's real stock of money. It is highly likely that the adjustment of money holdings of individual Saudis can be made only partially in each period because of lack of information on their part concerning developments in the economy, inertia, and the costs involved in making adjustments.[1] Furthermore if (as is likely to be the case), the desired money balances of Saudis should depend on expected (or permanent) income or other expected values of certain variables, it would take time for them to revise their expectations in light of the economic conditions they were currently experiencing.[2]

It is also quite likely that individuals in Saudi Arabia, given their long-run desired money balance and their money balance position in the previous

259

period (year), would attempt to minimize the costs associated with their current money-balance position.[3] In this case, the costs involved would consist of those required in altering portfolios and those associated with being out of equilibrium.

The first are commonly referred to as transactions costs and usually increase with changes in money balances.[4] The second are those of foregone yields on assets or the cost-increased illiquidity and risks (depending on whether the current money balance position exceeds or falls short of the desired position for the same period). It is usually felt that these costs increase with the discrepancy between the individual's desired and actual portfolio position. They can be depicted as:

$$M = ML + a(MD - ML) \qquad (15.1)$$

where ML = actual money supply lagged 1 year; MD = the amount of money currently demanded; a is assumed to have a value between 1 and 0 and represents the speed of adjustment between the actual and desired values.[5]

The expectation lag, on the other hand, can be thought of as a function of the anticipated value of a certain variable (such as income) and the actual value of the previous period. It also includes a component based on the error made in previous forecasts. In other words, in each period, the expectation of Saudis is likely to be revised in proportion to the size of error committed in the expectation made during the previous period. For example, in the case of income expectations, this error learning mechanism can be expressed as:[6]

$$YE = YEL1 + b(Y - YEL1) \qquad (15.2)$$

where YE = a measure of expected income; $YEL1$ = expected income last year; Y = actual income in the current time period; b = the average change in expectation and taxes—a value from 0 to 1.

Empirical evidence to date for other countries suggests that the speed of adjustment in expectation depends primarily on the costs associated with inaccurate information and the individual's attitude toward risks. It is argued by many writers that this lag can be ignored in developing countries. This is presumably because both uncertainties and risks tend to be high in these areas.[7] It seems just as logical, however, to argue that if in fact the majority of entrepreneurs and households in those countries have higher uncertainties and are greater risk averters, there could be a relatively longer expectation lag (that is, a smaller b), particularly because risk averters would act in a conservative manner in adjusting their portfolios.

Clearly the existence of either lag and their lengths in Saudi Arabia should be treated as an empirical matter. Toward this end, a long-run demand for money function was specified as directly related to expected income (YE) and inversely related to the expected degree of credit restraint (CR) and the expected rate of inflation (INF), or

$$M = d(YE) - c(CRE) - d(INF) \qquad (15.3)$$

Here credit restraint was defined as the ratio of private credit to nonoil income.[8] It has a negative sign because it is likely that when commercial bank credit is tightened, individuals conserve on their money balances, whereas in periods of easy credit, they may keep excess balances (because of their low opportunity costs).

Inflation was defined as the rate of inflation in the previous year minus the rate of inflation in the year prior to that.[9]

If we assume that money holders have identical expectations with respect to income, inflation, and the degree of credit restraint then the demand for money can be expressed as:[10]

$$M = [(1 - a) + (1 - b)ML - (1 - a)(1 - b)ML2$$

$$+ abc(CR) - abd(INF) + abe(Y)] \qquad (15.4)$$

If only the demand adjustment lag is operative, then the actual value of a and b must be $0 < a < b1$ and $b = 1$. In this case equation 14.5 becomes:

$$M = (1 - a)ML + abY + ab(CR) + ab(INF) + aeY$$

If only the expectation lag exists, then b must be greater than 0 but less than 1 ($0 < b < 1$) and $a = 1$. In this case the equation becomes:

$$M = (1 - a) + (1 - b)ML - (1 - a)(1 - b)ML2 + beY$$

$$- bc(CR) - bd(INF) \qquad (15.5)$$

If neither lag exists, then the equation reduces to

$$M = eY - c(CR) - d(INF) \qquad (15.6)$$

The magnitude and statistical significance of the coefficient of the lagged money is a demand for money function and can therefore be used to evaluate the existence and length of either the expectation lag or the demand adjustment lag.

When money lagged for one and two periods are both introduced in the function, the coefficients can be used to measure both lags.

The results (equations 15.7 to 15.9) for various specifications of the demand for money function indicate the possibility of the existence of both lags; that is

$$M = 0.826(ML) - 0.215(ML2) + 0.373(GDPN) - 0.54(CR) - \quad (15.10)$$
$$(3.27) \qquad\qquad (-1.00) \qquad\quad (8.4) \qquad\qquad (-2.90)$$

$$- 0.034(INF)$$
$$(-1.67)$$

$$b = 0.174; a = 0.260; r^2 = 0.9989; DW = 2.663$$

$$M = 0.829(ML) - 0.483(ML2) + 0.628(GDPN) - 0.038(CR) \quad (15.11)$$
$$(2.63) \qquad\qquad (-2.03) \qquad\quad (6.67) \qquad\qquad (-1.71)$$

$$- 0.028(INF)$$
$$(-1.17)$$

$$b = 0.172; a = 0.583; r^2 = 0.9984; DW = 2.533$$

$$M = 0.369(ML) - 0.245(ML2) + 0.860(DAN) - 0.043(CCR) \quad (15.12)$$
$$(2.07) \qquad\qquad (-1.92) \qquad\quad (14.31) \qquad\quad (-3.88)$$

$$- 0.030(INF)$$
$$(2.86)$$

$$b = 0.631; a = 0.388; r^2 = 0.9996; DW = 2.302$$

where CR = private credit/nominal nonoil income; INF = rate of inflation; (t) − rate of inflation (L). All coefficients are in standardized (beta) values.

The results give interesting insights into Saudi portfolio behavior. Apparently, while it is costly for individuals in the kingdom to be out of equilibrium, it is also costly for them to make adjustments to restore equilibrium. Deficiencies in their money holdings imply excessive holdings of other assets. The costs associated with restoration of equilibrium must therefore depend (among other things) on liquidity and the ease of convertibility of other assets.

We know that because of Islamic codes and the lack of government debt, there are few financial assets available. Most assets other than cash would be real (that is, physical, such as land and gold). The deficient financial structure therefore may explain the somewhat slow portfolio adjustment process observed during this period.

To summarize, if the speed of adjustment depends on adjustment costs, it will take longer for wealth holders in Saudi Arabia than in most countries to adjust their money holdings (that is, a smaller value of *a*) because nearly all other components in their portfolio are dominated by real assets. Clearly, it takes an individual more time to make a land or a house transfer than to make a switch between a checking account and a savings account.

Our results are, therefore, contrary to the assertion made by many writers that monetary lags are negligible in countries where there is a lack and variety of financial assets. The Saudi tradition and willingness to substitute real assets for money is apparently a major reason for that country's deviation from the normal developing country pattern.

Money Supply

The most interesting monetary pattern is the acceleration in the growth rate of the money supply (*M*1) after 1971. While the annual growth rate was 10.1 percent over the period 1960–1971, it rose sharply to about 43 percent in 1972, 40 percent in 1973, and 41 percent in 1974, reaching a peak of nearly 90 percent in 1975. Over the 1972–1979 period, the average annual growth rate of *M*1 was 46.5 percent.[11]

Equally interesting is the observation that the monetary stock series closely resembles that of high powered money—the monetary base (*MB*):

$$M1 = 1.17MB + 0.36 \qquad (15.13)$$
$$(70.93) \quad (1.50)$$

$$r^2 = 0.9972; \ F = 5030.88; \ DW = 1.7036$$

The relationship between the money stock and the monetary base is an important one. In the chapter 16 projections of the growth in the money supply are made from estimates of the likely growth of the monetary base.

The most important component (see table 15–1) of the supply of money base in Saudi Arabia is clearly the level of foreign reserves. During the 1960–1977 period, the minimum contribution of foregin reserves to the monetary base was 125.76 (1960). In 1974 this source rose to 1,178.50 percent. Until 1971 there was a rather stable pattern with foreign assets contributing on the average 232.56 percent to the monetary base. This stability was apparently disturbed by a number of factors including the oil price increases in 1973–1974.

The public sector component of the monetary base consists of the net claims of SAMA over the government. Since the government did not borrow from SAMA during the 1960–1979 period, this figure was negative, indicating that government deposits exceeded the stock of government liabilities with SAMA.[12] In the accounting sense, therefore, SAMA became an increasing net debtor to the government.

Table 15–1
Saudi Arabia: Sources of Money, Base 1960–1977 (billions of riyals)

Year	High-Powered Money	Foreign Assets (010)	Government Deposits (010)	Other Net SAMA Items (010)
1960	0.66	0.83 (125.76)	0.24 (−36.36)	0.07 (10.61)
1961	0.69	1.07 (155.07)	0.38 (−55.07)	— (0.00)
1962	0.79	1.20 (151.90)	0.40 (−50.63)	0.01 (−1.27)
1963	0.98	2.35 (239.80)	1.26 (−128.57)	0.11 (−11.22)
1964	1.02	2.68 (262.75)	1.49 (−146.08)	0.18 (−17.69)
1965	1.14	3.40 (298.25)	1.96 (−171.93)	0.30 (−26.32)
1966	1.26	3.66 (290.48)	1.95 (−154.76)	0.45 (−35.71)
1967	1.44	4.25 (295.14)	2.44 (−169.44)	0.37 (−25.69)
1968	1.66	3.92 (236.14)	1.83 (−110.24)	0.42 (−25.30)
1969	1.79	3.53 (197.21)	1.09 (−60.89)	0.66 (−36.87)
1970	1.82	4.02 (220.88)	1.39 (−76.37)	0.82 (−45.05)
1971	2.19	6.95 (317.35)	3.65 (−166.67)	1.11 (−50.68)
1972	2.87	11.99 (417.77)	8.26 (−287.80)	0.86 (−29.97)
1973	4.34	16.99 (319.47)	11.89 (−273.96)	0.78 (−18.40)
1974	6.00	70.71 (1,178.50)	62.40 (−1,040.00)	2.31 (−38.50)
1975	11.84	136.98 (1,156.93)	121.57 (−1,026.77)	3.56 (−30.07)
1976	19.13	180.84 (945.32)	125.15 (−654.21)	36.57 (−191.47)
1977	31.14	208.27 (668.82)	133.75 (−429.51)	43.39 (−139.34)

This process began with the introduction of the government's stabilization program in June 1958. The liquidation of the debt received priority. Although complete data for that period are not available, it is clear that through fiscal 1961 the budgeted increase in expenditures was held well below the anticipated increase in revenues. In addition, by early 1960 the government had repaid virtually all of its debt to SAMA; by the end of 1961 practically all the internal debt had been liquidated and a beginning had been made in repayment of the external debt.[13]

As noted, oil revenues affect both the domestic and external components of the money base.[14] Any changes in oil revenue will change government revenues, thereby changing the net position of the government with SAMA. Because oil revenues are denominated in dollars, a change in this figure will also produce a similar change in the foreign reserves of the bank.

The relationship between oil revenues, government deposits, and the monetary base distinguishes the Saudi Arabian economy from most developing countries. In the usual case, the private sector is the main or sole recipient of export earnings. Given relatively fixed exchange rates, these earnings increase the foreign assets of the central bank. They will also have a direct and equal expansionary effect on the supply of bank reserves (and hence on the supply of money).

Because the government is the main recipient of export earnings in Saudi Arabia, there is not a direct link between foreign exchange earnings, changes in foreign reserves of the central bank, and changes in money base. The ramifications of the kingdom's unique monetary situation are seen most directly in the manner in which the country's money supply is determined, and are best understood by examining the consolidated balance sheet of the government and SAMA.

From the liability side of this consolidated balance sheet, one can obtain a relationship describing the use of the monetary base (MB):[15]

$$MB = SCOB + LRD + ERB \qquad (15.14)$$

where $SCOB =$ currency in the hands of the public; $LRB =$ legal reserves of the commercial banks; and ERB represents the excess reserves of these banks.

Correspondingly, from the asset side of the consolidated balance sheet the sources of the monetary base can be identified as:

$$MB = SFA + GNAC + BAC + EAC \qquad (15.15)$$

where $SFA =$ foreign assets held by SAMA less the loans and credits received from abroad; $GNAC =$ claims on the government less the government deposits with SAMA; $BAC =$ SAMA's advance and rediscounts to the commercial banks; $EAC =$ other items on the asset side less the import registration deposits of the private sector and contingent liabilities.

The items of the balance sheet have been rearranged to reflect the separate components of the monetary base. In this regard, it is important to distinguish between the external sources (determined by the conditions in the balance of payments) and the internal sources (which depend on the government's budgetary position and the commerical banks' borrowing from SAMA).

External sources of the monetary base consist mainly of SAMA's net foreign asset holdings (SFA), which in turn depend essentially on the country's balance of payments position over time and is reflective of transactions in both the current and capital accounts.

Under the system of fixed (or pegged) exchange rates, the balance of payments acts as a constraint on the country's supply of monetary base. The exact way in which the situation in the balance of payments affects the changes in SAMA's foreign assets is:

$$\Delta SFA = FCOB + \Delta(FLB - FAB) + \Delta(FLG - FAG) \qquad (15.16)$$

where $FCOB$ denotes the current account balance, $(FLB - FAB)$ represents the net foreign liability of the banks, and $(FLG - FAB)$ is equal to the net foreign government debt (Δ is the yearly difference).

In deriving these relationships, it is implicitly assumed that the nonbank public in Saudi Arabia does not hold foreign assets or incur foreign liabilities. It is also assumed that private corporations do not issue securities or bonds to foreigners. These assumptions are indeed justifiable because of the very initial stages of capital market development in the kingdom.

The balance of payments on current account ($FCOB$) is equal to the total exports of goods and services minus imports of goods and services. In Saudi Arabia where oil is the major export and the dominant source of gross domestic product, the level of imports can be safely assumed to be dependent on their level, or:

$$FCOB = aGORFS + b \qquad (15.17)$$

where $GORFS$ denotes oil revenues and a and b are constant parameters.

The internal components of the monetary base consist of the government debt (when rarely incurred) to SAMA, $GNAC$, and the banks borrowing from SAMA. Because the bond market is insignificant, the government's rare deficits were financed mainly through increases in the government debt with SAMA ($GNAC$). In theory the government could also have placed securities either abroad ($FLG - FAG$) or with the banks ($BLG - BAG$); that is,

$$GDFICIT = \Delta GNAC + \Delta(FLG - FAB) + \Delta(BLG - BAG) \qquad (15.18)$$

where $GDFICIT$ denotes the government deficit.

The government deficit itself is defined here as government expenditure, $GENAN$, minus government revenue, $GRFS$, (being composed of oil revenue, $GORFS$, and nonoil revenue, $GNORFS$):

$$GDFICIT = GENAN - GORFS - GNORFS \qquad (15.19)$$

The manner in which oil revenue affects the monetary base in Saudi Arabia is seen best through an examination of the adjusted monetary base (BA), defined as:

$$BA = B - (FLB - FBA) - BAC - EAC \qquad (15.20)$$

The advantage of analyzing BA as a means of determining the money-supply process in Saudi Arabia is that it is composed only of items not influenced by the commercial banks.

Substituting for B from equation 15.15 yields:

$$BA = SFA + GNAC - (FLB - FAB) \qquad (15.21)$$

Taking the differences and substituting for *SFA* and *GNAC* from equations 15.18 and 15.16 and utilizing equations (15.17) and (15.19), we obtain an expression that defines the change in the adjusted monetary base as a function of oil revenue and government expenditure, or:

$$\Delta BA = (a - 1 - x)GORFS + (1 - x)(GENAN - GNORFS) + (b - y)$$
$$(15.22)$$

It follows from equation 15.21 that the way that the oil revenue affects the change in the adjusted monetary base depends on two parameters *a* and *x*. For oil revenues to have a positive effect on the monetary base, all that is required is for $a > (1 - x)$.

What might seem as a contradiction in terms would be the reverse situation where $a < (1 - x)$ would result in oil revenues having a negative influence on the money base.

Estimation yields:

$$\Delta BA = +1.49 - 0.0698 GORFS + 0.48(GENAN - GNORFS) \quad (15.23)$$
$$(11.65) \qquad\qquad (10.82)$$

$$r^2 = 0.95$$

implying a value of 0.411 for *x* and 0.520 for *z*.

Further, since $(1 - z) = 0.48$, oil revenues in fact had a negative effect on the change in the money base.

The values for *x* and *z* are realistic, since from the equations:

$$COB = (x)GORFS + b \qquad\qquad (15.24)$$

$$COB = -2.07 + 0.66 GORFS \qquad\qquad (15.25)$$
$$(11.79)$$

$$r^2 = 0.91$$

and

$$\Delta GENAN = (z)GDFICIT + a \qquad\qquad (15.26)$$

$$\Delta GENAN = 0.58 + 0.76 GDFICIT \qquad\qquad (15.27)$$
$$(7.72)$$

$$r^2 = 0.80$$

Again, it seems somewhat paradoxical to argue that increased oil revenues would actually reduce the money base. Looked at in terms of the relationships individually depicted by x and z, however, the result is plausible; z can be interpreted as the proportion of the government surplus (deficit) that is deposited either with SAMA or the commercial banking system.

Due to the attractiveness of foreign investments, we would expect z to be somewhat less than 1. On the other hand, x can be interpreted as the marginal effect of oil revenue on the current account balance of payments. Given the significance of oil revenues in the country's national income accounts and the kingdom's high marginal propensity to import, x should be relatively small. Other formulations (equations 15.28 to 15.35) confirm these conclusions.

$$\Delta BA = 1.60 \Delta GENAN - 0.21 \Delta GORFS - 0.08 \qquad (15.28)$$
$$(15.05) \qquad\qquad (-4.12) \qquad\qquad (-0.09)$$

$$r^2 = 0.9515 \qquad F = 117.60$$

$$\Delta MB = 0.39 \Delta GENAN + 0.05 \Delta GORFS - 0.09 \qquad (15.29)$$
$$(10.34) \qquad\qquad (2.44) \qquad\qquad (-6.28)$$

$$r^2 = 0.09340 \qquad F = 84.88$$

$$\Delta BA = 1.40 \Delta GENAN - 0.92 \qquad (15.30)$$
$$(9.89) \qquad\qquad (-0.74)$$

$$r^2 = 0.8827 \qquad F = 97.82$$

$$\Delta MB = 0.43 \Delta GENAN + 0.09 \qquad (15.31)$$
$$(10.88) \qquad\qquad (0.26)$$

$$r^2 = 0.9011 \qquad F = 118.44$$

$$BA = 1.22 GENAN - 2.73 \qquad (15.32)$$
$$(27.76) \qquad\qquad (-2.72)$$

$$r^2 = 0.9834 \qquad F = 770.49$$

$$\Delta BA = 1.52 \Delta GENAN - 0.17 \Delta OGDPN + 0.07 \qquad (15.33)$$
$$(11.39) \qquad\qquad (-2.45) \qquad\qquad (0.05)$$

$$r^2 = 0.9233 \qquad F = 66.23$$

$$MB = 0.15GENAN + 0.44GENANL - 1.33 \qquad (15.34)$$
$$(2.61) \qquad\qquad (5.81) \qquad\qquad (-4.24)$$

$$r^2 = 0.9973 \qquad F = 2591.44$$

$$\Delta MB = 0.19\Delta GENAN + 0.33\Delta GENANL + 0.21 \qquad (15.35)$$
$$(4.73) \qquad\qquad (7.30) \qquad\qquad (0.85)$$

$$r^2 = 0.9611 \qquad F = 173.05$$

Some further justification for this finding might be sought on the ground of interpreting the negative influence of oil revenue on the change in monetary base as an indication of the action of monetary authorities in sterilizing the effect of foreign reserves in monetary base.

To illustrate this point of view further, it is of interest to analyze more precisely the behavior of the Saudi Arabian monetary authorities in their attempt to offset the effect of foreign reserves on monetary base. An estimate of the degree to which the monetary authorities adjust the domestic component of monetary base to changes in the external component can be obtained from regressing the change in monetary base (MB) and adjusted monetary base (BA) and SAMA's foreign assets (SFA) on the change in SAMA's foreign assets (ΔSFA).

$$\Delta(MB - SFA) = -0.85\Delta SFA + 0.40 \qquad (15.36)$$
$$(-51.97) \qquad (0.26)$$

$$r^2 = 0.9948 \qquad F = 2700.52$$

$$\Delta(BA - SFA) = -0.74\Delta SFA + 2.52 \qquad (15.37)$$
$$(-6.46) \qquad (0.87)$$

$$r^2 = 0.7486 \qquad F = 41.68$$

According to these estimates (equations 15.36 and 15.37), the Saudi Arabian monetary authorities on the average adjust the domestic component of the monetary base by 85 riyals out of each 100 riyal change in foreign reserves, and the domestic component of the adjusted monetary base by about 74 riyals out of each 100 riyal change in foreign reserves. These results clearly indicate that the Saudi Arabian monetary authorities have been relatively successful in sterilizing movements in foreign reserves. This conclusion is certainly open to question.

Note that part of the negative effect of the variation in foreign reserve on domestic component of monetary base can be attributed to the fact that the oil revenue, by nature, affects both the domestic and external components of the monetary base; that is, any increase in the oil revenue increases the foreign reserves held by SAMA, while at the same time (given the level of government expenditure) decreases the claims of the central bank over the government.

This automatic sterilization process is of utmost importance in understanding the nature and the mechanism of monetary policy in Saudi Arabia. However, it cannot be denied that the conscious actions of the central bank mainly through the exercise of its control over the commercial banks, such as changes in legal reserves requirements and in advance and discounts to the banks, have been quite effective in offsetting the movements of foreign reserves on the domestic component of monetary base.

The higher estimate (0.85) for ΔSFA obtained when regressed on the monetary base (as compared with 0.74 when regressed on the adjusted base) is partial evidence of the effectiveness of SAMA in this regard. This follows from the fact that the amount of banks' borrowing from SAMA is included in the definitions of the monetary base (MB), while excluded from the adjusted monetary base (BA).

However, granting the imperfection of instruments of monetary policy, there may still be a considerable degree of sterilization. Ultimately, the question is an empirical one, and the evidence presented seems to tentatively indicate that the Saudi monetary authorities have been somewhat successful in neutralizing balance-of-payments fluctuations.

Whether the authorities should continue to be as concerned over the money supply and its growth is a question that can only be answered after simulations of the economy have identified a number of trade-offs associated with its control. These are examined in chapter 16.

Conclusions

A second important conclusion emerging from the analysis was the significant contribution of the monetary base to the growth of money stock. A complete understanding of the process of money-supply determination in Saudi Arabia thus ultimately requires an analysis of the factors determining the growth rate of monetary base.

Most of the literature on the interaction between domestic and international components of the money supply deals with developed countries and whether, given their high degree of capital market integration, central banks can exercise effective control over the money supply. Advocates of the monetary approach to the balance of payments contend that central bank control is limited by the fact that changes in the domestic component of the money supply will tend to be offset by counterbalancing foreign exchange flows.

While the capital markets in Saudi Arabia are certainly not as closely integrated with the rest of the world as are those of many of the advanced countries, the degree of control over the domestic component of the monetary base, and thus SAMA's ability to sterilize reserve flows, has been questioned on the grounds that its instruments of monetary policy available are very limited in their effectiveness.

The applicability of the monetary theory of the balance of payments, together with the determination of inflation, are dealt with in chapter 16.

Notes

1. Thomas Mayer, "The Structure of Monetarism (I)," in Thomas Mayer, *The Structure of Monetarism* (New York: Norton, 1978), p. 2.
2. See the general framework developed in Thomas Sargent and Neil Wallace," Rational Expectations and the Theory of Economic Policy," *Journal of Monetary Economics* (April 1976): 169–185.
3. E. Feige, "Expectations and Adjustments in the Monetary Sector," *American Economic Review* (May 1967).
4. W.J. Baumol, "The Transactions Demand for Cash: An Inventory Theoretic Approach," *Quarterly Journal of Economics* (November 1952).
5. Feige, "Expectations and Adjustments."
6. Chorng-huey Wong, "Demand for Money in Developing Countries," *Journal of Monetary Economics* (January 1977): 72.
7. J.O. Adekunle, "The Demand for Money: Evidence from Developed and Less Developed Economies," International Monetary Fund, *Staff Papers* (November 1971).
8. For alternative means, see Wong, "Demand for Money," p. 65.
9. Following A. Harberger in "The Dynamics of Inflation in Chile," *Measurements in Economics: Studies in Mathematical Economics and Econometrics in Memory of Yehuda Grunfeld* (Stanford: Stanford University Press, 1963), pp. 215–296.
10. Wong, "Demand for Money," p. 73.
11. All data on the money supply is taken from International Monetary Fund, *International Financial Statistics*, various issues.
12. Said Hitti and George Abed, "The Economy and Finances of Saudi Arabia," International Monetary Fund, *Staff Papers* (July 1974), p. 287.
13. Ibid.

14. For an excellent elaboration Cf. David Morgan, "Fiscal Policy in Oil Exporting Countries, 1972–1978," International Monetary Fund, *Staff Papers* (March 1979), pp. 55–86.

15. For an application of this approach to another oil-exporting country, see M. Pailami, "The Determination and Control of Money Supply in an Oil Exporting Country: The Iranian Experience," MIT Energy Laboratory, *Working Paper No. MIT-EL 78-027WP* (Revised February 1979).

16 Macroeconomic Adjustments—the Balance of Payments and Inflation

One of the most dramatic developments following the OPEC price increases of 1973–1974 has been the balance-of-payment's position of most countries. In particular, the balance-of-payments' accounts of Saudi Arabia have shown abnormally large surpluses on current account, balanced primarily by a massive accumulation of foreign exchange.

This development has a number of important implications for the conduct of the government's economic policy, for the balance of payments in an open economy plays an important role in determining changes in the stock of domestic money. International reserve inflows, for example, will increase the domestic stock of money if they are added directly to the money balances of residents, or if they are exchanged for domestic currency at the central bank.

It is quite possible that reserve flows are an important factor, and perhaps at times the dominant one, in determining changes in the kingdom's domestic stock of money. This observation raises questions as to the major determinants of Saudi Arabian reserve flows, and what role if any government policy can play in affecting these movements. To arrive at some tentative conclusions as to the nature of this adjustment mechanism in the Saudi Arabian context, estimates are made of the determinants of the kingdom's long-run reserve position. This analysis is undertaken in light of recent developments in the monetary theory of the balance of payments.

A related adjustment of importance in forecasting the economy is the manner in which the imbalance between aggregate supply and demand has been reconciled through price changes. Since 1972, the rate of inflation experienced in Saudi Arabia has been much higher than during the preceding two decades. Saudi authorities have continually stressed that the current inflation is largely a result of the (unavoidable) transmission of world inflation into the domestic price system. On the other hand, SAMA has indicated that part of the blame for domestic inflation must lie with the highly expansionary expenditure programs introduced by the government following the 1973 oil price increases and the resulting increase in the gap between aggregate demand and supply.

The nature of the inflationary process in Saudi Arabia must be identified and quantified before a number of fundamental long-run decisions, such as the rate of oil production, the level of government domestic spending, and the value of the riyal/dollar exchange rate can be intelligently made. In attempting to identify the type and sources of inflation experienced particularly after

1972 in the kingdom, three main questions need to be addressed:

1. To what extent has recent inflation been imported rather than domestically generated?
2. Precisely what role have government expenditures played in creating and sustaining inflationary pressures?
3. Has the country's underlying monetary mechanism been fundamentally different than that experienced in most other developing countries, and if so, in what way and with what implications for stabilization policy?

Saudi Arabian Balance-of-Payments Accounts

That the Saudi Arabian government receives virtually all the oil revenue and at the same time determines the volume of imports and how the remaining surplus will be invested abroad, makes it difficult to arrive at an estimate of the country's balance-of-payments position. More precisely, the distinction between the capital account and foreign exchange reserve items (on which the official definition of payments disequilibrium is based) usually is based on the assumption that the individuals or groups who make investment decisions (which are recorded in the capital account) are different from those who undertake residual or accomodating transactions (which appear as foreign-exchange reserve flows). Because of the government's unique role, this assumption is obviously not valid for the kingdom. Thus it is not at all clear what the best measure of the country's balance-of-payments surplus would be.

For example, between 1974 and 1976 the country ran an accumulated current account surplus of just over $54 billion. Only about $23 billion in foreign exchange reserves were, however, accumulated during the same period.[1] Since the government made almost all of the other $31 billion in foreign investments, the distinction between foreign exchange reserves and the remainder of Saudi Arabia's foreign assets is at best arbitrary. It is, therefore, somewhat misleading to suggest that Saudi Arabia had a payments surplus of only $23 billion during this period.

Given the institutional environment in Saudi Arabia, it might be more reasonable to use the current account as the measure of payments disequilibrium. By this measure we get a surplus of $54 billion for Saudi Arabia during the 1974–1976 period. Clearly, this measure conflicts with the notion that foreign exchange reserves are supposed to be highly liquid, since it is not reasonable to view Saudi investments in long- and medium-term assets as constituting reserves.

On the other hand, the "basic" balance-of-payments format (where the balance of payments is measured as the sum of the current and long-term capital accounts) avoids this problem by placing such nonliquid investments above the line as autonomous items.[2] Short-term investments are placed below the line with official foreign exchange reserves. Since the vast majority of Saudi investments were in short-term assets during this period, the difference between the current account and the "basic" balance-of-payments results would have been quite small. As more and more of the kingdom's long-terms revenues flowed into investments, the difference between the two accounts would become considerably larger.

More fundamentally, however, the use of the "basic" format still leaves the question of whether Saudi medium- and long-term investments are really autonomous. Does the kingdom really have a preference of investing abroad, or are officials doing so only because huge current account surpluses make it neccessary to put the resulting surplus funds somewhere other than in the domestic economy? The latter interpretation argues that these investments are in fact accommodating, and consequently that the current account is the best measure of Saudi Arabia's payments position seen from this perspective. The $54 billion figure appears to be a far better estimate of the Saudi payments surplus during the 1974–1976 period than the $23 billion figure suggested by the official settlements accounts.[3]

The fact remains, however, that whatever final measure is chosen, the definition of Saudi Arabia's balance-of-payments surplus will, unlike the case in most countries, be essentially based on a set of arbitrary definitions. There can be no presumption that at any particular point in time will it necessarily reflect with any degree of accuracy the usual autonomous and accommodating forces implied in the balance-of-payments statements.

A Framework for Analysis

One way of avoiding making arbitrary definitions of the country's balance of payments is to use the monetary approach to the balance of payments. The main characteristic of this approach is to group and classify all the items in the balance of payments into: (1) the money account, and (2) the trade-plus-capital account. Based on the principle of double-entry accounting, these two accounts are equal. By combining trade and capital items, this approach thus avoids any artifical distinction as to what items should be considered autonomous or accommodating.

In general the approach emphasizes the budget constraint imposed on the country's international spending and views the various accounts of the balance of payments as the "windows" to the outside world, through which the excess of domestic-flow demands over domestic-flow supplies and vice-versa are cleared.[4]

Accordingly, surpluses in the trade account and the capital account, respectively, represent excess flow supplies of goods and securities, and a surplus in the money account reflects an excess domestic-flow demand for money. Consequently, in analyzing the money account (or the more familiar rate of increase or decrease in the country's international reserves), the monetary approach focuses on the determinants of the excess domestic-flow demand for, or supply of money.

Clearly, a consistent use of the budget constraint implies that the money account—the current rate of change of reserves—can be analyzed in terms of the determinants of all the other accounts: at the simplest level of aggregation, the goods and capital accounts. The monetary approach, however, stresses an analysis in terms of the behavorial relationship directly relevant to the money account, rather than an analysis in terms of the determinants directly related to the other accounts (and only indirectly to the money account via the budget constraint).[5]

The monetary approach should, in principle, provide a picture no different from that obtained by summing an analysis of the individual capital and trade accounts.

To facilitate applying the approach to the Saudi Arabian balance-of-payments data, it is assumed that:

1. Transactions recorded in the kingdom's balance of payments are essentially a reflection of monetary phenomena. Emphasis is therefore placed on the direct influence of excess demands for or supplies of money on the country's balance of payments.

2. The demand for and supply of money are stable functions of a limited number of variables. This is an empirical proposition, confirmed by the analyses in the previous chapter. Changes in the money supply are, of course, not the only factors that affect the balance of payments. It is nevertheless assumed that real variables affect the balance of payments indirectly by first affecting the demand for or supply of money.

3. It follows that the analysis of the effect of a policy or other change must begin with an analysis of how this change generates a divergence between actual and desired money balances or affects such a divergence when it already exists.

4. As noted the approach does not rely on an analysis of the individual balance-of-payments subaccounts; it is sufficient to aggregate individual components (goods, services, transfers, short- and long-term capital) into a single category—"items above the line." This procedure is pragmatic in that it recognizes that an excess supply of or demand for money may be cleared through the markets for either goods, services, or securities. If the balance of payments is viewed within this framework, the pitfalls of placing emphasis on any of the kingdom's particular subaccount are avoided.

5. An accurate analysis of the kingdom's balance of payments can only

be made in the long run. The approach recognizes that short-run analysis is often complicated by the fact that the assumed adjustment mechanisms are incomplete during this time frame. For example, the adjustment of actual money balances to their desired levels does not occur instantaneously, but rather requires the passage of time.

6. The balance-of-payments adjustment process under the previous assumptions is automatic. More specifically, any balance-of-payments disequilibrium or exchange rate movement reflects a disparity between actual and desired money balances and will automatically correct itself. Any balance-of-payments imbalance or exchange rate change is thus assumed to be a phase in the automatic adjustment process. It follows that attempts by the Saudi authorities to counter these processes would merely increase the forces that give rise to the adjustment ultimately required for a return to equilibrium.

7. It follows that attempts by SAMA to neutralize the effect of international reserve flows on the domestic money supply are not possible in the long run. The long-run success in neutralizing the effects of international reserve flows implies that the Saudi authorities would be willing (since the country usually has a surplus) to trade investment and consumption goods for foreign currency balances. The accumulation of these balances by Saudi Arabia would represent a nonmarket-induced transfer of wealth away from the kingdom to foreign consumers. There is no reason to assume that the government would pursue such a policy in the long run.

To summarize, the monetary approach used to examine Saudi Arabia's balance-of-payments stresses that:

1. The kingdom's balance-of-payments problems are monetary problems in a monetary world economic system. It follows that these problems need to be analyzed by a model that explicitly specifies monetary behavior and integrates it with the real economy, rather than by a model that concentrates on real relationships and treats monetary behavior as a residual of real behavior.

2. Money is a stock, not a flow. Therefore, the model stresses that monetary equilibrium and disequilibrium require analysis of stock equilibrium conditions and stock adjustment processes.

3. Although money can be obtained from two alternative sources—(a) the expansion of domestic credit and the exchange of goods or assets for international money, and (b) conversion of international into domestic money via the monetary authority with fixed exchange rates—only the second would affect the kingdom's balance of payments.

It should be emphasized again that the focus of the analysis is the overall balance of payments, and not only the balance of trade (many writers in different contexts have confused the two and write indifferently about the trade balance and the overall "official settlements" balance).

The Model

The basic proposition that Saudi Arabia's balance of payments is determined by a mechanism that restores equilibrium between the supply of and demand for money, can be illustrated by the following simple algebraic model.[6]

In equilibrium money supply is equal to money demand or:

$$MS = MD \qquad (16.1)$$

Assuming the money multiplier to be fixed (and for convenience equal to one), equation 16.1 can be written as:

$$MD = MB \qquad (16.2)$$

where MB is the equal to the monetary base; that is, the sum of net foreign (R) and SAMA's domestic assets (D). Therefore:

$$MB = R + D \qquad (16.3)$$

Assuming the demand for money in Saudi Arabia to be a function of nominal income (Yn) and the interest rate (i), MD can be written as:

$$MD = f(YN, i) \qquad (16.4)$$

Equating equations 16.3 and 16.4, transforming from levels to changes, and solving for the change in foreign reserves, ΔR, yields:

$$\Delta R = -\Delta D + fY\Delta Yn + fi\Delta i \qquad (16.5)$$

where ΔR is the balance-of-payments surplus (or deficit), and fY and fi are the rate of change of money demand with respect to income and interest, respectively.

An alternative formulation could be obtained by assuming the demand for money to be homogeneous of degree 1 in prices, so that:

$$MD = Pf(Yr, i) \qquad (16.6)$$

Here Yr is real income and P is the domestic price level. Equating equations 16.6 to 16.3 and transforming to percentage rate of change yields:

$$\dot{R}(R/MB) = -\dot{D}(D/MB) + ey\dot{Yr} + ei\dot{i} + \dot{P} \qquad (16.7)$$

Here ey and ei are the income and interest elasticities of the demand for money, a dot over each variable symbolizes a percentage rate of change, and (R/MB) and (D/MB) are weights.

Implicit in the model is that causality runs from money demand to money supply; that is, attempts by SAMA to increase the money supply (MB) (by changing, for example, the level of domestic assets) above the quantity demanded will result in an outflow of reserves. Similarly, an increase in the demand for money will result in a reserve inflow.

It is also clear from this formulation that the kingdom will tend to gain international reserves as its real income and domestic price level rise (nominal income). Similarly, it will lose international reserves if SAMA attempts to expand the money supply by increasing domestic assets (or as the interest rate rises).

These conclusions logically follow from the assumed effect of increases in interest rates and prices on the demand for or supply of money; that is, increases in real income induce a rise in the demand for money, while increases in the interest rate reduce that demand. Furthermore, an increase in the domestic price level reduces the real money supply and induces an inflow of reserves.

While this conclusion may seem at odds with standard Keynesian theory, the effects of both the interest rate and price level follow from the assumption that, in monetary equilibrium, domestic inflation and interest rates are closely linked to and primarily determined by changes in the respective world rates. Consequently, reserve flows induced by price or interest-rate differentials between Saudi Arabia and other countries in the short-run Keynesian world are absent in this longer-run equilibrium approach.[7]

Absence of price or interest-rate differentials is also assured by the assumption of close substitutability among the goods and services of Saudi Arabia and its trading partners. In the limiting case of perfect substitutability (in the long run), interest rates and price levels would be fully equalized between Saudi Arabia and her trading partners.

The results (equations 16.8 to 16.10) imply that:

1. For all practical purposes, the supply of money under SAMA's control rather than the domestic quantity of money is ultimately determined by the flow of foreign reserves in conjunction with government budgetary decisions.

2. That foreign reserve flows can and do operate to restore equilibrium in the money market; that is, that the massive reserve inflows in recent years have been necessary to satisfy the increased domestic demand for money arising from the oil-price-induced increases in real income.

3. That any balance-of-payments disequilibria experienced by Saudi Arabia must inevitably be transitory; that is, the country's authorities may be able if they wish to "sterilize" acquisitions of international reserves, but they would eventually exhaust their stocks of domestic assets (including possibly

the ability to force domestic commercial banks to hold international assets instead of domestic assets).

4. The authorities would in this case be able to continue to sterilize reserve inflows only by lending the money back to foreign countries on noncommercial terms.

5. As long as real income continues to rise at rates that are rapid relative to those for the rest of the world, the demand for money in the kingdom will continue to rise relative to the demand for money in other countries. Assuming the government does not move dramatically toward budgetary deficits, this increased demand for money must necessarily come from additional reserve inflows.

Weighted Change in Foreign Assets

$$S\dot{F}A(SFA/MB) = -0.77ius + 3.94NO\dot{X}N - 0.81\dot{D}C(DC/MB) \qquad (16.8)$$
$$\phantom{S\dot{F}A(SFA/MB) = }(6.49) \qquad (3.78) \qquad\quad (15.36)$$

$$-\ 300.81\Delta DFGDP - 26.03$$
$$(2.07) \qquad\qquad\quad (1.03)$$

$$r^2 = 0.9969 \qquad F = 83.49$$

Change in Foreign Assets

(Current Prices)

$$\Delta SFA = -1.00DC + 3.98\Delta NOXN + 8.39\Delta DFGDP \qquad (16.9)$$
$$(31.72) \quad\ (5.11) \qquad\qquad (4.03)$$

$$-\ 1.12PC - 1.98$$
$$(-2.60) \quad (3.74)$$

$$r^2 = 0.9988 \qquad F = 1927.20$$

(Constant Prices)

$$\Delta SFAP = -0.99\Delta DCP + 0.69\Delta NOXNP - 0.03 \qquad (16.10)$$
$$(-91.60) \qquad\ (5.16) \qquad\qquad (-0.17)$$

$$r^2 = 0.9988 \qquad F = 4210.03$$

Credit

The money supply is traditionally regarded as one of the main explanatory variables for private-sector credit. This link is the basis for much monetary policy. Yet much discussion has centered around the fact that monetary policy acts with a lag. When decisions are taken to affect the money supply, there is usually a year's lag until the new credit conditions begin to affect the real sectors of the economy. As noted earlier, a strong link seems to exist from oil revenues to net foreign assets to government expenditure to the money base to the money supply. Several functional forms expressing the link between lagged government revenues (*GORFSPL*), exports (*FEXPTNAR*), and real domestic credit (*DCP*) were tested (equations 16.11 to 16.20) and confirmed this mechanism. Changes in domestic credit (ΔDCP) were related to real nonoil income (*NOXNP*) and changes in foreign assets ($\Delta SFAP$). Private credit (*PCP*) in turn was largely related to domestic credit and nonoil income.

Domestic Credit

(Constant Prices)

$$DCP = 1.39DCPL + 0.28GORFSPL - 3.47 \qquad (16.11)$$
$$(4.66) \qquad\;\; (1.79) \qquad\qquad\;\; (-1.18)$$

$$r^2 = 0.8313 \qquad F = 32.03$$

$$DCP = -1.45FEXPTNAR - 0.87GORFSPL + 11.89 \qquad (16.12)$$
$$(-2.34) \qquad\qquad (-2.96) \qquad\qquad (1.98)$$

$$r^2 = 0.8531 \qquad F = 37.75$$

$$\Delta DCP = 0.09NOXNP - 0.97\Delta SFAP - 0.44 \qquad (16.13)$$
$$(5.21) \qquad\quad (-137.80) \quad\; (-1.97)$$

$$r^2 = 0.9993 \qquad F = 9573.51$$

(Current Prices)

$$DC = -0.96GENAN - 0.92FEXPTNA + 10.23 \qquad (16.14)$$
$$(-3.55) \qquad\quad (-8.71) \qquad\qquad (3.39)$$

$$r^2 = 0.9826 \qquad F = 337.87$$

$$\Delta DC = -0.96 FEXPTNA + 5.43 \Delta NOXN + 4.72 \qquad (16.15)$$
$$(-3.82) \qquad\qquad (3.18) \qquad\qquad (0.92)$$

$$r^2 = 0.5552 \qquad F = 8.84$$

$$\Delta DC = 0.78 GENAN - 0.97 FEXPTNA + 10.23 \qquad (16.16)$$
$$(-3.55) \qquad\qquad (-8.71) \qquad\qquad (3.39)$$

$$r^2 = 0.9826 \qquad F = 337.87$$

Private Credit

(Constant Prices)

$$PCP = -0.02 DCP + 0.08 NOXNP + 0.80 \qquad (16.17)$$
$$(-3.95) \qquad (3.16) \qquad\qquad (4.38)$$

$$r^2 = 0.9171 \qquad F = 71.93$$

(Current Prices)

$$PC = -0.04 DC + 0.05 NOXN + 0.94 \qquad (16.18)$$
$$(-7.44) \qquad (3.03) \qquad\qquad (7.12)$$

$$r^2 = 0.9907 \qquad F = 637.42$$

$$PC = 0.23 NOXN - 3.66 DFGDP - 0.04 DC + 3.32 \qquad (16.19)$$
$$(2.52) \qquad\qquad (-1.35) \qquad\qquad (-2.98) \qquad (1.68)$$

$$r^2 = 0.9896 \qquad F = 381.68$$

$$\Delta PC = -0.06 \Delta SGD + 0.09 \Delta SFA - 0.03 NOXNL + 0.26 \qquad (16.20)$$
$$(-8.58) \qquad\quad (14.21) \qquad\quad (-5.02) \qquad\qquad (4.03)$$

$$r^2 = 0.9783 \qquad F = 165.62$$

Inflation

A number of variables and relationships have been hypothesized as possibly contributing to the country's recent inflationary episode. The following empirical analysis includes a discussion of the evidence on (1) the influence of foreign trade or openness variables on inflation, (2) the effect of excess demand on inflation, (3) the contribution of fiscal development variables to inflation. (4) the monetarist explanation of inflation, and (5) the process of reserve sterilization.

Openness and Inflation

Recent empirical work indicates that there is a relationship between the degree of national integration into the world economic system and inflation; that is, in general the more-open countries have experienced less price inflation.[8] Presumably openness serves as a kind of safety valve; domestic inflationary pressure spills over into the balance of payments in the open economy, thus necessitating less price inflation.

One way of testing for the effect of openness on domestic inflation is to test various formulations of a price equation with measures reflecting the degree of contact with the world economy included as one of the dependent variables. For example, several variables that might be included are: (1) the important–income ratio (ZAB), (2) the rate of change of the import–income ratio ($RZAB$); (3) the terms of trade (ratio of import prices to export prices, $ZITT$); (4) the rate of growth of the money supply (GMI); and (5) the rate of growth of real income ($GNOXR$) and expected inflation ($FAXL$).[9]

One would expect the import–income ratio to be negatively related to the rate of inflation; large increases in the money supply should be inflationary, especially during periods when the economy is operating at or near full employment. Similarly, a rapid rate of growth of income may cause inflation because of the creation of bottlenecks or a general difficulty to shift resources around at short notice.

Because a rise in the price of imports (and indirectly perhaps exports) will tend to induce a rise in the general price level, the terms of trade should be positively related to the rate of inflation. Finally, it may be assumed that the change in openness will be negatively related to the rate of price increase.[10]

The rate of inflation (the rate of change in the nonoil GDP deflator) was regressed on the previously noted dependent variables for the period 1961–1978. The final result (equation 16.19) goes somewhat against our initial hypothesis. The sign of ZAB is positive perhaps reflecting the fact that as Saudi Arabia increased imports after 1973 to offset domestic shortages, world prices were simultaneously increasing. Clearly, the OPEC price increases and world inflation are closely related. Interestingly enough, the monetary growth (either of $M1$ or $M2$) was not significant; therefore four largely exogenous nonmonetary variables—ZAB, GWP, $GNOXR$, and $FAXL$ account for nearly 99 percent of the fluctuations in the rate of Saudi Arabian domestic inflation.

Deviations from the Trend as a Measure of
Excess Demand

It is often argued that at least three characteristics of countries at Saudi Arabia's level of development limit the effectiveness of deviations from the trend ($DTNOXR$) as a measure of excess demand.[11] These are the high share of agricultural products in both production and consumption, the high rates of inflation, and the uneven growth of productive capacity. Saudi Arabia, still considered a developing country, is abnormal in not having any of these particular features. The agriculture sector is quite small; until the 1970s there was only negligible inflation. Because of oil revenues and the resulting relative lack of an effective foreign exchange constraint, productive capacity has proceeded at a somewhat even pace.

A second limitation of the usefulness of $DTNOXR$, often cited as a measure of excess demand, is that it incorporates the assumption that productive capacity grows at a constant rate.[12]

While this will not necessarily be true in developed countries, it is often far less likely to be the case in developing countries, given their dependence on unstable export earnings for the purchase of imported capital goods. Saudi Arabia, however, does not suffer from limitations on imports. In addition its rate of capital formation has tended to be constrained simply by a rather constant level of absorptive capacity rather than a fluctuating rate of foreign exchange earnings.

Implicit in the use of $DTNOXR$ is the notion that when the growth of output rises above its long-run trend, domestic productive capacity is being strained, and prices therefore must rise for output to expand. Admittedly this assumption is best suited to an advanced economy in which the production and consumption of goods consist largely of industrial products for which supply is flexible enough to respond to short-run shifts in demand. Because in most developing countries production and consumption are concentrated heavily on agricultural products (which in the short run are more subject to fluctuations in domestic supply than in domestic demand), it is questionable whether the $DTNOXR$ formulation of inflationary pressures would be satisfactory. Again in Saudi Arabia's case the relatively small agricultural sector means that the country should not experience such a high degree of short-run rigidity, and that therefore the $DTNOXR$ approach might be somewhat more applicable.

A third reason commonly used for doubting the applicability of $DTNOXR$ as an accurate measure of demand pressure in developing countries is their generally higher rates of inflation and money supply growth.[13] Within a limited range changes in short-run demand pressure will tend to result partially in higher nonagricultural output and price increases. Presumably, there is a point beyond which an increase in demand will result in higher prices only. Again, it is often argued that this point is probably surpassed more often in a developng country because of their higher rate of money supply increase (and the likelihood that, with the greater share of agricultural production in GDP, their short-run elasticity of supply is lower).

Again an examination of Saudi Arabia's monetary expansion indicates that the kingdom experienced increases in liquidity more or less in line with the more advanced countries.

If we accept the fact that most of the arguments against using $DTNOXR$ as a measure of excess demand are not applicable for Saudi Arabia, the question remains as to the best structural form for testing the effect of this variable on domestic prices. Several formulations were tried, with the final ones (equations 16.12, 16.13, 16.16, 16.17, and 16.18) yielding significant and positive results.

The results confirm that abnormally high rates of growth in the kingdom have been associated with periods of price increase. Of interest is the fact that changes in the GDP deflator ($\Delta DFGDP$) are much more sensitive to $DTNOXR$ than changes in oil prices (equation 16.17). $DTNOXR$ by itself only accounts for about 60 percent of the changes in the GDP deflator.

Excess Demand and Domestic Inflation

The tests for openness and deviations from the trend suggest that a useful framework for the analysis of inflation in Saudi Arabia would be a direct examination of the link between real expenditures and domestic price change. Real demand in Saudi Arabia is determined in part by factors that depend on aggregate supply, and in part by factors that are independent of supply. This approach assumes that it is in fact the factors which bring demand and supply into balance that are ultimately responsible for the economy's domestic price changes. For purposes of analysis, real demand is defined in terms of expenditures in constant prices and includes: planned expenditures, private expenditures, foreign expenditures for exports, and imports.

Planned expenditures are defined here as consisting of government consumption and gross domestic investment.[14] Part of gross domestic investment, such as social services and education, grows more or less in line with GDP in Saudi Arabia. But the other component of investment is defense. Obviously defense expenditures cannot be regarded as determined by economic factors, although they are conditioned somewhat by economic capacity.

With these considerations in mind several variables were created and used in the regression equations for domestic price changes. They included (in constant prices):[15]

Table 16-1
Saudi Arabia: Inflationary Mechanisms (Two-Stage Least-Square Estimates)

Variable	Estimated Equation	r^2	F
The GDP Deflator (DFGDP)			
1. DFGDP	$= 3.45 WPIND - 0.03 ADNP - 1.64$ $(14.31) \quad (-6.72) \quad (-9.02)$	0.9662	185.88
2. DFGDP	$= 0.11 EXCESS + 1.55$ $(15.51) \quad (22.14)$	0.9207	46.44
3. DFGDP	$= -0.02 ADNP + 0.14 DANP - 0.09$ $(-3.14) \quad (11.26) \quad (0.06)$	0.9485	119.80
4. DFGDP	$= 0.94 DFGDPL + 0.63 WPIND - 0.52$ $(10.31) \quad (4.17) \quad (-4.58)$	0.9826	394.97
5. DFGDP	$= 24.43 DTNOXR - 0.96$ $(12.25) \quad (10.41)$	0.9077	150.08
6. DFGDP	$= 5.19 DTNOXR + 0.71 DFGDPL + 0.61 WPIND$ $(1.93) \quad (4.86) \quad (4.38)$	0.9865	316.15

Change in GDP Deflator (DDFGDP)

7. $DDFGDP$ = $-0.09FSMIAS + 0.21FSMIDA + 0.15FSMIPI + 0.01$
   $\quad\quad\quad (-2.35) \quad\quad\quad (3.76) \quad\quad\quad (2.02)$

   0.9765   15.65

8. $DDFGDP$ = $1.01WPINDL - 0.19DFGDPL - 0.73$
   $\quad\quad\quad (7.62) \quad\quad\quad (-2.87) \quad\quad (-8.02)$

   0.9114   66.86

9. $DDFGDP$ = $0.61WPIND - 15.7DWPIND + 1.98DTNOXR$
   $\quad\quad\quad (4.54) \quad\quad\quad (-3.95) \quad\quad\quad (1.94)$

   0.9385   61.01

10. $DFDGP$ = $5.21DTNOXR + 0.42DWPIND$
    $\quad\quad\quad (4.00) \quad\quad\quad (0.80)$

    0.6096   11.71

11. $DDFGDP$ = $5.65DTNOXR - 0.07$
    $\quad\quad\quad\quad (4.83) \quad\quad\quad (1.20)$

    0.5929   23.23

Inflation (INF)

12. INF = $40.29ZAB + 0.53GWP + 1.55GNOXR + 0.98FAXL - 27.75$
    $\quad\quad (2.81) \quad\quad (2.23) \quad\quad (6.00) \quad\quad\quad (7.37) \quad\quad (4.93)$

    .9865   316.15

$FSM1AS$ = incremental aggregate supply
$FSMPA$ = planned absorption
$FSMPI$ = planned impact
$FSM1DA$ = incremental domestic adsorption
$FSM1PI$ = incremental planned impact

Also included were:

$FWPIND$ = world inflation
$ADNP$ = real domestic supply
$DTNOXR$ = deviation of real nonoil GDP from its trend
$DANP$ = domestic adsorption

In equation 7, table 16–1, $FSM1PI$ and $FSM1DA$ were found to be statistically significant and account for nearly 80 percent of the observed change in the nonoil GDP deflator.

An approximation to this approach looks at the excess liquidity created in the process of demand expansion (see table 16-2).

$$(EXCESS = M1/NOXNP)$$

In contrast to the assumptions here, using the monetary approach to study inflation in Saudi Arabia would undoubtedly lead one to begin with the fundamental proposition that the kingdom's inflations is merely an interaction of market supply and demand for money (and nonfinancial objects). Put differently, price movements are viewed by this model as systematically dependent on current and immediate past evolutions of the interaction between supply and demand conditions.

The starting point of this analysis is the basic monetarist model derived from the equation of exchange.[16] More specifically, it assumes a simple money demand function of the following form:

$$M/PY = Y^a C^b$$

where M is the (exogenously determined) nominal stock of money; P is the price; Y is a measure of real income; and C is the expected cost of holding real balances. Equation 16.21 is solved for P and expressed in terms of growth rates or (depicted by G prefixing the variable):

$$INF = RM1 - (1 - a)GY - bGC$$

Equation 16.22 incorporates the basic elements of the monetarist approach to inflation: money, real income, and the expected cost of holding real balances. In addition this formulation captures the basic methodological bias

Table 16-2
Saudi Arabia: Inflationary Pressures (Two-Stage Least-Squares Estimates)

Variable	Estimated Equation	r^2	F
FSMIAS	$= 0.71DZNANP - 1.40DPINNOP + 1.29DEXPTNAR + 0.05DMSFAR + 0.36$ $(10.75)\quad(-2.98)\qquad\quad(11.36)\qquad\qquad(3.63)\qquad\quad(1.69)$	0.9602	66.33
FSMDA	$= 6.57GINP + 1.50PINP + 1.32GCNP - 0.11$ $(3.53)\qquad(3.03)\qquad(7.03)\qquad(-0.33)$	0.9949	774.92
FSMPI	$= 0.94GINP + 0.73PINP - 0.11ZNANP + 1.39GCNP - 0.13$ $(4.67)\qquad(2.33)\qquad(-13.26)\qquad(13.09)\qquad(0.99)$	0.9906	271.93
FSMIDA	$= 0.76DGENANP + 0.98DPCNP + 1.60PINP + 0.18$ $(7.99)\qquad\quad(4.36)\qquad\qquad\qquad(0.78)$	0.8873	34.13
FSMIPI	$= -0.03DMSFAP + 0.05GORFSPL + 0.04$ $(2.15)\qquad\quad(4.89)\qquad\quad(0.02)$	0.7103	15.92
EXCESS	$= 10.30MBP + 1.27BAP - 5.74NOXNP + 11.55$ $(3.39)\qquad(2.97)\qquad(-3.09)\qquad(1.64)$	0.9207	46.44
EXCESSC	$= 0.04MI + 0.05NOXNP + 0.00$ $(8.53)\qquad(3.86)\qquad(0.00)$	0.9896	666.20
ADNP	$= 6.82ZNANPL + 27.97M1PL - 12.58$ $(-8.73)\qquad\quad(11.53)\qquad(3.44)$	0.9450	111.59
DANP	$= 0.82GENANP + 1.50PENANP - 1.43$ $(6.92)\qquad\qquad(7.74)\qquad\quad(-1.92)$	0.9956	1470.47
MBP	$= 0.24GENANP + 0.37DENANP - 1.22$ $(3.53)\qquad\qquad(3.01)\qquad\quad(-2.82)$	0.9801	319.94

of the monetarist school; that is, the equation has a limited number of variables, and the nature of relationships is clear and straightforward. The growth of money relative to output and cost of holding real balances will generate an increase in the rate of inflation. The growth of real income will cause decreases in the rate of inflation (via absorbing money in the increased demand for real balances). Similarly, the rate of inflation is assumed to be inversely related to the expected cost of holding real balances.

Equation 16.22 assumes instantaneous adjustment of monetary changes and no money illusion. Therefore, the tested form of the monetarist equation is:

$$INF = a + a_1 GM1 + a_2 GM1L - GYNOXR + FAXL \qquad (16.23)$$

where *GYNOXR* is the growth of real nonoil income; *GMIL* is the lagged growth of the money supply; and *FAXL* is the inflation rate lagged 1 year minus the inflation rate lagged 2 years.

The basic monetarist contention is:

1. That the causal relation runs from money to prices and output.
2. Any persistent increase in money relative to output is a sufficient condition for inflation.
3. The magnitude and length of inflation is dependent on the magnitude and persistence of monetary growth.
4. The occurrence of inflation is independent of the level of employment in the economy.
5. It is the increasing growth rate of money that yields inflationary pressures.

The major assumptions of the monetarist model are valid for developing economies such as Saudi Arabia in the sense that the structural conditions, institutions, and usual governmental actions vis à vis the economy are not in any way incompatible with the model. For example, in such economies expansionary monetary policies are frequently pursued to utilize idle resources. This often results in monetization of the rural economy.

The monetary explanation appears to perform very poorly over this period. By itself the rate of growth of money (*RM*1) only explained 47.30 percent of the observed rate of inflation. Also when combined with other variables, *RM*1 often has a negative sign. In fact better results were obtained by simply regressing the rate of world inflation on domestic inflation. By itself world inflation accounts for about 75 percent of the fluctuations in domestic inflation. Lagged world inflation, however, does not significantly contribute to the regression equation when introduced with current world inflation. This variable (*GWPL*) does, however, become significant when regressed with the growth of money.

Of the other variables examined in this context, expected inflation (defined here as the difference between last and the prior year's inflation) was highly significant and positive when regressed on current period inflation. This indicates that the cost of holding money is an important element influencing behavior in Saudi Arabia.

The inadequacy of the monetarist model in explaining the rate of inflation in Saudi Arabia raises the question as to whether the money supply is an exogenous variable in the kingdom. If the money supply increases in response to other forces, such as industrialization, some inflation will be an inevitable result of the structural factors underlying changes. The evidence in the following section suggests, however, that the Saudi authorities can sterilize reserve flows, and that the money supply should therefore be viewed as a policy-determined exogenous variable.

Conclusions

Standard analysis of the balance of payments in OPEC countries is usually based on real variables (oil sales and prices on the one hand, import-demands on the other) and focuses on the current account in the balance of payments. The approach developed here considers those factors which affect monetary equilibrium—income prices, interest rates, and domestic assets—and does not focus exclusively on any one component in the balance-of-payments account.

The desirability of considering more than just the current account arises from the increasing importance of the capital-account activities of the country. Because of the international investment activity of the Saudi Arabian government, the country's balance-of-payments accounts may no longer be analyzed in terms of current account balances alone. The broader view of our approach offers a framework for analyzing the balance on the entire account, an approach that focuses on long-run changes, and a model that appears to be consistent with recent events affecting the country.

Finally, the lack of a significant relationship between the growth of money and inflation raises some questions as to Saudi policy concern over the control of domestic liquidity. Two questions arise: (1) can the authorities control the money supply, and (2) should they pursue tight monetary control at the risk of slowing down growth?

Notes

1. Balance of payments figures are from International Monetary Fund, *Balance of Payments Yearbook*, various issues.

2. These definitions are from R. Stern, *The Balance of Payments: Theory and Economic Policy* (Chicago: Aldine, 1973), 2.

3. See Robert Dunn, "Exchange Rates, Payments Adjustment, and OPEC: Why Oil Deficits Persist," Princeton University, International Finance Section, *Essays in International Finance*, no. 137 (December 1979): 7–8, for an excellent discussion of this point.

4. Jacob Frenkel and Harry Johnson, "The Monetary Approach to the Balance of Payments: Essential Concepts and Historical Origins," in Jacob Frenkel and Harry Johnson, *The Monetary Approach to the Balance of Payments* (Toronto: University of Toronto Press, 1976), p. 22.

5. Ibid.

6. The notation follows that of Robert McNown and Myles Wallace, "International Reserve Flows of OPEC States: A Monetary Approach," *The Journal of Energy and Development* (Spring 1977): 267–278.

7. Ibid., p. 270.

8. See M.A. Iyoha, "Inflation and Openness in Less Developed Economies: A Cross Country Analysis, *"Economic Development and Cultural Change* (October 1973): 31–38; and M.A. Akhtar, "An Empirical Note on Inflation and Openness in Less Developed Economies," *The Philippine Economic Journal* (1976): 636–649.

9. *FAXL* is the expected rate of inflation, defined here as the inflation rate in the previous year minus the inflation rate in the year prior to that. See A. Harber, "The Dynamics of Inflation in Chile," in C. Christ, ed., *Measurement in Economics* (Stanford: Stanford University Press, 1963), pp. 219–250.

10. Akhtar, "Empirical Note on Inflation," p. 637.

11. An excellent survey of these issues is given in Edmund Sheehey, "On the Measurement of Imported Inflation in Developing Countries," *Weltwirtschaftliches Archiv* (1979): 68–78.

12. Ibid.

13. Ibid.

14. Following Arthur Smithies, *The Economic Potential of the Arab Countries* (Santa Monica: Rand Corporation, 1978), p. 21.

15. See Smithies, *Economic Potential*, for a detailed definition of the items making up each variable.

16. See Harberger, "Dynamics of Inflation," for a detailed discussion of the assumptions underlying the model.

17

An Appraisal of Saudi Arabia's Growth Prospects

The economic development strategy over the next two decades will most likely be (in light of existing problems) a continuation of the patterns established in the Second Plan. Previous chapters have concluded in general that given the alternatives this is a prudent strategy. It is also a strategy that has certain unambiguous implications concerning what levels certain economic variables must attain or be constrained within before its eventual success will be assured.

The quantification and discussion of the key macroeconomic relationships involved in the strategy was undertaken in the last four chapters. The following sections combine a number of the most important variables into an overall model of the economy (which in turn is decomposed into several submodels). The model is constructed so that it is capable of identifying the simultaneous interaction of these variables over time. Thus it is able to determine, among other things, whether the economy will be close to achieving the long-run growth objectives implicit in the strategy.

Basic Issues in the Model's Construction

The requirements imposed on the forecasting model developed are largely concerned with assuring that a number of key economic elements and forces are explicitly accounted for. For example, the model must be capable of presenting elements of traditional macroeconomic demand and at the same time recognize the supply constraints typically found in OPEC-type economies. Justification for the inclusion of demand is not difficult. Considering the government's activities vis à vis the economy, it has been shown that the public sector is a major consumer of the country's output.

At the same time, the government through its investment program is attempting to alter the supply constraints facing the private sector. Thus both aspects must be made to coexist within the framework of the model. While these points seem rather obvious, their actual application in the Saudi Arabian case involves a number of subtleties that need to be elaborated on before the actual presentation of the forecasts.

Finally, it is not sufficient to design a model. Some allowance for structural change must be incorporated within the projections. Unfortunately, precise identification of the kingdom's new activity patterns is subject to a high degree of error in light of the limited observation period following the increased petroleum revenues.

Along these lines it has been argued that since oil revenues have attained their present-day magnitude only recently and since this occurred (in 1973–1974) in such a discontinuous manner, we might expect a significant structural change in investment spending patterns to have occurred in the kingdom during the last few years.

If this is in fact the case, we might expect to find some of the country's absorptive capacity problems lying in the inability of the government to maintain the pace of expenditure, especially its investments in line with increases in oil revenues.

To test this theory, the following function was estimated:[1]

$$GE = a + A1OR + A2DOR$$

where GE = measure of government expenditure, OR = oil revenues, and D = a dummy variable assuming values of 0 (1960–1973) and 1 (1974–1978). Hence $A2$ would indicate if the government investment-spending coefficient with respect to oil revenues $A1$ had undergone any significant change.

The results (see table 17–1) indicate that:

1. The coefficients for $A1$ are always significant, and those of $A2$ insignificant. This certainly further confirms the hypothesis that oil revenues are a statistically significant variable explaining government investment behavior. The generally large statistics indicate that a large proportion of the variation in government expenditures may be attributed to the fluctuations in oil revenues.

2. The relationship between government expenditures and oil revenues did not undergo a structural change in 1974.

3. The propensity to spend is not equal but is in general larger out of lagged revenues and larger for consumption than investment.

4. The long-run propensity to spend is considerably higher than the short-run propensity for all three measures of government expenditure (investment—GIN; consumption—GCN; and total expenditures—$GENAN$).

At least one study concluded that the kingdom's absorptive capacity had undergone a structural change after 1973 simply because it concentrated on the relationship between current oil revenues and lagged revenues. The present study finds no significant structural change, and further there is no evidence of a declining ability of the government to maintain its level of expenditures. While it is true the propensity to spend out of lagged revenues is greater than current revenues, the amount is not great and should be of little concern.

Table 17–1
Saudi Arabia: Test for 1973–1974 Structural Change

Government Expenditure Variable	Measure of Oil Revenue	A1	A2	a	r^2	F
GIN	GORFS	0.220 (6.92)		−0.655	0.73	47.82
GIN	GORES	0.323 (9.37)	−0.099 (0.23)	−1.079	0.74	22.60
GIN	GORFSL	0.280 (13.50)		−0.647	0.92	182.37
GIN	GORFSC	0.401 (15.74)	−0.116 (0.47)	−1.141	0.92	88.86
BCN	GORFS	0.312 (12.71)		0.683	0.90	161.67
GCN	GORFS	0.506 (14.93)	−0.187	−0.117	0.91	77.73
GCN	GORFSL	0.367 (23.73)		1.418	0.97	563.06
GCN	GORFSL	0.649 (27.92)	−0.272	0.253	0.98	309.17
GENAN	GORFS	0.532 (9.48)		0.026	0.84	89.79
GENAN	GORFS	0.828 (10.97)	−0.285 (0.37)	−1.194	0.84	42.69
GENAN	GORFSL	0.647 (20.08)		0.758	0.96	403.20
GENAN	GORFSL	1.053	−0.392	−0.920	0.96	203.36

Type of Government Expenditure	Measure of Oil Revenue	C1	C2	Long Run Elasticity	r^2	F
GIN	GORFS	0.065 (9.23)	1.196 (8.06)		0.9504	143.82
GIN	GORFSL	0.146 (11.98)	0.829 (9.17)	0.854	0.9819	611.76
GCN	GORFS	0.121 (6.47)	0.849 (10.95)	0.801	0.9892	688.36
GCN	GORFSL	0.211 (8.21)	0.572 (4.69)	0.491	0.9890	673.11
GENAN	GORFS	0.167 (9.23)	1.029 (10.05)		0.9792	352.36
GENAN	GORFSL	0.346 (11.22)	0.693 (11.28)	1.127	0.9959	1833.96

Basic Features of the Forecasting Model

The model consists of a system of stochastic equations and identities containing the key economic variables. The latter fall into two main categories:

   1.   Endogenous variables—those that are jointly determined in the system and are influenced by other economic variables;

   2.   Exogenous variables—those that are not influenced by the system and whose values are assumed to be given. These consist of the following types:

a.   Variables external to the system, such as international prices and oil production rates.

b.   Lagged variables, including predetermined lagged endogenous variables (whose values before the current time period are given).

c.   Policy variables, whose values are determined by the government such as tax rates, foreign exchange rates, and government expenditures.

The policy variables are not entirely endogenous, since the economic behavior of the system often requires their modification by the government, but we refer to them as endogenous because the government can determine the size and timing of changes in them in accordance with its policy objectives.

The substitution of values for the exogenous variables enables one to obtain a solution of the model; that is, a calculation of values for all the endogenous variables. The model can then be used for forecasting. Treating the policy variables as exogenous makes it possible to compare the results of alternative policy measures. We employed the model both for describing and explaining past developments and for prediction. The first forecasts were made in connection with the proposed Third Five-Year Plan for 1980–1985. The implications of the plan were examined with the help of the model. One of the chief advantages of a formal model of this type is that it makes it possible to investigate various alternatives to the original plan and thus to analyze the sensitivity of the economic variables to changes in recommended policy measures (for example, the effect of an increase in the number of foreign workers in the kingdom).

As noted earlier there have been attempts at building more disaggregated models for the Saudi Arabian economy over the past few years.[2] It is proposed here that the process of quantitative modeling be started by expanding the basic Keynesian structure of aggregate demand and supply relationships and estimating the structural relationships by the econometric method (to account for the simultaneous relationships between many of the economic variables).

The construction of such a model may be of substantial interest in its own right. The parameters of the individual equations do have a number of policy implications and also yield insights that a nonquantitative examination of the economy would not be capable of deducing. The primary reasons for constructing the models are that they can be utilized for multiplier analysis, policy simulation, and prediction. Exploration of these properties of the Saudi Arabian model presents more opportunities for analysis than might be expected for the typical developing country.

A word of caution is called for about interpreting the model's results, however. By its nature the model constitutes a schematic framework of the economy based on a series of identifiable interrelationships that existed in the past (rather than on what is specific to the year that is to be influenced by economic policy). The best method of combining schematic information and insights into the new, special trends operating in the economy is not known. Nevertheless, since the model is based on the maximum amount of information obtainable on the various aspects of the economy, it can serve as a useful tool, although certainly not the only one for shaping the economy.

In summary, the model is based on the assumption that:

1. Only a limited number of exogenous variables determine all the kingdom's basic macrovariables.
2. Government expenditures follow a pattern similar to that over the 1960–1979 period.
3. There are no major alterations in world economic conditions during this period.

The Forecasting Model

The institutional characteristics and the historical background of Saudi Arabia presented in the previous chapters provide a foundation for the econometric forecast presented in this chapter. From these exercises we try to determine whether: (1) the kingdom's current development strategy is in fact a feasible one, and (2) what constraints are likely to be met in pursuing this strategy, particularly during the Third Plan period (1980–1985).

Model Characteristics

The model examines the economy from the point of view of the resources and requirements of implications associated with alternative growth scenarios. The forecasts determine the inflation rate and foreign work-force implications of alternative spending rates. The overall workings of the model are shown in the flow chart.

Structural Equations

While a detailed description of the equations used in the forecasting model can be found in the previous four chapters,[3] note that the model itself incorporates a number of interesting features that are particularly relevant for a country like Saudi Arabia. These include special equations to reflect:

1. The total dependence of government revenues and expenditure on oil revenues.
2. Consideration of the special duality the oil sector creates (the split of GDP into nonoil GDP and oil GDP).
3. The basic Keynesian nature of the major economic forces present (the importance of real factors and the endogenous nature of the money supply functions) and the almost total endogenous nature of the economy given oil production and oil prices.

The model's (see tables 17-2, 17-3, 17-4, 17-5, 17-6, and 17-7) were estimated with annual data for the 1960 to 1978 period. Variables were measured in 1970 constant prices.

All the equations are estimated by two-stage least squares and therefore we are not reporting the Durban-Watson statistics (bearing in mind that this task was designed for regression equations where the explanatory variables are exogenous). Suffice to say, however, that when estimated by ordinary least squares the same set of equations and variables showed no signs of correlation of the residual terms.

For convenience and manageability, the model was broken down into a set of self-contained blocks consisting of:

1. Oil-government expenditure Keynesian national income forecasting model in constant prices (see table 17-2).
2. Oil-government expenditure Keynesian national income model in nominal prices (see table 17-3).
3. Sectoral model in constant prices (see table 17-4).
4. Sectoral model in current prices (see table 17-5).
5. Monetary survey model (in current prices) (see table 17-6).
6. Commerical bank behavior model in current prices (see table 17-7).

Although a number of equations are used in more than one model, each model is designed to focus on a particular set of policy problems, such as employment and inflation.

The model differs from the usual two-gap focus on the role of capital assimilation and supply in that it emphasizes formation, demand, and investment opportunities in the process of the country's economic growth.

The model's structure therefore permits a somewhat broader definition of absorptive capacity than is usually found in forecasts of this type; that is, stress is placed on defining absorptive capacity in terms of the optimal adjustment of the growth rates of all factors of production.

This approach is especially appropriate in analyzing capital absorption in Saudi Arabia. The country's capital is: (1) for all practical purposes accumulated outside the national economy proper; (2) originated in the enclave oil sector with its few and ineffective direct linkages to the rest of the economy characterized by narrow resource base and structure (precluding the operation of the normal relationship between supply and demand in the capital market).[5] In such a setting, labor managerial skills, other cooperant factors of production (and perhaps commitment to development) and not capital are the major constraints in the pace of economic growth.

Viewed somewhat differently the country's investment process undoubtedly will continue to entail an important element of learning; that is, the kingdom's relatively low absorptive capacity must be attributed at least in part to the relatively low rate of post investment. The relationship between past rates of investment and prospective rates is intricate and complex because a higher historical rate not only implies greater familiarity and practice in investment field, but also a larger economic system that would be able to assimilate considerably greater amounts of capital. Some of the bottlenecks and difficulties confronting the country in its attempt to absorb greater volume of capital have to some extent been alleviated through labor importation and the attraction of foreign management, and to a lesser extent foreign entrepreneurship.

Indeed if the absorptive capacity of the country is broadly conceived as that magnitude of oil revenues necessary to sustain a feasible level of public expenditures consistent with the government's preferences and objectives (without strictly differentiating between investment and consumption outlays), there is a wide range of values that can be realistically forecast as within the range of the authorities implementation capability. If a problem of absorptive capacity is likely to develop in the future, it would most likely be because of the inflationary effect of the government's expenditure (and thus its voluntary reduction) rather than an allocation constraint.

The major assumptions implicit in the model equations have been discussed at length in the previous four chapters. In large part the model reflects the overall picture of an economy characterized by a number of rigidities in the pattern of resource use. As the economy continues to grow and expand, immobility should gradually give way to a greater degree of adaptability in both the utilization of factor inputs and in the composition of goods produced during any given time period.

Because factor substitution at the present time is somewhat limited, imports of both labor and capital have special significance in determining

Table 17–2
Saudi Arabia: Basic Keynesian Macroeconomic Model—Constant Price Block

Variable	Estimated Equation	r^2	F
PCNP	$= 0.32 NOXNP^c - 1.67 DDFGDP^b + 0.68 PCNPL^c - 0.37$ 　　(4.07)　　(-2.53)　　(4.27)　　(-0.82)	0.9704	134.94
PINP	$= 0.37 DNOXNP^b + 1.13 DDFGDP^c + 0.14 GRNANPL^c - 0.19 DPCNPL^a + 0.37^c$ 　　(2.21)　　(3.84)　　(6.35)　　(-1.75)　　(4.30)	0.9864	199.62
TINP	$= 0.77 GENANP^c - 0.20$ 　　(28.07)　　(-0.80)	0.9813	787.84
GINP	$= 0.31 NOXNPL + 0.21 GORFSPL + 25.63 DTNOXL - 6.94 DDFGDP$ 　　(3.02)　　(3.16)　　(3.48)　　(-3.33)	0.9667	79.81
ZNANP	$= 0.85 GENANP + 0.92 PCNP + 12.16 Z2TT - 15.87$ 　　(5.98)　　(3.87)　　(9.18)　　(-9.33)		
GORFSP	$= 1.88 EXPTNAR - 11.09$ 　　(7.19)　　(-2.95)	0.7870	51.71
SNP	$= 0.44 FFP + 0.466 GNPNP - 1.68$ 　　(10.95)　　(33.12)	0.9950	1292.90
FFP	$= 0.81 GNPNP - 0.61 ZNANP - 0.29 EXPTNAR - 2.30$ 　　(8.84)　　(-17.89)　　(-1.94)　　(-4.74)	0.9780	177.63
NOXNP	$= 0.04 KP + 12.51 EMPT - 7.34$ 　　(3.73)　　(14.70)　　(-7.88)	0.9921	814.10

$$INF = 0.45GWP^a + 53.55ZAB^b + 1.50GNOXR^c + 0.71FAXL^b - 31.65 \qquad 0.9733 \quad 100.40$$
$$ (2.10) \quad\ (3.54) \qquad\quad (6.30) \qquad\quad (8.12) \qquad (-5.56)$$

$$OGDPNP = 2.38EXPTNAR - 9.99 \qquad 0.7875 \quad 55.59$$
$$ (7.46) \qquad\quad (-2.34)$$

$$DFGDP = 0.71DEGDPL + 0.61WPIND + 5.19DTNOXR - 0.31 \qquad 0.9865 \quad 316.15$$
$$ (4.86) \qquad\quad (4.38) \qquad (1.93) \qquad\quad (-2.04)$$

$$DNOXNP = 0.03DKP + 8.60DEMDT - 0.18 \qquad 0.8554 \quad 38.44$$
$$ (1.89) \quad\ (2.09) \qquad\ (1.48)$$

Identities

$$GENANP \ = \ GCNP + GINP$$
$$DDFGDP \ = \ DFGDP - DFGDPL$$
$$GDPNP \ = \ NOXNP + OGDPNP$$
$$GNPNP \ = \ GDPNP + NFPNP$$
$$KP \ = \ TINP + TINPL + TINPLZ$$
$$DKP \ = \ KP - KPL$$
$$DEMPT \ = \ EMPT - EMPTL$$

Note: See text for identity of symbols.

( ) = t test

[a] Significant at 90% level.

[b] Significant at 95% level.

[c] Significant at 99% level.

Table 17–3
Saudi Arabia: Keynesian Macroeconomic Model—Current Price Block (Two-Stage Least-Square Estimates)

Variable	Estimated Equation	r^2	F
PCN	$= 0.27NOXN + 3.71DDFGDP + 0.51PCNC - 0.72$ (2.65)　　　(2.40)　　　　(1.82)　　(1.11)	0.9924	480.03
PIN	$= 0.45DNOXN - 5.11DDFGDP + 0.22PENAN - 0.49$ (3.06)　　　(−3.27)　　　　(4.65)　　(−2.01)	0.9943	640.03
GCN	$= 0.60FEXPTNAL - 38.8DDFGDP + 0.05FGCI - 1.41$ (22.45)　　　　(−14.91)　　　(2.47)　　(−4.77)	0.9971	1260.04
GIN	$= 0.48FEXPTNAL - 40.79DDFGDP - 2.31$ (19.74)　　　　(−13.32)　　(−7.10)	0.9871	457.59
GENAN	$= 0.100GORFS + 1.31NOXNL - 4.54$ (13.28)　　　(3.54)　　(−6.55)	0.9926	809.64
TIN	$= 0.76GENAN - 0.29$ (101.25)　　(−1.68)	0.9987	10,250.84
ZNAN	$= 1.18PENAN + 8.57ZITT - 0.06DDC - 11.60$ (31.82)　　　(3.17)　　(−3.29)　　(−4.41)		
DZNAN	$= 0.42DGENAN + 0.62DPENAN + 0.23$ (5.97)　　　　(5.90)　　(0.86)	0.9846	383.98
NOXN	$= 0.58K + 8.70EMPT - 6.70$ (18.90)　(2.59)　　(−1.82)	0.9932	872.88
DNOXN	$= 0.81DMI + 0.45DGENAN + 0.24$ (3.50)　　　(4.50)　　(0.91)		
MI	$= 0.41MIL + 0.43NOXN - 16.11PCYN + 0.03FAXL + 2.05$ (3.99)　　(12.55)　　(−3.48)　　　(3.49)　　(2.11)	0.9996	6271.10

$$OGDPN = \underset{(609.70)}{0.98}FEXPTNA - \underset{(-2.51)}{0.25}$$

0.9999   371,739.70

$$SN = \underset{(17.96)}{0.47}GAPN + \underset{(90.39)}{0.43}GNPN - \underset{(-6.62)}{1.37}$$

0.9993   9151.93

$$PENAN = \underset{(31.09)}{0.71}GENAN + \underset{(6.39)}{3.30}$$

0.9867   966.40

$$GDPN = \underset{(47.10)}{1.11}OGDPN + \underset{(12.20)}{1.16}GENANL + \underset{(2.41)}{1.75}$$

0.9990   6308.47

$$DDAN = \underset{(5.08)}{0.70}DGENAN + \underset{(3.47)}{1.84}DMI + \underset{(1.13)}{0.46}$$

0.9912   678.34

$$GAPN = -\underset{(8.90)}{0.92}FGCI - \underset{(9.44)}{0.90}FPCI + \underset{(13.52)}{0.93}DSFA + \underset{(1.35)}{0.64}$$

0.9787   168.38

$$FPCI = -\underset{(-7.44)}{3.64}GENAN + \underset{(10.65)}{110.94}DFGDP - \underset{(-11.05)}{95.97}$$

0.9849   392.12

$$FGCI = -\underset{(-4.15)}{3.39}GENAN + \underset{(3.42)}{0.36}FEXPTNA + \underset{(2.39)}{2.61}GENANL + \underset{(0.01)}{0.03}$$

0.9116   37.81

$$FCI = \underset{(8.25)}{0.46}FEXPTNA - \underset{(-3.53)}{0.35}FPCIL - \underset{(-3.37)}{7.48}$$

0.8851   46.21

$$CABP = -\underset{(-3.03)}{8.85}ZNAN + \underset{(6.52)}{1.48}FEXPTNA + \underset{(2.52)}{5.62}GENAN - \underset{(-0.02)}{0.06}$$

0.9341   51.94

$$PI = -\underset{(-14.57)}{0.42}ZNAN - \underset{(-199.12)}{0.97}DC - \underset{(-2.68)}{0.43}$$

0.9999   878.26

$$MSFA = \underset{(7.49)}{139.00}DFGDP - \underset{(-8.71)}{12.04}NOXN + \underset{(6.55)}{9.40}ZNAN - \underset{(-6.29)}{86.90}$$

0.9958   875.31

Table 17-3 (continued)

Variable	Estimated Equation	r^2	F
DMSFA	$= -0.98DDC + 0.78DNOXN - 1.13DPC + 0.04FAXL - 0.02$ $\quad(-65.59)\quad(38.28)\quad\quad(-5.54)\quad\quad(3.05)\quad(-0.29)$	0.9999	37,022.73
FSFA	$= 141.86DFGDP - 12.73NOXN + 9.48ZNAN - 88.14$ $\quad(7.57)\quad\quad\quad(-8.87)\quad\quad(6.56)\quad\quad(-6.32)$	0.9955	818.09
FSDFA	$= -0.97DDC + 0.60DNOXN - 0.45DPC + 0.42FAXL - 0.10$ $\quad(-130.37)\quad(59.52)\quad\quad(-4.44)\quad\quad(7.02)\quad(-2.37)$	0.9997	143,556.5
GORFS	$= 0.82FEXPTNA - 4.79$ $\quad(17.77)\quad\quad(-1.70)$	0.9604	315.63
GNORFS	$= 0.22NOXN - 0.56$ $\quad(35.60)\quad\quad(-3.74)$	0.9898	1267.53
GRFS	$= 0.56FEXPTNA + 0.97NOXN - 6.79$ $\quad(6.18)\quad\quad\quad(4.03)\quad\quad(-2.99)$	0.9812	312.88
FPSBPX	$= 7.73DPC - 1.36GENAN - 0.74$ $\quad(4.20)\quad\quad(-14.35)\quad(-0.41)$	0.9515	117.67
DC	$= -1.07GENAN - 0.88FEXPTNA + 10.04$ $\quad(-3.87)\quad\quad(-8.01)\quad\quad(3.48)$	0.9841	370.92
PC	$= -0.04DC + 0.52NOXN + 0.94$ $\quad(-7.44)\quad\quad(3.03)\quad\quad(7.11)$	0.9907	637.42
DPC	$= -0.06DSGD + 0.09DSFA - 0.03NOXNL + 0.26$ $\quad(-8.79)\quad\quad(14.57)\quad\quad(-5.14)\quad\quad(4.13)$	0.9794	124.07
DDC	$= -0.88FEXPTNA + 4.03DNOXN + 5.37$ $\quad(-5.90)\quad\quad\quad(3.86)\quad\quad(1.72)$	0.8423	32.04

$$SGD = \underset{(-7.77)}{-1.18DEFICIT} + \underset{(2.73)}{36.15DDFGDP} + \underset{(4.97)}{0.29GNDEX} - \underset{(-0.78)}{1.02}$$

0.9948   696.50

$$BA = \underset{(27.76)}{1.23GENAN} - \underset{(-2.72)}{2.73}$$

0.9834   770.49

$$DBA = \underset{(9.88)}{1.40DGENAN} - \underset{(-0.73)}{0.91}$$

0.8824   97.58

$$DDFGDP = \underset{(8.03)}{3.85MEXCESSL} - \underset{(-2.37)}{0.05SMIAS} - \underset{(-7.54)}{1.31}$$

0.8712   40.58

$$DNOI = \underset{(11.88)}{0.99DSFAL} - \underset{(-6.09)}{0.51DNOIL} - \underset{(-8.38)}{0.83DGDPNL} + \underset{(1.95)}{1.28}$$

0.9517   72.26

$$FOPSTBB = \underset{(4.53)}{0.64GNDEX} - \underset{(-6.69)}{1.62GENDXL} + \underset{(8.92)}{63.26DDFGDP} - \underset{(-11.04)}{21.24DPC} + \underset{(3.72)}{3.99}$$

0.9269   31.72

$$FNSBP = \underset{(-6.72)}{-0.39GNDEX} - \underset{(-2.92)}{0.23PSBPMSD} - \underset{(-5.12)}{3.07}$$

0.9410   95.64

$$M2 = \underset{(3.28)}{0.02GDPN} - \underset{(-4.03)}{2.51DDFGDP} + \underset{(7.66)}{1.03M2L} + \underset{(0.01)}{0.01}$$

0.9943   639.15

$$GNDEX = \underset{(1.92)}{0.46DEXPTNA} - \underset{(-2.61)}{0.48OGDPN} + \underset{(9.86)}{64.04DFGDP} - \underset{(-2.18)}{26.86DDFGDP} - \underset{(-11.40)}{53.42}$$

0.9992   3315.77

$$FPTBB = \underset{(-5.38)}{-0.17DNOXN} - \underset{(-1.92)}{0.05DGENAN} - \underset{(6.66)}{0.56}$$

0.9771   255.58

$$FBBP = \underset{(19.28)}{1.61FEXPTNA} - \underset{(-5.97)}{4.78ZNAN} - \underset{(-4.59)}{38.66DDFGDP} + \underset{(4.35)}{2.49GENAN} - \underset{(-3.59)}{4.19}$$

0.9928   342.38

$$FCOLTBP = \underset{(-9.29)}{-6.81DDFGDP} + \underset{(4.66)}{0.06GENAN} + \underset{(0.68)}{0.11}$$

0.9059   57.59

Table 17-3 *(continued)*

Variable	Estimated Equation	r^2	F
FDIBP	$= -3.41DNOXN + 7.25DSIN + 29.90DDFGDP - 1.61$ $\quad\;(-4.79)\qquad\;(4.77)\qquad(3.61)\qquad\quad(-1.58)$	0.7061	8.81
FUTBP	$= -2.31NOXN + 1.35GENAN + 1.71PENAN - 0.72ZNAN + 2.36$ $\quad\;(-5.55)\qquad(8.11)\qquad\;(5.17)\qquad\;(-4.19)\qquad(3.76)$		
FNMCBP	$= -1.63DNOXNL - 14.55DDFGDP + 1.38$ $\quad\;(-13.55)\qquad(-7.20)\qquad\;(3.06)$	0.9892	550.54
CABP	$= 1.80FEXPTNA - 2.79ZNAN - 79.49DDFGDP + 68.80ZITT - 75.38$ $\quad(27.57)\qquad\;(-16.25)\qquad(-15.44)\qquad(8.47)\qquad(-9.08)$		
PSBPMSD	$= -1.04DDC - 0.70FEXPTNA + 2.68$ $\quad\;(-5.76)\qquad(-9.32)\qquad\;(0.97)$	0.8882	47.69
FGEXTCFX	$= 69.64DFGDP - 1.15GNPEX + 0.77DDC - 60.94$ $\quad(12.22)\qquad(-7.79)\qquad(12.40)\qquad(-12.42)$	0.9888	324.23

Table 17–4
Saudi Arabia: Macroeconomic Model Sectorial Submodel—Constant Price (Two-Stage Least-Squares Estimates)

Variable	Estimated Equation	r^2	F
CONP	$= 0.13NOXNP + 0.18ICONNPL - 0.25$	0.9852	433.32
MANP	$= 0.17ICONNPL + 1.14$ (5.82)　　　　　(9.59)	0.7073	33.83
DP	$= 0.54POP + 0.05GENANP - 1.91$ (6.25)　　　(3.86)	0.9806	329.40
TP	$= 0.29NOXNP - 0.84$ (43.16)　　　(−12.09)	0.9925	1862.64
EP	$= 0.05NOXNP - 0.10$ (22.04)　　　(−4.43)	0.9720	485.61
TDP	$= 0.34ICONNPL + 0.23IONPL + 0.55$ (22.97)　　　　(4.10)　　　(8.01)	0.9829	353.04
AGP	$= 0.03NOXNP + 0.79$ (12.29)　　　(33.25)	0.9151	150.93
DEP	$= 0.50DNOXNP - 0.01$ (3.26)　　　　(−0.23)	0.4320	10.65
DAGP	$= 0.62DPOP - 0.08$ (2.92)　　　(−2.15)	0.3779	8.50
DDP	$= 0.09DNOXNP + 0.08$ (2.92)　　　　(2.02)	0.3791	8.55
DCONP	$= 0.30DNOXNP - 0.07$ (6.79)　　　　(−1.15)	0.7672	46.13
DTDP	$= 0.27DNOXNP - 0.03$ (9.89)　　　　(−0.84)	0.8749	97.88
DTP	$= 0.35DNOXNP - 0.07$ (14.29)　　　(−2.09)		

the kingdom's growth path; that is, as domestic factors cannot readily be adjusted to produce substitutes for imported producer goods, some minimum proportion of imports (both labor and capital) is required to utilize the country's domestic resources in an efficient manner.

As in the two-gap analysis contained in chapter 15, it is assumed that because the kingdom has some structurally determined rigid relationships between factor inputs, it is impossible for the economy to achieve its full growth potential without a certain amount of imported goods and services.

Table 17-5
Saudi Arabia: Macroeconomic Model Sectorial Submodel—Current Prices (Two-Stage Least-Squares Estimates)

Variable	Estimated Equation	r^2	F
AG	$= 0.07NOXN + 0.53$ (46.26) (15.73)	0.9940	2139.91
DAG	$= 0.09DNOXN - 0.30AGL + 0.25$ (16.70) (−6.27) (6.06)	0.9886	519.37
MAN	$= 0.12NOXN + 0.50POP - 2.40$ (69.99) (12.59) (−10.50)		
D	$= 0.18NOXN + 0.29$ (86.94) (5.99)	0.9983	7558.03
DD	$= 0.17NOXN + 0.04$ (40.16) (1.26)	0.9940	2139.91
CON	$= 0.84CONL + 0.19ICONN - 0.05$ (6.39) (6.97) (−0.57)	0.9975	2441.25
DTD	$= 0.21DNOXN - 0.01$ (21.82) (−0.16)	0.9734	476.08
T	$= 0.20NOXN + 0.29TL - 0.52$ (21.54) (4.62) (−16.01)	0.9996	16,228.59
E	$= 0.03NOXN + 0.34EL - 0.04$ (8.97) (2.48) (−3.39)	0.9980	2953.34
DE	$= 0.17DNOXN + 0.04$ (40.16) (1.27)	0.9920	1612.93
DT	$= 0.25DNOXN - 0.04$ (43.24) (−0.95)	0.9931	1869.71

The country's factor proportions problem has, of course, been relieved over the last several years with exports expanding sufficiently to assure the supply of the required imports. This solution may now be precluded with the imposed foreign labor ceiling. In this regard the kingdom's situation is in sharp contrast to the case of most countries in which it is the inability to develop effective substitutions for traditional exports (through some kind of new combination of domestic factors) that ultimately retards growth. As with most developing countries the problem of underdevelopment faced by the kingdom is essentially that of rigidites in resource use.

The forecasts from this type of export-based model can be used to derive a number of policy implications. There are, for example, several implications pertinent to the kingdom's economic planning and the efficiency of the Third

Plan. More generally the model is used to make a broad assessment in quantitative terms of the rates of economic growth implied by alternative export growth rates. As constructed, the model should provide reasonably reliable orders of magnitude on the basis of specified assumptions about the magnitudes of the various parameters to allow for probable future changes in the kingdom's economic structure. The gap between savings and investment can, for example, be used to determine the need for possible policy changes.

For example, the model also makes several critical assumptions about the kingdom's absorptive capacity.The analysis focuses on the role of capital in expanding the productive capacity of the economy. While capital availability is recognized as a prerequisite for the country's economic growth, emphasis is mainly on the relationship between capital assimilation and capital formation. Specifically, the notion that the kingdom's economic growth is principally constrained by capital is qualified. It is assumed that the kingdom faces little difficulty in absorbing small or moderate volumes of capital over a period of a few years (as it did in the 1960s and early 1970s). On the other hand, the country is likely to encounter serious impediments in maintaining a noninflationary environment at a substantially higher volume of capital.

In sum the forecasting model described here is suitable in selecting optimum planned growth rates and the associated levels of investment requirements. It is especially useful in assessing the realism and consistency of such documents as the Third Five-Year Plan; that is, it is designed to examine the implications of planned changes in the economy's structural parameters, especially the marginal propensities to import foreign workers and productively absorb investment, variables that reflect the government's general objectives of economic development.

Limitations of the Model

The following forecasts of the Saudi Arabian economy made through use of the model do not attempt to incorporate the influences of the rest of the world on that economy; that is, it is assumed implicitly that the range of values assigned to oil prices and oil exports do not create any feedback effects on the kingdom from the consuming countries.

Clearly, analysis of the method of determination by the Saudi government about the manner in which Western economic performance should influence oil decisions would be of great interest. Properly conceived, a study of the government's decision on pricing and production would be an extremely complex undertaking and beyond the scope of the current study. Analysis of that problem would require an extensive discussion of a number of political factors pertaining to both Saudi Arabia's relationship with the United States and the West, and also the kingdom's interaction with other OPEC countries.

Table 17-6
Saudi Arabia: Monetary Survey Relationships (Two-Stage Least-Squares Estimates)

Dependent Variable	Estimated Equation	r^2	F
MSQM	$= 0.10NOXN - 0.02PEMUSTB - 0.002$ $\quad (66.52) \quad\quad (-8.59) \quad\quad (-0.06)$	0.9974	2655.71
MSFA	$= -0.99DC + 0.60NOXN - 1.79$ $\quad (-172.43) \;(39.26) \quad (-9.46)$	0.9999	13,611.59
MSGD	$= 1.526ORFS - 0.646ENAN - 1.09$ $\quad (18.47) \quad\quad (-4.55) \quad\quad (-0.61)$	0.9890	628.42
MSOI	$= 1.74NOXN - 1.46CISR - 34.75INF - 8.12$ $\quad (66.52) \quad\quad (-5.68) \quad\quad (-3.83) \quad (-6.68)$	0.9799	211.23
MSPC	$= 0.02MSFA + 0.10NOXN + 0.67$ $\quad (4.65) \quad\quad (6.46) \quad\quad (4.26)$	0.9874	500.04
GRFS	$= 0.49FEXPTNA - 4.90$ $\quad (20.40) \quad\quad (-1.64)$	0.9652	415.99

$$NOXN = 0.49FK + 13.90EMPTZ - 11.66$$
$$ (16.51) \quad (3.35) \qquad\;\; (-2.55)$$
0.9923   904.37

$$DDFGDP = -0.08FSMIAS + 0.20FSMIDA + 0.10FSMIPI + 0.01$$
$$ (-2.52) \qquad\quad (4.15) \qquad\quad (1.94) \qquad\quad (0.15)$$
0.7963   16.94

$$DC = -1.08FEXPTNA - 0.35GENAN + 9.44$$
$$ (-9.32) \qquad\quad (-1.48) \quad\; (2.61)$$
0.9755   267.35

$$DFGDP = 0.11EXCESS + 1.55$$
$$ (15.51) \qquad (22.14)$$
0.9450   240.71

$$EXCESS = 10.30MBP + 1.27BAP - 5.74NOXNP + 11.55$$
$$ (3.39) \qquad (2.97) \qquad (-3.09) \qquad (1.64)$$
0.9207   46.44

$$FMBP = 0.24GENANP + 0.37PENANP - 1.22$$
$$ (3.53) \qquad\quad (3.31) \qquad\quad (-2.28)$$
0.9801   319.94

$$FSCOB = 0.38GCN + 0.38$$
$$ (63.42) \quad (3.51)$$
0.9963   1021.63

Table 17–7
Saudi Arabia: Commercial Bank Behavior (Two-Stage Least-Squares Estimates)

Dependent Variable	Estimated Equation	r^2	F
CBPC	$= 0.15 NOXN + 7.13 INF + 0.30$	0.9918	848.41
CBDD	$= 0.28 NOXN + 0.29 CBR - 2.61 INF - 1.02$ $(11.65)\quad(3.09)\quad\quad(-2.27)\quad(-6.64)$	0.9985	3554.31
CBQM	$= 0.19 NOXNP + 0.66 DFGCP + 0.10 CBR - 1.34$ $(13.28)\quad\quad(6.91)\quad\quad(7.86)\quad(-17.33)$	0.9988	3738.24
CBFA	$= 0.12 NOXN - 0.01 DC - 0.43$ $(8.37)\quad\quad(-2.74)\quad(-2.42)$	0.9815	372.36
CBR	$= -0.16 FMSGD + 0.20 FMSFA - 0.12 DMSFAL - 0.20$ $(-3.05)\quad\quad(7.08)\quad\quad(-2.30)\quad\quad(-0.43)$	0.9436	72.44
CBGD	$= 0.03 CBR + 0.07$ $(14.69)\quad(5.27)$	0.9350	215.84
CBCA	$= 0.03 NOXN + 0.03 CBR - 0.04 MI + 0.03$ $(4.02)\quad\quad(4.23)\quad\quad(-2.47)\quad(1.29)$	0.9965	1250.53
CBFL	$= 0.31 NOXN + 3.63 INF - 0.26 XNAN - 0.89$ $(2.76)\quad\quad(2.68)\quad\quad(-2.13)\quad\quad(-2.89)$	0.9734	158.68
CBOI	$= -0.20 NOXN + 0.21 ZNAN + 0.76$ $(2.98)\quad\quad(2.99)\quad\quad(4.50)$	0.3900	4.47

The treatment of petroleum revenues and their feedback on the Saudi economy is only one of many possible limitations of the forecasting model. Another deficiency is the omission of any consideration of nonoil exports. Not including these new export-oriented industries is equivalent to assuming that the government's development strategy is bankrupt. This, of course, is not the case, and the reason for their omission is simply due to the fact that they would involve quantum jumps in nonoil exports, because the model is forecast on an annual basis, much more accurate information about when they could come on stream would have to be available before they could be incorporated into the model.

Forecasting Procedures

As noted before, the methodology used here to arrive at a set of realistic forecasts of the economy and its macroeconomic components consisted of:

1. Estimating the structural equations depicting the basic economic forces at work in the kingdom.
2. Specifying growth rates for the exogenous variables—export prices, world price levels, and domestic oil production.
3. Running the model on a simultaneous equation basis to account for the interrelationships between the endogenous variables;
4. Determining critical areas of resource deficit (surplus).
5. Choosing the policy variables that have to be modified.
6. Specifying the level of policy variables (within the realm of reasonableness).
7. Rerunning the model with the new policy package.
8. Continuing the process until an equilibrium was reached.

Forecast for 1978

Forecasts for 1978 were made largely to test the model. The equations in the models presented earlier were reestimated using data for the 1960–1977 period rather than for 1960–1978. Actual figures for 1978 were substituted into the exogenous portions of the model. The exogenous variables, together with the actual lagged variables for 1977 were used in generating 1978 values for the endogenous variables. The results were quite encouraging (table 17-8) and indicate the structural soundness of model construction.

The sensitivity of the model was then tested by altering several exogenous variables and calculating the appropriate multipliers (table 17-9). For example, a 1 riyal increase in the previous years' government expenditures would increase total investment this year by 0.76 riyals, real money supply (MIP) by 0.03 riyals, and so forth. These tests made it possible to predict the

Table 17–8
Saudi Arabia: Forecast for 1978

Variable	Actual Value	Forecast Value	Percentage Difference
NUXNP	20.14	20.70	+2.78
NUXN	88.23	88.27	+0.05
TINP	17.76	16.74	−5.74
MIP	11.23	11.25	+0.18
DFGDP	3.83	3.91	+2.09
ZNANP	34.61	33.84	−2.22
GCNP	10.74	10.38	−3.35
SNP	22.81	23.42	+2.67
FK	154.77	147.45	−4.73
GRNAN	87.52	90.26	3.13
PCNP	11.64	10.80	−7.22
EXPTNA	139.54	139.78	+0.17
EXPTNAR	20.95	21.54	+2.82
GENANP	19.98	20.41	+2.15
KP	40.19	41.77	+3.93
GINP	9.24	8.65	−6.39
PINP	4.86	4.45	−8.44
PENANP	15.89	15.27	−3.90
MZP	13.25	13.41	+1.21

Table 17–9
Impact Matrix

Variable	GENANPL	GORFSPL	KPL	EMPT	CPPDF	CPPDFL
TINP	0.76	0.07	—	—	—	—
MIP	0.03	0.003	0.08	3.50	—	—
NOXNP	0.08	0.01	0.20	8.72	—	—
ADNP	0.01	0.01	0.02	1.05	—	—
ZNANP	0.76	0.07	0.05	1.99	—	—
DCP	—	−0.87	—	—	−14.80	−11.15
MSFAD	0.17	0.88	0.01	0.44	16.66	12.55
GCNP	—	0.03	—	—	5.95	4.48
GORFSP	—	—	—	—	19.19	14.46
SNP	0.06	−0.03	0.16	6.87	17.78	13.39
ΔZNANP	0.76	0.07	0.05	1.98	—	—
PCNP	0.02	0.01	0.04	1.85	—	—
DANP	0.01	0.01	0.02	1.05	19.19	14.46
GENANP	0.96	0.09	—	—	—	—
KP	0.40	0.04	1.05	—	—	—
SPP	2.06	−0.23	0.16	6.87	17.79	13.39
GDPNP	0.08	0.01	0.20	—	23.74	17.88

consequences of any departure from the historical growth path. After the model was complete with the equations estimated through 1978, preliminary not complete data for 1979 was released by the Saudi Arabian Monetary Agency. Using values for the exogenous 1979 variables and the lagged values of the estimated 1978 figures, a 1979 forecast was made. The generated values were all within 7 percent of the actual figures with most within 3 percent, again confirming the general predictability of the model.

Forecast of the Third Plan Period (1980–1985)

Forecasts for the Third Plan Period were made by incorporating a linear programming routine with the model equations. Theoretically, the model then became capable of depicting the shape of the country's production-possibilities surface for each of the five plan years. The shape of this surface was not fixed but instead was a function of: (1) expected demand patterns; (2) resource availability; (3) choice of techniques; (4) patterns of supply, including import substitution; (5) income growth; and (6) relative prices of goods and factors. Because the future production possibilities were predicted by the economic model, the prediction then became a function of another factor: (7) the structure of the model itself and the assumptions related to the technique of solution.

The endogenous generation of future production-possibility surfaces for an economy that can be used to predict alternative efficient patterns of production and resource allocation requires the model to incorporate some degee of choice. The linear programming algorithm that solved a set of linear inequalities for a constrained maximum developed for this problem was characterized by its ability to choose among alternative activities.

For a programming model of this type, it seemed better to maximize a general welfare function subject to other more precise national goals (which were included in the system as constraints). If there is a conflict among goals, the general level of welfare and efficiency in the system are not ignored as the government concerns itself with the trade-off among policy objectives.

The objective of maximum nonoil GDP growth subject to inflation and foreign labor constraints was chosen mainly because it seemed to portray best the government's interest in the kingdom's long-term socioeconomic stability. It is important to note that global profit maximization is not the real objective of the country. Indeed, Saudi Arabia's foremost concern is with the economy's ability to generate real economic development in the domestic nonoil sector without dependence on foreign workers or disruption of valued social institutions.

Table 17–10
Rates of Growth of Exogenous Variables

Variable (Symbol)	Low	Medium	High	LP
Employment (*EMPT*)	3.0	5.0	7.0	1.16
World inflation (*WPIND*)	3.0	5.0	7.0	5.0
Terms of trade (*Z2TT*)	0.0	0.0	0.0	0.0
Export prices (*EUV*)	0.0	1.0	5.0	1.0
Crude petroleum exports (*CPPDF*)	0.0	1.0	5.0	1.0

Note: *LP* = Linear programming-optimization result.

These considerations were introduced into the model in their simplest form; that is, given the goal of higher income growth, how fast can the kingdom's economic expansion occur while the country simultaneously reduces its dependence on foreign workers and contains the rate of domestic inflation? More specifically, the objective function is formally stated as: what is the maximum rate of real nonoil gross domestic product that can take place without additional foreign workers entering the kingdom and the rate of domestic inflation rising above 5 percent? Put differently, what specific increases would occur in nonoil GDP and the various macroeconomic aggregates if the inflation and employment constraints were relaxed?

In terms of the specific assumptions incorporated into the model figure 1 forecast, labor productivity, in line with Third Plan targets, was assumed to increase by 7 percent per year.

The other main exogenous variables are: (1) employment, (2) world inflation, (3) terms of trade, (4) export prices (*EUV*), and (5) crude petroleum exports (see table 17–10).

Forecasts of employment depend on the number of net Saudi workers entering the work force plus net immigration. High, low, and medium forecasts were also set at 3.0, 5.0 and 7.0 percent per annum, respectively, for comparison with the Fifth Plan (*LP*), which was set at 1.16 percent per annum.

Preliminary runs established that as constructed, world inflation and the terms of trade variables were not critical to the model's results. They are thus included only for completeness, with no attempt made to reconcile the inconsistency betweeen the terms of trade being set at 0.0 before the domestic inflation rate was determined. Again as indicated in trial runs, terms of trade fluctuations seem to have relatively little effect on the final results.

The volume and price of petroleum exports are forecast to increase at 1.0 per annum (with the high and low runs 0.0 and 5.0, respectively, set for comparison basis).

Given these exogenous values, an ex-ante prediction technique was used

Table 17–11
Saudi Arabia: Macroeconomic Forecasts for the Third Plan Period

	1980				1985			
	High	Medium	Low	Optimum	High	Medium	Low	Optimum
PCNP	16.10	15.87	15.66	15.47	31.13	29.25	27.79	26.45
GCNP	12.55	12.54	12.55	12.53	17.91	17.42	17.00	17.43
TCNP	28.65	28.41	28.21	28.00	49.04	46.67	44.79	43.88
TINP (ex ante)	18.71	18.62	18.74	18.64	27.51	25.55	25.87	25.55
TINP (ex post)	21.63	21.44	20.90	21.08	38.87	33.11	30.97	31.62
SNP (ex ante)	22.11	19.74	20.72	19.77	33.97	26.35	24.84	24.34
SNP (ex post)	30.58	27.99	28.09	26.90	43.42	31.46	29.68	28.67
Domestic gap (ex ante)	3.40	1.12	1.98	1.13	6.46	0.80	−1.03	−1.21
Domestic gap (ex post)	8.95	6.55	7.09	5.82	4.55	−1.65	−1.29	−2.95
PINP	5.71	5.53	5.34	5.17	9.78	8.90	8.49	8.20
GINP	11.45	11.36	11.48	11.37	17.21	15.24	15.03	15.23
GENANP	24.00	23.90	24.03	23.90	35.12	32.66	32.91	32.66
NOXNP	26.60	25.90	24.86	24.59	49.36	45.60	42.81	40.27
OGDPNP	31.87	29.78	30.71	29.61	41.91	31.53	30.70	31.35
GDPNP	58.47	55.68	55.57	54.20	91.27	77.13	73.51	71.62
NFP	0.76	0.72	0.72	0.70	1.19	1.00	0.96	0.93
GNPNP	59.23	56.40	56.29	54.90	92.46	78.13	74.47	72.55
External gap (ex ante)	12.30	9.48	11.14	9.96	18.99	5.48	5.37	8.05
External gap (ex post)	8.95	6.55	7.20	5.82	3.36	−2.65	−2.25	−3.88
ZNANP (ex ante)	42.37	42.37	41.96	41.60	66.68	62.74	61.46	59.86
ZNANP (ex post)	45.72	45.30	45.90	45.80	82.31	70.87	69.08	71.79
FEXPTNAR	53.91	53.13	52.38	50.92	85.67	68.22	66.83	67.91

to forecast the time path of the endogenous variables. The lagged endogenous variables were integrated beginning with the 1979 figures. The linear programming (optional) run was then performed, given the employment 1.16 and inflation 5 percent constraints (see table 17–11).

The model's results indicate that growth coupled with a sharp rise in the number of Saudis going through higher education and training will clearly put a strain on indigenous labor supplies. However, the Planning Ministry plans to keep the demand for extra labor to a minimum. Some 300,000 new civilian jobs will be created that will be filled by movements of labor from construction and agriculture as well as increases in skilled expatriates and the local labor market.[6]

The model indicates the plan's envisaged spending increases could aggravate inflation once more. Controlling inflation, however, will be more difficult in the Third Plan than in the Second, where it was successfully combated by fiscal policy, administrative controls, and encouragement of immigration from other Middle East countries and Asia.

The adverse effects of curbing government spending will be greater in the 1980s because of the dependence of a growing number of enterprises on low-cost government finance and the business generated by public-sector projects. A considerably larger bureaucracy using up scarce supplies of skilled Saudi manpower would be required to administer a comprehensive mix of wage and price controls.

In general, the forecast is optimistic concerning Saudi Arabia's ability to achieve the Third Plan's objectives. Failure to meet the plan targets would probably stem from the government's inability to manage the economy using traditional macroeconomic policy instruments, such as the level of government spending, rather than any particular constraint. In this respect the kingdom is moving into a crucial state of its development where the drive to industrialize will become increasingly difficult to halt, divert, and even manage.

Long-Run Forecasts

The model is important primarily for short-run simulations, but it can also be used for longer-run forecasts. Dynamic forecasts for 1985 to 2000 were therefore also made under the same three assumptions for the endogenous variables used in the Third Plan forecast.

Seen in this long-run context the results produced a number of interesting patterns, including:

1. Over the period 1978–1990, real nonoil growth varies from a low of 10.7 percent per annum in the low oil-export forecast to 12.74 in the high oil-export, unconstrained foreign labor case.
2. The rate of growth of capital formation is high in all three forecasts, not varying by more than 1 percent between the high and low forecasts.
3. Government investment rates of growth are considerably greater than public consumption growth in all forecasts.
4. Inflation is sensitive to the rate of growth varying (again over the 1978–1990 period) from 10.34 in the low forecast, to 13.04 in the high forecast.
5. Private expenditure grows at a somewhat slower rate than public expenditure, with private consumption growth greatly exceeding the growth in private sector investment.

6. The growth in money (*MB, M1P, M2P*) are nearly in line with nonoil income.
7. The ex-ante savings gap dominates the trade gap for all forecasts, with the gaps tending to increase at lower rates of growth.
8. The trade gap tends to be positive throughout the forecast period for all forecasts where the medium and low rates of growth yield a small ex-poste negative gap.
9. These trends continue over the 1990–2000 period, with the general pattern being one of a gradual deceleration of most macro variables to a stable growth path.
10. Thus by 2000 the average annual real nonoil growth for 1978–2000 has declined to 11.42 percent per annum, 10.10, and 7.66 for the high, medium, and low forecasts, respectively, with an inflation rate of 11.98, 10.68, and 8.52, respectively.
11. For the period 1990–2000 itself, these rates are 9.86, 8.47, and 7.48 for nonoil GDP and 10.97, 9.53, and 7.32, respectively, for inflation.

All scenarios indicate that the domestic gap declines from a positive to eventually negative position over time. The size of surplus is thus a function of the size of government revenues as well as of its expenditure pattern over time. Greater surpluses in the early years allow the building up of a stock of wealth (while the absorptive capacity remains low). This implies that if the absorptive capacity expands, the economy could draw upon its foreign portfolio, enabling it to maintain rapid growth even if for some reason oil revenues began to decline. It is those early year surpluses that increase significantly the size of the total financial surplus.

Before too many conclusions are drawn, however, it must be pointed out that the projections made by models of the two-gap variety used here are quite sensitive to the assumed values of the savings investment and import functions. Also there is a great degree of variation in judgment about the extent to which domestic production can be increased to substitute for imports. It would be advisable to appraise such variables as imports separately for different broad categories of goods (since the emerging import structure would reflect the process of adaptation of domestic resources to a multitude of factors, such as market conditions and technological possibilities).

Conclusions

The results of the forecasts for 1980–2000 and the optimization procedure for 1980–1985 suggest the following:

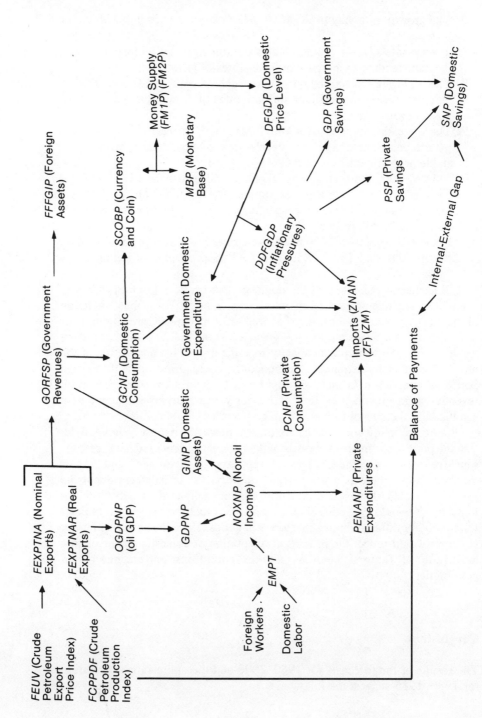

Figure 17-1. Saudi Arabia: Macroeconomic Flows and Linkages

1.   Using a macroeconometric model as well as an operational concept of absorptive capacity it was possible to determine Saudi Arabia's growth potential and financial position according to several oil scenarios.

2.   Oil revenues are seen to affect the economy both positively and negatively. On the positive side, they are still the major growth-propelling factor. On the negative side, they are capable of producing excess liquidity and resulting inflation.

3.   Economic growth in Saudi Arabia should be able to be maintained at rather high levels without excess inflation, while at the same time the foreign work force is gradually reduced. Inflationary pressures remain a major problem for the Saudi Arabian economy, however, especially when we consider the deflationary measures required for its elimination.

4.   To maintain a steady growth path over the short, medium, and longer term, oil revenues must be divided optimally between those funds destined for internal use (according to absorptive capacity) and those destined for foreign investment.

Notes

1. A structural test along these lines was suggested in Ragaei El Mallaklt and Mihssen Kadhim, "Absorptive Capacity, Surplus Funds, and Regional Capital Mobility in the Middle East," *Rivista Internazionale di Scienze Economiche e Commerciali* (April 1977): 308–325.

2. Again, the best of which is developed in Faisal S. Al Bashir, *A Structural Econometric Model of the Saudi Arabian Economy: 1960–1970* (New York: John Wiley, 1977).

3. See appendix A for a list of all the variables.

4. As developed for example by Jaroslav Vanek in *Estimating Foreign Resource Needs for Economic Development* (New York: McGraw-Hill, 1967).

5. See Said Hitti and George Abed, "The Economy and Finances of Saudi Arabia," International Monetary Fund, *Staff Papers* (July 1974): 247–306.

6. Ministry of Planning, *Third Development Plan* (Riyadh: MOP, 1980), ch. 5.

18 Summary and Conclusions

The OPEC price increases had several important effects on Saudi Arabia: (1) it provided the kingdom with the means to fundamentally change the status quo between itself and both the producing companies and the consuming countries; (2) the kingdom's economic power was suddenly increased, but its vulnerability also rapidly increased as the government became accustomed to a larger source of revenues; (3) the interdependence between the kingdom and other producers and consumers became more unstable in both the political and economic senses as frictions developed betweeen these groups, and (4) because of (1) through (3), the kingdom sought a development strategy that would enable it to achieve a feasible interdependence between itself and both the consuming and producing nations.

Several possible strategies were both logical and feasible:

1. A rapid increase in the production of crude oil.
2. A continuation of mainly crude oil production, but based largely on domestic needs.
3. A policy of diversified industrialization.
4. A policy mix consisting of moderate industrialization, international banking, and development of service sectors—government employment.
5. A largely retainer strategy consisting of regional investment of oil revenues and moderate domestic development.
6. A high-growth strategy of petroleum-based industrialization combined with high and steady levels of oil exports.

Each of these strategies has certain advantages and disadvantages. Clearly, the strategy of expanding the production and export of crude would increase revenues, but at the same time it would also increase the kingdom's vulnerability. Similarly, a reduction in output and production for domestic needs would reduce foreign labor demand, but it might simultaneously encourage the development of substitutes by the consuming countries.

Ultimately, of course, the kingdom opted for a strategy of viable interdependence whereby domestic investment of oil revenues in heavy industries (made possible by high levels of export) was seen as the best means of achieving some sort of balance between efficiency and vulnerability. Through government investment of oil revenues, the authorities sought structural change capable of: (1) increasing the ability of the country to use more of its oil resource domestically (so that the kingdom's dependence on oil exports could be curtailed); (2) increasing the country's ability to produce and trade products derived from oil; (3) enabling the country to trade and bargain on relatively equal technological and economic grounds, and (4) making the country less vulnerable to the effects of severe market fluctuations or sudden changes in the politics of the consuming countries.

While the econometric model in the previous chapter indicated this strategy to be optimal and feasible ,given the country's socioeconomic goals and priorities, it is still true that:

1. The kingdom is almost totally dependent on oil exports and on the effect of these oil revenues on the domestic economy.
2. The strategy is largely a resource-based, capital-intensive process of industrializaiton, with agriculture playing a largely passive role of maintaining structural balance, and the noneconomic one of enduring some level of food self-reliance.
3. The strategy requires careful preplanning and identification of profitable investments (particularly since the break with past patterns of growth has been so radical).
4. The strategy has been deficient in assessing realistically the manpower and education requirements of such industries.
5. Little attention has been given to the identification of efficient import substitution industries for which market size is adequate for efficient production.

These factors are capable of creating a number of potential problems, which if left unattended could undermine the country's entire development effort.

Potential Development Problems

There are several problems that are potentially serious enough to warrant government action. It is difficult to prioritize these difficulties in terms of relative importance for concern. A tentative ranking based on factors discussed in the previous chapters would be:

1. A worsening of the world food situation;
2. Deterioration of the income distribution
3. The foreign worker situation
4. Sector uncertainty about the role of the government in the economy
5. Those problems requiring reforms in planning procedures

Worsening of the World Food Situation

The world food situation will likely continue to deteriorate over the next 20 years as population pressures begin to make themselves felt and the amount of usable land per capita declines.[1] While existing technology should be able to offset this trend, the inability of many developing countries to implement productivity increases (largely because of political reasons) will mean lagging output. The result will be increases in scarcity, whereby food, even if available, will sell for relatively higher prices; that is, the terms of trade for Saudi Arabia might deteriorate.

Of course, a dismal worldwide agricultural performance is not inevitable. Given the seriousness of the problem, however, several actions should be undertaken. These include: (1) the attainment of a certain minimal capacity to produce and stockpile supplies of its basic food items; and (2) the construction of facilities to achieve at least 6 month's self-sufficiency in storage. Financial conditions in 1981 would enable self-sufficiency to be obtained by the end of the Fourth Development Plan, and perhaps even earlier. In short, the phase of rapid industrialization that the kingdom is currently passing through should be accompanied with the provision of agricultural supplies (though not necessarily through broad-based domestic agricultural production).

Deterioration in Income Distribution

Though no official data are available,it is clear that Saudi Arabia (as with many other developing countries) is finding that rapid growth results in a worsening of the distribution of income. Unless action is taken soon the deterioration may become particularly severe in the 1980s as industrialization speeds up. As is typically the case in countries at this stage of development, gaps are appearing between various income groups and regions in the kingdom, as well as between the country's urban and rural population. In the long run the country certainly will have the resources at is disposal to alleviate the situation. (Its small and relatively homogenous population makes this task easy.)

There is no reason that a conflict between equity and efficiency has to arise even though in its eagerness to promote growth the government has tended to allocate oil revenues to areas (Jubail, for example) where only a very few Saudis are able to directly benefit.[2] So far, therefore, Second Plan industrial investments have resulted in only a limited number of potentially efficient areas. These locations have prevailed at the expense of the less-developed and often more heavily-populated areas (the Asir, for example). While it is clearly inefficient to counter completely the forces of economic efficiency solely on the basis of social efficiency criteria, it is also clear in light of the Iranian experience that a balance must soon be struck on both human and political grounds to prevent a disruption of the social fabric.

In this regard Saudi Arabia is somewhat fortunate that by developing at a later point in time the kingdom can avoid many of the mistakes made by Iran. There is no question that a major lesson to be learned from Iran's development strategy is that even though the level of income for most of the population may be increasing fairly rapidly, discontent is likely to arise if the gap between regions or urban/rural or even particular groups continues to widen. Adverse income distribution patterns of this sort ordinarily will not cause a problem if corrected early. Increasing income disparity can, however, cause mass alienation, as in the case of Iran. This is most likely to occur during periods such as in 1981 when expectations of future living standards are accelerating (because of the knowledge and accumulation of that wealth in relatively few hands).

Income distribution considerations translate themselves into the setting of targets to minimize the urban/rural income gap and the achievement of better interregional balances. Investments along these lines can be easily justified, given the potential social strains associated with the kingdom's present strategy. This conclusion holds even though the resulting investment pattern might reduce the kingdom's overall economic growth potential.

The Foreign Worker Dilemma

Associated with the strategy of the Second Plan has been the almost total reliance on foreign workers and foreign expertise for plan implementation, although the Third Plan sets as its main goal the elimination of the kingdom's dependence on foreign workers. While this objective is certainly admirable, it is difficult to imagine (at least during the next decade) how the industrial complexes at Jubail and Yenbo can be anything but dependent on foreign technicians. Most Saudi migrants to these complexes will not have the skills or inclination necessary to man a large percentage of the new job opportunities opening over the next 10 years.

These Saudis can always find public employment. It is clear that if the kingdom is ever to evolve away from a retainer state to a productive dynamic economy, complexes like Jubail will not be sufficient. A complementary startegy would involve locating industries more evenly through the kingdom. These would presumably require more skills than the majority of Saudis will be likely to possess as vocational training begins to make an impact. While possibly inefficient from a pure economic point of view, in the long run the lower social costs of these industries compared with the Jubail-type strategy may make these industries easily justifiable.

The government's emphasis on education in the Third Plan is undoubtedly the best one for eliminating the foreign worker problem.[3] Investments in education and training do, however, have long gestation lags. If education is to be stressed as a way of providing productive jobs for the Saudis at Jubail and Yenbo, then the Saudi planners (because of the long gestation lags involved and the necessity of proper timing of projects to productively employ workers) must identify as quickly as possible the final projects (and their timing) that will be located at these sites.

Role of the Government

To efficiently implement its long-run development strategy, it will be necessary for the authorities to define more precisely than they have thus far the role of government in the economy. To be sure, the existence of a large influx of oil-based revenues implies a large role for the public sector. By the same token it has been publicly stated that when the basic infrastructural investments in the kingdom have been completed (sometime in the Fourth Plan), the role of the public sector will decrease rapidly relative to that of the private sector.

The forecasts of the previous chapter indicate, however, that the private sector may not be in a position to generate the type of demand needed to maintain the growth rates capable of being attained in the kingdom. This is particularly true of private investment, whose rate of growth tends to lag behind that of real nonoil income in all of the forecasts.

In principle, therefore, while the government's intention of encouraging the private sector to assume responsibility for most production in the kingdom is a wise one given the inefficiencies usually associated with public sector involvement, reduction of the government activities should not proceed too rapidly. There is a real risk of deflation if the government contracts its investment too rapidly. This problem is reinforced by the apparent accelerator mechanism underlying private investments; that is, a reduction in the rate of growth would have a compound contracting effect on private investment.

While it is clear, therefore, that the kingdom's strategy of achieving an international comparative advantage in the area of industrial production is correct and that this strategy must eventually rest on the abilities and dynamism of the private sector, the government must, however, clearly convey to the private sector that its continued activity in the economy is necessary for stabilization purposes. Otherwise there may be a number of misunderstandings over the true scope of the government's economic involvement that would cause the private sector to be even more reluctant than it has been to undertake investments in manufacturing.

In any case the government should have little trouble in finding areas to spend money in directing the path of the economy toward the creation of a more normal economy. These include:

1. Investing in health and education necessary to maintain and increase the human element in the development process (while at the same time contributing to improvements in labor and managerial quality).
2. Participating initially in heavy industries where the private sector may be reluctant to venture.
3. Subsidizing regional investments in backward areas to mold the future spatial configuration of population and economic activity in a manner more compatible with existing sociocultural factors.

Planning Reforms

There is a great need to revise the country's system of planning to fill in the current gap in decision making that exists not only between the various ministries in Riyadh, but also between decision makers in the capital and provinces. Again, the Iranian experience illustrates the ramifications of overcentralized decision making. Thus, qualified individuals at the regional and city level presumably well acquainted with local problems must be drawn into the decision-making process to a much greater extent than in the past.

The major institutional problems in this area that need to be examined by the Saudi authorities include: (1) the scope and capability of the planning system; (2) the implementation of decentralization policies involving decisions designed to increase participation of more Saudis in the development process, and (3) the necessity of administrative reforms.

In view of the very high goals set for the kingdom's social and economic system over the longer term, and the pressures associated with reaching these goals, it is clear that not only private sector efficiency but also increases in public-sector efficiency are of paramount importance. The kingdom's overly bureaucratic planning procedures must be streamlined to reduce the time delays involved in project identification and the subsequent awarding of contracts. Reforms should also help reduce the duplication of effort and the numerous cost overruns that currently characterize the Saudi development effort. Better coordination of expenditure plans between ministries would also help (through stricter budgetary control) to reduce inflationary pressures.

The question of reforming the public administrative apparatus is an efficiency question that needs to be examined on a longer-term basis. Eliminating red tape is important as a complementary factor in the strategy of development outlined here, especially with respect to creating private-sector enthusiasm and dynamism. Within the public sector there should also be a reform in the incentive system for employees. If the government is forced to increase its scope in the economy of activity due to the natural conservatism of the private sector, then it must be able to attract and retain highly qualified managers. Clearly, for the government to expand its capability in the economy, it must revise its incentive system to reward individuals more on the basis of ability and performance.

Conclusions

While Saudi Arabia's economic future is undoubtedly a rosy one, the Iranian experience has demonstrated how fragil oil-based economies really are. A charting of the kingdom's likely growth path is quite pretentious and should be done only in the context of the caveats discussed above (plus, of course, all the political, social, and military ones so often seen in the popular press). One thing that is clear is that it is difficult to see how the role of the government will decrease even over the longer term.

If in fact the kingdom has a comparative advantage only in large-scale capital-intensive industries, the government may have to remain involved in economic activities in which the private sector, because of risk or size of investment reasons, will always be reluctant to enter. Clearly, however, this involvement is possible without compromising the kingdom's commitment to a procapitalist, laissez faire model of development, nor in any way would it encroach on any of the tenets of Islam. In all regards the country is truly fortunate.

Notes

1. See Radha Sinha, "the World Food Problem: Concensus and Conflict," *World Development* (May–July 1977): 371–382, for an excellent discussion of these issues.

2. See Montek Ahluwalia and Hollis B. Chenery, "A Model of Distribution and Growth," in H. Chenery, *Redistribution with Growth* (London: Oxford University Press, 1974), pp. 209–235, for a proof of this proposition.

3. Ministry of Planning, *Third Development Plan* (Riyadh: MOP), ch. 5.

Appendix A:
Variables and
Their Properties

The variables listed here were used in the analysis and forecast of the economy. They cover the period 1960 to 1978 and are based on annual data. To make the listing briefer, the following conventions were used in the presentation of the equations in the main body of the study:

1. Constant prices are of variables deflated with the GDP deflator, 1970 = 100.0, and are represented by a P at the end of the variable; that is, $NOXNP$ is real or constant nonoil income, whereas $NOXN$ is nonoil income at current prices.
2. Δ is an operator, referring to the difference between two successive time periods; that is, 1970 minus 1969.
3. A L at the end of a variable means it is lagged 1 year, while a $L2$ at the end refers to a lag of 2 years.
4. A dot over the variable—for example, $N\dot{O}XN$—indicates the percentage rate of growth.
5. Symbols beginning with D (except $DFGDP$ and DC) refer as in (2) to the difference in yearly values.

Table A–1
Variables and Their Properties

Symbol	Variable Name	Characteristic	Possible Policy Variable
PCN	private consumption	endogenous	no
$NOXN$	nonoil GDP	endogenous	no
$DFGDP$	GDP deflator	endogenous	no
PC	private credit	endogenous	yes
INF	rate of change in nonoil price deflator	endogenous	no
GCN	government consumption	endogenous	yes
$DTNOX$	deviation from trend in nonoil GDP	endogenous	no
$GORFS$	government oil revenues	exogenous	yes
$FEXPTNA$	exports, current prices	exogenous	yes
$FEXPTNAR$	exports, constant prices	exogenous	yes
$GENANP$	total government expenditures	endogenous	yes

Table A–1 (*continued*)

Symbol	Variable Name	Characteristic	Possible Policy Variable
GNORFS	government nonoil revenue	endogenous	yes
TIN	total investment	endogenous	yes
ICON	investment in construction	endogenous	yes
GIN	government investment	endogenous	yes
PIN	private investment	endogenous	no
ITRN	investment in transport and communication	endogenous	yes
PENAN	total private expenditure	endogenous	no
SP	private savings	endogenous	no
M1	Currency plus demand deposits	endogenous	no
M2	M1 plus quasi-money	endogenous	no
Z1TT	terms of trade (GDP deflator/import prices)	exogenous	no
Z2TT	terms of trade (consumer price index/import prices)	exogenous	no
GNDEX	domestic government expenditure	endogenous	yes
DC	domestic credit	endogenous	yes
ZNAN	imports	endogenous	no
K	capital stock	endogenous	yes
GRFS	total government revenue	endogenous	yes
SN	total savings	endogenous	yes
FZNANP	real imports	endogenous	no
F	domestic gap ($SNP - TINP$)	endogenous	yes
CAPFP	domestic gap ($SNP - TINP$)	endogenous	yes
FCAPF	domestic gap ($SNP - TINP$)	endogenous	yes
SG	government savings	endogenous	yes
DAN	domestic absorption	endogenous	yes
ADN	domestic supply	endogenous	yes
CR	private credit/nominal nonoil income	endogenous	yes
MB	monetary base—high-powered money	endogenous	yes
SFA	SAMA foreign assets	endogenous	yes
SCOB	currency and coin	endogenous	yes
LRB	legal reserves of commercial banks	endogenous	yes
ERB	excess reserves of commercial banks	endogenous	no

GNAC	claims on government less government deposits with SAMA	endogenous	yes
BAC	SAMA advances, rediscounts to banks	endogenous	yes
EAC	other commercial bank assets	endogenous	no
GDFICIT	government deficit (surplus)	endogenous	yes
BA	adjusted monetary base	endogenous	yes
B	monetary base	endogenous	yes
COB	current account balance	endogenous	no
MS	money supply ($M1$)	endogenous	yes
MD	money demand ($M1$)	endogenous	no
IUS	U. S. treasury bill rate	endogenous	no
FSMIAS	incremental aggregate supply	endogenous	yes
FSMPA	planned absorption	endogenous	yes
FSMPI	planned impact	endogenous	yes
FSMIDA	incremental domestic absorption	endogenous	yes
FSMIPI	incremental planned effect	endogenous	yes
FWPIND	world inflation	exogenous	no
EXCESS	$M1/NOXNP$	endogenous	no
FAX	expected inflation $INFL - INFL2$	endogenous	no
ZAB	imports/GDP	endogenous	no
GNOXR	real growth nonoil GDP	endogenous	no
FF	domestic gap ($SNP - TINP$)	endogenous	yes
GWP	growth in world prices	exogenous	no
CON	value added, construction	endogenous	yes
MAN	value added, manufacturing	endogenous	yes
D	value added, public administration	endogenous	yes
E	value added, electricity	endogenous	no
TD	value added, trade	endogenous	no
AG	value added, agriculture	endogenous	no
T	value added, transport and communications	endogenous	no
FNSBP	net services, balance of payments	endogenous	no
FUTBP	unrequited transfers, balance of payments	endogenous	yes
FPTBP	private unrequited transfers, balance of payments	endogenous	no
FGTBP	government unrequited transfers, balance of payments	endogenous	no

Table A–1 (*continued*)

Symbol	Variable Name	Characteristic	Possible Policy Variable
FNMCBP	nonmonetary capital, balance of payments	endogenous	no
FCMBP	private nonmonetary capital, balance of payments	endogenous	no
FDIBP	direct investment, balance of payments	endogenous	no
FCOLTBP	other private long-term capital, balance of payments	endogenous	no
FOSTBP	other private short-term capital, balance of payments	endogenous	no
FGCMBP	government (net) nonmonetary capital	endogenous	yes
NOI	commercial bank other net assets	endogenous	no
GNPN	gross national product	endogenous	no
GAPN	domestic gap ($SN - TIN$)	endogenous	yes
FPCT	private external capital flows	endogenous	no
FGCI	government external capital flows	endogenous	yes
FCI	total external capital flows	endogenous	yes
CABP	current account balance of payments	endogenous	no
MSFA	foreign assets (monetary survey)	endogenous	yes
FSFA	SAMA foreign assets	endogenous	yes
FPSBPX	private sector, balance of payments	endogenous	no
SGD	government deposits with SAMA	endogenous	yes
FBBP	balance of payments, goods and services	endogenous	no
FTBP	trade balance	endogenous	no
FEOBP	errors and omissions, balance of payments	endogenous	no
FBPT	total balance of payments	endogenous	no
PSBPMSD	private sector, monetary impact	endogenous	no
FGEXTCFX	government domestic expenditures	endogenous	yes
MSQM	quasi-money, monetary survey	endogenous	no
MSFA	foreign assets, monetary survey	endogenous	no
MSGD	government deposits SAMA, monetary survey	endogenous	yes
MSOI	other assets, monetary survey	endogenous	no
MSPC	private credit, monetary survey	endogenous	no
CBPC	private credit, commercial banks	endogenous	no

CBDD	demand deposits, commercial banks	endogenous	no
CBQB	quasi-money, commercial banks	endogenous	no
CBFA	foreign assets, commercial banks	endogenous	yes
CBR	reserves, commercial banks	endogenous	yes
CBGD	government deposits, commercial banks	endogenous	yes
CBCA	capital accounts, commercial banks	endogenous	no
CBFL	foreign liabilities, commercial banks	endogenous	no
ĊBOI	other items, commercial banks	endogenous	no

Appendix B:
Saudi Fiscal and
Hijra Year Dates and
Gregorian Equivalents

Table B-1
Saudi Fiscal and Hijra Year Dates and Gregorian Equivalents

Saudi Fiscal Year (1 Rajab to 30 Jumad II)	Begins[a]	Hijra Year	Begins[a]	Hijra Months[b]
1385–86	25 Oct 1965	1385	1 May 1965	Muharram
86–87	16 Oct 66	86	21 Apr 66	Safar
87–88	4 Oct 67	87	11 Apr 67	Rabi I
88–89	23 Sep 68	88	30 Mar 68	Rabi II
89–90	12 Sep 69	89[a]	19 Mar 69	Jumad I
				Jumad II
1390–91	2 Sep 1970	1390	9 Mar 1970	Rajab
91–92	22 Aug 71	91	26 Feb 71	Shaban
92–93	10 Aug 72	92	15 Feb 72	Ramadhan
93–94	30 Jul 73	93	4 Feb 73	Shawwal
94–95	19 Jul 74	94	23 Jan 74	Dhul-Qi'dah
				Dhul-Hijjah
1395–96	9 Jul 1975	1395	13 Jan 1975	
96–97	28 Jun 76	96	2 Jan 76	
97–98	16 Jun 77	97	22 Dec 76	
98–99	6 Jun 78	98	11 Dec 77	Gregorian
99–1400	26 May 79	99	30 Nov 78	months[b]
				January
1400–01	15 May 1980	1400	19 Nov 1979	February
01–02	4 May 81	01	9 Nov 80	March
02–03	23 Apr 82	02	28 Oct 81	April
03–04	12 Apr 83	03	17 Oct 82	May
04–05	2 Apr 84	04	7 Oct 83	June
				July
1405–06	22 Mar 1985	1405	27 Sep 1984	August
06–07	11 Mar 86	06	27 Sep 85	September
07–08	28 Feb 87	07	4 Sep 86	October
08–09	17 Feb 88	08	24 Aug 87	November
09–10	7 Feb 89	09	14 Aug 88	December

[a]Dates are approximate for future year.

[b]See *Statistical Yearbook* 1393 A.H. (1973), pp. 13–14, for starting dates of Hijra and Gregorian months in past years.

Bibliography

Abdullatif, Sheikh Ahmed. "A Strategy for Investing the OPEC Surplus." *Euromoney* (August 1980): 23–24.

Abdul-Rauf, Muhammad, *The Islamic Doctrine of Economics and Contemporary Economic Thought: Highlight of a Conference on a Theological Inquiry into Capitalism and Socialism*. Washington: American Enterprise Institute, 1978.

Abolfathi, Farid et al. *The OPEC Market to 1985*. Lexington, Mass.: Lexington Books, D.C. Heath and Company, 1977.

Abu-Laban, Baha, and Abu-Laban, Sharon. "Education and Development in the Arab World." *Journal of Developing Areas* (April 1976): 285–304.

Adekunle, J.O. "The Demand for Money: Evidence from Developed and Less Developed Economies." International Monetary Fund, *Staff Papers* (November 1971).

Adelman, I., and Morris, C.T. "A Factor Analysis of the Interrelationship between Social and Political Variables and Per Capita Gross National Product." *Quarterly Journal of Economics* (November 1965): 558–60.

Adelman, M.A. "The World Oil Cartel: Scarcity, Economics and Politics." *Quarterly Review of Economics and Business* (Summer 1976): 7.

Ahluwalia, Montek, and Chenery, Hollis B. "A Model of Distribution and Growth." In *Redistribution with Growth*, edited by H. Chenery, pp. 209–235. London: Oxford University Press, 1974.

Akhtar, M.A. "An Empirical Note on Inflation and Openness in Less Developed Economies." *The Philippine Economic Journal* (1976): 636–649.

A'La Mavdavdi, S. Abul. *The Economic Problem of Man and Its Islamic Solution*. Lahore: Islamic Publications, 1978.

Al-Bashir, Faisal S. *A Structural Econometric Model of the Saudi Arabian Economy: 1960–1970*. New York: John Wiley, 1977.

Al-Farsy, Savad Abdul-Salam. "King Faisal and the First Five Year Development Plan." In *King Faisal and the Modernization of Saudi Arabia*, edited by Willard A. Beling, pp. 58–71. Boulder: Westview 1980.

Anderson, Sir Norman et al. *The Kingdom of Saudi Arabia*. London: Stacey International, 1977.

Ali, Anwar. *The Role of the Saudi Arabian Monetary Agency*. Jidda: SAMA, 1971.

Almon, S. "The Distributed Lag Between Capital Appropriations and Expenditures." *Econometrica* (January 1965): 188.

Amuzegar, Jahangir. "Atypical Backwardness and Investment Criteria." *Economica Internazionale* (August 1960).

_____. *Comparative Economics: National Priorities, Policies and Performance*. Cambridge, Mass.: Winthrop Publishers, 1981.

_____. "Ideology and Economic Growth in the Middle East." *The Middle East Journal* (Winter 1974): 3–7.

Arab Economist. "Saudi Arabia Moves to Diversify Economy: Industrial Development Has Priority." (August 1977): 24–29.

Asfour, Edmond et al. *Saudi Arabia: Long Term Projection of Supply and Demand for Agricultural Products*. Beirut: Economic Research Institute of American University, 1965.

Askari, Hossein, and Cummings, John. *Oil, OECD, and the Third World: A Vicious Triangle?* Austin: Center for Middle East Studies, 1978.

Azzam, Henry. "Analysis of Fertility and Labor Force Differentials in the Arab World." *Population Bulletin of the United Nations Economic Commission for Western Asia* (June 1979): 45.

Banker Research Unit. *Banking Structures and Sources of Finance in the Middle East*. 2d rev. ed. London: The Financial Times Business Publishing, Ltd., 1980.

Baumol, W.J. "The Transactions Demand for Cash: An Inventory Theoretic Approach." *Quarterly Journal of Economics* (November 1952).

Becker, G. "A Theory of the Allocation of Time." *Economic Journal* (September 1965): 493–517.

Behrman, Jere, and Klein, L. "Econometric Growth Models for the Developing Economy." In *Induction, Growth and Trade, Essays in Honour of Sir Roy Harrod*, Edited by W.A. Eltis et al., p. 169. London: Oxford University Press, 1970.

Berntson, Lyle Schertzad Byron. "The New Politics of Food." *World Development* (May–June 1977): 627–28.

Bertram, G. W. "The Relevance of the Canadian Wheat Boom in Canadian Economic Growth." *Canadian Journal of Economics* (August 1973).

Birks, J.S., and Sinclair, C.A. "International Labor Migration in the Arab Middle East." *Third World Quarterly* (April 1979): 87–88.

_____. *International Migration and Development in the Arab Region* (Geneva: International Labor Office, 1980).

_____. "The Domestic Political Economy of Development in Saudi Arabia." In Centre for Arab Gulf Studies, University of Exeter, *State, Economy and Power in Saudi Arabia*. A Symposium, July 4–7, 1980.

_____. *The International Migration Project, Country Case Study: Saudi Arabia*. Durham, England: University of Durham International Migration Project, 1978.

Bishtawi, Adel. "Arab Banking Survey." *Saudi Business and Arab Economic Report* (October 5, 1979): 13–15.

Braibanti, Ralph. "Saudi Arabia in the Context of Political Development

Theory." In *King Faisal and the Modernization of Saudi Arabia*, edited by Willard Beling, pp. 36–37. Boulder: Westview Press, 1980.

_____, and Al-Farsy, Fouad Abdul-salam. "Saudi Arabia: A Development Perspective." *Journal of South Asian and Middle Eastern Studies* (September 1977): 7, 8, 21.

Buchan, Jamie. "Water Supplies." *Financial Times* (April 17, 1978): 21.

Buchanan, James. "Farming in the Eastern Province," *Saudi Business and Arab Economic Report* (November 23, 1979): 34–38.

Cargill, Tom. *Money, the Financial System and Monetary Policy*. Englewood Cliffs, N.J.: Prentice Hall, 1979.

Caves, R.E. "Export Lead Growth and the New Economic History." In *Trade, Balance of Payments and Growth, Essays in Honor of Charles P. Kindieberger*, edited by J. Bhagwati, pp. 433–442. Amsterdam: North Holland, 1971.

Central Department of Statistics, *Consumer Expenditure Survey in Five Cities of Saudi Arabia, 1397/1977*. Riyadh: Ministry of Finance and National Economy, 1979.

_____. *Consumption Expenditure Survey in Rural Areas of Saudi Arabia, 1397/1977*. Riyadh: Ministry of Finance and National Economy, 1979.

_____. *National Accounts of Saudi Arabia 1386–1387 through 1391–1392, A.H.* Riyadh: Ministry of Finance and National Economy, 1973.

_____. *Statistical Year Book*. Various Issues.

Central Planning Organization, *Development Plan, 1390 A.H.* Riyadh, n.d.

_____.*Development Plan 1390 A.H.* Riyadh, 1970.

_____. *Socio-Economic Development Plan for the Eastern Region of Saudi Arabia (1975/76–1979/80)*. Riyadh: Ilaco Consultants, 1975.

Chenery, Hollis. "The Application of Investment Criteria." *Quarterly Journal of Economics* (February 1953): 78.

_____. "Comparative Advantage and Development Policy." *American Economic Review* (March 1961): 28–31.

_____. "Land: The Effective of Resources on Economic Growth." In *Economic Development with Special Reference to East Asia*, edited by Kenneth Berrill, p. 19. London: Macmillan, 1965.

_____. "Restructuring the World Economy." *Foreign Affairs* (April 1975): 242–262.

_____, and Strout, Alan. "Foreign Economic Assistance and Economic Development," *American Economic Review* (September 1966): 679–733.

Choucri, Nazli, "Demographic Changes in the Middle East." In Joint Economic Committee, Congress of the United States, *The Political Economy of the Middle East: 1973–1978*. Washington: U.S. Government Printing Office, 1980.

Cleron, Jean Paul. *Saudi Arabia 2000*. New York: St. Martin's Press, 1978.

Conlisk, J., and Huddle, D. "Allocating Foreign Aid: An Appraisal of a Self-Help Model." *Journal of Development Studies* (July 1969): 245–251.

Cranes, Robert. *Planning the Future of Saudi Arabia: A Model for Achieving National Priorities.* New York: Praeger Publishers, 1978.

Davidson, Paul. "Causality in Economies, A Review." *Journal of Post Keynesian Economics* (Summer 1980): 576–584.

Dawisha, Adeed. "Internal Values and External Threats: The Making of Saudi Foreign Policy." *Orbis* (Spring 1979): 129–43.

Dequin, H. *The Challenge of Saudi Arabia.* Singapore: Eurasia Press, 1976.

Doran, Charles. "Three Models of OPEC Leadership and Policy in the Aftermath of Iran." *Journal of Policy Modeling* (September 1979): 414–415.

Draper, N.R., and Smith, H. *Applied Regression Analysis.* New York: John Wiley, 1966.

Dunn, Robert. "Exchange Rates, Payments Adjustment, and OPEC: Why Oil Deficits Persist." Princeton University, International Finance Section, *Essays in International Finance No. 137* (December 1979): 7–8.

Dutta, M. *Econometric Methods.* Cincinnati: South-Western Publishing Company, 1975.

Economist Intelligence Unit. *A Study of the Middle East Economies: Their Structure and Outlook into the 1980s.* London: The Economist Intelligence Unit, 1978.

Edo, Michael. "Currency Arrangements and Banking Legislation in the Arabian Peninsula." International Monetary Fund, *Staff Papers* (July 1975): 510–38.

El Mallakh, Ragaei. "Where Does OPEC Money Go?" *The Wharton Magazine* (Winter 1980): 34–39.

El Mallak, Ragaei, and Kadhim, Mihssen. "Absorptive Capacity, Surplus Funds, and Regional Capital Mobility in the Middle East." *Rivista Internazionale di Scienze Economiche e Commerciali* (April 1977): 308–325.

El-Sherbini, A.A. "Problems of Arid Agriculture in West Asia." *World Development* (May–June 1977): 441–446.

Eshag, Eprime. "Quantification of Disruptive Effects of Export Shortfalls." *Tahqiqate e Eqtesadi* (Winter 1971): 29–64.

Evans, Michael K. *Macroeconomic Activity: Theory Forecasting and Control.* New York: Harper & Row, 1969.

Feige, E. "Expectations and Adjustments in the Monetary Sector." *American Economic Review* (May 1967).

Fekrat, M. Ali. "Growth of OPEC Type Economics: A Preliminary Theoretical Inquiry." *Economia Internazionale* (February 1979): 82.

Ferber, Robert. "Consumer Economics: A Survey." *Journal of Economic Literature* (September 1973): 1303–1342.

Ferguson, C.E. *The Neoclassical Theory of Production and Distribution.* London: Cambridge University Press, 1971.

Ford, J.L. *The Ohlin-Heckscher Theory of the Basis and Effects of Commodity Trade.* New York: Asid Publishing House, 1965.

Frenkel, Jacob, and Johnson, Harry. "The Monetary Approach to the Balance of Payments: Essential Concepts and Historical Origins." In *The Monetary Approach to the Balance of Payments*, edited by Jacob Frenkel and Harry Johnson, p. 22. Toronto: University of Toronto Press, 1976.

Friedman, M. *A Theory of the Consumption Function.* Princeton: National Bureau of Economic Research, 1957/1958.

Ghadar, Fariborz. *The Evolution of OPEC Strategy.* Lexington, Mass.: Lexington Books, 1977.

Greenberg, E. "Fixed Investment." In *Topics in Applied Macroeconomics*, edited by David Heathfield, p. 97. New York: Academic Press, 1976.

Halliday, Fred. "Migration and the Labor Force in the Oil Producing States of the Middle East." *Development and Cultural Change* (July 1977): 263–292.

Hambleton, H.G. "The Saudi Arabian Petrochemical Industry: Its Rationale and Effectiveness and the Social Political Implications." In Centre for Arab Gulf States, University of Exeter, *State Economy and Power in Saudi Arabia*. A Symposium, July 4–7, 1980.

Harberger, A. "The Dynamics of Inflation in Chile." *Measurements in Economics: Studies in Mathematical Economics and Econometrics in Memory of Yehuda Grunfeld.* Stanford: Stanford University Press, 1963.

Hartshorn, J.E. *Objectives of the Petroleum Exporting Countries.* Nicosia: Middle East Petroleum and Economic Publications, 1978.

Harvey, Nigel. "Money Changers: Serving the Public without Rules." *Saudi Business and Arab Economic Report* (July 25, 1980): 20–25.

Hayami, Yujiro, and Ruttan, Vernon. *Agricultural Development: An International Perspective.* Baltimore: Johns Hopkins Press, 1971.

Hill, Emid. "Saudi Labor and Industrialization Policy in Saudi Arabia." Paper presented at Center for Arab Gulf States, University of Exeter, *State, Economy and Power in Saudi Arabia*. A Symposium, July 4–7, 1980.

Hirschman, A.O. *The Strategy of Economic Development.* New Haven: Yale University Press, 1958.

Hitti, Said, and Abed, George. "The Economy and Finances of Saudi Arabia." International Monetary Fund, *Staff Papers* (July 1974): 247–306.

Hoagland, J. "Saudi Arabians Push $100 Billion Development Plan." *The Washington Post* (April 13, 1975).

Howe, J. Tripp. "The Riyad Bank." *Saudi Business and Arab Economic Report* (May 9, 1980): 20–21.

_____. "Saudi Banking," *Saudi Business and Arab Economic Report* (June 6, 1980): 22–29.

Hubday, Peter. *Saudi Arabia Today*. New York: St. Martin's Press, 1978.

Industrial Studies and Development Center. *A Guide to Industrial Investment in Saudi Arabia*. 5th rev. ed. Riyadh: ISDC, 1977.

_____. *Non-Oil Manufacturing in the Private Sector: Present Conditions and Projections for the Second Plan*. Riyadh: ISDC, 1974.

International Monetary Fund. *Balance of Payments Yearbook*. Various issues.

_____. *International Financial Statistics*. Various issues.

_____. *International Financial Statistics* (May 1980): 96.

Iyoha, M.A. "Inflation and Openness in Less Developed Economies: A Cross Country Analysis." *Economic Development and Cultural Change* (October 1973): 31–38.

Jaidah, Ali M. "Downstream Operations and the Development of OPEC Member Countries." *Journal of Energy and Development* (Spring 1979): 305.

Japan Cooperation Center for the Middle East. *Analysis of Demand and Supply of Manpower in the Arabian Gulf Countries—An Excerpt*. Tokyo: JCCNE, 1976.

Keran, Michael, and Al Malik, Ahmed Abdullah. "Monetary Sources of Inflation in Saudi Arabia." Federal Reserve Bank of San Francisco, *Economic Review* (Winter 1979): 17–22, and Supplement, p. 14.

Kerr, Malcolm et al. *Inter-Arab Conflict Contingencies and the Gap Between the Arab Rich and Poor*. Santa Monica: Rand, 1978.

Kirschen, E.S., ed. *Economic Policies Compared: East and West*. Vol. I, *General Theory*. New York: American Elsevier Publishing Company, 1974. 8–44.

Knaverhase, Ramon. "Social Factors and Labor Market Structure in Saudi Arabia." Yale University Economic Growth Center, *Discussion Paper No. 247*, May 1976.

_____. *The Saudi Arabian Economy*. New York: Praeger Publishers, 1975.

_____. "Saudi Arabia's Economy at the Beginning of the 1970s." *The Middle East Journal* (Spring 1974): 126–127.

Koyck, L.M. *Distributed Lags and Investment Analysis*. Amsterdam: North Holland, 1954.

Kuh, E. *Capital Stock Growth: A Microeconometric Approach.* Amsterdam: North Holland, 1963.

Kuhand, Edwin, Schmalensee, Richard. *An Introduction to Applied Macroeconomics.* Amsterdam: North Holland, 1973.

Kurabayashi, Y. "The Impact of Changes in Terms of Trade on a System of National Accounts: An Attempted Synthesis." *Review of Income and Wealth* (1971): 285–297.

Landau, Louis. "Savings Functions in Latin America," In *Studies in Development Planning*, edited by Hollis Chenery, pp. 299–321. Cambridge: Harvard University Press, 1971.

Leff, Nathaniel H., and Sato, Kazvo. "Macroeconomic Adjustment in Developing Countries: Instability, Short-Run Growth, and External Dependency." *The Review of Economics and Statistics* (May 1980): 170–179.

Legum, Colin, ed. "Deficits in Saudi Arabia: Their Meaning and Possible Implications." *Middle East Contemporary Survey.* Vol. II, *1977–1978.* New York: Holmes & Meier Publishers, 1979.

Liano, T.D. "The Relative Share of Labor in the United States Agriculture." *American Journal of Agricultural Economics* (August 1971).

Long, David E. "Saudi Arabia." In Joint Economic Committee, Congress of the United States, *The Political Economy of the Middle East: 1973–1978.* Washington: U.S. Government Printing Office, 1980.

_____. "Saudi Oil Policy." *The Wilson Quarterly* (Winter 1979): 90–91.

Looney, Robert E. *The EconomicDevelopment of Iran.* New York: Praeger Publishers, 1973.

_____. *Income Distribution Policies and Economic Growth in Semi-industralized Countries: A Comparative Study of Iran, Mexico, Brazil, and South Korea.* New York: Praeger Publishers, 1975.

_____. *Iran at the End of the Century: A Hegelian Forecast.* Lexington: Lexington Books, D.C. Heath and Company, 1977.

_____. *A Development Strategy for Iran Through the 1980s.* New York: Praeger Publishers, 1977.

McNown, Robert, and Wallace, Myles. "International Reserve Flows of OPEC States: A Monetary Approach." *The Journal of Energy and Development* (Spring 1977): 267–278.

Malone, Joseph. "Building a Constituency: Non-Petroleum Activities and Programs of the Arabian American Oil Company." Paper presented at Center for Arab Gulf Studies, University of Exeter, *State, Economy and Power in Saudi Arabia.* A Symposium, July 4–7, 1980.

Mansfield, Peter. *The Middle East.* 5th rev. ed. New York: Oxford University Press, 1980.

Mayer, Thomas. "Plant and Equipment Lead Times." *Journal of Business* (April 1960): 127–132.

_____. "The Structure of Monetarism (I)." In *The Structure of*

Monetarism, edited by Thomas Mayer, P. 2. New York: Norton, 1978.

_____, and Sonenblum, S. "Lead Times for Fixed Investment." *Review of Economics and Statistics* (August 1955): 300–304.

Metwally, M.M. "Market Limitation and Industrialization in Arab Countries," 1979. Mimeographed.

_____, and Tamaschke, H.V. "Oil Exports and Economic Growth in the Middle East." *Kyklos*, no. 3 (1980): 499–521.

Middle East Economic Digest. "Foreign Labor Dominates Key Sectors— And Some Will Remain Indefinitely." Special Report on Saudi Arabia (August 1978): 53–54.

Mikesell, Raymond. "The Contribution of Petroleum and Mineral Resources to Economic Development." In *Foreign Investment in the Petroleum and Mineral Industries*, edited by Raymond Mikesell, pp. 3–28. Baltimore: The Johns Hopkins Press, 1971.

_____. "Monetary Problems of Saudi Arabia." *Middle East Journal* (Spring 1947): 172–173.

_____, and Zinser, James. "The Nature of the Savings Function in Developing Countries: A Survey of the Theoretical and Empirical Literature." *Journal of Economic Literature* (March 1973): 1–26.

Ministry of Agriculture and Water. *A Guide to Agricultural Investment in Saudi Arabia*. Riyadh: MAW, 1979.

Ministry of Planning. *The Second Development Plan 1395–1400 A.H.* Riyadh: Ministry of Planning, 1975.

_____. *The Second Development Plan 1975–1980*. Riyadh: Ministry of Planning, 1976.

_____. *The Construction Industry in Saudi Arabia*. Riyadh: Ministry of Planning, 1977.

_____. *Third Development Plan*. Riyadh: Ministry of Planning, 1980.

_____. *Third Development Plan, 1400–1405 A.H.* Riyadh: Ministry of Planning, 1980.

Modigliani, F. "The Life-Cycle Hypothesis of Saving, the Demand for Wealth, and the Supply of Capital." *Social Research* (Summer 1966): 160–217.

Mohsin, Mohammad. "Feasibility of Commercial Banking without Rate of Interest and its Socioeconomic Significance." *Islamic Quarterly* (December 1978): 151–157.

Morgan, David. "Fiscal Policy in Oil Exporting Countries, 1972–1978." International Monetary Fund, *Staff Papers* (March 1979): 55–86.

Morgan, Theodore. *Oil Prices and the Future of OPEC*. Washington: Resources for the Future, 1978.

Mosher, A.T. *Creating a Progressive Rural Structure*. New York: Agricultural Development Council, 1969.

Moughrabi, F.M. "The Arab Basic Personality: A Critical Survey of the Literature." *Journal of Middle East Studies* (1978): 103.

Muslehuddin, Muhammad. *Economics and Islam*. Lahore: Islamic Publications, 1974.

Nankani, G. "Development Problems of Mineral-Exporting Countries," The World Bank, *World Bank Staff Working Paper No. 354*, August 1979.

Naqui, Syed Nawab Haider. "Ethical Foundations of Islamic Economic Study." *Islamic Studies* 27 (1978): 105–136.

_____. "Islamic Economic System: Fundamental Issues." *Islamic Studies* (Winter 1977): 332–335.

Nyana, Solayman S. "The Islamic State and Economic Development: A Theoretical Analysis." *Islamic Culture* (January 1976): 1–23.

Nyrop, Richard et al. *Area Handbook for Saudi Arabia*. 3rd rev. ed. Washington: Superintendent of Documents, 1977.

Otani, Ichiro. "Inflation in an Open Economy: A Case Study of the Philippines." *IMF Staff Papers*, 1975, pp. 379–418.

Pagoulatos, Angelos, and Timmons, John. "Management Options in the Use of Exhaustible and Nonrenewable Natural Resources." *Rivista Internationale de Scienze Economiche e Commerciali* (June 1978): 489–507.

Pailami, M. "The Determination and Control of Money Supply in an Oil Exporting Country: The Iranian Experience." MIT Energy Laboratory, *Working Paper No. MIT-EL 78-027WP*, rev. February 1979.

Pendleton, Scott. "Developing Qatif." *Saudi Business and Arab Economic Report* (October 17, 1980): 22–25.

Pitchford, J.D. *Population in Economic Growth*. New York: American Elsevier, 1974.

Poleman, Thomas. "World Food: Myth and Reality." *World Development* (May–June 1977): 384.

Population Division of ECWA. "Demographic and Socio-Economic Situation in Countries of the ECWA Region, 1975." *Population Bulletin of the United Nations Economic Commission for Western Asia* (January 1977): 3–11.

Preston, Samual. "Mortality, Morbidity, and Development." *Population Bulletin of the United Nations Economic Commission for Western Asia* (December 1978): 68–69.

Ragab, Ibrahim. "Islam and Development." *World Development* (July/August 1980): 513–521.

Rahman, Afzul-ur-. *Economic Doctrines of Islam*. Vols. I, II, and III. Lahore: Islamic Publications, 1974.

Rashid, Ali, and Casady, Robert. "Methods and Preliminary Estimates from the Saudi Arabian Multipurpose Survey." Paper presented at the *41st Session of the International Statistical Institute*, New Delhi, December 5–15, 1977.

Royal Commission for Jubail and Yenbo, Directorate General for Jubail Region. *Community Programming: Permanent Community for Jubail Industrial Complex*. London: Colin Buchanan and Partners, 1977.

Rugh, William. "Emergence of a New Middle Class in Saudi Arabia." *The Middle East Journal* (Winter 1973): 18–19.

Saad, Nassar. "Agricultural Demand, Supply, and Prices with Special Reference to Arab Countries." *L'Egypte Contemporaine* (October 1976): 39–64.

Sargent, Thomas, and Wallace, Neil. "Rational Expectations and the Theory of Economic Policy." *Journal of Monetary Economics* (April 1976): 169–185.

Saudi Arabian Monetary Agency. *Annual Report*. Various issues.

———. *Annual Report 1399 (1979)*. Jeddah: SAMA, 1980.

Saudi Business and Arab Economic Report. "The Barriers Faced in Private Sector Economic Development." (November 30, 1979): 11.

Sayigh, Yusif A. *The Economies of the Arab World* (New York: St. Martin's Press, 1978). 167–178.

Sayigh, Yusif. "Problems and Prospects in the Arabian Peninsula." *International Journal of Middle East Studies* (February 1970): 51–56.

Schultz, T. Paul. "Fertility Patterns and Their Determinants in the Middle East." In *Economic Development and Population Growth in the Middle East*, edited by Charles Cooper et al., pp. 400–447. New York: American Elsevier, 1972.

Shaikh, Abdul Zuades et al., *Outlines of Islamic Economics*. Indiannapolis: Association of Muslim Social Scientists, 1977.

Sharshar, A.M. "Oil, Religion and Mercantilism: A Study of Saudi Arabia's Economic System." *Studies in Comparative International Development* (Fall 1977): 46–64.

Shaw, R. Paul. "Migration and Employment in the Arab World: Construction as a Key Policy Variable." *International Labor Review* (September–October 1979): 589–605.

Sheehey, Edmund. "On the Measurement of Imported Inflation in Developing Countries." *Weltwirtschaftliches Archiv* (1979): 68–79.

Shirreff, David. "IMF Encourages Saudis to be Big Spenders." *Middle East Economic Digest* (October 1979): 6–7.

———. "Manufacturing: Rich Incentives Ensure Quick Returns," *Middle East Economic Digest*, Special Report (July 1980): 39.

———. "Reclamation Scheme Flourishes at Al-Hassa Oasis." *Middle East Economic Digest* (January 26, 1979): 7.

———. "Strict Society Keeps Rein on Growing Work Force." *Middle East Economic Digest*, Special Report on Saudi Arabia (June 1979): 7–8.

Shourie, Aron. "the Use of Macroeconomic Regression Models of Developing Countries for Forecasts and Policy Prescription." *Oxford Economic Papers* (March 1972): 1–35.

Sidahmed, S. "The Lost Labor." *Saudi Business and Arab Economic Report* (January 9, 1981): 22–24.

Siddiqui, M.N. *Some Aspects of the Islamic Economy*. Lahore: Islamic Publications, 1978.

Simon, Julian. "Population Growth May Be Good for the LCDs in the Long Run: A Richer Simulation Model." *Economic Development and Cultural Change* (January 1976): 309–337.

Sinha, Radha. "The World Food Problem: Consensus and Conflict." *World Development* (May–June 1977): 371–382.

Sisley, Timothy. "The Evolution of the Private Sector." *Saudi Business and Arab Economic Report* (February 15, 1980): 22–24.

_____. "Farming in the 1980s." *Saudi Business and Arab Economic Report* (January 11, 1980): 30–31.

_____. "Saudi Arabia: The Contemporary Political Scene." In Centre for Arab Gulf Studies, University of Exeter, *State, Economy and Power in Saudi Arabia*. A Symposium, July 4–7, 1980.

Smithies, Arthur. *The Economic Potential of the Arab Countries*. Santa Monica: Rand Corporation, 1978.

Solow, R.M. "Intergenerational Equity and Exhaustible Resources." *Review of Economic Studies* (October 1974): 29–47.

Stern, R. *The Balance of Payments: Theory and Economic Policy*. Chicago: Aldine, 1973.

Szyliowicz, Joseph. "The Prospects for Scientific and Technological Development in Saudi Arabia." *International Journal of Middle East STudies* (August 1979): 355–372.

Tabbara, Riad et al. "Population Research and Research Gaps in the Arab Countries." *Population Bulletin of the United Nations Economic Commission for Western Asia* (December 1978): 3–32.

Teece, D.J. "Technology Transfer by Multinational Firms: The Resource Cost of Transferring Technological Knowhow." *The Economic Journal* (June 1977): 242–261.

Theil, H. "On the Theory of Economic Policy." *American Economic Review* (May 1956).

Thesiger, Wilfred. *Arabian Sands*. New York: Dutton, 1959.

Timbergen, J. *On the Theory of Economic Policy*. Amsterdam: North Holland Publishing Company, 1952.

Tourk, K.A. "The OPEC Cartel: A Revival of the 'Dominant-Firm' Theory." *The Journal of Energy and Development* (Spring 1977): 321–328.

Turner, Louis. "Industrial Development Strategies in the Arab Gulf States." In *Issues in Development: The Arab Gulf States*, edited by May

Ziwar-Daftari, pp. 210–211, 213, 215–219. London: M.D. Research Services Limited, 1980.

_____, and Bedore, James M. *Middle East Industrialization*. Farnborough: Saxon House, 1979.

UNCTAD. *Major Issues in Transfer of Technology: A Case Study of the Pharmaceutical Industry*. Geneva: UNCTAD, 1975.

_____. *An International Code of Conduct on Transfer of Technology*. New York: UNCTAD, 1975.

Vanek, Jaroslav, *Estimating Foreign Resource Needs for Economic Development*. New York: McGraw-Hill, 1967.

Vernon, Raymond. "Comprehensive Model Building in the Planning Process; The Case of the Less-Developed Economies." *Economic Journal* (March 1966): 57–69.

Vidal, Frederico. "Development of the Eastern Province: A Case Study of Al Hasa Oasis." In *King Faisal and the Modernization of Saudi Arabia*, edited by Willard Beling, pp. 90–91. Boulder: Westview Press, 1980.

Wassink, Darvin. "Economic Development with Unlimited Finances: Foreign Exchange Surpluses in OPEC Countries." *Rivista Internationale di Scienze Economichee e Commerciali* (December 1978): 1086.

Weinbaum, Marvin. "Political Risks in Agricultural Development and Food Policy in the Middle East." *Policy Studies Journal* (Spring 1980): 735–738.

Weinstein, M.C., and Zeckhauser, R.J. "The Optimal Consumption of Depletable Natural Resources." *Quarterly Journal of Economics* (August 1975): 371–392.

Wells, Donald. *Saudi Arabian Development Strategy*. Washington: American Enterprise Institute, 1976.

_____. *Saudi Arabian Revenues and Expenditures*. Baltimore: Johns Hopkins Press, 1974.

Whelan, John. "Al-Bank Al-Saudi Al-Fransi: Fully Committed to Saudiisation." *Middle East Economic Digest*, Special Report (July 1980): 69–70.

Wilson, R.J.A. "The Evolution of the Saudi Banking System and Its Relationship with Bahrain," 1980. Mimeographed.

Wong, Chorng-huey. "Demand for Money in Developing Countries." *Journal of Monetary Economics* (January 1977): 65, 72–73.

Worthington, E. Barton. "Water, Science and Technology in the Middle East." In *Technology Transfer and Change in the Arab World,* edited by A.B. Zahlan, kpp. 223–235. New York: Pergamon Press, 1978.

Yong, Arthur. "Saudi Arabian Currency and Finance," part 1. *Middle East Journal* (Summer 1953): 361–380.

_____. "Saudi Arabian Currency and Finance," part 2. *Middle East Journal* (Autumn 1953): 539–556.

Yotopoulos, Pan, and Nugent, Jeffrey. *Economics of Development: Empirical Investigations*. New York: Harper & Row, 1976.

Zakat and Income Tax Department. *Regulations for Income Tax, Road Tax, and Zakat*. Riyadh: Ministry of Finance and National Economy, 1978.

Index

About the Author

Robert E. Looney is associate professor of National Security Affairs at the Naval Postgraduate School, Monterey, California. He has been a faculty member of the University of California at Davis, the University of Santa Clara, and the Monterey Institute of International Studies. He has also been a development economist for the Stanford Research Institute and has served as an economic adviser to the governments of Iran, Saudi Arabia, Mexico, and Panama. Dr. Looney has published numerous articles in professional journals and is the author of *The Economic Development of Iran* (1973), *Income Distribution Policies and Economic Growth in Semiindustrialized Countries* (1975), *The Economic Development of Panama* (1976), *Iran at the End of the Century* (Lexington Books, 1977), *A Development Strategy for Iran through the 1980s* (1977), *Mexico's Economy* (1978), and *The Impact of World Inflation on Semidependent Countries* (1979).